What People are Saying

"I totally enjoyed the format with the vignettes and stories, mixed with the poetry. Your poetry is beautiful and often just plain exquisite. The humor is beyond wonderful and will be an amazing treat for those meeting you for the first time in this book."
—Schyleen Qualls, writer, producer, actor, and spoken word performer

"I love your poems of upbeat uplifting paeans to clear thinking. Keep them coming."
—Ken Babbs, author of *Cronies,* adventures with Ken Kesey, Neal Cassady, The Merry Pranksters, the Grateful Dead, et al. A biographically intrepid trip.

"You are such a word wizard that I could not possibly ever match your expression of the depth of personal pain. Hauntingly spherical."
—Juan C. Garcia, PhD, LMFT

"I couldn't put it down. I cried and laughed so much I peed in my pants."
—Wilma Kampe, Substance Abuse Counselor

Zen MATADOR

THE FINE ART OF TRANSCENDING THE BULL

The unabashed, unabridged,
under the bridge, under the influence Edition

The Memoir of

Tomás Chavez

ISBN: 979-8-9929646-0-8 (print)
ISBN: 979-8-9929646-1-5 (E-Book)

Green Dolphin Books
7889 Lichen Dr, 226
Citrus Heights, CA 95621

The name **Green Dolphin Books** was chosen as a reflection of my sensibilities as to the romantic, the majestic, and the adventurous spirit of a grand new frontier, as in the 1944 historical novel *Green Dolphin Country*, by Elizabeth Goudge.

The name is also a reference to my reverence for the consciousness inherent in all sentient beings, as exhibited in the superior intelligence of whales and dolphins. "The dolphin is the most classic of fishes, the favourite of Apollo, and sacred to that bright divinity."—John Vinycomb in his 1909 book *Fictitious and Symbolic Creatures in Art.*

And, not least, the name is an expression of my passion for the jazz idiom, mirrored in the melodious "Green Dolphin Street," which was first heard as the haunting and subtle refrain for the 1947 movie based on Elizabeth Goudge's book. The tune inspired recordings by such icons as Miles Davis, Ella Fitzgerald, Tony Bennett, and Sarah Vaughn, each rendition terribly lovely and rich … in a word, mellifluous.

Please do check out the penultimate Miles take of "Green Dolphin Street" on the *Kind of Blue* album. That 1959 vinyl vanguard, it is argued, is the quintessential jazz long-play with a sextet ensemble that included trumpeter Davis, saxophonists John Coltrane and Julian "Cannonball" Adderley, pianist Bill Evans, bassist Paul Chambers, and drummer Jimmy Cobb. Take a listen … it'll tell you a lot about me. *Miles Davis Kind of Blue* full album 1959 – YouTube

CONTENTS

DEDICATED TO THE ONES I LOVE

I am literally in awe of the fine human beings who I've had the immense fortune of hanging around with over the years. Sitting next to me in West Fresno at Columbia Elementary School with turn-of-the-century wooden desks with holes for the ink bottles, or in smoky bars with jars of hard-boiled eggs and pickled pigs' feet they came, fabulous funky folks who were, as Kesey had it, "on the bus."

There's not enough room on this page to list them and, I fear, not enough brain cells remaining to capture the memories of them all. (You gotta see the scanned pictures of an alcoholic's brain … makes you wanna drink!)

Where to start? "Well, to begin with, you should start at the beginning," advised Glinda, the Good Witch in *The Wizard of Oz*. So I'll try it chronologically (with some exceptions), not by order of influence or affection … I love 'em all. And I'll make the commentary brief… they all know what I'm talkin' 'bout. And for those who've passed away, well, I'll catch you on the flip-flop.

> Don Stevenson, Director of the Fresno Boys Club back in '51.
> The Boys: Morris, Edgar, Frank, Roger, and Steve—To the bone!
> Gina, Tyler, Emily, and Mona—I mean, wow, you guys are like family.
> Dru Isanda, Co-pilot on my flights of fancy
> Ken Kesey, who invited me to The Swamp
> Father Jack Fulton who said, "God is love" and slipped me a hundred bucks.
> Jess Rodriguez … Can you say uber-exuberance?
> Dr. Juan C. Garcia, a curandero to the marrow.
> Tino Esparza, who was more than a friend.
> And finally, this book is dedicated to my hilarious bud
> Fat Dennis Riley (FDR), who never met a pie he didn't like.

FOREWORD: AN UNEXPECTED LETTER

I offer the following kind letter from a friend of old, Schyleen Qualls. A spoken word artist par excellence, she has written for and performed in hundreds of projects for film, television, and radio, here and abroad. (If you're a fan of poetry readings, you'll surely appreciate her performances on YouTube.)

All of this to say I'm most grateful for her praise as regards my memoir, though I'm fairly nervous that it may raise expectations. In reviewing my bio, she offers you a menu of accolades worthy of a 5-star restaurant but, hey, this is but the opening day of the humble Chez Tomasso.

In any case this was an unsolicited letter, just her spontaneous response to the work I sent her early on. There is a very popular Mexican song titled *Sabor a mi*, which loosely translates to, "a taste of me." Odd, but you can even remember the taste, the scent, the feeling of closeness of a past lover even though the affair was many years ago.

Setting aside the compliments and the condiments, I am hopeful this letter serves the purpose of offering a slight taste of the fare about to be served. Bon appétit!

> Dear Tomás. I just got back from Denver yesterday. My mother is doing much better and is home from the hospital. While Mom was in the hospital, I was able to read your manuscript. I loved the book!
>
> I totally enjoyed the format with the vignettes and stories, mixed with the poetry. Your poetry is beautiful and often just plain exquisite. Your honesty, insights, reflections are all written with that special way that is pure Tomás.
>
> The humor is beyond wonderful and will be an amazing treat for those meeting you for the first time in this book. The writing is honest, even heart-wrenching, and easily transports the reader into the stories and moments of the journey you share with us.
>
> In a very tender and revealing way you allow us to see the man who has lived his life with integrity and joy in spite

of all the darkness and difficulties. And you introduce us to a whole cast of characters that, in our brief moments of reading about them, we feel we know. What a wild, fulfilling, challenging life you have had, Tomás, and thank God you have taken the time to share some of it with us.

There is something so universal about being on this earth and learning to love ourselves through the gift of our challenges. We all go up and down, but something in our spirit keeps us hoping that we will continue to heal ourselves.

I'm truly grateful to you for being such a dear friend and for the beautiful experiences and people you brought into my life years ago. I think that the book will give the reader new insights into their own lives, since we all have some kind of addiction we are living with and hoping to conquer.

It was an honor to enter your world and to have the pleasure of imbibing your God-given gift of weaving stories and creating magic with words.

With Love,
Schyleen Qualls

INTRODUCTION

This is the memoir of a life-long "seeker" (a term meaning one who searches for Ultimate Truth … whatever that means), a hardcore yet grateful alcoholic, and a forever finger-snapping beatnik. Like cool, daddy-o!

By grateful alcoholic I mean that my addiction, in spite of all the damage caused by my excessive drinking (Mea culpa, mea culpa!), has also been a major factor in many of the positive aspects of my life. You might call it unintelligent design.

Good things happened now and then regardless of my derelict ways, my reckless bohemian persona, and just maybe because of them … I'll never know. My outrageous style often brought me into serendipitous contact with wonderful friends, great ideas, amazing support, and even intimate experience with that which jazz giant John Coltrane called *A Love Supreme.*

I am grateful to be alive, grateful for a handful of marvelous friends, and grateful to the Big Guy for going out of His way to love me in spite of my countless shortcomings and trespasses. It appears He's not such an uptight cat after all (I know, "He" could well be a "She" or an "It"… but more likely all of the above. Hey, go with the flow, dude … or dudette.) And He, from a Zen standpoint, might well be a moot point in a seemingly pointless process … ellipses ad infinitum.

But I must say, it is Spirit that has so often lifted me out of the unmindful and deadly morass while languishing in the lush life, Spirit who has come to my rescue. Years ago Carl Jung, the founder of analytical psychology, insightfully pointed out the irony that the way to overcome alcoholism (alcohol being dubbed "spirits") is through the Holy Spirit, "Spiritus contra spiritum." In essence, to conquer our addictions we need our higher power—a transcendent intervention—to lovingly swoop us up and fly us out of our downward spiral. We need to humbly ask, though sometimes She just gracefully embraces us.

You must understand that in my hey-daze, the '60s to mid-'70s, it was thoroughly in vogue to be loaded on some damned thing—acid, mescaline, pot, shrooms, and a plethora of mind-melting morsels—at work, at play, ubiquitously blasted, totally toasted. Psychedelics, though, were never the choice of lazy brains. So it is not the least bit surprising that arguably the most dangerous and devastating of them all—plain ol' booze—was and still is the most popular.

That's because folks just wanna have fun, just wanna escape from whatever's bugging 'em, want that wild fermented sugar high. I really get that, but brews do not make Bud wiser, just stupider. That crap is pumped into the brains of unborn children, lonely and feeble old folks, and everyone in between by billions of advertising dollars and a lobby that has the morals of a jiving, conniving, street-corner pimp.

But to be clear, regardless of my philosophical flippancy, it is my mystical meandering that remains a token of my devotion to The Love Supreme. (An atheist, I eventually concluded, is a person who doesn't believe in himself).

This book is also a shout out to the basic goodness in the world, dismissing the dismal daily dose of what's wrong with everything. If you say the cup is half empty, man, that sucker is bone dry. But if you see it as half full, then indeed your cup runneth over.

Hey, and let's smile a bit. As my lanky, countrified friend HL Moore, with a wry smile—as in rye whiskey—and a whiny Appalachian twang, used to say, "God looks at things through your eyes—are you showing Him a good time?" In those way wild days HL and I had a hell of a good time, all of course to please God.

By the way, I once asked HL what HL stood for, just what did those two letters mean? He looked at me like I must never have been up in those remote hillbilly mountains and then replied, "Nope, that's it, buddy, my name's HL." Well, hell, HL!

As autobiography, the book reflects the remarkable and not-so-accidental meetings with a host of marvelous characters—*characters with character!*—who have brought hope, great joy, and laughter into my life. Many of them, I must confess, I met in dark taverns at oddball hours. W. C. Fields once lamented, "A woman drove me to drink and I didn't even have the decency to thank her."

The point here is that this work is not preachy, not about alcohol bashing, but more an honest portrayal of life in this mode—including all the crap that comes with it. Com-mode, you might say. And there is no doubt it is about addictions of all sorts from a first-hand standpoint, about my lifelong embracing of the very elements that brought a flair to the affair yet, like all horrid habits, also caused an immense amount of suffering to myself and others.

It is said that "in vino veritas"—in wine there is truth, or at least a certain unabashed intimacy that loosens the heart strings of our being and the zippers of our pants. There is surely no shortage of friends and lovers who have consummated their bonds after a glass or two … or three. And many a writer has scribbled his/her creative concoctions under the vino volcano. A somewhat related fact is that hidden beneath a thin veneer of our allegedly civilized neo-cortex is a real asshole who comes out to wreak havoc when we've had one too many.

The reference to the bull in the sub-title *The Fine Art of Transcending The Bull* is in fact two-fold: from early 11th century Zen teaching there exists the poetic allegory of "The Ten Bulls," each one representing a stage of evolution in consciousness, of taming the bull. By the time "the ox herder" reaches the eighth stage he has attained pure enlightenment.

That is because in this state of awareness the seeker becomes a bodhisattva, an enlightened being attuned to the ultimate non-duality of it all, the all-pervasive Isness understood as the Great Void of Buddhism. From the Ten Bull verses of Kuòan Shiyuan, the eighth bull stage is thus described: "Both bull and self transcended. Whip, rope, person, and ox—all merge in No Thing. This heaven is so vast no message can stain it."

As to the second meaning, well, it's hardly complicated and sure ain't subtle. Yep, pretty straightforward: I'm talkin' bullshit, b-u-l-l-s-h-i-t, bullshit! This bull represents the lengthy list of lamentable lies, those that are used to manipulate us and those we tell ourselves and are victims of; the obvious and the insidiously subliminal lies; and those from a source of plain ol' ign'ance. Some folks talk shit 'cause they don't know no betta'.

But first and foremost, it's about my own conscious and subconscious BS. Our mind has an amazing capacity to obfuscate and vacillate, whereas on one hand it inflates itself like a puffer fish to appear bigger than it really is, and on the other it glosses over what deeply hurts us. Yes, we humans have a nearly miraculous mechanism for covering over the dark and hurtful things we ourselves have done. By writing from the heart, as honestly and spontaneously as I'm capable, I've had to look deeply into myself, forcing me to confront some things I've avoided through much of my life, actions only for the ears of my priest.

And so in doing my best to face my demons, by confronting them directly, they have weakened considerably and with the aid of a lot of therapy and a decent home life most have succumbed to a healthy dose of sanity and relative peace. Thank God that this is even possible.

The following observation is from an article by Aura Glaser, Ph.D., a dharma teacher and psychologist: "Jung commented that we don't become enlightened by imagining beings of light but by *making the darkness conscious.* [my italics] The great Persian poet and Sufi mystic Rumi summarized it well, "When you embrace hurt, it becomes joy."

In this metaphor of a matador, the bullfighter is that in us that is passionate, compassionate, and evolving in consciousness; is that daring soul who lives on the precipice of the Matter-horn, precariously surfing an avalanche of danger, destruction, and damnation. The bullfighter is potentially heroic though often fearful and not fully assured—yet, yes, he's the guy who takes the proverbial "bull by the horns."

Now in my mid-seventies, I offer this collage of memories, poems and prose pieces in hopes that it might in any way be helpful to another human being—a laugh, a lift, an insight, maybe even a little support with our mutual stuff.

Jazz Riff. As inferred, one of Saint Coltrane's greatest works is an entire side of an album titled *A Love Supreme.* Back in '64 this phenomenal piece was composed spontaneously in one sizzling set. What a mesmerizing, swirling Dervish creation!

So if you're a budding jazz enthusiast or maybe a young person who is working on your Bachelor of Bohemia degree, here's one very hip album: Easy to find, maybe now's the time: *A Love Supreme*, John Coltrane, YouTube.

ACKNOWLEDGMENTS

Dru Isanda, for ongoing formatting, editing suggestions, tossing in her two-cents worth (whether asked for or not), and being the Rock of Gibraltar when all else was crumbling.

David Stanford, for his thoughtful editorial suggestions and a bit of i-dotting and t-crossing. Most important is that he did point out some parts that were repetitive. It's a better read for it … Thanks, Dave!

Dr. Juan Garcia, who must have felt that this work had a bit of merit because, without the slightest request, the guy sent me a $1,000 check for the publishing fee and said, "Do it."

The small army of doctors, nurses, and therapists of the West Coast VA hospitals, to whom I am extremely grateful. I have staggered into their emergency rooms throughout my life, primarily as a consequence of extreme alcoholism. They have patched me back together after several near-death situations—at least a dozen. A cat only has nine lives! And speaking of cats …

Louie, my furry, yin-yang kitty who has laid in her little bed right next to my computer throughout the years, all the time teaching me the valuable practice of Zen sleeping. I promised her a lifetime supply of catnip and tuna once this thing hits best-seller status. She just yawned.

THOROUGHLY SUPERFLUOUS NOTES

- **Rosetta Stoned.** You may be well advised to skip the ramblings of this segment altogether, but frankly it's a kind of Rosetta stone for the rolling stream you are about to enter. In fact, you might be well advised to roll up your pants before crossing ... but keep your boots on.

- **As stated**, this book is an autobiography in collage form. I throw in the proverbial kitchen sink (unmitigated miscellaneous minutiae I managed to muscle up); corny and campy jokes which, needless to say, I picked up in many a smoky bar.

- **The "F-word"** in here is for *Food* ... though, on more occasions than I care to admit, where that other bawdy F-word fits I'm out to use it ... you might say an out-of-bawdy experience.

- **The sequence** of the writings is chronologically ordered for the most part. It is not quite disjectī membra poētae, the scattered "limbs of a dismembered poet"—no, there is a bit of method to the madness. Here and there between the chapters of the newly written material (the vignettes), I'll insert a poem, a drawing or a photo. My intention here is that these motley injections will, hopefully, push the story forward.

- **Many of the poems** were written decades ago. A clever way, I must say, to finally get some of that musty old stuff published. "The older author is constantly rediscovering himself in the more or less fossilized productions of his earlier years."—Oliver Wendell Holmes.

- **Drunkish.** I'm amazed that I remember as much as I do. I'm reminded of a Norman O. Brown line that I first read when I was in my hippy-dippy Santa Cruz period: "Nothing in the mind is ever forgotten but can be brought to light again under the right conditions ... the mind is the eternal city." I've spent most of my life in a drunken stupor, with more blackouts than I care to remember ... but then I don't have to worry about that, do I?

- **I sometimes write** in the parlance of years past, not always politically correct, but, hey, this is also about that slice of history and that was the jargon of the time. Example: I use the word "chick" which was rarely viewed as demeaning, nope, it was cool … like, "She's a cool chick" or, like, in the lyrics of the sizzlin' Julie London tune, *Fever*, "Chicks were meant to give you fever, be it Fahrenheit or Centigrade." That song, by the way, was originally recorded by Little Willie John back in '56. His rendition never hit it big time because, as the saying went, "If you white you alright, if you brown stick around, but if you black stay back." This is a bad-ass jam! Check it out: "Fever"—Little Willie John—YouTube.

- **Oldies but Goodies.** By the way, I include a lot of references to old tunes throughout the book. They were and are an integral part of my life, I mean '50s and '60s sounds. By listening to my music, blasts from the past, you can check out my groove even now … and you, dear reader, will probably get a kick out of these old vinyl memories no matter what your age. Just ask the Wolfman, Jack!

- **Iconoclastic blasts.** This isn't a popularity contest, it's about being as honest as I can, all the time acknowledging that even I—Moi?—am as full of shit as the only port-o-potty at a crowded Texas rodeo.

- **Not just a spent youth** but to a great extent a spent life. For every poem, vignette, and sketch here, how many hundreds have blown in the wind, Mister Dylan? Figuratively and literally my piecemeal scribblings were placed like little paper boats into the stream of suchness. Getting booted out of my pads and leaving some pretty good shit behind with angry unpaid landlords on my ass or jealous lovers wielding salami slicers may have had a little to do with it.

- **Confuseling.** If at times things seem a little confusing, a bit erratic, and maybe out of sequence, it's probably because they are. This writing is a spontaneous reflection of the cacophonous drumbeat of my earlier life, hardly a harmonious symphony but more often the blaring clash of disparate, desperate notes. Oh, and I tend to be a bit redundant but that's only because I tend to repeat myself over and over again and again.

- **If truth be told** there is nothing in here, to the best of my knowledge, that is untrue—well, almost nothing. As they say, "Life is stranger than fiction," and my life has been sufficiently strange and shocking and wonderful and magical that my real job here is to report it as factually as I can, no need for embellishment.

- **I use the word "vignette"** in place of "chapter" because the flashbacks that are the fabric of this work, the short memory pieces (Do I have a short memory? Short what?) just don't qualify as your traditional chapters. Besides, the French word vignette sounds a little classier, more cosmopolitan, like the difference between autobiography and memoir. "Voulez-vous un bonbon, Mademoiselle? C'est si bon!" (Translation: Would you like a bonbon, you fine thang? It's soooo good!)

- **A little light on the matter.** You'll also find that much of the material is "light," as in lightweight, shallow, frivolous and utterly paltry (I like to think of it as "easy reading") … and here and there you'll find pieces that are light as in "I see the light." Hallelujah, brutha'!

Book One

ANOTHER COUNTRY

An Ignominious Birth Wrought with
Mystery, Myopia and Menudo

1944 to 1970, Mas o Menos

Photo Courtesy of Glenn Nagel Photography

Another Country

Being a swarthy sort who could pass for any number of nationalities, I'm often asked, "Where are you from?" Love that question. It gives me a chance to reply, "Another country." Invariably they of course inquire, "What country is that?" And I respond, "West Fresno." They usually laugh and I think, "Hell, I wasn't kidding!"

I've sometimes thought of Fresno as a chunk of transplanted antebellum Alabama, with its prickly cotton bolls and stooped over bodies, racism, and terrible hardship. When I was a kid, Fresno had all of those elements and I sure picked my share of cotton, grapes, and every other conceivable fruit and vegetable to be gathered. Fresno was indeed the hub of "The Food Basket of The World," that being the great San Joaquin Valley.

Crime of course comes with an oppressive environment like that, as does the devastating impact of cheap, formaldehyde-concentrated wine in every little grocery store, and heroin peddlers creeping around the old buildings of our community. In so many ways Fresno still has all the multi-layered poverty of a Third World nation, yet remains filled with wonderful folks who have endured and nurtured beautiful families through the years.

1944. The place of my conception was a funky hotel above a grimy theater, The Ryan, now Cuca's Mexican Café in Chinaman-less Chinatown. The hotel, I've been told, was a brothel back during the Second World War when I was born. Though not in business for decades it still stands in Fresno's ghetto, housing the ghosts of military men out for a good time, farm workers with pockets of cash, and nervous white men from across town, spirits listening to the joyous sounds of live mariachis from below and a radio blaring a sultry "Harlem Nocturne."

My parents, according to my birth certificate, were a 21-year-old soldier and an adolescent girl, 18, young people who may have cared for each other but didn't want a child. Their names were Abraham Chavez and Mary Hernandez. My middle name is Jesús. Abraham, Mary, and Jesus … good Buddhist family.

I find the possibility of my parents' first meeting in a less lewd environment entirely plausible, if for no other reason that only a few blocks east was the very popular Rainbow Ballroom. Still in the midst of the Second World War, Fresno was packed with military troops at Hammer Field and Camp

Pinedale, and the Rainbow had to be their "big band" destination on any given weekend. Romances blossomed in that intimate hall, where sometimes a thousand couples danced into the night. Maybe that's where they met.

Was my mother a prostitute? My foster mother said yes, but she was a serious boozed-out psych case, bless her perennially sauced soul. As to my "blood parents," I can only surmise there were any number of real reasons for their decision to drop me at some doorstep. In any case, I was quickly sent to an orphanage where I wailed with the rest of the little ones. I often wonder if my real parents were drinkers, or if their parents were.

I don't remember the orphanage days at all, but by the time I was four I was fostered. In retrospect, I think I was much better off at the orphanage.

Fraxinstein

The once thriving multi-racial Chinatown, the hub of West Fresno, has been long deserted by damn-near every ethnic group, except for the poor Blacks, Mexican immigrants (Border Brothers), Central Americans, Vietnamese, and Hmongs who moved in decades later. The others all left quite systematically according to the color of their skin: first the originally settled Anglos, including the Germans, then Italians, the Armenians, even the poor-ass Okies, followed by the Chinese and Japanese—that seems to be the general sequence. The original Native Americans from this area, the Yokuts, were hardly heard of and I think we all know why.

The name Fresno comes from the Spanish, and means "ash tree," genus fraxinus, because of the abundance of these botanical rabbits that once grew along the San Joaquin River. Some folks have taken a cheap shot with the below-the-belt punch of "Fres-not"—maybe because it has been America's drunkest city, fattest city, poorest city, most car jackingest city, to name a few of the Visitors Bureau highlights.

But the fact is, for all of its faults, Fresno is just like most burgs across the U.S. and that, Sir or Madam, ain't necessarily a compliment. By ripping out the old neighborhoods and building the soulless fortresses of the 'burbs, the definition of *neighbor*-hood is largely lost, and of course the ghetto remains much as it was sixty years ago. Where's all that redevelopment money? I think we know that too.

Photo courtesy of Ben Pease

The Altar of My Mis-Conception

This is the corner of F and Kern, the Nippon Building directly across from the great Buddhist temple. It lies in the heart of what was once Fresno's thriving "Golden West Side," a euphemistic tag made popular by the raspy, Wolfman Jack-ish voice of R&B DJ Happy Harold of KGST radio on the daily "Happy Harold's House of Blues."

The first floor now includes Cuca's Mexican café, specializing in Wienies con Huevos. Is that Freudian or am I weird? ... Don't answer that. The café is where, back in the '40s and '50s, the musty old Ryan Theatre once stood ... The Ryan where an old drunk put his hand on my knee in 1953.

Admission for kids was 10¢, for which we'd watch a cartoon, a terribly outdated newsreel, and a couple of ancient movies. I mean those flicks were oldies in the '50s, re-re-re-runs, starring guys like Tom Mix, Buster Crabbe, Johnny Weissmuller and classic gangster films with Edward G. Robinson, James Cagney, and a young Humphrey Bogart.

Without fail those aging celluloid strips would snap halfway through and you'd hear the flip-flip-flip of the reel until the Asian guy running the projector would wake up and fix it. Above was the Ryan Hotel, where a few years earlier my mom and pop played "Hide the Sausage."

Here is a passage by haiku master Basho (1644 to 1694), who composed great writings inspired by his considerable travels afoot. I find this particular piece eerily reminiscent of my own oddly ordained hatching:

> As we walked along the Fuji River we came upon an abandoned child, about two years of age and crying pathetically.

I wondered if his parents, finding the waves of this floating world as uncontrollable as the river, had abandoned him here, thinking his life would last only as long as the dew. The child looked as fragile as bush clover petals that would scatter, today or tomorrow, in the first autumn wind. I took some food from my sleeve and threw it to the child as we passed.

Somewhere Under the Rainbow

Here's the Rainbow Ballroom in a previous incarnation. Originally on "I Street" (now Broadway), it was built as The Fresno Natatorium, an indoor swimming complex back in 1918. In '24 it was transformed into Central California's most happening dance hall, replete with a sparkling, spinning ball in the center where I recall shaking my booty on many occasions.

In its heyday this venue played host to some real heavyweights, not the least being the likes of the big bands of Glen Miller, Harry James, Woody Herman, Tommy Dorsey and The Duke himself, Duke Ellington.

Later it would host the Latin big bands … I mean this is the music we Chicano kids could dance to, had the steps, like to the Afro-Cuban sounds of Perez Prado* (known as the "King of Mambo" … *Que rico el mambo!*)

And later still, shake a leg with legendary rock acts including Creedence Clearwater, Carlos Santana Blues Band, Fleetwood Mac, Janis Joplin, and Ike and Tina Turner. Not too shabby for funky Fresburg. And let us not forget Ray Camacho and the Teardrops, Tex-Mex Rrrrroke-en-Rrrrroll, who were indirectly responsible for many Mexican babies (and maybe directly).

*Prado's recording of "Cherry Pink and Apple Blossom White" featured a bad-ass *gabacho* trumpeter, Billy Regis, who knocked the hell out of the high notes. In '55, the tune reached Number One—that's Numero Uno—for 10 weeks in a row on the *Billboard* chart. I must have heard it a thousand times since then, and never stop lovin' it! Proto-salsa. Check it out, *ese*. Just Google Cherry Pink, Perez Prado, YouTube.

The Foster Family Fiasco

Oedipus Mex, 1948. The very first event that I can recall was when I was about four. It took place on the porch of our home at one of the Mosesian orchards where we were pickers and packers. This very old but reasonably well-kempt house, with wooden floors that curved from decades of many a wet mop, had a back porch without glass windows, just screens to keep out the countless fruit flies.

I was playing outside in a puddle of mud when I decided that a very fine thing to do would be to go and kiss my mother, my newly acquired foster mother. I quickly found her. She was doing the wash, by hand, using a washboard in a cement sink. I pulled at her dress and asked for a kiss. She picked me up and kissed me. She didn't even mind my muddy hands all over her clean white dress.

Throw Daddy under the Train. The second memory is when I was about five. The three of us—foster parents John and Linn, and Yours Truly—were sitting around the dinner table. I had a considerably older foster brother, Eddie (eight years my senior), but he was probably screwing around with his buds in that small railroad work camp. As it turned out, my foster dad had found a decent job as a flagman with one of the railroads that came through, the Southern Pacific, or just SP. The company provided small mustard-colored shacks along the tracks for the workers and their families, with all the coal they could use to heat the places.

The incident at the table was a picture of what I was to witness for the rest of my young life: them using the foulest imaginable language … "You fucking Okie whore," "you Spic son-of-a-bitch," etcetera ad nauseam. Same arguments, again and again, … how he rescued her from a hell-hole dive bar, how she was caught screwing someone, the two of them all this time guzzling the cheapest and worst rot-gut wines imaginable.

The bickering on this particular night reached a common violent boiling point. The wiry *gabacha* grabbed an empty bottle and threw it at him; she missed but kept throwing things. Being short and fast, the little guy was a tough target. He swerved and ducked as bottles smashed against the walls, spreading flying glass everywhere—just like in the cowboy movies.

That sadistic little monster then, out of nowhere, turned to me and slurred in his slight Mexican accent, "You see how she is! You see how she is? Screw her, I've had it! I'm going down to the tracks—the railroad tracks—an' just lay there 'til the next train runs over me!"

My eyes shot wide open as did my mouth. I finally had a family, and I was already going to lose my dad. I fell to my knees and, teary eyed, begged him not to do it. That bantam-brained bastard never had the slightest inclination to leave that crazy bitch and his beloved bottle, was never leaving the pathetic game they played, night after night.

Notes

- About foster Father John—You don't know the half of it, but I forgave him many years ago. To be fair, the poor guy never had a chance. The last of nine kids and the runt of the litter, he was raised in an illiterate Mexican family down in Southern Cal at the turn of that century, 1903. He himself was illiterate, couldn't spell or write his own name.

  And being a short, dark, older Metzican here in White America, I have no doubt this layered oppression could not have been good for what was left of his crumbled self-respect. I remain pissed off about the factors that got him to where he lived out his tragic life … and being married to a wild, booze-crazed White chick sure as hell wasn't a plus.
- There's a word used in modern psychology regarding folks who, either physically or mentally, have been severely abused, and that word is battered. I really understand the meaning on both counts. It bothers me that when the abuse is primarily mental it so frequently falls under the radar and is allowed to continue.
- Linn's favorite quote: "Wish in one hand and shit in the other and see which one gets filled first." Move over Oprah, now that's positive thinking!
- John's favorite line directed to me from the time I was seven: "You're a little queer, ain't you?" Well, yes, I guess I was a bit unusual.
- "Folie à deux": "a delusion or delusional system shared by two individuals, usually a husband and wife." From *A Dictionary of Psychology.*

Karmic Encounter

1948. My first meeting with an East Indian (as differentiated from Native American "Indian" or "Fresno Indian," pejorative for an Armenian in the Fresno area) was at the old Mosesian farmhouse where I lived briefly when I was five or six.

There was an aging Hindu man that I still have a grainy picture of tucked away somewhere. He's standing alone next to our house with his long, white beard and dirty pants—but a very clean turban. I remember walking with him, one of my earliest memories, and asking who he was and what he did. He said he was "The Irrigator."

These were sizable fields and orchards, with rows as long as my eyes could possibly see. He would open those massive water pipes with their steering-wheel-sized faucets and the water would gush out into the ditches, somehow wondrous for a small child.

I remember walking by his side, barefooted, squishing my toes in the mud while he brought the mighty Euphrates together with the Ganges and the Nile. Perhaps it was he who taught me the true meaning of the dot on the forehead of his people.

The First Kick Boxer

1952-ish. We would sit around the flimsy dinner table, sometimes the four of us but usually three, them with a glass of wine, or on occasion a bottle or can of your basic beer. On this very special occasion (it was my 6th birthday, woo-hooo!), beer was the beverage of choice, and Lucky Lager was the brand, the brand with the big red X across the label (for good reason I now know). My single birthday gift was a miniature glass beer mug. It was designed to look like the real thing but was a tiny version, about the size of a shot glass.

We ate our usual meal of home-made beans, tortillas, and some sort of a tomato sauce concoction with onions, garlic, oregano and any kind of cheap meat cooked into it. But this day, this very special day, they poured me a foaming glass of … of … of Lucky Lager! Man, that was smooth. "Can I have anotha', suh," I begged with my best Oliver Twist accent. Pour some more, por favor!

One, two, three … I loved it! Then, Bam!, like a lightning bolt it hit and they, my parents-of-sorts, of course thought it was just f-ing hilarious, this little kid swerving like a swirling dervish and doing double-back flips. Their laughter really pissed me off, and so I raced out to the back porch and into the back yard where I encountered a bunch of cardboard boxes that had been stacked there.

Those boxes had never seen such fury … I kicked the hell out of every one of 'em! My buzzed-up parents stood on the porch watching me, still laughing hysterically, which pissed me off all the more. Take that, you cardboard piece of shit!

By the way … the next year my parents out-did themselves with a gift that made me feel like a full-grown, for-real man. One morning about a month before my birthday, early October, I found myself out in a drizzly cotton field. We found warmth standing around a couple of old car tires that had been set aflame. The smell and black smoke of the rubber was unpleasant, but the heat was most welcome.

There's no getting around it, picking cotton was very hard work, stooped over and moving your fingers as fast as you could to fill that damned canvas cotton sack strapped over your shoulder. Then dragging it all the way to a large, 12-foot-tall trailer where you would weigh the sack, climb a ladder to the top of the trailer, walk across a plank, and dump the cotton out of your bag—that itself was no picnic. The length of those bags ranged, generally about 20 feet for women and teenagers, 25 to 30 feet for men. When full the larger ones could easily weigh well over a hundred pounds, the very long ones even up to two hundred and more. Dragging those damned things down the endless rows in the hot sun was, pun intended, a real drag.

Well, anyway, my family and a handful of others stood around that noxious fire smell as we waited for the rising sun to burn off the small amount of morning mist on the cotton. Since we were paid by the pound the growers wouldn't have to cough up quite as much for our labor. I remember a pretty standard 2½ to 3 cents per pound, and that little bit of extra weight of the water would have the growers shitting bricks. In other words, a hundred pounds earns you three-fuckin'-dollars! … and grown men would spend half a day reaching that point.

So, about this time of the morning my foster parents pulled me over to them, and offered a present all wrapped up in a used Fresno Bee newspaper. It was like some kind of warped Christmas gift. They said something to the effect of, "Hey, we got you something very special for your birthday coming up."

Man was I excited! I shredded that paper in seconds, and there it was: *my very own mini cotton sack*, a five-footer. Wow, I felt like a million … My very own cotton sack, just like the grown-ups!

Watermelon Boy

Well, this all started when I was just a kid, maybe eight or nine. So happens that on one of my family's sublime summer outings working in the cotton fields of Central California, I met another kid about my age, a girl who was out there just like me, a cotton-pickin' Mexican.

So one morning as I was up on that plank emptying my bag, here comes the next worker-bee. Turns out it's a she-bee, a young girl about my age. Well, you know me, even then I was immediately jabbering with her about whatever, really just plain fun. Well, next thing you know we both dove from the plank atop the cotton trailer into the half-full, maybe six-feet-deep pile of pure white cotton. We were soon wrestling around and gleefully screaming.

Well, of course, all good things gotta end, so it turns out when the next person, a heavy set, mustachioed man (Booo!), reached the plank to dump his 20-foot bag he basically told us to get the heck out of there and go back to our parents.

Soooo, come to find the little girl is back out there in the field with her family picking alongside my parents … and I'll be darned if they weren't friends. So where is this all going, you ask? Hell, I don't know, I mean that was about 70 years ago … Oh, yeah, the next day, which was either a Saturday or Sunday, a weekend for sure, we were to all get together at our house.

Turns out for the first time in my lifetime with these foster parents we finally had a half-decent home, I mean very old but with running water, separate bedrooms, and an inside toilet … how 'bout that. Now to get back to my story, my mom was busily preparing a meal for this gathering, don't recall what was on the menu, but her being White it probably featured white bread sandwiches of some sort. And on this warm day there was certainly no shortage of … *watermelon*, slices of it in the ice box (a kind of non-electric Ice Age refrigerator cooled by large blocks of ice.) Ah, ha!

As Mom was cutting some slices for the upcoming gathering—me and my parents and *my newfound friend* and her parents—I asked if I might have a piece of melon, and she said, fine, but there is something that I must remember. She appeared very serious about the matter. What she shared I really took to heart: "Tommy, here's your watermelon but whatever you do, don't eat the seeds!" Huh? Well why not, spitting them out would just slow me down. Then came the shocking reason: "Tommy, if you accidentally swallow a seed, even one, a watermelon will grow out of your butt!"

Holy shit, can't have that, especially with my little friend coming with her family. So I went out in the back yard and in record time that sweet watermelon slice had disappeared, me with the juice rolling all over my chin. As usual, I wiped my mouth with my t-shirt and that's when it hit me. I hadn't spit out any seeds, nary a one! Can you say psycho-so-matic?

Well, within an hour or so my Dad's friend along with his family show up, of course with my little friend in tow. I saw them pull up in front of the house and in desperation I sought an escape. I could hear chatter from the living room and the girl's voice asking where I was. Gasp! They must have spent half of eternity looking for me, and suddenly the closet door opened where I had been hiding in a corner.

"What are you doing in here?" asked my mother as I began to cry, tears flowing as if the worst thing ever had just happened to me. But I did manage to answer her: "Mama, you know what you told me about watermelon seeds? Well, it's true, I know, I can feel one already growing out of my butt." Boy, I sure didn't want my little friend to see me in this totally embarrassing state.

My foster parents weren't the most subtle or thoughtful people in the world, and soon the whole darned room was howling with laughter as they looked at me hunkered down in a corner of the small closet. Good thing kids are pretty good about quickly getting over such matters, especially if a nice slice of cold watermelon is offered.

Hey, check this one out: *Watermelon Man*, Mongo Santamaria, YouTube … reminds me of the head-boppin' *Lowrider* by the Latino band War, and Ray Baretto's *El Watusi.*

The Tragic Tail of Henny Penny

1953-ish. Have I mentioned that we were quite poor? How poor were we? Why, we were so poor the winos in the neighborhood used to drop their empty bottles into our back yard so we could recycle them … that's a fact, Jack. We were so poor …

Anyway, there was one category in which we weren't poor, and that's chickens. Yep, we had a couple dozen in the back yard right next to the alley, living in a makeshift coop hammered together with old two-by-fours and chicken wire. I was about six at the time, and I was mesmerized by all those chickens laying eggs every day. My job each morning was to get a basket and search for the eggs. My parents would save some for eating and sell the rest to neighbors.

One day I spotted a new chick, all bright yellow and fuzzy. We didn't have a dog or a cat, but I was quite attached to this particular little critter, so I asked my parents if I could keep him as a pet. They said OK, and in due time we figured out he was a she. Being a very creative kid, I chose to name her Henny Penny.

I soon separated her from the batch and built a cage for her out of a large cardboard box that I kept on the back porch. I cuddled her and treated her like she was a puppy. In record time that darned chicken was following me around the yard, and she even came when I called her (feeding her each time may been a bit of an incentive). I even developed my own original secret code to call her, "Here chick-chick! Here chick-chick!" I was amazed how rapidly she grew.

In a few months we had even more chickens, and I'd get up early, feed them, and gather all those eggs. But late one night as we slept some guys must've got pretty hungry or in need of a wine fix, because every darned chicken in that coop had been snatched … every one of' 'em except Henny Penny, who was tucked away in her own little cardboard crib.

This happened in November, I know because my birthday is in November, and it was also a few days before Thanksgiving. By that time of the month, you may rest assured that my alcoholic parents had drunk up the two welfare checks sent for the upkeep of my older brother and me. But even they felt an obligation to do the right thing, and so on a drizzly Thanksgiving afternoon all four of us sat down for a somewhat civilized dinner: biscuits, gravy, mashed potatoes … and what they said was a small turkey. Mmm-mmmm!

Well, I don't think I need go much further, but the obvious struck me and so I nervously went out to the back yard and Henny Penny was, of course, nowhere to be found. I didn't even eat the damned potatoes and gravy, my favorites. Folks say all dogs go to heaven, and I'm here to say some chickens do too.

Tarzan Meets the Neighbors

The comedian/activist Dick Gregory had a great line regarding his book titled *Nigger*: "Dear Momma, Wherever you are, if ever you hear the word 'nigger' again, remember they are advertising my book." When I first heard of that book, I was a young man in my early twenties. Little did I know that I'd meet and converse with this gentleman several times over the course of my life.

When I was seven, I had no real idea what the so-called N-word meant, and in fact, to the best of my recollection, there had been no black folks in my life. Living in those railroad shacks in West Fresno I can only recall Okie and Mexican boys that I would play with because they were the only ones around—the Wilsons and the Soto kids.

Then my old man got fired and we moved over to an old house on "E" Street, where the *Fresno Bee* newspaper now stands. Everything on that block was old, old houses with old Italian folks to the left and the right, Mrs. Minenna and Mrs. Capozzi, and old Mr. Green, who was black, across the street. He was a pleasant old coot, just sat on his porch in that creaky old rocking chair from morning to night, watching the old cars go clattering by.

Right next to him was a small, single-mom black family that I eventually came to know. I'm not sure of their last name, but the boy about my age was named Paul, Paul Wise. I forget his two sisters' names (oddly enough, I remember that the name of the baby in the family was Etienne). They were no different than the other snotty-nosed kids I had played with back at the railroad shanties except they were "black"... which never made sense to me because, in fact, that whole family was really brown.

Anyway, before I got to know them, I'd just play by myself, climbing up that big sycamore tree in front of the house and doing my best version of the Johnny Weissmuller Tarzan yodel, "Oh-ah-oh-ah-oooo-ooo!" Well, for some reason the kids across the street took umbrage with my bellowing and proceeded to pick up some good-sized rocks ... then they began throwing them, throwing them at me, me, *Tarzan, King of The Jungle.*

I was quick to respond, "You fuckin' little niggers!" I still have no clue where I got that but there's a real good chance it was from the Wilson clan. The more I screamed, the more rocks they threw. About this time my ruddy-faced, red-headed foster mother, white as the milk from a Hopalong Cassidy milk bottle, came out to the front porch and observed this exchange, them with rocks and me with words. "Oh, Tommy," called my mom, "come down here … I want to talk with you." Oh, shit! I knew that tone.

She said, very simply and very sternly, "Don't ever—*ever*—use that word again, you understand?" It was clear to me that it wasn't the F-word that she was referring to. She really didn't explain much but went on to spank the holy shit out of me. Crude but effective. (In this day and age—I know it ain't p.c.—but that whoopin' was well deserved.)

I never used the word again and cringe to this day when I hear it, whether it's from up-front white racists or punky black kids, used as if there's something cool or complimentary about it. It's hard to hate a word … but this one qualifies. Within a day or two, Paul and I had become best of friends, and we'd hang out up in that old sycamore trying to out-do each other with our best Tarzan screams, "Oh-ah-oh-ah-oooo-ooo!"

Give Pizza a Chance

> "The only hope for any of us is peace. Violence begets violence. Get out there and get peace. Think peace, live peace, and breathe peace and you'll get it as soon as you like. Okay?"—John Lennon

1951-ish. Radio, Radio. Radio, verrry good to me. I was eight or so when I first got my very own radio, a small, used thing but, hey, it was mine. In spite of the incessant ravings of my foster parents, and even louder than they, was my beloved little AM radio. From what I recall, the thing looked like it was right out of a 1936 Flash Gordon Sci-fi serial.

As I've said, we only had AM in those years but man, it was rich, full, and deeply human—and very little of the divisiveness we now see in most media. Better than television at the time with the humongous antennas or woefully inadequate rabbit ears, fuzzy snow-flake episodes of *The Cisco Kid* … Ai, Pancho!

Those and embarrassingly bad advertising, like "You'll wonder where the yellow went when you brush your teeth with Pepsodent" … or "Chinese Baby love Jello!" The Jello Peril? Radio wasn't better than TV just because of those things but better because it took a good imagination to fully appreciate.

In my case I became totally absorbed in those adventures, creating the images in my mind often based on the old movies I had seen or the stacks of comic books that I faithfully collected (I still dream about finding wooden boxes of wonderful old comics hidden in a musty cellar somewhere).

I would often lay comfortably in my bed with my comic book buddies at my side, radio blasting. But above the sound of my favorite programs, I could always hear my parents in the next room in their unholy, seemingly eternal battles (I do pray that in death they found peace and quiet). The good thing about that little box was that you could turn it up. The louder they got, the louder went my radio. That sucker had an unusually loud speaker—at least that's what I heard the grown-ups say—a pre-historic ancestor of the infamous boom-box.

I'd lay there, peanut butter-and-jelly spread on a home-cooked flour tortilla in one of my sticky hands, comic book in the other, listening to *The Lone Ranger* and his ass-kissing sidekick, Tonto (Tonto, by the way, in Mexican slang means fool or stupid—thanks a lot, Kemo Sabe!)

Did I tell you I met Jay Silverheels, the actor who played Tonto on TV and in the old movies? The cat was a bone fide In'jun, a First Nations Mohawk, a Native-Canadian. Met 'im at a bar in Santa Cruz—the original Catalyst, on Front Street—and, after the man was nice enough to buy me a drink, I had the audacity to ask him if he knew what Tonto really meant … ouch! Anyway, he just stood there, all stoic, like a wooden Indian … well? Didn't say another word, just stared into the mirror behind the bar … and the son-of-a-gun didn't buy me another drink either. Maybe I pissed him off … ya think?

By the way, the endearing name that the character Tonto calls The Lone Ranger is Kemo Sabe, which in Spanish is really "que no sabe." That roughly translates as "he who knows nothing" or "clueless" … Stupid and Clueless, dynamic duo indeed.

But I digress … on with the radio shows, like *Red Ryder and Little Beaver*, *The Inner Sanctum*, and, of course, *The Shadow*. My foster mom was also a radio addict. Most of her days were spent laying on the bed—we didn't have a sofa, let alone a living room—glass of cheap wine in one hand and roll-your-own cigarette in the other, with soap opera's tragic *Helen Trent* losing lovers like I was losing teeth. And now and then the news would come on, usually some incongruous-to-me reports on the raging battles in Korea. I couldn't care less, because I was occupied with my comic books, Ka-pow! and Rat-a-tat-tat!

One evening when my dad was out carousing, my mom needed to go to relieve herself but for whatever reason was afraid to go to the outhouse alone. An outhouse, mind you, was a wooden no-flush shitter and back in 1952 there weren't too many homes that didn't have a toilet within the house ...We lived only a couple blocks from downtown Fresno which, by the way, had the first mall in the nation, but we still had a fly and spider infested crapper! This putrid, rickety thing had been there since the time the house was built, I'm thinkin' since the early '20s and man, it smelled like it.

It sat right next to the alley and back then there were crazed and hungry folks who would wander up and down looking for empty bottles to sell or chicken eggs to steal. She'd just grab me by the hand and like a rag doll drag me along with her into the back yard where she'd do her business.

This particular evening, the sun had just set, a clear, warm summer twilight in Fresno, the heat having subsided to a comfortable—by Fresno standards—high-eighties. She went into the toilet and, rude as she was, left the door wide open—but then, hell, the cows and pigs don't close a door to take a crap, do they?

Anyway, that evening I spotted the first glittering star, probably a planet ... but who in my cosmos knew then? She, for the first time, shared with me the wonderful little nursery rhyme about wishing on the first star you see: "Star light, star bright, first star I see tonight, I wish I may, I wish I might, have this wish I wish tonight." Well, I didn't have to think at all. Without one iota of hesitation, I knew what that wish was for: *World Peace.*

How in the world does an eight-year-old kid come up with an idea like that? I don't recall going to church up to this age, and I don't believe I could possibly have understood the familiar passage from *The Beatitudes*, "Blessed are the peacemakers, for they will be called children of God." —Matthew 5:9, NIV.

More sensible to wish that I got a bicycle or a bee-bee gun, or that my parents stopped drinking. Nope, I've never understood that one. My only connection with that kind of sanity was the radio, where idealism and goodness still reigned as The Lone Ranger and Tonto rode the wild range ... Hi-Yo, Silver, and away!

Peace Piece. Many, many moons later, in the Orwellian year of 1984, I conceived of a meaningful directory that I titled *The Peace Catalog*. The concept was to create an anthology of articles from a variety of the top thinkers on the subject of World Peace, followed by a directory—literally "yellow pages"—on the topic.

I then wrote a little business plan and headed down to a bar near the University of Washington, Giorgio's, where a bunch of old commie professors and other well-educated crazies hung out. I presented my idea to a couple of profs with whom I had become acquainted and in short time managed to raise about $10,000 for publishing this unique book. I was fortunate to find a very bright graduate student, Duane Sweeney, to be the editor. He deserves the credit for accumulating most of the articles in the book, though I furnished the writings of certain famous writers with whom I was acquainted.

The name of the book, in fact the general concept, was inspired by Stewart Brand's *Whole Earth Catalog: Access to Tools*, a real breakthrough in terms of information on self-sufficiency, ecology, alternative education, holism, and do-it-yourself instructions for do-gooder projects. I just tried to apply that formula to world peace.

My catalog had damn-near everything you could imagine on the subject, including a directory of existing peace groups throughout the world, over 1,000 (mind you, this was pre-Google), and great articles sent to us by the likes of astronomer Carl Sagan, author Ken Kesey, poet Lawrence Ferlinghetti, and, hey, artwork by Pablo Picasso.

Always the punster, I called my fledgling publishing company *Press for Peace.* Once the catalog was published, I tried some guerrilla marketing techniques to peddle the book (frankly, that was because I didn't know a damn thing about getting the publication to the larger audience via traditional modes. I still groan.)

But one of my clever ideas was to have the book's coming out party at a nice pizza joint in the neighborhood and call the event "Give pizza a chance." I had the pizza guy use pepperoni and sausage to form the old school peace symbol. We, of course, invited the various members of the press, especially TV stations and the then vibrant newspapers, The Post-Intelligencer and The Seattle Times.

Well, I'm not sure of the sequence but what happened about three years later is that I found myself down in Santa Monica meeting with a prominent peace activist named Jerry Rubin. What a nice man. I gave him a copy of the catalog and we decided that getting a copy of the book to right-wing war-toy humdrum ham actor Sylvester Stallone might get some press. But the real schtick was the pizza bit.

So, Jerry took it a step further: he convinced a pizza joint buddy of his to bake a mega pizza with a giganto peace sign, again made out of pepperoni and sausage. He then delivered it to Stallone's doorstep, with a copy of *The Peace Catalog*. The message to Mr. Stallone was simple, just like the Beatles' tune, "All we are saying is *give peace a chance.*" Made the front page on one of the local rags...of yeah, the LA times. I recently found the article on the topic with this title: 'Peace Pizza,' Sent to Stallone, Symbolizes Protest of Violence, L.A. Times Archives, Aug. 14, 1988, 12 AM PT

Because of my marketing ignorance and, I hate to admit, my non-stop alcohol intake, I just couldn't move the thing. I eventually found a co-publisher but unfortunately the book never caught on. It was pretty academic and definitely a niche thing but still that was hardly the cause of its premature demise. Sadly, I was yet to make peace with my own demons and my lifelong nemesis.

I have learned that it is damn near impossible to attain world peace when so many powerful individuals are mentally and morally deranged, the great majority who are addicted to some damn thing—including money and power. They are always at war with others and with themselves. There is certainly a call for great heroism here, and I think it is the young people of the world who will save us from the old paradigm of a dual-istic mentality.

Before the book was printed, I asked a woman who was working on the project to go to a grade school and request that the kids do drawings of their image of peace for my book. Of about a dozen that were brought to me, I chose a wonderful piece of art by an 11-year-old kid named Winston Chu. With crayons he had drawn a very cool image of outer space, replete with planets and comets. And he had hand-lettered these words on his creation: "Peace should be like space … Endless." From the mouths of babes.

Sadly, a book like this is needed as much now as ever. I'm workin' on it.

The
Peace
Catalog
A Guidebook to a Positive Future.

The First Step

It saddens me so, those fingers ever pointing,
from the first evil gesture to the point of near extinction.

The old men with rat-a-tat brains,
the ones who relish re-runs of World War carnage—
Japs & Krauts & G.I. Joes all making ack-ack noises,
"Ah, now *there* was a war!"
No, they are not the ones.

Those same old men are now poor boys with bang-bang fingers
trapped in a circle of dangerous delusion,
prison bait who have lived too little and read not enough—
they are not the ones.

Are now camouflaged patriots who vote
with their heads rammed between
an assault rifle and a bible they pretend to understand…
they are not the ones.

But Jesus said, "Love thy neighbor,"
and Jesus said, "Love thy enemy,"
And so I guess the first step is to take my own finger
and put it on a button tritely marked, "Love is the answer!"

Slit my finger and with my blood sign a treaty
disbanding my own formidable army
of hatred and illness and fear,
make a corny pact with myself that says,
"Peace in the world starts with peace in the heart."

Take this step and try to remember
there are G.I. Joes in every uniform of every country
who all are an equal part of the one force
whose eye is everywhere and whose finger does not point.

What's Behind the Stars?

June, 1982. Here's a brief note to an old classmate, sent just before our 2nd high school class re-union.

Elena DLP,

How great it's been to read about all of you. I write to you specifically because of your interest in astronomy. Man, it was fabulous when we could really see those beauties in the ol' Wez Frez sky, before smog had taken hold. That's a wonderful hobby you have.

When I was about eight, I'd lay at night in my back yard and ask myself boggling questions, like "Where did the dinosaurs come from?" and "What's behind the stars?" In that early exercise of childhood inquisitiveness, I was in awe of that sweeping, twinkling blanket and think 'til my little brain was exhausted.

In trying to figure out what indeed is behind the stars, I remember picturing a dome-shaped brick wall that covered the entire universe, what I could see of it anyway. It looked like the aged Italian bread oven in the back yard of my next-door neighbor, Mrs. Minenna, there on E Street. (Not by chance, the remnants of a similar oven were still standing in my own back yard, an oven that must have been built in the '20s, which is about how old that house was.)

The massive brick wall, my imagined wall, was a humongous structure that encircled what I envisioned as the universe. Brick by brick by brick I built that sucker. That was my solution: a gazillion-sized ball made of bricks that encircled the starry heavens.

But damn, then I was confronted with yet another boggler: What the heck's behind that brick wall I had just constructed? If we go far enough out, we might find the answer. If we go far enough in, we might find the answer.

See you at the get-together! Your Tiger classmate,
Tommy

Bullfight at the Okie Corral

> "I will not see it! Tell the moon to come for I do not want to see the blood of Ignacio on the sand."
> —from *Weeping for the Death of Ignacio Sánchez Mejías*, an elegy written by the Spanish poet/activist Federico Garcia Lorca for his famous matador friend, who had been gored to death…at exactly five in the afternoon.

1953. As a child I had very, very few good times with my old man. Working in the vegetable garden was one of them. Drunk or not he'd get out there in the hot sun, get down on his knees, and plant his tomatoes, onions, and red-hot Fresno chili peppers. I'd poke along behind him, having the periodic privilege of sticking a seedling or seed into the freshly watered earth. And the following story is of another good time:

When I was a little kid, about eight or so, my dad took me to a bullfight. It was held in the heat of summer in a remote little outdoor arena with splintery bleachers, part of a small fairgrounds somewhere in the central San Joaquin Valley. The cruelty to the bull was certainly not a factor and there was no law against it. It was not until 1957 that only "bloodless bullfighting" was allowed in the U.S.

The place was packed, filled mostly with dirt-poor Latino workers and a few white farmers drinking from long-necked beer bottles. I was excited because it was absolutely rare for me to go anywhere with my foster father. Looking back, I can see why that was so, not just because of our overall poverty but the fact that every extra cent my parents had went into booze. In that context it was amazing that I went with him at all, but then—going along with the "there-are-no-accidents" theory—maybe I was there so I could write about it now.

The beers-of-choice back in those days—in our circle, in any case—were Lucky Lager and Pabst Blue Ribbon. "What'll you have? Pabst Blue Ribbon!," the jingle went. So, right on cue, as my dad chugged his brew and I chugged my root beer (root training for later life addictions), the music began, a live band playing a grand rousing tune, trumpets and trombones and tubas (oh, my!) … glorious stuff for a little kid in a dustbowl kind of place.

Then, slowly, came an introduction of the afternoon's heroes, the skinny guys in flashy gold-sequined tights and strange little hats, regal and cocky in their strut. God it was good, even in Outer Nowhere. For me there was a kind of beauty in the air.

But then I opened my loud brain and broke the trance. What's the point to all this I wondered, as kids often do. Is it a dance, a parade? I had seen the gaudy Catholic processions, a few dozen true believers marching down a small street now and then, bass drum pounding for Patron Saint So-'n-so, glittery and surreal, and this ceremony that I was witnessing felt a bit the same, a pageantry with the underpinnings of something tragic. But it still felt good—wonderful!—because it swept me away like a hokey cowboy movie or a Superman comic book.

The music made my skin shiver with goose pimples, just the regal sense of it, the high-note trumpet blares and sketches of Spain. The whole adventure raised me to a new level, made me feel like I was part of something great, bigger than me and my old man and all the bullshit I was growing up with.

This was a microcosm of life and death. Perhaps there was an historic connection—my Spanish blood—of some sort locked up in sub-cellular memory, a connection that remembers the iconography, images, smells, and feelings from dynamic, archetypal moments in our distant past. Perhaps this is a tale of the death of the moon so that the sun may rise again, the killing of separateness.

Whatever it all was, I liked it! I didn't think at all about how the bull felt, spear after spear plunging into its body until the bloody finalé, the bull, Christ-like, being sacrificed to bring heaven to a bunch of poor farm workers for a couple of hours on a sweltering afternoon. I washed down a handful of popcorn with a slug of root beer and, with the rest of us peasants, shouted a hearty "Olé!"

Transcending the Bull

God knows it's a good time to point the finger, most of America is doing it … the finger to the politicians, bankers (con men with Harvard ties), dope dealers (including the American Medical Association), and countless others. But I am here to say if there is "bull" to be fought, it is mine, it is my bull that must be brought down into the dust of trampled egos.

The truth of it is that this creature of attachment, of possessiveness, of addiction, is damn near undefeatable. The more we pick at him (the work of the picadors), the more pissed off and stronger he gets, edging closer to his moment of glory, a deadly gore to his arrogant adversary.

The wise bullfighter is aware of this. Like the controlled spontaneity, the planned accident, of a sumi-e artist, the bullfighter with a flowing yet well-rehearsed *veronica* steps aside as that snorting fool, wasting his massive advantage, goes flying into emptiness. I can almost hear that baffled animal, "What the …?"

A *veronica* is the movement a bullfighter gracefully makes while pulling his cape aside and stepping away from a charging bull. It is named for St. Veronica and a gesture with her handkerchief after wiping the bloody face of Jesus.

As we know, this "stepping aside" was a key element in the development of the early martial arts' schools. Hundreds of years ago, when monks—both Taoists and Buddhists—were attacked on the road, they discovered means of using their adversaries' own brute strength against them. As I understand it, they learned to quickly move aside, tiring the thugs out—the original "rope-a-dope." And, as the attackers were falling, the monks gave'em a good old Kung Fu chop. Right on, Grasshopper!

Most recently, I was still exploring various treatments for my alcoholism—at least I was trying, trying being trying—and sad to say still plunging my mind and body into a no-win arena.

The word matador, as you may be aware, is taken from the Spanish verb *matar*, meaning to kill. As *Zen Matador* this indicates the killing of ignorance, the killing of unhealthy ego, and the killing of harmful desires … easier said than done. Deep down I pray that I still have a few *veronicas* left in me.

The King of Chinatown

Circa '56 Black-and-White Photo of my Foster Father

On the sunny West Side of Fresno, in Chinaman-less Chinatown, the ghost of gritting teeth and broken bottles staggers in alleys and howls in the heat of the late afternoon … *Aye-yai-yai-yai-yai!*

The King of Chinatown, barefooted with his banker's vest and shirt of skin and cologne of musty brown alley smells, scans his domain through shot-glass spectacles, twirls in a little corrido-like spin, remembering La Gloria at the Las Palmas' *tardeada* in the summer of '52, La Gloria of The Knife and veins of roses ... *Aye-yai-yai-yai-yai!*

The King of Chinatown, annoyed with progress, flips off the thundering jet and surveys his collection of bottles and cans—a party will be held by all! —except Old Chino, who called him a peenchee sonnavabeechee and threw a blow at him, him, The King of Chinatown.

The King of Chinatown at six in the morn races to the run-down labor buses, upon entering throws *chingasos* for a front-row seat, hard money for the Big Dance, dreams of that glittering, spinning ball at the Rainbow Ballroom, he, all spiffy in his second-hand suit and two-tone shoes, remembers the wicked saliva of the skinny white chick and scratches on his numb back.

The King of Chinatown remembers when a fifth of tokay was 41 cents and when the skinny white chick laughed all the way to his room above the cantina; for a second he stops to cry but quickly wipes his mouth of suffering, scratches his parched balls and declares his royal stature ... *Ai-yai-yai-yai-yai!*

The Gift

When I was nine, I was in the third grade at dear old Columbia Elementary. It was a two-story brick schoolhouse built in the 1930s that just felt like a place of learning. The halls and rooms were warm and welcoming and, as it seemed, the teachers loved what they were called to do. Certainly, Miss Capozzi did, with that beaming smile each morning as we entered the classroom.

This particular day was special because we were getting out of school for the Christmas and New Year holidays. Miss Capozzi (who I had a big ol' crush on) said that we'd be working on a special project that, when completed, we could take home with us. What could it possibly be?

She told us to clear our desks and take out our crayons. This excited me because I really enjoyed drawing of all sorts. Then she gave each of us, may twenty kids or so, a piece of drawing paper, a size and length that we were unfamiliar with—maybe a foot tall and a couple feet wide.

Now, being just a day or two before Christmas, it made sense that we were asked to draw a picture filled with holiday images, you know, like candy canes, a Christmas tree, and a snowman with a carrot for a nose. I gleefully jumped into this kid-sized art project and filled in that empty sheet pretty quickly.

Next came a real surprise: each one of us was given an empty (too bad) ice cream tub. The thing was made of a cardboard-like material and was round like a small drum. I'd seen these containers before when we were served a scoop down at the Snow White ice cream parlor. I'd guess it was meant to hold about five gallons.

The pieces were all coming together, and when we had all completed our drawings, she gave us a small tube of Elmer's glue. She then instructed us to put the glue on the outsides of the ice cream tub and wrap our little masterpieces around the tubs. And voilà, there it was—a delightful trash basket for the home!

When school was out, I excitedly hurried home to our shanty with my creation, knowing it would be well received. After all, this was my one and only Christmas offering for my mother.

She was sitting there as usual, listening to a soap opera on the radio, a cigarette in one hand and a glass of wine in the other. I held my gift behind my back and told her I had something for her. When I showed it to her, I exclaimed, "Merry Christmas!"

I seem to recall there was a second of hesitation, just her curiosity, I guess, about what the heck it was. I told her that it was for trash, a Christmas trash basket (but of course). She nodded and looked it over. I mean in my mind it was a pretty nifty little thingamajig.

Then, out of nowhere, I just broke down in tears, I mean a real deluge. I told her that I was so sorry that this was all I had for her, that I couldn't give her a "real" gift. I was so embarrassed for how measly I felt the present was, not considering the genuine feeling that I'd put into it.

But after a nice hug from her and something to the effect that she really liked it, I was soon outside running in circles with a make-believe dog.

What My Boys Club Means to Me

> "I'm living proof that the Boys and Girls Clubs work."
> —Denzel Washington

1951. I'll never forget my first day at the Fresno Boys Club; I can't possibly. I was greeted by Donald Stevenson, the club director, Harvey, his assistant, and young Howard, a black kid who was Harvey's assistant. (Howard had been a club member since he was a kid himself).

It was my 7th Birthday and my foster parents had waited long for this glorious occasion. For 50¢ they enrolled me for a year in "The Club," pleased I am sure to get me the hell out of the house. I could hardly wait to get to that wonderful new family, from the time school let out until closing every evening at nine o'clock when I'd walk home by myself.

I recall a couple of times when a big car with an older white man would pull up slowly and ask if I'd like a ride home … probably well-meaning, after all, it was older white men who donated to build and maintain that loving clubhouse. But my instinct was to say thanks and keep on walking.

The Club at the time was down on Tulare and "C" Street, two relatively small oblong buildings that looked like they had been built during the Second World War or before. They were clean but considerably run down from the wear and tear of age and a few hundred kids flying across those wooden floors and stairs.

It was the stairs that provided my first and lasting memory. I had been playing outside on the basketball court when we were called into the building to check out for the night. I ran up those old stairs, maybe three of four of them, and tripped, my left index finger split wide open by a large, jagged splinter on one of the steps, a hazard for sure. Thank God there were no friggin' attorneys around.

Blood was gushing and Harvey and Howard saw to my wound, washing it off, putting on a generous pour of mercurochrome (ouch!), and wrapping it with a bandage of gauze and tape. Mr. Stevenson came up to me and said he'd give me a ride home. When we pulled up in front of my house there on E Street, we could hear my foster parents' drunken howling all the way out into the street. Mr. Stevenson had probably seen this scene before in the lives of so many of those ghetto kids.

The injury produced a permanent scar on my finger, which I value to this day (so when I give you the finger—flip the bird, as it were—I'm really just showing off my Boys Club initiation wound). The Club became my real home and dramatically changed my entire life. It brought me in contact with other kids in the same boat as me, and with adults who gave a damn. The club had a television set (imagine that!), all kinds of games, a workshop (which I was never interested in), and ongoing activities. There were fishing and camping excursions every summer, neat trips to the mountains during snow season and even warm-fuzzy Christmas parties with gifts for everyone, which I remember to this moment. I had none of these things at home.

Over time I became a bit of a spokesperson for The Club, a little fundraiser with my clean white Boys Club T-shirt. I'd go to dinners and give what became my stump speech: *What my Boys Club Means to Me.* When I was eleven, I was selected as *Boy of the Year* … Meant a lot to me, shaking the Mayor's hand and all … Even got a hug from ex-heavyweight boxer/movie star Buddy Baer. (The guy fought Joe Louis twice for the World Championship, lost both times. Still he was a hell of a puncher, with a record of 52-7 with 46 knockouts. His older brother, Max, had already been World Champ and his nephew, Max Junior starred as the big duffus, Jethro, on the sitcom, *The Beverly Hillbillies* … The three not-so-little Baers.)

As Boy of the Year, I went on TV the Saturday morning after I received my trophy, which I carried with me. I sat there, right next to Mr. Stevenson, Harvey, and Howard. The show producer let us know that he would pan the camera onto each of us and ask us what we thought about the club. He would start with Mr. Stevenson on the far right, then on to Harvey, Howard, and me on the far left (I was a leftist even then).

I had a plan. Howard was quite a lot older, and would have neat, intelligent things to say. When the camera finally got over to me, I'd start by saying, "Like what he said. Yes, I really agree with Howard." I was quite comfortable with this sequence.

The only problem was that after interviewing Mr. Stevenson, the cameraman for whatever reason swooped the camera right onto me. That really threw me off, to put it mildly. "And Tommy, what do you think about your Boys Club?" My mouth fell open, and I sat there staring into the lens, knowing that millions of my fans around the world were honed in, waiting to hear my clever words.

In that moment or so of dead silence, I learned a great lesson. But I was in too much shock to remember it.

P.S. In its 2007 "Philanthropy 400" report, the *Chronicle of Philanthropy* placed Boys & Girls Clubs of America in the No. 1 position among youth organizations for the 13th consecutive year. To donate visit: www.bgca.org

The Day I Lost my Marbles

1953-ish. As mentioned earlier, we had moved to a new neighborhood (which was really a very old neighborhood), there on the 1600 block of E Street. These were older houses built back in the '20s and '30s, and they still had functional narrow alleys where the garbage cans would be swooped up by hard-working men and where black widows hid in wooden garages still being used. There was something alluring and human about those little unpaved roads with wild berry bushes and loquat trees growing along the sides.

After being there for a couple of years, I realized there were two Italian boys about my age who lived just a block down the street. One was James Campese, who was my age, and the other was Allen Marquise, who as I recall was a year older. We kind of hit it off, as kids will, and they invited me over to one of their homes one warm summer afternoon. The purpose was to play marbles. Well sure, why not?

There were no garages in the front portions of those dwellings, just grass lawns but mostly dry, hard soil. So, we found a flat area in the dirt and with a stick and a string drew a pretty standard circle, maybe eight feet in circumference. We took out our marble bags filled with various types of these precious finger-sized toys—aggies, boulders (the big suckers), cat's eyes (they actually looked like cat's eyes, well, kind of), swirls, and even our steelies—solid metal shooters, though we all agreed we wouldn't use them. They were like guided missiles that would blast the glass marbles to pieces!

Even at that age, I was a decent player though I did lose to these two on that fateful day. After the final game when they had pretty much wiped me out, Allen seriously asked me, "Hey, Tommy. You know Joe?" Hmmm, never heard of the kid. I, of course, curiously replied, "Joe who?" Big mistake. That was my first experience with "the dozens," the fine art of insulting another kid in pure jest. The answer to that question as we all know is "Joe mama." They laughed like crazy, and I was mortified; I mean they had really "capped on" me.

By the time James, Allen, and I got to the 5th grade, I had become the Columbia Elementary Marble Champion, ribbons and all. Two years in a row! And I hate to admit it, but it was with great pleasure that, when the games with each of those guys was over, after I had literally left them in the dust, I'd point to them and jab "Joe mama!" What a guy!

Beef Stew by Candlelight

It was a common occurrence for me to see the trucks drive up to our shanty, the utility vehicles from the electric company, the gas company, and the garbage company. They were sometimes there to collect payment or give notice, but more often than not to flat- ass turn the service off for non-payment.

I watched a lot of old movies as a kid … I mean these flicks *were old then*, '30s and '40s pics. Most of them were black and white, terribly hokey mysteries, westerns and war sagas showing in those urine-scented theatres on the West Side—the Cal, Ryan, Lyceum, and the greatest of them all, the White Theatre, all averaging 10¢ for two to three movies and a bunch of old-school cartoons.

When the gas at home was turned off—as it frequently was, especially in the winter—and we had to bathe in cold water, my mom would say, "You know, Tommy, if you wash your face with cold water, you'll never get wrinkles." Yeah, sure, thanks … just pay the damned gas bill! But with my parents there was always a higher priority and that was their wine. We didn't have a TV bill because we didn't have a TV. In any case, on this particular stretch everything was out: electricity, food, water—The Triple Crown of Poverty. They did, however, have two food-related commodities on hand: one, a couple of boxes of canned and boxed crap (like Spam, powdered milk, and good ol' Rainbow bread) that they had picked up from some charity; and two, a large box of votive candles, the little fat guys you light for sick, dying, or dead friends or relatives. Who knows how those candles ended up there, probably a gift from the Catholic Church to light the place when the electricity was off.

So how were candles and food-related you ask? I recall that some of the larger cans in that charity box were beef stew, with decent chunks of meat, potatoes, and carrots in a gravy-like sauce reminiscent of a freshly opened can of dog food. Man, that was good, especially the way we cooked it when the lights and gas were off.

Basically, my parents would cleverly place four or five of those short votive candles beneath the burner grate in place of the gas burner and say three Hail Marys. Then they'd dump the beef stew into a cooking pot and put the pot on top of the grate. Just let this gourmet concoction heat for about 10 minutes, and voilà—*Beef Stew by Candlelight!* How romantic!

Creature from the Fink-Smith Wading Pool

"Not since the beginning of time has the world known terror like this!" —Trailer for the 1954 film *Creature from the Black Lagoon*

It was mid-summer, typically sweltering. I must have been in the 2nd grade or so, always wearing my beautiful (I thought so anyway) Fresno Boys Club T-shirt and brogan shoes. I would walk about three blocks to the local public playground—Fink-Smith—with two baseball diamonds, a couple of basketball courts, and a cool clubhouse with lotsa games. In the very center of it all was a wading pool for us young'uns that was maybe ten feet long and only about two feet deep at the very center ... for me it was like swimming in a vast, unfathomable ocean.

The pool was also a place to pee—how convenient—when you thought nobody was paying attention. I recently compared notes with some buddies of those years and come to find every one of us was doing it. Mmmm, lemonade!

I didn't know how to swim or, to my knowledge, did anyone else. We just crawled along the bottom and pretended. Or we basked by the edge of the pool and took in the rays, though I seriously doubt that any of us, mostly Latino and Black, needed a tan. I was quite adventurous as a kid and, on occasion, would venture into the deepest part of that boundless yellow sea. I had been to the movies recently and had seen a horrifying flick titled *Creature from the Black Lagoon,* which added to my excitement and terror as I explored the depths of the Fink-Smith pool.

So, there I was, by myself, all the way out in the very center, down at the very bottom of that vast and mysterious body of water. Kids have such great imaginations ... hell, I saw whales, sharks, and giant manta rays as I stared into the murky Devonian depths as long as I could hold my breath. Then in my peripheral vision I saw it coming, big and ferocious. I looked up and there we were, face to face, it glaring at me with an immensely evil look, claws bent as to slash, and mouth wide open with fangs protruding ... *The Creature from the Black Lagoon!*

It scared the holy shit out of me! I turned and scrambled back to the side of the pool. As I was pulling myself out, I looked back to the center and, with an enormous splash it popped up, laughing. It was John Henry Horton, the terror of the 2nd grade and my nemesis. Chalk one up, John Henry.

Flour Power

"The difference between a derelict and a man is a job."
—from the classic 1936 film *My Man Godfrey.*

Part 1. As I've noticed over the years, by and large if something is crazy it just gets crazier. Well, right now I'm rememberin' how bad things got worse with my maniacal parents, John and Linn, as they drank more and more over a prolonged period—we're talkin' decades. That cheap, rotgut wine truly warps your mind, as does excess drinking in general.

When John had a job with the railroad there was at least a smidgen of sanity … meals were somewhat timely, and my parents' raucous knock-down-drag-out fights weren't as frequent as in the months and years that followed. A job makes a world of difference, whatever it is … it is work and there's honor in a man or woman bringing home a paycheck. When the job was lost—and I can certainly see why John was fired—everything went straight to hell. More time to drink, more time to complain, more time for the two of them to reminisce about the good times but mostly the bad of their stretch together prior to fostering Eddie and me. (I also think that their non-stop emotional encounters laid the setting for late night making up … sick shit.)

I have said that they were very violent with each other. You have to understand that, one, this was a daily occurrence, and two, it became more violent as time went on. Using bottles, knives, and anything they could pick up to throw at one another, they fiercely went at it. Who needs big time wrestling?… Only this wasn't funny or phony. The fighting was combined with the added effects of unimaginative cussing … the proverbial broken record from times long past.

One evening when I was about eight, it reached a point that I just couldn't stand another moment of it. They were in literal fisticuffs in the cramped kitchen area when I noticed the large ten-pound can we used to store the flour to make our fresh tortillas … Give us this day our daily tort.

Ah ha! I opened the can and grabbed the long-handled aluminum grain scoop. By this time, they were rolling on the floor. I filled the scoop and aimed it at them, flinging the white powder directly into their faces … now that was a scene.

It actually stopped them during this round ... they just sat there, dumbfounded. But they, like the cockroaches that ruled the inner lining of that shack's walls, learned to adjust to me making a fuss with my little arsenal of flour-flingers, and the next time I tried it they just kept on fighting.

I share this vignette for one reason: to vividly portray just how thoroughly mad my parents were, and how easy it would be for me to just say fuck them and that horrendous horror chamber that was my home for fifteen years of my formative life. And even if I could finally understand what made them tick—the combination of extreme poverty, unemployment, lack of education, alcoholism and all the other elements that make for this wretched study—even if I knew their entire history and the history of the cultures that wrought (that should be *rot*) them, what is there to possibly gain by bitching about spilled flour?

Part 2. I'm a full-blown life-long liberal, but I gotta say I'm tired of some poor folks who spend their lives reacting and "acting out" as a result of a bad deal they got from the get-go, the fertile basis of extreme reaction that lays the ground for the worst of things. For some, it's day in and day out of unrelenting racism, sexism, and multi-phased oppression to deal with—oppression and all of its overt and covert ramifications leading to deadly ill effects on physical and mental health. I can really see how some folks just say fuck it and turn to violence and crime. I know, because I've been one of them. I don't condone it but I certainly know why.

This all is a long-winded way of saying this: No matter what hand we are dealt, at least we're here playing the game and for that alone we should be grateful. Most of us in this country have a chance, an opportunity, to attain a level of comfort but the degree of our success, our serenity, and our fulfillment overwhelmingly depends on our attitude. Sure, we are the result of our environment, but the point is with the right attitude and corresponding action we can do a lot to overcome being dealt some pretty lousy cards. Besides, you've just got to believe there's some thing, some force, that cares about us, and that it's possible to change our negative circumstances by focusing on the positive.

This is not a predetermined universe. Consider the unpredictable behavior of some subatomic particles at the quirky quarky quantum level that just flat-ass instantly disappear. Where the hell do they go? Or the head-spinning "spooky action at a distance" of what is termed "entanglement" where a mere thought can affect a particle light years away! (If, by the way, those ideas are looked at from an enlightened perspective then really it becomes a matter of matter at play in a boundless playground of consciousness, and therefore logical. "It's only logical," in the words of Mister Spock.

I bring up such subjects to infer that that things are not fixed, and *that translates on this level as us having choice in our lives.* But in spite of the confusion on one hand of unpredictability in much of the universe and, conversely, of the negative implications of a simplistic cause-and-effect mentality, we cannot give in to predetermination. I truly resent the notion that human beings haven't the capacity to attain and maintain control of their lives.

There's a terrific short literary essay titled *As a Man Thinketh* by turn-of-the-century author and poet James Allen, recently re-titled in a politically correct and modern fashion as *As You Think*, published by New World Library. Regardless of a person's background, this message is most profound and relevant as to our mental health, well-being, and hopefulness.

This line in Allen's introduction, I believe, pretty much sums it up:

> ... its object being to stimulate men and women to the discovery and perception of the truth that *'They themselves are makers of themselves'* by virtue of the thoughts which they choose and encourage; that mind is the master weaver, both of the inner garment of character and the outer garment of circumstance, and that, as they may have hitherto woven in ignorance and pain, they may now weave in enlightenment and happiness.

All of this said, nature or nurture, it's more than a flip of a coin ... though more difficult for some than others, we do have a say in the matter. See "Flip of a Coin" sketch below.

Flip of a Coin

Karma Miranda and My Banana, Split

Back in the '50s, the movies were always my getaway, at least on weekends. And my parents were more than happy to see me go. Heck, for 9¢ us kids could see three (Count them, three!) movies at the White Theatre, watch a handful of cartoons, and a "cliff hanger" serial from the '40s with Rocketman, Batman, or one of those futuristic heroes like Flash Gordon (all wearing baggy tights, mind you … no sissies here). Even movies featuring the psychedelic fruit-laced headpiece of the world-famed gyrating, chicka-chicka-boom of dancer/singer Carmen Miranda was sheer entertainment … The place was rockin'!

About that time—when I reached the sixth grade—it was my great honor (and worthy of any boy's resumé) that I became a "Traffic Guard." This meant that I got to wear a stupid little yellow hat, carry a "stop" sign on a post and, most importantly, had the power to stick that stop sign out to bring cars to a screeching halt to let the kids cross the street.

One day I made the costly mistake of being especially kind to a couple of classmates, Carmen and Virginia, because they were always smiling at me for some strange reason. I puffed out what there was of a chest and, quite gallantly I must say, stopped a string of cars during morning rush hour to allow the girls to leisurely sashay across the street. I can still hear those late-to-work drivers, "You little son-of-a…"

Well, anyway, one weekend later I went to the White Theatre, got a bag of popcorn and a couple of those big chewy candy bars that you could chaw on for an hour (they were called "Big Hunk"). Man, I was ready for Roy Rogers to kick some bad guy's tail! Roy, by the way, was a TV and movie hero back in the '50s, "The King of the Cowboys." But noooo …

Here come Carmen and Virginia, and they sit on both sides of me. They must have had a bet of some sort. Simultaneously they both leaned over to me, purring and wiggling like kittens on catnip. Virginia: "Ohhhhh, Tommy, I'm soooo cold." Huh? "Well here," sez I, quite the gentleman, "Take my sweater." Carmen: "Tommy, I'm soooo afraid, can you put your arm around me?" Wha …? I don't think so! I need both hands for my popcorn and Big Hunk … chaw, chaw, chaw.

I saw Carmen at school several months later and my chemistry must have changed a bit. I thought, hey, this *could* be interesting … maybe she'll go to the movies with me. That following Saturday I mustered up the courage, went just up the street to the doorstep of her house, and popped the "Will you?" question. She stared at me with an eyebrow mightily raised, put a hand on her hip, and with little pondering let me know that I, to quote her, *was not in her little red book.* I sat there at the movies that afternoon, just me and my Big Hunk … chaw, chaw, chaw.

The White Theatre – October, 1931

That Marvelous Misty Mansion

> "San Joaquin Valley's Largest Entertainment Center," said the marquee. "Opened in 1914, the White Theatre was one of many theatres that were once located in Fresno."
> —Cinema Treasures

9¢ Admission! This is what the White Theatre—that grand, marvelous, misty mansion—was like in '48, four years after I was born. For many years it was Central California's premier entertainment center, with an ornate ceiling, opera boxes, and a full three-curtains-deep professional stage (I know because I snuck back there many a time).

And true to old Fresno form, it maintained a sizeable upstairs balcony for Mexicans, Blacks, Chinese and all of us colored others from various mothers. Well, shit, at least they let us in. Movin' on up … literally!

By the time I got "to the White's", about 1950, newer movie houses—like the Warner, Wilson, Hardy, Tower, and Crest were in their heyday, turning this beautiful piece of history into a second-run hangout for wild kids and wayward winos. The reality is that this environment allowed some of us to taste within its very structure the wondrous beauty and glamour that was once reserved for "the other side," with its professional stage and opera boxes. When the lights dimmed, we were in Wonderland.

Buddy Lang's Garage & Gentlemen's Parlour

> "When purple-colored curtains mark the end of day I'll hear you, my dear, at twilight time."
> —from the lovely lyrics of *Twilight Time*. It had become a #1 smash hit, made popular by The Platters when I was in the fifth grade. With ocean buoys clanging in the background, I think of San Francisco at twilight whenever I hear it. Just google "Twilight Time" on YouTube for a lovely trip to the Bay.

1954. Buddy Lang, my second mentor and for-real employer, was one of the very few black men in Fresno at the time who owned his own business, Buddy Lang's Garage, no less. It was just up the alley from our house on E Street, thick with blackberry brambles growing up the crisscross metal fence that surrounded the property. It sat on a sizable corner lot cluttered with old cars with rusting engines and cracked windows. Buddy used those old clunkers for parts and as crash pads for some of his late-night clientele of gamblers and whores.

He hired me when I was about 10 or so as his … hmmm, flunky comes to mind, but I prefer *Boy Friday.* Basically I did what he asked of me: sweep the floors, clean the oily nuts and bolts in a small tub of overused kerosene, go to the Mom 'n' Pop store across the street to get change for the guys shooting crap in the back room, and at the same little market buy his saltine crackers, cans of sardines, and bottles of bourbon that were the staples of his daily diet; refill the pop bottles in that old pull-em-straight-up soda machine (10¢ then) and snag a free one on hot, summer days. And part of the gig was to just be around when that big, bad, very real man would stand there in his greasy overalls, swigging whiskey while leaning against one of the cars he was working on.

By mid-afternoon, the high school chicks would come walking home, passing his shop there on D Street. They always had that certain little swish in their gait, a motion I was unfamiliar with at my age. *Ah-oooow*, he would howl like a wolf, always laughing as the girls would, with feigned embarrassment, look the other way … but somehow I think they still appreciated the animal attention. *Ah-oooow!*

The poem below references Buddy, and also Rodney King, whose beating led to the Los Angeles riots of '92. The whole matter was the result of the totally biased judgment of an all-white jury regarding King's being beaten to a pulp by a group of cops, mostly Anglo, who were all acquitted in lily-White Simi Valley, home of Reagan's library … all acquitted!

I happened to live there in East Hollywood at the time, and it was flat-out eerie for the lights to be out and the streets to be empty each evening in a city of 14 million. But even the curfew couldn't hold back the truly explosive outbursts of the Blacks as parts of the city experienced riots and fires which we all watched each evening on all major TV stations.

After all of this, Rodney's famous quote still lingers, "Why can't we all just get along?"

On an entirely different note, Buddy appeared to have as much interest in such matters as one of his junkyard dogs. In his microcosm of West Fresno, racism was just the way it was. At least that's the way it seemed to me as a punk kid, though I found out decades later from old friends of his that Buddy was "woke" and did what he could to change that picture.

Adding to all of this, as I observed over my years of schlepping bolts, hammers, wrenches, and whiskey for the man, he did have more than his share of attractive women of all persuasions from both sides of the tracks, an equal opportunity entertainer. They'd show up in every kind of vehicle all perfumed up to get their transmissions lubed.

Tommy Boy, he called me. He treated me great and paid me well for the work I did for him. As I grew older, I got a little better at being his helper, but I really never had the aptitude for being a mechanic (flunked out of the Auto Mechanics class in high school, takes a lot of talent to do that, but the fact is I couldn't have cared less).

In short time Buddy had kind of adopted me and would now and then drag me along on his weekend jaunts to San Francisco, to The Fillmore, Da Mo', and down the endless streets of Oakland. (About which Gertrude Stein said, in the '30s, "There's no there there," but in the funky fifties there were certain hot spots with the blackest of blues, jazz, and no shortage of hot mamas.)

By the age of 11, I had never been to a city larger than Fresno, and had only seen the ocean in movies, like that mesmerizing Hitchcock flick filmed along the San Francisco coast, *Vertigo.* I'll never forget reaching the Bay

Bridge late one afternoon, twilight time, and for the first time I saw the twinkle of that great city off to my right as Buddy raced us across in his sparkling new '56 Plymouth Fury, white with gold-colored metallic streaks down the sides. My young heart pounded at the dazzling sights, the smell of the ocean, the pure beauty of my maiden voyage to a whole new world! It was love then and it is now. San Francisco, my heart's devotion!

In 1990 or so I was briefly back in Fresno. I was hanging out in a downtown casino where I happened to be sitting next to a peer of Buddy's, a big ol' sucka' named Leroy Brown, yep, bad, bad Leroy Brown. Upon mentioning my love of Buddy, to use Leroy's own words, he was "… an icon of West Fresno. That man would show up at get-togethers, church services, and business meetings all dressed up … but without no shoes!" I had noticed that myself some mornings while working at the garage, just lookin' down at those big ol' calloused feet. Why did he show up at times without socks or shoes? Where did he leave them? Where had he been the night before? Not likely with his church-mouse spouse. One hell of a character!

A true mentor, the parent I wish my parents had been more like, he was nonetheless still a serious drinker and a rogue in the best of ways, attributes I came to relish in my life-to-be. He drove his Baptist wife up the wall but somehow, she put up with it and, I know, deeply loved that good-hearted rascal. Hey … Why *can't* we all just get along?

P.S. Before Buddy went to that Great Dice Game in the Sky, I made it a point to track him down … thank God he was still kickin'. I found his home just up the road from where I had spent a couple of years of my teenage life, there on East Lemon Street. I knocked on the door, he answered, and he hardly recognized me … hell, I was just a little grease monkey flunky when he last saw me.

I had a simple gift bag for him, a can of sardines, a box of saltine crackers, and a large bottle of Old Crow Bourbon, the items I had brought to him hundreds of times as his little helper. In a very brief exchange, I was able to quickly let him know how important he was to me, giving me a great job as a kid, a sense of work ethics, and paying me damned well for it … not to mention the trips to the Bay Area, where my eyes were first opened to the City Lights.

Before Rodney King

Before Rodney King,
West Fresno remained a chunk of transplanted Alabama
with dewy cotton bolls and the same bent-over bodies
that built the pyramids and Taj Mahal.

Before Rodney King,
Buddy Lang left long cotton sacks for black Cadillacs,
popped straight shots of Old Crow,
shot dice and ate rice in a bustling hustling Chinatown,
Buddy Lang, a Bunyan-esque mean machine
whose tears would flow down that grease-covered face
at the death of a junkyard dog,
would more than once stagger home pulling out all the stops
and get the sure attention of the waiting cops
stroking their batons.

Before Rodney King,
Joaquin Murrieta and Three-finger Jack
swigged tequila/whiffed marijuana in the Roeding Park Zoo,
cruised their '49 Ford and explored
thoughts of freedom with hands of mud,
a flowery kaleidoscope of family and blood,
dreamed of a world that glittered like the Rainbow Ballroom
and smelled like Fitch's hair oil,
weaved their low rider across the manicured grass,
and got the general attention of the waiting cops
stroking their batons.

Before Rodney King and the Fires of Lost Angeles,
The Sacred Halls of Ivy were leveled
to a heap of rusty rubble even as the others stood,
and the White Theatre, that grand, misty, marvelous mansion,
once decent and elegant in its décor,
found itself on the wrong side of the tracks
and was buried in a musty dust;

Roy Rogers, John Wayne, Gene Autry and John Payne
shot a million Indians at the White Theatre
as little brown and black boys cheered,
Snow White became No-White
and the freeway devoured our spine.

Before Rodney King,
libraries were scarred and forever charred
in Alexandria and Berlin,
the Iroquois decimated the Huron,
Crusaders impaled bloody crosses
into the pounding heart of clout-less cults
and aborigines learned to die in a more civilized fashion;
Happy Harold sold white port & lemon juice
to welfare recipients on Whites Bridge Road,
and Sherley Anne Williams,
after kissing a dozen Raggedy Ann sisters good night,
carried Dostoevsky to bed;

Before Rodney King, Martin Luther King and César Chavez
knelt at the lotus feet of Mahatma Gandhi
as manacled multitudes marched on City Hall
with peaceful prayers for the waiting cops
stroking their batons.

East of Easton

> "All over Harlem, Negro boys and girls are growing into stunted maturity, trying desperately to find a place to stand; and the wonder is not that so many are ruined but that so many survive." —James Baldwin

It was the summer of '55, a Saturday morning, and already hot as hell in Fresburg. Good time to go swimming. I wanted to go with him, but my older brother Eddie, all 17 lanky years of him, wouldn't have it. I was 11 and it wasn't cool having a loud-mouthed kid hanging around when he was trolling for chicks with Junior Gibbs, a muscle-bound Black kid who was his best friend.

Eddie, as it turned out, was also Black—or as his National Guard card informed him, Negroid. When he first saw the card that came in the mail a few weeks after he had joined, he punched his fist through those stucco walls and ran outside sobbing.

He was a beautifully tan kid, a Hispanic mulatto of some sort, tall and handsome with tight thick curls and a rich, full smile. Black, because according to Whitey if you have even 1/8 black blood in you, you're black and that's that. Ironically, when Eddie was first fostered, my foster father thought the boy was pure Mexican—as if there's such a thing.

No, Eddie sure didn't want me cramping his style that day, especially since he had just broken up with the love of his life, Claudette Colbert of Easton roots. Her folks owned a rickety two-story house in a bayou-like setting a few miles due west of Fresno up Highway 41. Easton was an almost invisible town with one grocery store, one little market, and a bar. She, the ebony beauty he had so adored, his first and only love, Cleopatra reincarnated, had just had a child that Eddie thought was of his doing...turned out the baby wasn't his and it wasn't her first time either. Maybe that's why.

He had a sharp black '50 Ford coupe, with white walls and shiny moon hubcaps. He was stylin'. Turns out he and his ace-coon buddy, Junior, were heading out to the San Joaquin River to meet a couple of girls, swim and do whatever teenagers do. Before he took off that morning, he told me not to worry about that bothersome little redhead next door—Rory—who had expressed her undying love for me (but only when my hair was combed), that someday I'd come to appreciate those critters ... fateful words.

Several hours later, after a day with the Burris kids, I moseyed on home with my faithful dog Ring. As I neared my house, I noticed a handful of people standing on the front porch, including a cop ... very unusual indeed. For some reason I went around them and entered the front yard of our next-door neighbor, Mrs. Minenna, Rory's grandmother. Sometimes I would mysteriously find myself roaming around her yard, maybe because she often had Italian pastries that she baked in her backyard oven. This time she stopped me in my tracks and insisted I come into her house for dinner. Dinner? ... it was four in the afternoon.

I recall every moment like it was yesterday: the small wooden table in the kitchen, the wood-burning stove she still used, the pasta and homemade bread, and a glass of milk, her sitting across from me, sad faced. It was obvious that something was haywire, but what? I couldn't help but ask what was going on and she squared with me. "Tommy, I don't know how to tell you this," she quietly murmured as to soften the message, "but Eddie drowned this afternoon."

I really didn't—or didn't want to—understand, and responded by asking, "But is he dead, really dead?" She nodded her head, and it took less than a minute for me to jump up and go racing out of her house, through their back yard, into the alley, then into our back yard where an old. unpainted barn stood. I chose not to go up front into our house, I just walked around back there, stunned, with tears streaming down my face. "God, God, please don't let him die. I know you can change it. Please make him alive again, God."

They say the good die young, but I think that's just a platitude to ease the suffering of those who've lost a young person. And Eddie really was a good kid, and way, way too young.

After-Eddie Notes:

- After Eddie's death, foster Father John had a new piece of wisdom for me that he repeated with some consistency: "You'll never be the man Eddie was." A real zinger, right to the balls … You go, John!
- The day after Eddie's death I was given a shiny fifty-cent piece to go to the movies (25¢ was what I usually got). I remember I went to one of the upscale theatres, the Wilson. It was a Saturday afternoon and Disney's *Lady and The Tramp* was playing, corny spaghetti scene and all, two dogs slurping the same string of spaghetti … that's amoré!
- That darned film was so mesmerizing I actually forgot—was kindly swept away from—the fact that my anchor, my older brother, the only sane one, was no longer there to protect me. Looking back, I think I became frozen in time, stuck there in that comforting Technicolor womb for so much of my life to come.
- There's probably a psychological term for it, being stunted like that, but I had found an escape in those dark theatres and that escape was the wonder of just being a kid in Fantasy Land. In some ways, alcohol does that too.
- There is also a lesson that I have learned from this tragedy. In Eddie's desperation to live, he almost took Junior Gibbs down with him as Junior attempted to save him in the middle of the river. Drowning people are known hang on to whatever they can.
- I have noticed over the decades that this happens in different ways. People who are "drowning" in grief, despair, loneliness, and worry can take you

down if you let them. What a fine line between being compassionate for others and not allowing their pain to drag us down.

- I am saddened by the dismal condition of poverty-stricken people here and abroad—at times, the suffering of so many can itself be a devastating awareness. We are not equipped to take on the pain of the world, there is danger in that river. All the more reason to be strong and positive in our own lives, all the more reason to do the little things that we can.
- I would like to believe that if Eddie had lived, my life would have been more stable, a lot less angry, and not lost to the whims of forces beyond my control. I would not have been destined for a certain madness.

No Laughing Matter

> Turning and turning in the widening gyre
> The falcon cannot hear the falconer;
> Things fall apart; the centre cannot hold;
> Mere anarchy is loosed upon the world,
> The blood-dimmed tide is loosed,
> And everywhere
> The ceremony of innocence is drowned.
> —from *The Second Coming*,
> by William Butler Yeats

Winter, 1956. As a young kid I always had a pretty good little sense of humor, all the way back to grade school. My pals will tell you that. Typical sophomoric-at-best stuff, including the most painful of puns, but at that age the stupidest things were considered quite funny. The slapstick of Jerry Lewis, Laurel and Hardy, and The Three Stooges was roll-in-the-aisle, flat out hilarious. An added dimension could well have been a by-product of living in hell day to day.

Sometimes I think there's a good chance my incessant blathering was just letting off steam from the pressure I was under on the home front. Little kids don't understand the world of insanity, don't understand the gross inconsistencies caused by alcohol and drug abuse, nor of any abuse they are subjected to. They just feel deep down that something is terribly wrong and feel helpless as far as changing the larger world they're caught up in.

I vividly recall being in my 6th grade class on an early fall day, Mr. Bushby's class. I liked that old guy, tall, skinny, looked like a crane, the one on the Vlasic pickle jar with his old-fashioned reading glasses always on the tip of his nose. I liked him because he would often pin my drawings up on the wall for all to see, and because he'd laugh to himself at something he would say to us, though we seldom got the punch line.

This particular day a courier came to the class and gave a note to Mr. Bushby. It said that I was to report to the principal's office ... what the heck did I do this time? When I got there, I first noticed a relatively young woman, I'd say in her mid to late 20s. She was dressed in a plain business suit, but in spite of the stiffness of her attire she herself didn't seem terribly rigid. When I walked through that door, she looked at me with a demure smile and kind eyes as if to say, "I understand." She asked the principal, Mr. Riordon, if he would kindly leave the office.

"Tommy, my name is Miss X, and I'm with Social Services. We're the people who work with your parents to make sure that you're OK. Do you understand?" I answered yes, but really had no idea what she could possibly be talking about. However, I had been warned by my mother that "the welfare lady" was butting into our life, so this was cause for a bit of trepidation. "We're going to go for a ride ... Do you have your jacket and all of your things here that you need to take?"

The next thing I know we're traveling down the road in one of those terribly official-looking gray, four-door sedans, not heading to my home which was just up the street a bit, but out into the country. I recognized that southeastern direction because my family and I had worked in the orchards there in the summer. We soon reached a rural burg called Parlier which was on the outskirts of Reedley. Mile after mile we went, and further into the countryside. (Relativity note: For all of its population, Fresno is still a cow town; Reedley is a much smaller burg on the outskirts of Fresno, and Parlier is a yet smaller town on the outskirts of Reedley.)

As we drove along it finally came down to this: "You know, Tommy, we need to take you away from your foster parents for a while (she emphasized the word "foster"), and you're going to be in a whole new school. You'll have brand new clothes, and meet some really nice boys and girls ... Doesn't that sound great?" Again, I had no clue as to what this was all about but figured, well, it feels like she's a good person who actually cares a bit about me.

Within an hour we pulled into a long driveway and up to a sizable two-story house, a relatively new one. The country home was surrounded by a great deal of property, not an orchard but flat farmland with rows and rows of irrigated soil, some with seedlings just sprouting. We pulled up into the driveway. She walked around and opened my door and said something to the effect of "You'll like Mr. and Mrs. Y. They really love kids."

Miss X said that she would be back in a few days to explain this all to me, but that everything was all right and that I should just enjoy myself and my new surroundings. And she was absolutely right about Mr. and Mrs. Y. They were nice middle-aged white folks although their color really didn't matter to me one way or the other; I was used to a white mother. The fact is, as it turned out, they were kind, nurturing and … sober. Sober. That was a new one.

That very first night I was shown to my room, and then introduced to the other kids in the home, maybe five in all. Two of them were the children of the Y's and the others were relocated—if that's the word—foster kids like me. Two of them were my age, a boy and a girl. At dinner we all sat politely at the dinner table, a short prayer was said, and a full-course, healthy meal was served, even with a piece of pie for dessert. You know, I thought, this ain't bad, nope, not bad at all.

The very next day, Mrs. Y took me shopping for clothes. Such a thing had never happened to me in my ten whole years on this planet. Usually, items were bought one at a time, only as needed. She bought me an entire new wardrobe: new pants, shirts, underwear, socks, coat, and a shiny pair of shoes that I could only have dreamed of. The works. And here's the kicker: I did the shopping; it was what I chose. I have to say, this was really an entirely new experience, clean, fresh and good, like everything else that seemed to be taking place.

That afternoon, Mr. Y had me get into my "work clothes," the clothes I was wearing when I was taken there, primarily an old pair of jeans and of course my standard brogan shoes. This attire was perfect for what we were about to do: go out and irrigate those ditches. I had my own hoe, and he just asked me to do as he did, mainly pull mud and weeds out of the ditches so that the water would flow more easily … go with the flow. While we were working, he asked me if I liked it there and I said very much so. He asked if I might like to stay there and I said very much so. We finished our work and headed back to the house.

The next morning Mrs. Y drove me to my new school, me with brand-spankin' new everything, even my drawers. I sat at the back of the classroom and was introduced to the other students. A few seats in front of me were a handful of girls giggling and whispering. I heard only two words: "He's cute." What the …?

Three or four weeks went by and then one day, in the middle of my classes, I was summoned to the principal's office and there sits Miss X, who again asks for privacy. She says, "Tommy, this is important, please listen carefully to what I have to say." What she had to say was really hard for me to grasp. In essence, I had been removed from my foster parents' care not so much because they were full-blown violent street-corner alcoholic maniacs, and not because their mental abuse was extreme. Wouldn't you think that was quite enough? But that wasn't the case. According to Miss X, it was because my mother was accused of sexually molesting me.

Apparently for months welfare workers had spied on us, looking through windows and slits in doors. It is difficult for me to go back to that time, but in fact things, awkward things, had transpired on several occasions. Yes, it does come back, a history of it, fondling, and memories I would just as well leave in that dark, distant past. And even before that, incidents with my older brother Eddie in the bathtub. My complaints to my parents went unheard, them absolutely looking the other way as if nothing had ever been said and nothing had ever happened.

That evening Mrs. Y reminded me that I was going to court the next morning, and that I should contemplate overnight what I wanted to say to the judge who was to decide my fate. Heavy stuff for a little kid. The next morning, Miss X picked me up and cautiously drove me through the dense and dangerous tule fog that every year causes mangled tragedies, trucks filled with farm workers or drunk teenagers heading to a local party.

Onward to the Fresno County Courthouse, in this case as daunting as the thick fog we were driving through. On that ride into town, which seemed to last forever, the social worker let me know that I should listen very carefully to the judge's words. My mind was swirling trying to grasp the gravity of it all.

This was not a typical courtroom at all. No one had to rise as the judge entered the chamber. The only people there were the judge, his stenographer, Miss X, and to my surprise … my foster parents. The judge was a soft-spoken, low-key guy who did his best to explain to me at my level what was transpiring. In retrospect it felt as if it was even difficult for him to explain. It went something like this:

"Tommy, the reason you were taken away from your parents was because your mother has been accused of molesting you. Taking advantage of you … sexually. However, we can't prove that, so there's not much we can really do. In fact, young man, the whole matter is totally up to you. Please take a minute and talk with your foster parents."

There they were, perhaps as sober as I had ever seen them (meaning maybe not having had too much to drink that morning). My dad even had an old suit on, something I had never seen. She had a clean dress, and her hair, for a change, was neatly combed. She had tears in her eyes. They whispered that they missed me and that life was so lonely without me, especially since my older foster brother Eddie had drowned the previous summer. Would I please come home? You know, there was some real truth in their voices.

I went back to my seat next to the judge, and just sat there looking at them ... God, they were pathetic! What a sad, hopeless, helpless couple they were, how terribly, terribly tragic. My heart went out to them. What would they possibly do without me? And furthermore, that monthly check, my monthly check, is what they paid their rent with. And got their cheap wine with.

Compassionate perhaps, but maybe not the wisest of decisions ... Who's to say? I left the courtroom that afternoon walking between my foster parents, holding their hands. Such a rare experience. Needless to say, in record time they were back in the same old warfare mode ... Too bad earplugs weren't available then. You know, to this day I wish I had all those cool clothes that were left at the ranch house in Parlier.

Farewell, Sweet Pooch

I had already felt the loss of my older brother when he was only 18. His death was devastating as he was the sanest in the batch, and by his mere size he had some control over my parents' constant mental abuse.

But for me the most important part of that little family was my dog Ring, a Shepherd-Collie mix who was my bud since he was a tiny puppy. He had been my pet for about seven years when he was captured by the animal control folks. This happened on the first day of my entering the seventh grade. I was eleven years old. That morning, I walked a couple of miles up the road to an entirely new school. Ring, on that same day, was picked up wandering around the old grade school where he thought I was, since he had walked with me each school day, year after year.

When I finally got the message about his being snagged, I had no clue as to where to go or how to get him out, and I had no money or transportation. My thoroughly drunk parents were of no help whatsoever, and if they did have money for his release, it would have gone for booze anyway. Ring was my personal Puff, the Magic Dragon. I loved him immensely and I was helpless to save him.

Some unthoughtful kid let me know that when the Humane Society "puts down" (a nice way of saying "puts to death") un-adopted dogs they get processed to be used as soap! I still feel tremendous guilt for not having the depth or the wherewithal to rescue him. Of all of my family, I loved him the most.

God Fills in what you have Lost

My friend Mike, an ex-top-level cop, sent me a tiny notice he had found while doing a little research trying to find my real parents. From the *Fresno Bee* dated late November of 1944, it mentioned that four children had been born that week—one of them was yours truly: "Born to Mr. and Mrs. Abraham Chavez, a boy." Frankly, because I have never seen my biological parents, this was fascinating news to me. It totally confirmed the hidden away birth certificate that I found when I was in my mid-30s. It kind of said, hey, buddy, yeah, you were actually born.

This didn't come as a complete surprise because Mike had let me know he was trying to track down just who my parents were. His motives were both as a puzzle-solver and as a buddy. I'm not sure why, but this notice rattled my cage a bit. At some deep level I've tried to bury the whole matter. After all, they deserted me when I was first born, leaving me to the likes of my foster parents.

I don't believe this self-protective attitude and lifelong masking was conscious at all. I do know that by the age of seven, before my perennially-soused foster mom Linnie had unceremoniously informed me one evening that she and John weren't my real parents, I was somehow already aware that that was the case. It really didn't bother me, I didn't cry, I didn't care.

Besides, that same evening, she had also drunkenly shared in no uncertain terms that my "blood mother" was a prostitute … I think the word was whore. This part didn't mean a thing either, but she of course went on to explain what the word meant.

As my life has proceeded my mind needed to somehow fill in what was missing. The truth is that for my entire life I just blanked out anything to do with my parents, period. I told myself that I didn't give a fuck who they were, one way or another.

And I never tried to find out. I literally and psychologically buried my foster parents a long, long time ago and my blood parents even before that. But now I must confess, seeing that little announcement brought it all back. I'm sure it is why I got quite drunk that evening. I had been pretty good about my sobriety for a considerable span, several months, but the surfacing of this tiny notice somehow shook me up.

I called old friends, chatted about sports and just shot the breeze to escape the matter. The subject of this little discovery didn't come up in my conversations and it didn't really hit until that night while I tossed in my sleep. It came in the form of a dream in which my foster mother (quite sober in this dream) consoled me with this auspicious comment: "God fills in what you have lost."

From the mystic Sufis, an anonymous aphorism proclaims, "When the heart weeps for what it has lost, the spirit laughs for what it has found."

Arrested Development

> "What we call abnormality in this culture is actually normal responses to an abnormal culture. The abnormality does not reside in the pathology of individuals, but in the very culture that drives people into suffering and dysfunction."
> —Dr. Gabor Maté, author of *The Myth of Normal.*

Eventually the malaise of my less than *Leave it to Beaver* upbringing laid the ground for my behavioral sickness, a sickness that fit beautifully with my bars, whores, and open doors philosophy and lifestyle. A wasted mind is a terrible thing, and mine was wasted like a Freddie Fender ear bender. "Wasted days and wasted nights …" goes the song I heard and lived day after day, year after year.

November 5, 2014. I just read a pertinent article in The Fresno Bee titled, *Childhood trauma a hidden crisis in California and Valley*, by Barbara Anderson. I have no doubt this study applies across America. It seriously rattled my cage because it reminded me of all this ancient crap that I've done my best to drown with booze and bullshit.

Here's the gist of that article: First, that "Californians who experienced verbal, physical, sexual abuse or neglect in childhood are more likely to have long-lasting serious health problems …" No shit. I'm sorry, but to me that's terribly obvious … but I am glad it has surfaced scientifically. They say it's a "hidden crisis," but I think for all practical purposes it's an up-front epidemic. The stuff hospitals and prisons are made of.

"People who have had four or more traumatic experiences are more than five times as likely to suffer from depression, more than two times as likely to have chronic obstructive pulmonary disease, almost three times as likely to smoke and more than three times as likely to binge drink."

Further, the article tends to focus on "four or more traumatic experiences"; apparently that's when the experiences really begin to dent one's future, creating physical and mental health patterns. "Childhood trauma also affects education attainment and job security. An adult with four or more traumatic experiences is 21% more likely to be in poverty, 27% more likely to have less than a college degree and 39% more likely to be unemployed." The fact is that for yours truly most of these statistics have applied most of my life.

The report also found a high correlation between childhood traumatic events and involvement in the child welfare system: "An adult with four or more childhood traumatic events is 13% as likely to have been removed from home and placed in a child welfare system as someone who has not experienced childhood trauma." Child welfare system, aka foster homes.

You know, this study seems to focus on how fucked up a person can become after only four childhood traumas. In my childhood it was a nearly daily occurrence, a routine on many levels, and that's no bull ... non-stop monstrous madness. Can you imagine, until I was 14 or so I thought that was normal.

Well, if I was in that foster home for 14 of my formative years, and the traumatic incidents were only once a week (mind you, the knock-down drag-out fisticuffs and endless screaming of my foster parents was pretty constant), then let's do some simple math: At only one trauma per week, times 52 weeks per year (call it 50), times 14 years (call it 10), equals 500 childhood traumas!

So how the hell do you escape this degree of trauma and chaos? The answer is you don't. There are experiences from early childhood that can warp a person for the rest of his or her life. That I have been mentally ill for the lion's share of my adult life should come as no surprise. To those old friends who have seen me in my darker hours, well, I hate to say it but it was just par for the course. You can't fight what you can't see. The word "trapped" comes to mind and the whole matter horrifies me.

On the other hand, if a guy can somehow hang in there and keep weaving, dancing, dodging, keeping a distance from the blow that will put him out for the count, then maybe, just maybe, he'll become a champ rather than a chump.

With that, I most seriously thank God for the pioneers—Sigmund, Carl Jung. Bill W., and the countless others in the field of mental health who offer hope and promise to those of us who desperately need it. I sure as hell have! I've had more than my share of different types of therapy throughout my adult life, and without it I'd be in prison or dead. Period.

I recall one of my very first meetings with a wonderful shrink, Dr. David Newman, when I was a first-year student at San José State. Yeah, he had my number alright. Not so subtly, he said, "You know, Tomás, there is such a thing as healthy guilt."

Kintsugi

He was a lovely vase
dropped by his parents before he was born.
A samurai sword shredded his eyes
and tore open his heart—
He could not have known how broken he was.

He thought he was a begging bowl
and that is honorable and good,
but it would take a lifetime of patience
to reverently piece back
the shattered innocence
and mend its precious form.

To repair the slashes of betrayal
and stabs of incorrigible lust
it would take a steady hand;
It would take the fine black resin delicately rolled
from layers of molten lava
and the golden lacquer of the sun
to shape the splintered parts into priceless art.

He gathered those pieces wherever scattered,
saved them and treasured them.
It was many years until the time came
when he would meticulously mold
the fallen bits into a sublime vessel,
more beautiful for each scar.

A Lifetime in a Drop

Going into the seventh grade things changed considerably. New school, new friends ... and girls, girls suddenly seen in a considerably different light. Another change was that both junior high and senior high were in the same buildings, so we were always around "the big kids."

That first year at Edison Junior-Senior High, at age 11, I co-starred in the combined student body annual Christmas play. The setting was in a countryside during the time of Christ. It was about a crippled shepherd lad named Nicky—who I played—and his uncle Jed, played by a senior named Jimmy Sandoval.

One starry night Nicky puts his crutches down and goes to sleep out in the field. He dreams of angels singing over him—in the case of Edison High, beautiful black and brown angels singing praise of Jesus and His miracles. (These angels were from the school's advanced choir and boy did they have some voices, having been raised in Black church gospel choirs.)

The dream seems so real to little Nicky he thinks it really happened. He awakens and, so excited about the beautiful and heartening message of his dream, he leaps up and goes running across the stage to his uncle, screaming, "Uncle Jed, Uncle Jed, I've seen a miracle!" Mind you, the crippled kid is running *without his crutches* ... get the picture?

Well, even though most of the audience applauded, my newfound 7th grade buddies were howling about my flakey acting ... Those little rats! To this day I don't know what was so damned funny!

Now, about these buddies ... Later that year in our P.E. (Physical Education) class, we were being taught how to swim. Mr. Fitzgerald, the swim instructor, was a handsome young man and rumor had it that he was boning Miss Valasis, our English teacher. But I was more concerned about the swimming bit ... I was scared as hell because my brother had drowned that summer and I didn't want to even go near a bathtub. When time came to jump into the pool I stood there at the side, shaking like a leaf, tears flowing. Hell, no, I won't go! (Yep, I invented that Viet Nam mantra.)

Fitzgerald—the original Joe Cool with his movie star sunglasses—came over and personally took me into the shallow end of the pool. He started by showing me how to kick while holding onto the side. In record time I was paddling back and forth, eventually trying out for the Olympics in Munich. Not really, but I could make it across the short length of the pool.

Now, it turned out that not all of my newfound friends really were friends. Two of them, Raymond Fisher and John Henry Horton, were bullies. Raymond would beat me up "just 'cause" and John Henry was always looking for ways to terrify me. (Footnote here: When I met my new friend Eddie Perez, with whom I had seven out of seven classes in the 7th grade—go figure—he befriended me immediately and went on to beat the shit out of Raymond Fisher … Go get 'im, Ed!)

One day while we were all in the pool during a "free period," meaning we could pretty much do whatever we wanted, I found myself comfortably treading water—floating—in the center of the pool. Suddenly, like a giant octopus, John Henry of Creature-from-the-Fink-Smith-Playground fame grabbed me from behind and dunked me. I remember coming up for a bit, him still holding me from behind. Then down again. Laughing, he kept me under for what seemed like hours. God, I panicked!

Most of us have heard or read about a "near death" or "out-of-body" experience. Here I experienced my own life—*viewed it*—in one single second. My entire life—every bit of it, every iota, being born, being in the orphanage, ripping my finger open on my first day at the Boy's Club, *every minute detail* of every moment of my life with no breaks, no commercials, one continuous motion picture—flashed through my senses in a fraction of a minute, a fraction of a second. Absolutely amazing!

Mr. Fitzgerald came to my rescue, pulled John Henry away and asked if I was okay. I was still in shock, not so much about the dunking but about experiencing 11 years in a second of time. How could that possibly be?

Notes

- I met John Henry about thirty years later. He worked for me as a janitor at a large event I was producing out at the Fresno Fairgrounds. I thought about it but never thanked him for dragging me down into The Twilight Zone.
- Jimmy Sandoval, my uncle in the Christmas play, started a rock-n-roll group called *Jim Doval and the Gauchos* that made its way to produce an album or two, and performed on national television to an audience of millions … you go, Uncle Jed!

Border Brothers

1957. His name was David Santos and he and his parents, like a lot of the folks there in West Fresno, had recently arrived from Mexico. They had crossed the Rio Grande, or somewhere along the border, packed like sheep into one of the dangerous coyote trucks.

David's English was very broken, but he sure was trying. This was early in the 7th grade and our English teacher was a middle-aged Armenian gentleman named Harry Kachadoorian who, quite coincidentally, was quite hairy—a constant source of sophomoric amusement. Because of his Carpathian Mountain swarthiness, a penchant for dark suits, dark ties, and a straight-back style of combing his hair, us kids dubbed him "The Count," as in Bela Lugosi's *Count Dracula* … I vaaahnt to suck your blaaahd.

Anyway, one day Mr. Kachadoorian was systematically asking each of us to spell certain words, I guess to get a sense of our eenglitch proficiency and find out who might need a little extra mentoring. Well, when he got around to David, the word was pickle. "David," Mr. Kachedoorian asked, "Please stand up and spell pickle."

Silence. Silence. Then, in a low, soft voice "p…i…" Deep thought. "g…g" More thought. "e…l, p…i…g…g…e…l, Piggel," he proudly proclaimed. Damn, we cracked up! We were howling, falling out of our seats … Piggel??? That poor kid probably never ate a pickle—make that piggel—for the rest of his life.

The Hustler

> "Look, friend, I'm not trying to hustle. I don't never hustle people that walk into poolrooms with leather satchels. Don't try to hustle me."—from *The Hustler,* starring Paul Newman and Jackie Gleason. Damn … good … movie.

The Boys Club was always there in one way or another (free pool table, basketball court, and lotsa cool kids to play with), educating me in ways that school and home could not. For example, in the summer between the 7th and 8th grade—I was 12—they lined me up for a neat little gig: I was a "Zoo Guide." What this meant was that I would put on my zoo guide T-shirt and take small groups, kids and adults alike, around the Roeding Park Zoo, second largest in California at the time.

I shared what I had been taught about the various animals: "And this, folks, is an African elephant. Notice the ears? Bigger than its cousin the Indian Elephant." "This is a large, flightless bird, the ostrich, native to Africa, and here's his close relative, the rhea, who comes from the other side of the world, South America." And I pointed out the obvious difference between types of camels; the one-hump Aryan, also known as Arabian, and the two-hump Bactrian. (The common wisdom is that two humps are better than one).

How fortunate I was, when you think about it. What kid anywhere had regular access to this world of exotic animals and was taught about them, an unusual education as to the magnificent diversity of animal life brought from every continent on the planet, up close and personal with chimps, baboons, and gorillas. (An early course in anthropology—how could we not be related?)

Well, a couple of years later, the year I turned 14, I was called into the principal's office. That was not always a good thing but in this case it certainly was. Turns out kids back then could work at a young age, and the good ol' Boys Club had recommended me for a job hawking peanuts and Pepsi for a concessionaire named Red Klein. He was a middle-aged man, pot-bellied and pre-maturely balding.

Mr. Klein, as I respectfully called him, was a friendly, hard-working fellow who had a very lucrative business: he had the contracts for almost every entertainment venue in Fresno at the time, like Kearney Bowl and the Clovis Speedway (hardtops, midgets, and Indy 500 types, where I got to see legendary champ Billy Vukovich, as well as the sadistic-friendly "demolition derbies"), and also the Fresno Memorial auditorium (wrestling, boxing, concerts, and various cultural shows), and a half dozen lesser establishments.

As a peanut vendor I enjoyed acts that most kids from my 'hood couldn't afford, like the Ice Capades, the Barnum & Bailey Circus, the Harlem Globetrotters, professional dancers, musicians, and singers (frankly, I could've done without the all-white, flag-waving *Up with America* concert at the Memorial Auditorium; it was like Lawrence Welk on Quaaludes).

In that same venue I once got the honor of going backstage to hand a Pepsi to a young girl exactly my age (born the winter of 1944, we were about a week apart). She was so popular she'd had *as her opening act* in the UK an average little white band called *The Beatles.* Her name was Brenda Lee. What an experience and honor to have heard her on the radio that very morning and then be standing in front of her that afternoon, handing her a soft drink, all four foot nine inches of her ... She smiled even better than she sang.

My job was simple: wear a white paper hat, carry my wares in a tray—mostly soft drinks and peanuts—and yell my ass off at these various shows, "Pepsi, get yer ice-cold Pepsi!" Little did I know when I started that I could earn what amounted to a small fortune peddling these products—anywhere from $30 to $100 per event, on occasion even more. Back then it was an immense amount, especially for a kid my age ... I'd make more in a couple of hours than my parents could earn in an entire week working in the fields.

I assure you, they were pleased as hell to get their hands on most of those cash dollars. To be fair, they used some of it to buy food, but I know damn well most of it went for their hootch. So I learned to tuck away a buck or two, not much but enough to buy some of my own clothes and food.

We were called "hustlers," because that's exactly what we did: hustle our butts off, up and down those stairs, passing bags and cups back and forth, making change, and then running back to the station where they'd load us up again. I got pretty good at throwing bags of peanuts down those rows.

And when things were slow, I could sit down in a spare seat and watch terrific shows, like the great Pre-NASCAR hardtop races at Kearney Bowl featuring Marshall Sargent, the square-jawed quintessential hero, versus the villainous Al Pombo, a swarthy Sicilian who of course drove a shiny all-black racer. This was no bullshit ... They duked it out week after week, with the majority of that redneck crowd rooting for the "Dudley Do-right" Sargent character. Pombo was my man.

It was all great weekend theatre. Those flashy racers in memorable and dangerous competitions, and at the Memorial Auditorium I'd see up-and-coming boxers, along with some has-been pugilists that had been crème de la crème in their day. Guys like Sugar Ray Robinson and Ezzard Charles, and crowd-pleasing locals from Fresno and The Valley, like "The Little Professor" Gabe Terronez (who got knocked out at Kearney Bowl by national champ Emile Griffith ... Fresno wept.)

The auditorium also featured wrestlers who were still super-stars, like Gorgeous George. Gorgeous George was one hell of a showman, a break-through performer in his day. He wore a pink boa and would swish around the ring like a fairy princess. He would then proceed to pound the shit out of the "Good Guy." This never sat well in sexually repressed Fresno, with a bunch of illiterate clowns belching their anti-gay venom. Whenever one of the "good guys" smacked that gawd-daym queer, the crowd would go bonkers.

Anyway, one Saturday I got down to the auditorium right on time, around seven or so. The crowd was just arriving. I quickly had my work gear on, white shirt, my white paper hat, change apron, and tray strapped across my neck full of sodas. Up the same hall where I was walking to begin my sales came Gorgeous George, sans boa. I don't know how big he really was but to a relatively small kid he looked like a giant. I summoned up my courage to walk up and ask him a question I had been pondering for months. He stopped to listen.

"Excuse me, Mister George, but ...uh...can you tell me something?" I nervously inquired.

"Wha' dah ya need, kid?"

"Well, uh, uh," I stammered, "I've been watching you guys wrestle for a while now and it just seems, well ... uh, uh ... *phony.*"

Hardly diplomatic, and I thought, oh, shit, maybe I should've kept my big mouth shut. He stared down at me for a moment, me a working stiff just like him, and then says, "Hey, look kid, we all gotta make a living." I instantly got it, and that was cool: he was an entertainer. You know, like some Presidents.

That evening as I hawked my wares—Pepsi, get yer ice-cold Pepsi! —it looked like George ditched his scripted act, because he proceeded to literally beat the crap out of his opponent. I was there by the ringside, fists in the air, screaming "Get 'im, George!"

I sold for Mr. Klein's concession company for about three years, up until the summer leading to my Senior year. I'll never forget walking up the stairs at Kearney Bowl while the hardtops roared in circles, the low-brow crowd always hungry for a nasty crash. And there sitting with a couple of their boyfriends were two girls, Elena de la Peña and June Lujano. I'd had a crush on June for years, and felt embarrassed that I had this piddly job with a silly little hat. I quit about a week later. That's one of the stupidest damn things I've ever done. "Look, kid, we all gotta make a living."

Gorgeous note. By the 1960s George Raymond Wagner was an icon, not only of pro wrestling, but pop culture. Notable entertainers such as Little Richard, Bob Dylan, James Brown, and Muhammad Ali all would credit Gorgeous George's flamboyance as inspiration in creating their own entertainment persona.

Under the Bleachers, by Seymour Butz

Thanks to my way-too-often-naked foster mom, my voyeurism had peeked (sic) early on. While I was hustling soda at Kearney Bowl I got to watch top-notch racers, some of whom went on to become national stars, like two-time Indianapolis 500 champion Billy Bukovich— "The Fresno Flash." But I also watched the girls, and as the cars spun in mesmerizing circles every Friday, Saturday and Sunday night, there was always a break for the "Queen of The Speedway" pageant, a cheesy little ceremonious crowning that took place just before the evening's main event.

I was interested in the fact that the beauty queen and her lovely runners-up always wore short skirts and were generally seated a few rows up from the very front-center of the racetrack. I was turned on—like turned-on! —to this panty-licious spectacle by a fellow hustler, a young white dude who pulled me aside one evening and whispered "Pssst, hey, Tommy, wanna see some first-class drawers?"

It wasn't lost on me that these weren't ordinary knickers. I mean this was the Queen of the Scene, always a blondie with gorgeous gams, indeed a rare sight in West Fresno. (Oddly enough the race-ist track was located in that very ghetto ... Nobody on the other side of the tracks wanted their evenings disturbed by the rumbling and screeching of those loud-ass cars every weekend.)

And so it was that I suddenly became very patriotic, that is I'd wait for "The Star-Spangled Banner" to play and then scoot to that particular spot under the bleachers where the beauties, hand over heart, stood at attention ... and believe me, Mini-Me stood at attention as well. I suddenly understood the National Anthem lyric, "José, can you see?"

Well, to my extreme embarrassment one evening as I ogled the always immaculate under-garments suddenly there was a flashlight on me from behind. It was the regular rent-a-cop for the place, a middle-aged dude that I always sold Pepsi to. I thought, oh shit, how do I get out of this one? I immediately looked down to the ground with the lame excuse that I had dropped some money while working upstairs.

Wasn't necessary. With a big 'ol shit-eatin' grin the guy sez, "What color's she got on tonight ... white or pink?" That summer I'd say my prospects were looking up.

"What it is?"
asked the blackbird
of the dove;
The dove, he say,
"Man, what it is
is love!"

My One and Only Love

"The very thought of you makes my heart sing
Like an April breeze on the wings of spring,
And you appear in all your splendor,
my one and only love."
—from lyrics of "My One and Only Love"

My first love was Sharon Meyers. I first saw her when we were in the third grade. She was crawling up those monkey bars—love at first sight! And then, maybe a year later, I watched her gliding around the skating rink down by the Black Elks Lodge on F Street. Yep, she was The One alright!

She turned into a truly stunning young lady, influencing my taste in women throughout my life. Her mom was White, I was told, and her dad was Black, one of the very few doctors from the West Side. Both the mixed marriage and a Black doctor were rarities in those days. One warm afternoon when we were in the tenth grade I had the rare opportunity of walking her home from school. As we got closer to her home she looked over at me and said, "You know, Tommy, when you grow up you're going to be a very sophisticated gentleman."

Who the hell in tenth grade at Edison High School would say such a thing? (I hope that when I grow up I won't disappoint her.) Anyway, she, like the sensuous Lena Horne, Nancy Wilson, and Dorothy Dandridge, surely influenced my sense of beauty in the "fairer sex."

Of course, as I grew into my twenties and further into my addictions I was less discriminating, especially when I was blurry-eyed in some dark bar where I'd find myself going home with anything that crawled. I recall reading a piece of graffiti on a toilet wall in some funky beer joint that was an appropriate description of my sexual morality: "I'd fuck the crack of dawn if I could get up that early." The women who woke up with this wild man had to feel as repulsed as I did. Nothing a quick Bloody Mary wouldn't fix.

But, in spite of my alley cat dalliances and clitoral proclivities, over the years I have met and loved her again and again, *the epitome*, with different names, different shapes, different colors. A full-bodied beauty queen from Portland or a cutie pie pixie from Seattle; a redhead Irish lass from, well, Ireland, and a healthy midwestern girl, reeking of farm fresh goodness. Yes, and even an Irma La Douce look-alike whose grandmother accused her in Paris of being just that: standing in the doorway looking like a French whore. She was every bit as sensuous but hardly a professional.

Oh, and how could I forget an absolute knockout of Asian persuasion down in Santa Cruz who had the dubious fortune, Cookie, of listening to me reading poetry at a little restaurant on my 30th birthday. She was Japanese, if you please, immaculate with thick, shoulder-length black hair, a grad student who, as it turned out, had a meticulous little cabin up by the university famous for its banana slugs.

As we awakened the next morning I scribbled a ditty for her which is arguably the most repulsive, gag-me-with-a-chopstick, not sukiyaki but super-sucky, racially clichéd love note ever written:

> Blossom of The Cherry,
> Light of the Rising Sun,
> I bow beneath your almond eyes,
> Ichiban—Number One!

Again, I was smitten and, to use another cliché, in love with love. Throughout my life I actually believed my teen-brain lyric-induced romantic emotions, and it was way too easy to say, "I love you." Each time *she* was my first love, my history or hers be damned. How fortunate that my sincere, albeit needy and misguided, expression would periodically lead to a richer friendship after we had parted the sheets.

My point here, though, is that my "true love" was all of those wonderful women with their various temperaments, looks, and backgrounds—yet somehow, *she* was always the same. What she was and always has been is the muse herself, who, if it is our great fortune, comes to us in myriad forms—and what we men must always understand is that it is the muse who chooses.

Blue Note. Singer Johnny Hartman was indeed a heart-man. When I lived up in Seattle I hung out for a while with a buddy of his from New York, a classy dude named Teddy. Nice guy … said that Hartman was one of the first Black cats to have his own TV program, but they pulled him off the air because too many White chicks were literally throwing him their drawers. Yep, to hear his voice it's easy to understand why. Kick back and listen to "My One and Only Love," John Coltrane and Johnny Hartman, YouTube. The entire album is dangerously smooth.

The Boys

> "I have friends in overalls whose friendship I would not swap for the favor of the kings of the world."
> —Inventor Thomas A. Edison. Many of those friends, incidentally, I met at Thomas A. Edison High.

1958-1964. There at Edison High I had a cadre of cohorts, an intimate little circle of buddies, if you could call "intimate" hanging around in a totally dark room, pulling down your pants and lighting matches to your ass while you farted. Big Frank had a real flame-thrower! With all the greasy crap we had digested throughout the day, beans of course being high on the menu, we all cut some pretty good ones! Imitation, it is said, is the highest form of flatulence. Butt (sic) I digress …

In my little circle we were all just plain teenagers and few of us thought of ourselves as Hispanic, Latino, Mexican-American, not even Chicano. For the most part labels weren't in the mix … we were just American kids who happened to be of Mexican descent. Not until later in our lives, when we *crossed the tracks*, did we find out that indeed there was a difference, that there was White privilege and Brown oppression.

In spite of our overall Anglicization, we continued to do a lot of things that were of the Latin culture—like celebrating Mexican Independence Day with a background of live mariachis, and driving through the dense tule fog on Christmas night to eat sweet, home-made tamales after a late Mass. From early on, we went to dances where the bands played a mixture of salsa, mambos, cha-chas and good ol' rock 'n' roll, where the lovely Mexican girls were chaperoned in the basement of the St. Alphonsus community hall or at the Rainbow Ballroom.

To whatever degree of Mexican-ness we were, "The Boys" did however have very American first names, like *Morris* Martinez, *Edgar* Palomino, *Edward* Perez, *Frank* Quintana, *Steve* Santos, *Roger* Flores, etc. And I, of course, was *Tommy*.

As kids we all watched *Ozzie and Harriet* on black and white TV while eating our fried wienie tacos (Mexican hot dogs); as teens, we "dragged the main" like they did in Stockton à la *American Graffiti* in Big Frank's cool mint green '55 Chee-vee con moon hubcaps; and we all had wet dreams of Marilyn Monroe after seeing her nude photo on the wall at the Sensano brothers' barber shop … except for Big Frank, who had dreams of his mother's cooking. We all remain dear friends.

A Note on "Sabor a Mi." Within this latter time frame—1964, two years out of high school—there was a multi-hit hit vinyl album that became a must-have in all of our collections. It was titled *Amor,* and the most popular tune within that album was *Sabor a Mi* (essentially suggesting, "Have a taste of me, savor me.")

There have been numerous renditions of this very popular 1959 bolero. It has been covered by many of the great Mexican and Mexican-American singers over the decades, from the terribly rich voice of Javier Solis, to Luis Miguel, José Feliciano, Los Lobos, and El Chicano; and there have been a score of international versions, like that of the peppy gypsy-jazz group Monsieur Periné.

But my all-time, very danceable fave is on the *Amor* album. Here the great Trio Los Panchos provide the backup for the '60s pop diva who had hits on both the American and Latin charts, the delightful Eydie Gormé … make that gourmet. Treat yourself to this delish dish: *Sabor a Mi* by Eydie Gormé & Trio Los Panchos—YouTube.

This whole album of classic Mexican tunes was part of the fabric that connected us Chicanos to our past while we danced in living rooms and various dance halls, drank our Coca-Cola, and ate cheap burgers at the new McDonald's in Fresno. (By the way, the very first McDonald's franchise in the nation was right there on Blackstone Avenue … 10¢ for a burger, same for a bag of fries!)

So here's to Harriet Nelson (1909 – 1994, R.I.P.), most famed for her role in the TV series *Ozzie and Harriet*, with sons David and Ricky.

Adíos, Harriet, American Mom

The day Harriet Nelson died
The Amana freezer and a thousand TV dinners cried.
She was real, all right, and her loss makes us sadder,
we never knew when she was on the rag
and it didn't even matter.

She was always on cue, a real find—
The fact she was White never entered our mind.
The fact is *she was always there,*
Supportive, nurturing, like a mother bear,
Ready to patch the bleeding ego
Of the little next-door amigo.

Amid the sirens and sobbing,
and hammered fingers throbbing
like clockwork came the invisible pillar
of our ramshackle walls, she was the filler
of a million shanties, the once-a-week mom
for a rainbow of kids named Pancho and Tom.

From the whole block they'd come
with their pockets of candy,
peachy keen glee, sticky hands were dandy
glued to the front of the black-and-white screen
hot popcorn and Kool-Aid, a warm fuzzy scene.

We didn't miss a show, never, no never.
Harriet, we loved you, and need you more than ever.

The Kearney Bowl Dream: An Arcane Arcade

Summer, 1961. A 10-minute déjà vu all over again. I awakened with the dream still vivid in my mind: in it I had visited a little street fair, one of those tiny circuses you see in otherwise empty lots here and there. It had all the normal attractions: tossing ping-pong balls in little bowls to win a goldfish, shooting a basketball to impress a girlfriend, a Ferris wheel, acrobats, and clowns; cotton candy and hotdogs-on-a stick.

In this chimerical, Fellini-esque setting I walked through the entrance and went to my right. (Interesting that in all major circus walkways, expositions, trade shows, etc., wherever people walk into an area where there is a sequence of things to be seen, the great majority of us will go to the right.)

This dream reflected a truly small, local event, maybe a couple dozen arcade attractions at the most. In it I walked from booth to booth, listening to the barkers while taking in the glimmer and the delicious smells of childhood joy. But it was a tiny show—just one tight circle—and the end came as I returned to the entrance, which was also the exit.

The word *circus* at its root means circle, and that's what I had just walked in. A circle, by the way, like a square, is the basis of a mandala, the sacred iconic art of Hindu, Buddhist, and even Christian symbolism, with outer points equidistant to a central focus. In the case of Christianity, the Four Apostles compose the points of a square on the reliefs of some older churches.

That evening I was scheduled to work at the local racetrack, Kearney Bowl, hawking my sodas and peanuts to the large crowd that always packed the venue, maybe three thousand or so.

I walked to work—maybe a mile along a mostly dirt road—and arrived a little early this particular day. Upon arriving at the parking lot of the track I noticed a large portion of it had been cordoned off—set aside for a small ... circus. I had always loved these hokey types of freaky shows since I was a small fry at the Big Fresno Fair and, small as this event was, I was at least going to take a few minutes and enjoy the atmosphere.

The second I walked beyond the entrance of the fair I knew precisely what was about to happen next, detail by detail, sound to sound. As I walked by each exhibit, each game, ride, concession stand, I knew exactly what a person was going to do or say. I knew it because this was *precisely* what my dream had vividly depicted, and I knew it like I had been there before with a camera in my brain, recording every little iota of information.

A karmic circle, if you will, a ten-minute déjà vu. It was stunning in a quiet sort of way. I just kept walking until I reached the exit, which was also the entrance, and then things returned to "normal"—whatever that is.

I went to work that evening, sold my sodas, and didn't think a heck of a lot about the rather miraculous event that had occurred out in that mysteriously converted parking lot.

Raiders of the Last Ale

> In the Okefenokee swamp of Florida, the Walt Kelly cartoon character Pogo Possum is walking around one very hot day when he spots Al, the Alligator, kicked back under a fallen tree. Sez Pogo, "What are you doing under there?" Al answers, "Under where?" Final panel, Pogo sez, "It's too hot for underwear!"

1961. It was almost time for the summer vacation, already hot as hell in sweltering Fresno. Edgar Palomino and I were in our Junior year and about to become Seniors … woo-hooo! For some reason we were let out of school early that particular day and went directly to his house, not really planning what was about to happen.

Both of his parents were wonderful cooks, his dad winning a statewide chef award, and his mom being the head cook for grade schools and high schools in the West Fresno area. They always had a refrigerator filled with great leftovers, like her mouth-watering enchilada casserole. More important, however, was that there was often an ice-cold pack of beer in there (not Lucky Lager, but something a little more exotic, like Olympia).

I really don't remember the brand, and it wouldn't have made a difference. I do recall Ed heading straight for the fridge and grabbing a couple of bottles. He had never done this before; like my psychedelic mentors to come, I think he just wanted to "turn me on."

We scooted to his room and closed the door with prayers that his parents or older brothers wouldn't show up. This was to be the first drink I was to have since the fateful and well-documented Cardboard Box Incident when I was six.

I recall Ed sitting in a chair and my sitting on the edge of his bed. We were yakking and laughing and farting and guzzling—what the hell, let's have another one! We grabbed a couple more, and went back to his room, him on the chair and me on the bed and then, Bam!, I fell back, kicked my legs straight up, did a flip across the bed, and let out a whoop like a horny cowboy in his first whorehouse. This time I didn't kick boxes around, but just swerved my way home wearing a shit-eating grin.

Mrs. Palomino's Enchilada Casserole

As some of us graduated up the ladder from grade school to junior high and then to high school, one thing was consistent: Mrs. Palomino's enchilada casserole, and periodically her enchilada pie. Why was it consistent? Well, when we were wee ones, there at old Columbia Elementary, that wonderful two-story brick play pen, who was the cook who prepared our lunches? You got it … Mrs. Palomino. "Mrs. Palomino, can I please have seconds?" "Well of course, Tommy, but first blow your nose."

Then of course came Edison Junior High (Now Erwin Middle School) … "Mrs. Palomino, can I please have seconds?" "Well of course, Tommy, but first blow your nose," and then Edison Senior High—Go Tigers!—where, almost miraculously, we had the good fortune of having … you got it! … Mrs. Palomino as our lunchtime chef. Needless to say, once a week we got a good helping of that scrumptious enchilada concoction.

Nutritious Notes: Mr. Louis Palomino, Edgar's dad (aka Crab Louie) was once awarded the prestigious *California Chef of the Year* Award. With this in mind, I must acknowledge the following international chefs and gourmands, friends of Mr. and Mrs. Palomino, who have generously contributed to the aforementioned casserole recipe:

Ann Chilada, Kay Cedia, Chill E. Bean, Al Bondigas; Kwak O. Moley; M.N. Udo; Sal Monela; and the great Italian chefs Shelly Verdi and Cheech A. Roni. And let me not forget the top-notch home cooks Ben Venido and of course Fresno's own Tom Ollie Pye.

A Ticking Time Bomb

Ever since I was squirming around in that menagerie of measley (sic) mongrels, the Fresno Orphanage for Booted-out Babies (FOFBOB), I was a ticking time bomb. It is readily apparent in what my foster mother once told me as to how I came about having the name Tommy. It wasn't from Tomás or Thomas or Tom. Nor that I was born on Thanksgiving day … Tom as in turkey. It wasn't from any of those names.

No, it was Tommy as an abbreviation of "atomic!"… because when they first saw me in my little cage I was already a molecular explosion, a split atom bouncing off the walls, a vision of fission to be sure.

The big word back in '45, especially after the horrendous Hiroshima and Nagasaki bombings, was *atomic*. They named me after a fucking bomb! Ah-Tommic … an ignominious beginning to be sure.

A few years back—during the summer of 2010—Roger Palomino, an older brother of my old friend Edgar of the Stolen-Beer-Bottles fame, came to my house to visit along with a mutual friend, Dr. Juan Garcia. I hadn't seen Roger for almost forty years. We hadn't really known each other well when we were kids. I was just the frenetic friend of his younger brother. But as Roger tells it, the one thing he remembered of me when we were in our early twenties is that I was "always very angry." No shit.

The truth is I've been boiling mad most of my life—it's the stuff that madness, as in flat-ass crazy, is made of. So even before those maniacs became my foster parents I was already jacked up to the max on natural speed. I have been that way since I can remember.

And it seems to coincide with that empty-orphan feeling I have at times … It's like walking down a set of stairs and not knowing if the next stair will be there, a constant fear of "the rug being pulled out from under." As my young life went on, hurtful and constantly traumatic events added to that insecurity, and a certain lack of stability arose that only made it worse.

At last I can now see why, but it has taken me a lifetime to get over much of that nightmarish melodrama. Apart from that, as a "person of color" raised in poverty, the more I learned about this society's racist basis the more pissed off I became. As the Black protests in the deep South became more intense and then as the various social movements of the early '60s continued to escalate, so did my anger.

And so did my alcohol consumption, as if I needed an excuse. One thing I have learned over the years is that if you don't resolve old stuff it continues to fester with explosive results. We don't forget a damned thing! We may painstakingly cover shit over, like a cat in his confining litter box, but sooner or later the poop will pop.

The Wrath of Grapes

> "They are not long, the days of wine and roses:
> out of a misty dream our path emerges for a while,
> then closes within a dream."
> —from "Vitae Summa Brevis," by Ernest Dowson, 1896

I sometimes cry when I think of them, that miserably lost couple, John and Linn. I cry because I feel sorry for my maladjusted, wine-addicted foster parents. Okies from Muskogee they were, only from Kans-ass, right out of their version of the Dust Bowl, at the same time in American history, the Dirty Thirties. From eerily empty Kansas they came out in a Model T Ford in which they had chased rabbits across the bleak flatness of those arid prairies; now they were chasing a dream, California, better than the bare no-where of Edson Hardly-on-the-Map Kansas.

My foster parents were old enough to be my grandparents, him being born in 1902 and her in '05. She had a 6th grade education (pretty good for the time and place), but he couldn't write his name ..."X" marked the spot. He was a short, squat, very "Indian" looking man, with teeth that had worn down to his gums from grinding them night and day. She was a couple of inches taller, a skinny white chick with red hair and freckles, a bit Irish one would think. Linnie Mae Warner.

What unimaginably screwed-up people, lost in the unwashed Mason jars they often drank from. They had no clue what was to come, but they were full-blown crazies who spent their years tragically linked in the haze and rippled daze of those smelly little rooms we lived in, he a barnyard musician at some earlier time and she a cantina floozy that he met along the way.

All people have their good sides, but by the time they fostered me they were already riddled with the toxin of rapidly processed dirt-cheap 20% alcohol wines—tokay, muscatel, white port—a certain death trap. Their addiction was so all-encompassing that they would verbally and physically fight over this crap, night and day, to see who got the last drop. They would secretly put marks on the label of the bottle with their fingernails to see who had sneaked a drink, and that was often the cause of another uproar. (The deadly formaldehyde level of these horrid wines was many times that of legal limits ... See notes below.)

After John was fired from Southern Pacific we moved from house to house, and each time the place was shabbier. In that sense we too were migrant farm workers, moving from hovel to hovel in that same West Fresno ghetto. From the 9th grade into my senior year, we lived in a stuccoed shack-in-the-back with chicken wire and newspapers as insulation. 41 East Lemon. When the lights went out you could hear the cockroaches scurrying through the papers, probably looking for the comic section for stress release from listening to my parents bicker all night long.

John and Linn used the welfare money given them to take care of me to buy their poison and would often send me to the little rip-off market in the area—Red Front, on Thorne Avenue—to pick up their fix, a bottle of wine and a pack of Chesterfield cigarettes when they could afford it (other than that, roll-your-own with cigarette papers and a can of Bugler tobacco).

Mister Goldman, the storeowner, would give them credit and by the time the monthly welfare check arrived it was already spent ... such a deal! I often begged him not to sell the shit to them, but he would just say that if he didn't someone else would ... and he was right. With regularity we were forced to move because even the slumlords couldn't handle their night and day rampages. Screaming, fighting and, finally—thank God! —sleeping when they had exhausted themselves from their wino tantrums.

I was with them until I was old enough to join the Army, by which time I was frothing at the mouth to get the hell out. As it turns out, I think I was a "natural alcoholic," meaning I was born with that proclivity, but the 13-or-so years with those maniac parents might have had a little to do with why I pounded the drinks down so heavily as an adult. Yah think?

Fermenting in Fresno: I recall decades ago reading in *The Fresno Bee* that the amounts of formaldehyde in certain wines right out of the San Joaquin Valley were several times the level that was legally allowed. I gather it was the cheapest process of food preservation, so screw the people who drank it. Formaldehyde has also been used for the embalming of humans and pickling cucumbers (perhaps that's where the term "pickled"—meaning drunk on your butt—came from).

So when people like my foster parents have been thoroughly saturated with this carcinogenic junk, all one desires is more of it to kill the pain caused by it! As a full-blown alkie, every time I see the excellent film *The Days of Wine and Roses* I break down because I know it is so true.

Rotgut Capital of the World

As a kid, six to sixteen, I would schlep back and forth through those Fresno alleys to the local grocery store to get my parents their daily bottle because they were too damn drunk to walk that far … one fuckin' block! The other winos in those alleys, mostly black folk, generally had a little something colorful to mutter as they got fucked up in the heat of the day.

Summer after summer they were plastered on WPLJ (acronym for White Port and Lemon Juice). Hate to say it but on a broiling Fresno afternoon that syrupy crap tasted pretty damn good.

Another po' man's drink was Thunderbird. The winos made up a little ditty that they'd ask one another: "What's the word? Thunderbird. What's the price? Twenty twice." Forty friggin' cents to blast your brain and shred your kidneys simultaneously! On KGST radio Happy Harold, the wayward R&B DJ, the black sheep of his white family, would play the shit out of the WPLJ tune and then, with his raspy Wolfman Jack-ish voice, hawk the latest cheap-o wine prices on "The Sunny West Side of Fresno!" The man knew his market.

Check out "White Port and Lemon Juice" sung by the Bel-Aires and years later by Frank Zappa. And here's another funky version, from 1955, "White Port 'n' Lemon Juice" by doo-wop group The Four Deuces, YouTube. Get down, Leroy Brown!

A Bus Stop Named I'm Tired

> Question: "Why do Mexicans have large nostrils?"
> Answer: "So they have something to pick during
> the off-season."

Over the years I've done a lot of rote work, meaning doing pretty much the same thing in the same damn fields and orchards over and over again—row after row, season after season. Oddly enough, that work as a kid being driven out to fields in labor buses trained me well for other enterprises … row after row.

So in spite of it all, that fieldwork has been converted to a great survival skill. You've got to make the most of what you've been conditioned with, what you been given this time through the mankind mill … in my case, much later in life, I used this resilience to tediously make my phone calls to long lists of sales leads.

Just a note: I do wish that more youngsters in America were allowed to work—not grueling work, just real work for decent pay—because not having this training, this early work ethic, will surely put them at a disadvantage in the emerging world.

Pretty Woman

> "Pretty woman, walking down the street/ pretty woman, the kind I like to meet/ pretty woman, I don't believe you, you're not the truth/ no one could look as good as you … Mercy!"
> —"Oh, Pretty Woman," song and lyrics by Roy Orbison

I have no idea who she was, not really. I only knew her name was Blanca, because of her relatively light skin. She went to another high school, and she and her family spoke mostly Spanish and kept very much to themselves. The common denominator was Roy Orbison … Rrrrrr-owww!

I first laid eyes on her the early summer between my 8th and 9th grade while we worked in Joe Tanaka's peach and plum orchards, going up and down those wooden ladders to snag the ripening fruit. There was always a radio blaring in the background, sometimes Mexican music but usually the local "Top Ten"—which was really more like the top fifty, and they'd always throw in hits from years before. Probably because at that time there really were "disc jockeys" playing vinyl 45s, alphabetically stacked at the DJs fingertips, and older folks still loved the hits from earlier years and would call in requesting them.

You'd hear the same songs day after day, a real hodge-podge of tunes from all parts of society, whoever made it to the top…country singer Teresa Brewer's "How Important Can It Be?"; Chuck Berry's way-danceable "Nadine"; Domenico Modugno's "Nel blu dipinto di blu" (the quintessential "Volare" melody before the Dean Martin and Gypsy Kings renditions); one hit wonders "Sukiyaki" by Japanese crooner Kyu Sakamoto and "Stranger on the Shore," by Britisher Mister Acker Bilk; and of course the ubiquitous Roy Orbison. Year after year that strange lookin' cat with his oversized, tinted reading glasses and his distinctive falsetto to the nigh-operatic notes would somehow knock a home run, like "Pretty Woman," "Crying," and "Only the Lonely."

And as the tunes kept rolling we'd pick that fruit, summer after summer … and each year it occurred to me that Blanca was getting a heck of lot prettier. Her tight-knit family, maybe five or six of them, would huddle at lunch time just a few feet from my little family of three, and I'd just chaw on my burrito or white bread boloney sandwich and stare at her, hoping to catch her eye. It finally happened in the summer going into the 11th grade, with Roy doing the Hawaiian-esqe *Leah* tune …"I gotta go diving in the bay, gotta get a lot of oysters, find some pearls today to make a pretty necklace for Leah." Man, that flew me out of that orchard and onto some tropical island with beautiful Blanca at my side. (Maybe that's where my attraction to Hawaii began.)

At that point I made the executive decision to tell her I liked her and ask her to meet me at the movies someday (which wasn't very likely in that we had no phone and I doubt her family did). Nonetheless the time came and I pulled my comb out of my back pocket and ran it across my wavy black hair, straight back with a little flip in the front for what I thought was my Tony Curtis look.

I thought over my approach a couple of times, and then I was ready, Teddy. But by the time I walked towards her the whole family was already getting into their dust-covered station wagon. She was the last to jump into the back seat and I caught her eye ever so briefly. We didn't have the chance to say a thing.

I'd like to think there was a little yearning in her heart … there sure was on my part. I never saw her again, but whenever I hear The Big O's "Leah" I am swept back to that beach where Blanca and I laid in the sand as the warm ocean caressed our toes.

> In the tradition of the awesome, the frightening, the menacing "I Was a Teenage Werewolf," now comes the equally mediocre…

I was a Teenage Beatnik

Fresno, Fall of '61. I was in my Senior year, Danny a mere Junior. When we reached the front of our school that sunny morning we just out of nowhere decided to ditch classes and spend a day goofing off. So we headed over to his pad with our orange PeeChee folders in one hand and a soda in the other. To get from Point A (Edison High) to Point C (Dan's pad), we had to go through Point B (the downtown area, the new Fulton Mall).

Well, as it turned out this particular day, we spotted a brand-spankin'-new, freshly waxed, blazing red Chevy convertible, top down, parked in front of a store close to the newly built mall. We were innocently walking by it ... honest. We admiringly looked it over, and lo and behold the keys were in the ignition! The owner had walked into a store and left the keys in the friggin' ignition ... Hello.

We walked a few steps in the direction of Danny's house, stopped, looked at each other, and with some kind of psychokinetic power (psychopathic might be more like it) we non-verbally communicated, I mean it was like as if some powerful mysterious force took control of our feet, I mean we made a 160-degree U-turn and headed right to that shiny red car. With zero hesitation I jumped in the driver's seat, turned on the key, and I'll be damned if the tank wasn't full to the brim. Still no words.

Then something quite beyond my good Catholic upbringing forced me to ask: "Danny, you ever been to San Francisco?" The distance between San Francisco and downtown Fresno is about 190 miles. Danny, like myself, was a peasant who hadn't seen much of anything except the little towns surrounding Fresno where we'd go each summer to pick fruit. I'd at least had the good fortune of having been taken to The City a couple of times, courtesy of my mentor Buddy Lang. Danny didn't have to say a damned thing for me to get his response.

Two Mexican teenagers in a stylish brand-new car—red convertible, mind you, with squeaky-clean whitewall tires—on our way to the Big City ... damn! We flew through those hick towns down Highway 99: Madera, Merced, Turlock, Modesto ... then crossed over ... Tracy, Livermore, Hayward. I still don't know how we got there without being pulled over or how we got there at all. We were truly clueless and could hardly see ourselves in this pretty dramatic scenario. These two punky Chicano kids racing down the highway, radio blaring, top down, had not a notion of what the hell we were in the thick of ... *but damn it was fun!*

Time flies when you're just groovin' and suddenly, we were at the front of the Oakland Bay Bridge ... *almost there.* Then in a flash, to the left of us and to the right, sat several Highway Patrol cars. That was the first time it dawned on me that we might just possibly have done something wrong and that there was a very good chance that we'd pay dearly for it. Shit!

On top of the cops' presence there was a small matter we hadn't counted on: the fee at the toll bridge. I don't remember ... 25¢, 50¢ at the most ... whatever it was, it was a fortune to us. We had to scramble through our pockets ... nickels, dimes, pennies, anything. When all was said and done, we had barely enough to pay our way through. Those cop cars apparently were there for some other reason, not for these two criminal masterminds who had just escaped Minimum Security at the Edison High Reformatory for Stupid Asses.

After my adrenaline had settled down a bit, I said to Danny, "Danny, we gotta get rid of this thing ... man, we could be in deep shit. Let's look for a place to leave it." The first exit dropped us off in an exciting part of town, what I later came to find was North Beach, North Beach which oddly enough had been my destination since the 7th grade when I first learned about my kookie heroes, The Beats. (By the way, that exit no longer exists thanks to the Loma Prieta Bay Bridge World Series earthquake.)

Almost out of gas, hey, there's a spot. I parked the car and asked Danny for a blank sheet of paper from his Pee-Chee folder and a pencil. He gave them to me, and I proceeded to write, in big, fat letters, "FOR SALE." I placed that sheet of paper under the windshield wiper, left the keys in the ignition as we found them, and said, "Danny, let's get the hell out of here!" (Over the years I've wondered what idiot stole that car next.)

We walked around a while taking in the sights and smells and checking out the denizens of this dazzling new world ..."Toto, I have the feeling we're not in Fresno anymore." Here they were: enigmatic characters wearing berets, well-dressed professional women in high-heels and suits, animated Chinamen hawking their vegetables and fish, striptease barkers beckoning horny sailors, and one sweaty older guy who wanted to take us up to his room for God-knows-what but, being the "older brother," I nixed it.

We ended up on an uphill street called Upper Grant. Of all fucking things, there it was, right there on the corner of that alley by the oldest saloon in the city with its swinging doors and alley cat smells, a street sign that said

"Fresno"! A little alleyway, a short block long, right off of Upper Grant. A dead-end. Fresno. Damn! That street sign is still there.

Another cat, a mid-aged streetster in that very alley shared his sandwich with us. The dude was genuinely helpful after we told our harrowing story about the bridge, the cops and all, said he liked our style and gave us a few bucks for a Greyhound bus to get back home.

Little did I know that those impressions had already cast my fate and that I would spend many a year in that very saloon, in that milieu and lifestyle for which I've had a propensity since my earliest teenage years.

In Carnations. By the time I was in the 7th grade back in'57 I would literally stop and smell the roses. I *knew* on some level I was a bit of a poet, a beatnik, and a seeker of spiritual wisdom. Don't ask me how because nothing in the intellectual poverty I grew up in remotely suggested this direction. The entire matter has led me to consider reincarnation as a real possibility. In that very same year a cat named Jack was truckin' through Fresno on a journey into history.

Kerouac Kwote: "I stuck my head out of the window and took deep breaths of the fragrant air. It was the most beautiful of all moments. The madman was a brakeman with the Southern Pacific [Railroad] and he lived in Fresno; his father was also a brakeman. He lost his toe in the Oakland yards, switching, I didn't quite understand how. He drove me into buzzing Fresno and let me off by the south side of town. I went for a quick Coke in a little grocery by the tracks, and here came a melancholy Armenian youth along the red boxcars, and just at that moment a locomotive howled, and I said to myself, Yes, yes, Saroyan town."—from *On the Road*, by Jack Kerouac, 1957

Facing de Feet

In 1961 and '62, I was part of the California State 1-A Champion Edison High track and field team (No. 1 Water Boy and Equipment Schlepper). I was pretty fast, but my black brothers were flat-ass beauty in motion at those San Joaquin Valley and State-wide track meets, leaving their competitors literally in their dust.

It occurred to me way back then that there was something not quite right about the images on those dull yellow Pee-Chee folders we all carried: not one black or brown face! We had faithfully used them since junior high, and yet something was rotten in the State of Subliminal Segregation. It finally occurred to me that Pee-Chee was a play on "Peachy"—hence the yellow color—a term that in those days was peachy keen, i.e. way cool. What wasn't cool is that for all of those years there wasn't a single drawing of a Black, Chicano, or Asian kid playing sports on their covers.

See if you can find the famous Black Olympians Jesse Owens or Rafer Johnson in the art. Johnson, by the way, was from a funky little redneck burg just south of Fresno, Kingsburg, no less … the only Black family in that whole damn town, and that was back in the '50s. But guess who's coming to the Olympics?

I remember as a kid reading about him, front page of the Frez Bee he was. Rafer Johnson became the 1960 Olympic champion in Rome in the decathlon! And it was in '60 *and* '61 that my little school, Edison High, with its superb Black and Latino athletes won the California State Track Championship … no mean feet.

Further, Fresno was home to the annual world-class track meet, the West Coast Relays. No shortage of us darkies there, but did those frickin' folders ever reflect that reality? I don't think so.

Photo by Ben Pease

Doing the Mashed Potatoes at the Old Buddhist Temple

1961. In Chinatown, on Kern Street right around the corner from the Cal Theatre, stands the Fresno Buddhist Temple, graciously styled as to give a sense of the majestic "old country" while bringing a touch of American architecture of the day. Designed in 1919 by a young architect named Toyokichi Kurahashi and an associate named William C. Hays, it was the marvel of a thriving Chinatown. The funding came in large part from Japanese immigrants who had been gradually arriving since the 1880s.

They had originally built a wooden temple that, I gather, mysteriously burned down one day. Within a year the new brick building, essentially three stories, was a glistening testament to a resilient culture. (I can almost hear the Japanese equivalent of "Burn *this* down, asshole!") What a grand building, built from the pennies of peasants. The church and grounds, as I recall, were always immaculate, with an aura of hidden depth.

However, when I was 16 or so these details were irrelevant … I was an airhead, so shallow I thought the whole world was like E Street, where I lived in West Fresno. I only knew two things about the temple: on weekends my buddies and I (Morris, Frank, and Steve) would jump the wire fence and hit that cool outdoor basketball court the Buddhists had built behind their church and, two, on rare occasion, maybe once a year, my small group of buddies would get an invite from the Japanese girls at Edison High to go shake our booties at one of the dances in the temple hall.

In fact, as part of the after-graduation drunken marathon—'62! Whoop-de-do! —we all bounced from party to party to party and, as I hazily recall, ended up with those same basketball buddies doing the mashed potatoes on the slippery floor of the Buddhist Temple … I tell you, Michael Jackson had nothing on James Brown as far as getting up on your toes, hand subtly on your crotch while smoothly gliding backwards. Even Fat Frank could get down … Go Frank, with your bad self!

The only thing I remember from that point on was puking on the Buddhist Temple fence and losing my band pin, given as a medal of sorts for my years of service as a trombone player in the Edison Marching band, pep band, orchestras, dance band, oh, yeah, and the Christmas brass ensemble … my band pin! Puking on the Buddhist Temple fence! How Zen is that?

And speaking of James Brown, here's one of the tunes that had us breaking out in a cold sweat: "I feel Good," James Brown, YouTube. The man had some bad steps … The hardest workin' man in show biz'ness!

From Beer to Return as Pee

"Maybe back in the days of the pioneers a man could go his own way, but today you got to play ball."—Burt Lancaster as Sgt. Warden in the film *From Here to Eternity.*

Summer of '62. The fat recruiting sergeant in Fresno—Sergeant Null was his name, go figure—had guaranteed that when I joined the Army I would be sent directly to Hawaii. I had developed a real longing for a fantasy isle like this, perhaps from seeing commercials of hula girls swaying their hypnotic hips or reading books like James Michener's *Hawaii* (God, it still calls!) But I know it had a lot more to do with getting away from suffocating Fresno and the insanity of my foster parents.

After high school graduation I wasted no time signing up. I was first sent to Fort Ord, located near Monterey Bay, for Basic and Advanced Training (in my case it was to enhance my typing skills preparing me to become a supply clerk). After that four-month stretch I was shipped out (in this case flown) to Hickam Air Force base near Pearl Harbor, and then bussed to the center of the island of Oahu, to Schofield Barracks.

The place had been made famous by the James Jones novel *From Here to Eternity* and by the film based on the novel. When recently watching the old flick I could see Schofield hadn't changed much: the three-flight barracks, the mynah birds, and the kitchen police duty—KP. And I'll bet the WWII dogfaces also ate powdered eggs and shit-on-a-shingle (a gravy-ish chipped beef on toast—pretty tasty, come to think of it), and drank all the chocolate milk you could guzzle. Man, I was in heaven!

On weekends, when I wasn't doing extra KP for being a fuck-up, I'd put on my civies and head into Honolulu. Ten cents a dance on Hotel Street where the emphasis was on *Ho...Ho*-no-lulu?). But better yet, to Waikiki, where the service men had a terrific recreation hall called Fort DeRussy. That place had been there before the Second World War, a splendid getaway right on the beach, with pool tables, cheap hot dogs, and dances on the weekends with Hawaiian girls and stateside chicks who were often accompanied by their horny moms. Ahhh, Bernadette, Koko Crater Coquette ... but that's another story.

Back home I had gotten used to getting a great beer buzz with my buddies before we would take off to the dance hall, the Rainbow Ballroom, where the swirling, sparkling ball hanging dead center from the ceiling would mesmerize us young Latin Lovers. But I was only 17 there in Hawaii and had yet to cultivate an older dude who'd buy the hooch for me.

My only alternative was the little beer garden at the DeRussy Rec Hall where they only served 3.2, a "Near-Beer" with a tiny fraction of the real stuff. I'd get there early on the weekends and order a pitcher, then another and another. By seven I had a mini-buzz and was ready for the big dance but spent most of my time pissing. Good thing I wasn't an alcoholic.

Thank you, June Lujano

As I've mentioned, the 7th Grade at Edison Junior/Senior High was the beginning of six consecutive years in the same school. It was amazing in so many ways: new kids, so many of them, including those giants in the 11th and 12th grades. This was all to me an exciting and magical environment, "The Sacred Halls of Ivy"... not to mention my evolving horny toad chemistry.

Enter June Lujano. When I first saw her that very first year she was wearing a skirt that made her look like a striped bass—same colors, stripes down the side, similar smooth, slinky figure. I was between a rock and a hard place, with the emphasis on hard. I kept thinking about those beautiful fish I used to catch on trips to Friant Dam ... and then I'd see June walking past.

One day one of her girlfriend's busted me. I overheard her say, "Junnie, Tommy's looking at your shape." Well, flash forward to the end of our sophomore year, filling out forms as to which classes we'd take in our June-ior year. June and a lot of other girls of course took typing. Typing? Well, I figured, this was maybe my best chance of getting next to her, I mean literally. I signed up, one of only two boys in the entire class (the other, Joe Winston, was there for God knows what reason, but he seemed to be having a gay old time).

I got to classes early that opening fall day, wearing a well-ironed shirt that I carefully pressed *twice* ... Hey, June's gonna be there. I was probably the first kid ready to head into that typing class, with the idea that I would sit as close as possible, right next to her if I could. Well, I got that seat and as the year went on, I got really good at typing. I wasn't a jock, just a trombone player in the band, which doesn't exactly qualify one as a babe magnet but hey, in that junior year I got up to 45 words per minute on those heavy old typewriters, Smith Corona, Burroughs and the like.

It was almost a contest, "Who can type the fastest without error?" On occasion, the teacher would mention who in the class was getting the best results—sad to say my digital prowess didn't impress her. I tried again in my senior year, and actually got up to 62 WPM ... pretty impressive for a spaced-out scatterbrain with the bulk of my attention on June's legs. She ended up dating a football player, Rufo Vaquilar, and I ended up learning to do the twist, the mashed potatoes, the jerk, and the pony, all which served me well here and there, as a very young man still in high school and later in the Army at USO dances in Hawaii.

That spring of '62, just like in the movie *American Graffiti* which took place in 1962 in the small town of Modesto about 114 miles north of Fresno, most of us graduated and went our own way. I just needed to get the hell out of Fresburg. I also joined the Army because I had been guaranteed that I'd be sent to Hawaii where, no doubt, I'd meet beautiful Hawaiian girls with whom I'd of course have good Christian fellowship.

Little did I know that damned near every young man was being sent to Hawaii to be trained in the jungles there, jumping into the tropical mud in preparation for warfare in Southeast Asia—The powers-that-be knew it perfectly well back then. Even at our lowly level we heard the buzz ... *Viet Nam.*

I was a supply clerk. Why? Because I could type 62 words per minute on a manual typewriter and believe me there were few other kids who could do that. After being on the island for a few months and crawling around in the fern-covered tree-canopied jungle with our camouflaged helmets and heavy 9-pound M1 rifles (which were about to be upgraded to M15s and then to the standard M16s), we were informed we'd be shipping out soon ... "Advisors," yeah, right. The 25th infantry Division, Tropic Lightening with that great insignia of a golden lightning bolt, was the first Army division to go into 'Nam.

About that time a messenger came midday to our company sergeant, a Master Sergeant, who in turn brought me into his office...Oh, shit, not again. Anyway, says he, "Private, you have to go down to the Adjutant General's office. They want to talk with you." Adjutant General?...isn't that about serious legal crap? Double Oh Shit...this time I've really done it!

I show up, salute an officer or two—the place was crawling with officers! —and I'm asked to go into a room where there's a desk, a typewriter, and a fat sergeant (love that Army chow) staring at me. He says, "Put some paper in and just type what I say." Huh? Anyway, he starts slowly dictating and I'm hammering those keys and slapping that return lever like a speed freak cleaning his house. My heart was mega-pumping the coffee and glasses of chocolate milk I had chugged that morning, I mean tweeker-level jacked up!

He says, hey not bad, not bad at all. He leaves the room for a few minutes then he and a young officer, a first lieut, walk in and the lieutenant says, "Well, Private, welcome to the Adjutant General's headquarters. You'll be transferring companies and working here in the clerk's corp." Top secret clearance, khaki shorts and short sleeve shirts—no stinkin' heavy metal helmets here. Even the damn lieutenants carried swagger sticks.

The AG company was in some ways elite, maybe thirty of us in all as I recall, some could well have been the sons or relatives of senators and millionaires. This was during the draft and all young men were in one of the services, one way or another. I'm not proud of it but you know damn well that kids like these seldom go to the front line, nor does their commanding staff. My typing skills had probably saved my brown ass, and so that's why I titled this piece "Thank you, June Lujano."

A Typing Exorcise

Now is the time for all good men...
Now is the time for all...
Now is the time for...
Now is the time...
Now is the...
Now is...
Now...
...
..
.

A Note for my Homeboys

I am proud of our classmates from Edison High Class of '62 who served valiantly, even re-upped, like Sergeant Gerald Hernandez, Captain Leonel Alvarado, Major Rufo Vaquilar, and Corporal Tommy Arredondo, who died on his first tour. There may have been more, these are just the ones that I am aware of.

I recently spoke with Gerald for the first time in several years. I mentioned that I was a poet and he said he had written a poem many years earlier. At the time he was a young man of 22 getting out of his first stint in Vietnam. The guy re-upped twice after that. Here it is, raw and real as you can get:

Written by Sgt. Gerald J. Hernandez
United States Marine Corps at the D.M.Z.
Republic of South Vietnam, September 15, 1966

This poem is dedicated to the men and women of our armed forces who served and gave the supreme sacrifice.

No One Knows

The days are short, the nights are long
in this futile search for the Viet Cong.
Fighting is fierce, the death toll is high
for an undeclared war we do not know why.

Who is the enemy who brings us such fear?
Is he the old woman in the village who tries to sell us beer?
Could he be that young man in the fields attending his cows?
Or is he that little kid who says, "Hey, G.I., you give me one chow."
We see them every day and yet we don't know
which one of these persons is our deadly foe.

We come to this faraway land, most of us young, some of us old
all with the same purpose, and all with the same goal
to be tough and hang in there, and hope to survive
so we can leave this hell hole, not dead but alive.

Most are boys when we come to this place
but leave here much wiser and older, you can tell by their face,
a face that has aged with the perils of war
and doubt in our minds about who we are fighting for.

I'll be leaving soon, "I'm short list!" I shouted,
it's someone else's turn to stand up and be counted.
I just hope and pray that in later years
our sons' wives will not have to shed tears,
tears for their loved one who is not coming back home,
back home to the family he left all alone.

How many more lives must we lose before we realize
that peace for mankind is not won by deceit and lies.
I'm leaving now, my time coming to a close
but I still haven't answered my question
because "no one knows."

Hitch Hike, Baby

> "I'm goin' to St. Louis, but my next stop just might be L.A.
> (Hitch hike) Now what'd I say? (L.A.)
> Got no money in my pocket so I'm gonna have to hitch hike
> all the way (All the way) Yeah (Hitch hike baby)
> —Marvin Gaye, '62, backed by Martha and The Vandellas.
> YouTube it, baby!

Part One. The Army, thank God for it, taught me a thing or two. Bottom line was I really needed some adult discipline, something I had seldom had growing up. And one of the better skills it taught was the frugal art of hitchhiking.

Well, they didn't teach it per se but I did learn from fellow soldiers who, on their weekend passes or more extensive leaves, used the real economy route. Amazing what a uniform and a smile will do. Even sans uniform, it served me well over the years, hitching from San Diego to Canada, always being picked up quickly, which pissed off other hitchers who had been standing there for hours. (It's about the thumb, dude, and the smile and the swagger … and making eye contact, if you can. It's about being cool.)

We didn't make much in those days, in fact as a buck private (no stripes), I seem to recall back in '62 the monthly check was about 70 bucks. Well shit, when you got your little leaves to go see your girl or your family there's no way in hell you're gonna spend cash money when you're endowed with the Almighty Thumb … Hitch hike, baby!

Over a short period of time I got really good at it, especially in uniform. At that time it wasn't a hippy phenomenon at all, mostly straight or adventurous young men like Jack Kerouac's *On the Road.* Lot of military or ex-military guys would pull over and open the door.

On one of these earliest jaunts, heading out one evening from Fort Ord back home to Fresno (about 150 miles away), I was dropped off in the sleepy farm town of Salinas, made famous by Steinbeck's *Of Mice and Men.* There was sure as hell no other reason for fame, at the time a funky little burg with all the fine elements of West Fresno.

I needn't inform you that the first thing this boy did was to find a close-by dive, smoky and smelly, my kind of joint. They didn't give a damn about my age, maybe the uniform loosened them up. After a couple of drinks, I meandered around the corner looking for something that, to that date, I had never had. Hell, I had my first and only wet dream back at Fort Ord, eight grueling weeks of forced celibacy … even the Five Sisters didn't have a chance.

Then bam!, there she was, right on that corner, bulging every which-a-way, hot red dress so tight she looked like an over-stuffed tomato … Well, all right! Probably early thirties, a haughty hot mama, hand on hip. "Hey soldya boy, you wants a date?" A date? Hey, I thought she was serious. Maybe, just maybe, after a prolonged period of meaningful courting I might just stand a chance. Hmmm. "Well, sure Ma'am," sez I, "I'd love to date you."

Well, the next thing I know she drags me upstairs in a rundown hotel, she going door to door pounding the hell out of each one of them. Each time the response from the lady in the room was quite the same: "Leave me ta hell alone, bitch, I's busy!"

Double Hmmm. Then she sez, "Thaz al'right, come on now, soldya boy, I be takin' care of yo' ass." Immediately we find ourselves in an alley behind the hotel, she trying to open the door of any car parked back there. Finally, she finds one that is unlocked, a four-door clunker. She just up and jumps into the back seat, pulls her dress up and her drawers down. And here it comes, damn near broke my heart, "Soldya boy, you gots a hanky, yeah you do."

As part of the uniform we always carried a sharp, folded white handkerchief in our coat pocket. Well, she snatched—so to speak—that damn thing out, rapidly rubbed it across her tawdry twat smelling of sweat and cheap perfume, threw it on the floor, and then warned me in no uncertain terms that I had better to hell hurry up because the cops were always patrolling that particular alley.

Whatever bit of a hard on I had went south, and I sez, "Hey, I'm sorry Ma'am, but I'm kinda' late, gotta' be goin'." She sez, "Look now, shee-it, you can't be doin' that, Soldya Boy … gimmee some Goddam money!"

I asked what her price was, and she said ten dollars. Ten Dollars? To be honorable, I said "Look, here's a five-er," handed her a crisp five-dollar bill and, choosing not to retrieve my deflowered handkerchief, headed back to the highway, thumb out with my virginity still intact.

Part Two. I got to Fresno, West Fresno, 'round 'bout midnight or so. Some older black dudes that I had seen on that very same corner for years, "E" Street and Tulare, were shooting craps on the sidewalk … seven come eleven! Well, I had always been pretty good wit' dem bones and, dumb as cum, figured now that I be a man, I gets to play wit' da big boys.

So I pulled out a few bills, got down on my knees, and sure as hell I was hot, rollin' those dice and snappin' my fingers at each roll. Time and again I hit my number and time and again those suckas took my fuckin' money … Waz up with these cheatin' muthahfuckas? I challenged them and they in unison said no way, that I had crapped out. Wha??? I didn't want to get my soldya butt kicked so I said screw it, and with the little money I had left I headed a few blocks down the road to see my parents and crash.

About that time one of the younger characters on that corner, a guy who had known my older brother years before, asks me if I'd like a nice lady to go to bed with, "You likes Colored girls, White girls, Chinese girls, shee-it, I gots 'em all." From his pocket he shows me pictures of a couple of scantily dressed babes, as if they're in his stable. Well, thinks I, my luck's finally coming together. Okey-dokey, let's take a look at these fine ladies.

We head around the corner to a very old motel, just a bunch of little shacks side by side. Then here it comes, he sez, "Say soldya boy, I's gonna take care o' yo' young ass, but fu'st I wants yah to he'p me. See, one of these gaddam hos be ripping off my customahs, an' I needs to find who da hell da bitch be. While they be fuckin' she be stealin' all they muthahfuckin' money!" Why that double-crossing prostitute, the nerve!

"So look here now, all I wants is fo' you ta give me whatevah money you gots and I marks it with a pen … that way I be knowin' who da bitch be." Makes sense to me, why sure, sir.

Well, as soon as I pull the bills out of my pocket, he snatches them in a blink of an eye and rushes into the door of one of those tiny motel rooms. I sat there like the full-blown fool I was, waited for about a half an hour still thinking about that beautiful blond he was going to set me up with.

Finally, it occurred to me that the son-of-a-bitch might have ripped me off—big time duhhh—so I go and blam on the door. Some other big sucka' opens the door, all belligerent, and asks who the hell am I. I tell him what happened and he, now looking like he wants to kick my soldya boy ass, sez, "Ain't nobody here, get the fuck outta here, man!" Ah, home, sweet home.

Oh, My Little Soldier Boy

"You were my first love and you'll be my last love
I will never make you blue, I'll be true to you
In this whole world you can love but one girl
Let me be that one girl, for I'll be true to you."
—from "Soldier Boy," as sung by The Shirelles (1961)

Winter, 1962. Iris Elaine Washington. Damn, I loved that girl, brief as it was, truly innocent first-time stuff. A pretty girl, mellow caramel, fine as wine on the slim side, a certain elegance about her style.

Met her at a bus stop, me in uniform with my privates showing (that is, I was still a buck private in this man's Army, no stripes). I had just finished basic training and was being shipped out from the Oakland Army Terminal. I wasn't sure of my ultimate destination other than I was getting the hell away from Fresno and supposedly was going to Hawaii.

Anyway, I had a few days of leave while at the terminal, and one of those drizzly evenings I found myself standing at a busy bus stop having no idea whatsoever where I was going. Yet it turned into a sweet experience I'll never forget.

That's when I first saw her, standing there in a light rain. You know, the proverbial "love at first sight." She was about my age, so terribly poised and fresh, waiting for the bus—just like the innocent song "Yes, I'm ready," by Barbara Mason. Man, I had no choice. I was clueless as to introducing myself, so I just moseyed up and pretended that I was getting on the same bus … Well, I was. And I did. Fortunately, in that fairly crowded bus, she sat where there was an empty seat next to her. Did she sit there purposely?

Soon we were headed up that lengthy boulevard, 14th, and something clicked, something good. I surely had no finesse in chatting up the chicks, but we managed to introduce ourselves and just kept on with our small talk. We did have a lot in common really, background to some extent—West Fresno and East Oakland were and are both ghettoes with similar goings-on—but the real commonality was our spunk, our humor, our vibrant youth. We instantly hit it off.

At one point she let me know that she'd be getting off soon. She stood up and pulled the cord above to stop. I was tormented with the idea that I might never see her again. She looked down at me with a sweet smile and asked, "Would you like to meet my mother?" Would you like to meet my mother? I have seldom heard lovelier words.

I clearly remember walking up to her house, an older building reminiscent of homes I had visited in West Fresno, nothing fancy but solid, the kind of place where white folks had lived decades before. She opened the front door and we walked into her living room where her mom was sitting on the sofa watching TV. We were introduced, and after a pleasant but brief conversation her mom excused herself, saying she had had a long day.

Iris turned off the TV and threw on a few mellow records, like the then popular Shirelles album. We settled into that comfortable old sofa, talked, and gradually held hands. She asked if I liked to dance … like to dance? That original Shirelles album, The Shirelles who launched the "girl group" genre and stole the hearts of many a young man, was mostly composed of slow numbers, the romantic stuff, yes, but also little cha-chas, like "Will You Love Me Tomorrow" and "Tonight's the Night." And of course, "Dedicated to the One I Love."

The slow tunes were romantic as hell. "Closer … closer … you really got a hold on me, really got a hold on me," went some old lyrics and that is precisely what was happening. I had danced with girls back in high school, but this was something else. After moments of gentle gyration we'd sit between songs and smooch on the couch, a very natural meeting of perfectly matched lips. And then, like all good things, the voice from the back room, "Iris, girl, it is getting a bit late, say goodnight now."

As it turned out we dated three or four times before I had to ship out. Never got beyond smooching and I never pushed it. But you know, that's really all I wanted, I couldn't have asked for more. It was the wonder of the present and the possibility that this was the beginning of something wonderful. We promised that we would write and that I'd be back soon to create something special.

I was soon shipped out to Schofield Barracks, Hawaii. She wrote regularly, and I think I responded just once. Terrible. You see, I had fallen in love again, this time with a voice and an image. I was in love with Shirley of The Shirelles that I had heard hundreds of times on records and radio, who ironically was singing in the background back when Iris and I made out on her mom's couch; I was in love with Shirley's voice and image on the cover of several albums (lead singer and namesake of that very popular group made up of four lovely high school friends, Shirley being the leader of the pack).

As things would have it, a few months after being at Schofield I got wind of a big concert in Honolulu, featuring a couple of warm up one-hit wonders, The Cascades with "Rhythm of the Rain" and Paul & Paula with "Hey, Paul"… but the headliner was the multiple-hit Shirelles). Wow! … and double Wow! It was on a weekend and I had just been paid. I put on my one and only sports jacket, the same one I had graduated in several months earlier, tied the knot on that skinny little tie, gave my shoes an extra pop—and yes, I'm ready!

I grabbed a military bus and as we weaved our way down the hill past Pearl Harbor and into Honolulu, I sipped whiskey from a small bottle tucked snuggly into my inner coat pocket. And then within an hour or so, quite magically, there she was, just twenty feet away: Shirley! Triple Wow!!! There and then I made an executive decision: When the curtain closed for the final act I would just flat-ass sneak backstage, a habit I had developed back at the White Theatre when I was a huckleberry kind of kid. And I did just that.

"What are you doing back here?" growled the husky white guard. "Uh, well …" Think, Tom. I then blurted out, "Well, uh, uh … I'm the manager of The Shirelles." (Note: The only reason I came up with that whopper is that in my senior year in high school I was the so-called manager of a local R&B band called The Rebel Brothers, four young Mexican kids with a black lead singer who did a damned good impersonation of James Brown. Got them a gig or two.)

Guard: "Oh, yeah, and I manage Elvis." Then with a shitty sneer he orders, "Just hold on here for a second." Next thing I know, here she is, my latest true love, I mean like a foot away … *Thee* Shirley of *Thee* Shirelles, no less. Damn, Sam!

To make his point the guard says with a considerable smirk, "Ma'am, this young man's sayin' he's your manager." She puts her hand on one of those booty-licious hips, looks me up and down, and says as I hold my breath … she says, with sultry southern softness, "Uh-huh, that *is* my manager."

She asked me to hang on for a minute, returns with the others, and then we're limo'd to her pad, a swank suite in a hotel on Waikiki … the rest is history … of sorts.

God, I hate to cop to it but not much happened, a mild smooch or two, yes, that's about the most I could truthfully brag about to my buds back on The Mainland (although I think I stretched that story a taste back then, yep, just a hair, as in pubic).

There were a bunch of kids up in that sizable hotel suite that night, pretty crowded with fans who had an "in," as in "I'm in with the in crowd." *Thee Hotel* where the group was staying was the world-famous Royal Hawaiian and just being in that venue was a fine experience, a setting I was to return to again and again. Moxie moves mountains.

As weeks and months went by Iris continued to send me letters but I was too shallow and self-absorbed to respond. As fate would have it, I saw her about five years later at a political rally in Berkeley. We were demonstrating on two interweaving picket lines, she in one and I in the other. What a pleasant surprise when we came face to face!

We said hello in those brief interactions as we paced with our signs and chants and agreed to get together immediately afterwards. The rally was broken up by the cops and our rendezvous wasn't to be. I think we were both swept up in the power struggle and politics of the times and, sad to say, we never re-connected. A part of my heart still lingers on that Berkeley sidewalk.

Oldies and still Goodies: "Soldier Boy," "Dedicated to the One I Love," and "Will You Love Me Tomorrow?" by The Shirelles, and "Yes, I'm Ready," by Barbara Mason. YouTube these sentimental journeys and try to find them as videos … even better if you got that someone to share with.

My First Lei

And what memoir would be complete without a tale about the writer's first fuck? I guess I could be a little more delicate, but … well, you'll see.

It all began one night … Well, actually it began one day, there at Schofield. I had been assigned the task of Kitchen Police yet again because, frankly, I was a pretty bizarre kid—you know, like getting back to base late from beach parties, even AWOL a couple of times—and KP and pass restrictions were often my punishment, really most lenient in retrospect. Thank God I had my understanding sergeant because no other unit would have tolerated the shit I pulled.

Such as making a few bucks via usury, loaning guys money when they were flat-ass broke, generally within a week from the time they got their measly monthly check. This is really a shameful practice, even the Bible says it's so, but it was a way to make a buck or two … or two hundred. The troops were generally broke and/or horny within a week from the time they picked up their checks, and brother, cash is king!

I had learned from an older guy, a three-stripe sergeant whose girl was named Ruth (though she was always dumping him, at which time I jokingly said he shouldn't become Ruth-less, a grumpy gimpy drunk who went on crazy sprees—we got along just fine.) I was already starting to scribble little ditties on pieces of scrap paper and the fellow said I could be a good writer in time, maybe the next James Jones. I had no idea what he was talking about.

He was a lifer, been in over twenty years, and still a three-stripe sergeant because he, like me, was one hell of a screw-up and a hard-core drinker. A good guy, good at his job there in Tropic Lightning Division HQ, a nutso alkie who everyone loved. He's the cat who showed me the ropes about lending money.

Usury: charging my pals and their pals one hell of an interest for the little loans I'd give them...often up to 50%! That's how I was able to send my buddy Eddie Perez that $500 when he wanted to have his first kid in a decent hospital rather than the place where most of us peasants were popped out, that being the Fresno County Hospital. And that's how I was able to rent my tiny bachelor pad, a really cheapo studio apartment in the basement of a rundown hotel—but it was right there, right there on frickin' Waikiki! My Out-of-Fresno dream was almost realized.

It's a good thing I had befriended that fat, black, gay Staff Sergeant (three strikes against him in those days), because he's the guy who signed the weekend passes. And that particular weekend, having mercy on my foolhardy soul, he came in while I was pearl diving (washing dishes) and says hey, how'd you like a pass? I love yah, baby! So, after the final greasy pot was cleaned, maybe five-ish, I donned my civies, threw on what I thought was a classy after-shave, Aqua Velva ... I still like that cheap crap...and rambled down to "The Key," Waikiki that is.

It was at this time, me being a 19-year-old lightweight hustler, that for whatever mysterious reason I had become closely acquainted with a bartender—imagine that—at a remarkable and historic hotel, yes, the one-and-the-same Royal Hawaiian. When first constructed this was truly splendorous, a lovely pink pearl right there on the beach where the hula girls I had dreamed of would sway their hips on the surf lanai every night for the rum-filled tourists.

Built by the Matson Navigation Company (Matson Lines now) in 1927, this was a prime destination for moneyed travelers from around the world. It was for kings and presidents and movie stars and rock-n-roll legends ... and it was for a certain Army private who had little cash but a shitload of chutzpah.

I'd go into that beautiful old place wearing a flowery silk shirt and pretend to be Hawaiian—Royal Hawaiian, but of course. Being a dark, curly-headed Mexican it wasn't too difficult for me to pass as local, 'til I opened my mouth. The bartender and piano player got a kick out of it. I'd do my flaky version of a pidgin accent—You know da kine?—and do my best to convince tourists that I was the real thing. It worked most of the time because those folks had never seen a real Hawaiian, let alone a friggin' fig-pickin' Mexican from Fresburg.

Now this particular night there I was, midnight-ish and already many Mai-Tais to the wind—what incredibly syrupy crap but loaded to the brim with three different kinds of rum, a mega-buzz and a sure hangover! I'd always ask the piano man to play a medley from West Side Story … *Mah-reee-ah, I just met a girl* … and that night in she walked. Well, not quite Maria, but an older fox, graying, petite, and wearing very tight leopard-skin leotards. Mrrr-ow on the prowl, a cougar at my jugular.

Talk about ready! The chick was juicily over-ripe. She sashayed straight up to the piano bar where I had found my weekend perch and ordered one of those sickeningly sweet cocktails. I honestly have little memory of her face, fairly attractive I guess, and there was nothing that I recall that stood out personality-wise—a well-to-do older lush, bless her kinky soul.

All I really remember is that she was white and had that lean, hungry look. She was definitely an older broad and when you're a kid like I was there's a near repugnance for anyone over 40, even 30, sexually anyway. These days I'd jump those ol' bones in a New York second … if I could jump.

This was new territory and I didn't know what to say or how to say it. I cannot lie, my leopard hunting skills sucked—but she just sat there and smiled. I find it hard to imagine how truly full of shit I was, but that woman was not interested in my vast repertoire of worldly knowledge. Nope, I don't think so at all.

Wellll … It didn't take long for me to mention that I had a little apartment close by and not even that long for her to put her arm around mine and drag me out the door. The bartender had a little smile, and the piano man played the "Tonight" tune from *West Side Story* … "Tonight, tonight, it all began tonight …" Fitting, huh?

It was pretty hazy from that point on, a blur of Mai Tais, curiosity and out-of-hand mutual horniness. So the next thing I recall is she's lying on my couch, flat-ass naked, just checking me out. Unpolished in such matters, I—how embarrassing—didn't know what the fuck to do … literally. Hey, you don't kid about confessions like this—not a clue. Well, yeah, I took my clothes off but, uh, what's next?

Yeah, now what, stupid? She was kind of stunned, I guess, with the realization that I was a flat-out virgin. So she graciously took it step by step, "No, not there, not … there! Yeah, here … slow … slow. Here, baby." Next thing I know I'm flopped on top like a fuckin' bean-bag, just kind of laying there with all my weight directly on her. "No! No! Use your arms, lift your chest up, yes, honey, like that." Mmm, says I.

Now again I really hate to admit it but within seconds it was all over, I mean shot the wad, completed the evil deed of the wicked seed. Jeezuz-friggin'-shit, is that all there is? All those years of wondering, fantasizing ... bam! ... over in a flash.

As I lay there, buck naked, blown out by the speed of it all, she, catlike, slipped out the door. I fell asleep and the next day I thought, yeah, it was quick alright but still light years better than Willy and the Hand Jive.

The Day JFK Went Away

November 22, 1963, early afternoon. For those of us living when President Kennedy was assassinated, the shocking event is forever imprinted in our memories. Most of us remember the exact time and place, and we remember the details of what we were doing.

Some of The Boys and I were driving around Fresno, looking to get a couple of six packs and go cruising in Roeding Park. Big Frank, Morris, Edgar, and myself. As usual, we were in Frank's sparkly green '55 Chevy. We were all underage, 20 or so, but I was the one chosen to go into the Tower District supermarket to score the beer. The guy behind the counter always let me slide.

I was headed to check out with my cart of chips and a couple of six-packs of 16-ounce Olys (Olympia Beer) while a black and white TV behind the counter announced the news. The President has been shot! The President has been shot! The checker turned up the volume. There was a melee of reporters and screaming and general panic. So shocking that the whole matter was a blur, it just couldn't be, not here.

This particular president meant a lot to us young liberal Hispanics ... he gave us hope and encouragement. It finally felt like something very good was in progress and all would be well.

I went back to the car and loaded the goodies into the back seat. I said something to the effect of "You're not going to believe this, just not going to believe it! The President has been shot!" Everybody shook their head and looked at each other as Frank proceeded to turn on the radio. In those years, the only radio signal worth a shit was AM. We listened a lot to KYNO because of the Rock n' Roll format.

The Beatles were a relatively new phenomenon, and frankly I didn't like them because I felt, like Elvis, they were stealing a lot of black folk's music. Besides, I just thought they were soulless, a cute group of I-wanna-hold-your-hand teeny-boppers. But that day such pettiness was thoroughly irrelevant. That day I recall a Beatle tune being interrupted with that same announcement I had heard on the TV.

We were all stunned and sat there outside the market glued to the radio. It was not much later that it came that the shots were fatal, to the head. We went on to the park and changed stations to what was then KGST that featured Happy Harold's House of Blues, a very, very black program that played great R&B, like Ike and Tina Turner, early Etta James, and some very funky cuts that were out of the late '40s and early '50s.

I mean this was an hour later and Harold's raspy voice still hadn't announced the events of the President's fateful motorcade. The funk-ayyy music went on and the crummy commercials were announced by Happy Harold his-own-damn-self, still pitching the cheap wine that was being sold at a local West Fresno liquor store. Harold made up his own spots on the spot. Not a damned thing about the assassination of the President of the United States, even hours later ... That was our 'hood back when.

Top-Secret Kennedy Era Note. Few know that I was heavily involved with the protection of this country back in '62, especially during the Bay of Pigs. As an Army private training at Fort Ord near Carmel-by-the-Sea, I was assigned to protect our nation by guarding a bridge over the freeway that led to the base. I had no doubt the Cubans had snuck ashore from a Russian submarine and were about to invade the Pebble Beach Golf Course. A 17-year-old space-case, I was issued a loaded M-1 rifle ... Let me assure you, those damned Commies weren't gonna cross my bridge! Thank you for your service.

Uncle Bob in The 'Loin

Question: What's the definition of a gay Irishman?
Answer: A guy who prefers women to whiskey.

1964. Oakland Army Terminal again, where some of us took off from and where most of us with the grace of God returned to, as I did that day. Lot of kids coming home from 'Nam and some of us luckier guys from Hawaii. We all went through the rituals of paper signing, being discharged, etc. And then suddenly there you are, nothing but a duffle bag filled with your "civies"—civilian clothes—and a couple hundred bucks in your pocket. I was now 20 and still didn't know shit from Shinola.

I was wearing that same ruffled blazer sport coat I had graduated from high school in a few years earlier. I threw the bag over my shoulder and headed out to hitchhike, not knowing exactly in which direction. I wanted to see my old buds back in Fresno but dreaded being with my dying foster parents in that squalid environment, the ones I so wanted to get away from—God, from Waikiki back to fucking Fresno. A real downer. Then there it was, the Sign from Above ... quite literally! It was a very large sign close to the freeway: Fresno, 180 Miles, San Francisco 4 Miles. Hello. This was not a flip of a coin.

It didn't take a friggin' genius to make that decision, thumb out and blam, I was in the heart of it all, on Market, feeling the hubbub of a then-thriving and upscale city street, beautiful and sophisticated way beyond my callow self. Cable car clangs. North Beach bums with bright, open eyes. And gorgeous people, men and women and all of the above like I had never seen.

I was a kid in a candy shop, but my cash didn't go far, a few meals, a night or two in a cheap hotel, and drinks, drinks, drinks ... even though I was still underage no bartender gave a damn. And you could get one hell of a cocktail for 50¢ ... for a po' boy from Fresno I was in absolute Heaven!

I, like everyone else in the nation, was well aware of the tabloid crap about those weirdo beatniks of San Francisco but a little off the radar (you'd need to have gay-dar) was the growing homosexual population, then fittingly centered in the bustling Tenderloin district. For some reason I remembered the black/gay/overweight sergeant whom I had befriended back at Schofield Barracks, befriended because most of my fellow flunkies were so uptight about him ... good old racism and probably some repressed stuff still alive and well in this-man's-army. The sergeant who had helped me get onto the Attorney General's staff, who very well may have saved my life. Wish I could remember that sarge's name.

There in The City in record time I had shot my wad, wad of money that is, and found myself back in an off-Market bar I'd been hanging out in before I hit the skids. I had run out of bucks the night before, a broke-dick countrified kid without the slightest inclination of what was coming up next. I finished my final drink and headed around the corner to the Greyhound bus depot where I had stashed my duffle bag in one of the lockers.

Me without a pot to piss in and without a plan, not even the bucks for a ticket to Fresno … though I was aware that there was always the Almighty Thumb. It was pretty late in that swirling turnstile when Greyhound busses were still almost classy. I sat on a bench, hand on my chin like Rodin's *Thinker* wondering what the fuck's next? Enter Uncle Bob.

He was an older gent, probably mid-fifties, well dressed, looking every bit the stereotypical '60s White businessman in a grey flannel suit, tie, and all. He approached me and asked where I was headed. I said hell if I know, would like to stay but out of moolah. He says don't sweat it, are you hungry, let's go grab a bite. I had no clue whatsoever where this was leading … a real big duh … just a nice guy, a meal and maybe a flop and so, hey that's cool … what's for dinner?

We grabbed a cab and headed up the road a few blocks … left the duffle bag in the locker. I don't remember the name of the joint, but it was really a low key luck club, a Chinese restaurant and bar, dimly lit like most were in those days with plush leather chairs and booths … kind of fancy with a baby grand and a chubby, well- dressed black cat playing and singing Johnny Mathis type stuff, "Misty," "Moon River," show tunes and the like. A Chinese joint with a groovy piano bar … huh?

We sit at a table, my sponsor buys drinks … What'll you have, he asks. Just out of Hawaii, I of course order a Mai-Tai, quadruple rum, light on the ice. He had a martini. As my eyes became accustomed to the room, it occurred to me that there weren't a hell of a lot of chicks in there … in fact *none.* The food was off the hook and that piano player had it down. My host's name was Bob, Uncle Bob I dubbed him. Never overtly put the hit on me up to that point, but by this time I knew it was coming.

Within a few hours we hit three or four more joints in The 'Loin, all gay, a full throat buzz at full throttle. And even though it was his unquestionable intention to get me in the rack, there was nothing pushy whatsoever about his demeanor. I found out that he worked in the oil industry somewhere in the Middle East and that he spent the bulk of his year there. In retrospect, he was a very bright, kind and considerate man, genuinely trying to help a down-and-out kid (perhaps with a little ulterior … make that *exterior* … motive).

Not that there wasn't the wish, but only once did it surface. He knew I had nowhere to go that evening so of course he offered a stay at his apartment. When we got there, an urbane setting with a harp in the center of the living room and a panoramic view of the bay, he asks "Another drink?" Why not? And then of course *The Question.*

I answered respectfully: "Bob, I appreciate everything, but it's just not my thing. No worry, I'll split so as not to bother you." He didn't push an iota, gave me a blanket and pillow, said good night, and went to his bedroom; I flopped on the sofa. Part of it was, he later confided, that he liked my company and felt a bit puffed up when we'd walk into one of the bars that he frequented, him with a fairly handsome young dude to show off to his hungry little clan.

This went on for about a week, hitting places where guys looked like Rock Hudson and/or Marilyn Monroe ... gayer than a teddy bear's picnic. He turned me on to North Beach, to the classic poem *Howl*, and actually introduced me to a couple of Beat poets like Bob Kaufman (who said nothing but just nodded) and the ever famous/infamous Allen Ginsberg (whom I was to meet a handful of times later in my life ... but that's another story). In reality, he turned me onto San Francisco's off-beat underground, and that's saying a lot. One morning we got up, had coffee and he said, "Tom, I'm leaving in a couple of days, but I have a little gift for you."

That morning he called a cab, I grabbed my duffle bag, and we headed out, me not knowing what he had in mind. I figured he was dropping me off at the Greyhound. We drove over to Market Street, toward the bus depot, but then continued onward and turned left at the then-upscale Macy's, up Powell-of-streetcar-fame. About four blocks up on the left side was a hotel, which is still there, now rundown but back then a very nice place with a view of the adjacent Union Park, right around the corner from Lefty O'Doul's, SF's iconic baseball bar, and down the street to the Geary Theater. How exciting! From Fresno's alleys of the valley to this, arguably one of the most desirable corners on the whole damn planet.

We walked into the lobby and Uncle Bob paid cash—cash!—for two months' rent. That was $400 a month for a room, a fair amount then—hell, you could rent a large apartment for a hundred bucks a month back in Fresno. We then went up to the room Bob had reserved, a cozy space with a nice little balcony overlooking the cable cars and the park ... everything I could have possibly dreamed of.

He then thanked me for the time we had spent and gave me a couple hundred bucks—which was also a small fortune in those days—to live on and get me settled. Double-Damn! I hugged him and said thanks. He said, "See, you can be nice."

A Grave Matter

I'd gotten out of the Army early, before my three-year stint was up, with a hardship discharge due to the fact that both of my foster parents were close to death and could use a helping hand. They were much beyond helping in the sense of "saving," and when I got back, I was so much into the bottle myself I wasn't of much help anyway. I still have guilt about the matter. My buddy Steve Santos tried to console me by pointing out that they were both so thoroughly wasted that there really was little I could possibly have done.

By this time my foster father John was old and feeble, yet he could always muster up the energy to trundle down to Chinatown and pull up a stool at a dive called Los Siete Mares where he'd shoot the breeze with his long-time buddies, like Jesús Comenaro, my Godfather.

John died within a year of my returning home. Oddly enough, the death of this little man was not directly from booze but from staggering home one afternoon, loaded to the gills, and being beaten to a pulp by a gang of young Mexican thugs with names like El Porky, Shorty, and Magoo. I grew up with little assholes like that—11, 12, 13 years of age—who'd gang up on a weak person for the thrill of it, break windows and do anything destructive—vicious young punks who would inevitably end up in jail or the pen.

My mother died within a year of that, with only one lung—emphysema—yet still smoking like a chimney, and still chugging that rot-gut wine. Hard core. I think she died of loneliness though, without her crazy little playmate. Pobresita. My dreams got stranger.

Way back then I had no idea how very difficult it is for older folks to break away from years of addiction ... and there sure as hell weren't any detox centers for the very poor.

Pockets of Pathology

(Snapshot of a Chicano bad-boy, circa '57)

He liked to hold his hands in his front pockets, pants low,
head low like he was staring at his feet hidden under the oversized, well pressed khaki pants, his short, wiry frame dwarfed by the oversized, well pressed Pendleton shirt.

The handsome young man, all 13 years of him, was already
un puro vato loco mad dog psycho whom the moppy-headed cholas swooned over and his juvenile gang admired
and feared, proud leader of that rabid little pack.

His short, shellacked hair-do covered with a tight net,
his taut lips and amateur tattoo of a Con Safos cross
on his right hand caught in the web between the index finger and society all made him appear very cool.

His cocky closed-lip smile for the girls camouflaged
an unceasing glare penetrating the statue of the Virgin Mary,
his slow, loose walk and manicured style
all made him appear cool, very cool.
He was so cool no one knew he had never been loved.

Back to Bleaker Street

Fresno, '64. When my courtesy-of-Bob stint as a heart-of-the-city dweller was over, I ended up back in good ol' Fresno doing farm work again. Farm work! Something to quickly get a little cash into my pocket. This, after Waikiki and San Francisco. I distinctly recall being out there a couple of days in the mid-day sun hoeing cotton and thinking fuck this, it just ain't worth it, gotta be another way. Washing dishes, washing cars, anything, but get me to hell out of these fields!

I just up and left that field in the middle of the day, didn't try to pick up whatever I had earned, and hitch-hiked back home. Home was now the chicken wire and stucco job where I had spent my high-school years still living with my crazed foster parents. The roaches now had grand kids. Things hadn't changed much, including the bathroom, the one with the slugs slithering across the walls, and the half-full milk carton with my mom's tobacco-laced spit.

What I most recall about my little room was that as dismal as it was, to my amazement, it was quiet. My parents were a bit older and quite sick (as I touched on earlier—unbeknownst to me they were in fact near death), so their hostilities had subdued considerably. They were still drinking heavily, but just didn't have the energy for the knock-down-drag-outs of previous years.

No phone, no radio, for sure no TV … What's a guy to do? Well, aside from an occasional date with Mother Palm and The Five Sisters, there were those things called books. And the downtown Fresno Library was top-notch at the time, relatively new and well stocked. What strikes me as strange is that the books I chose to check out were a little odd for a 20-year-old Chicano kid from West Frez, certainly an oddball collection.

To name a few: *How to Win Friends and Influence People*; *The Power of Positive Thinking*; and a quick-read chick book titled *Bonjour Tristesse* by Françoise Sagan … What a hodge-podge. I even picked up a sizable paperback by Nikos Kazantzakis titled *The Last Temptation of Christ*. The author imagined Jesus as the "Son of God," replete with the capacity to perform miracles, but at the same time the "Son of Man," in the sense that he also had earthly desires. At a point he even yearned for the life of a mere mortal … wife, children, and home.

I was deeply touched by the work and was brought to tears by the foreword where I first imagined Jesus as human. Somehow that version made a lot of sense, a tortured soul with a terrible tug from both heaven and earth. He was for me far more personal and reachable with his complexity, his urges, and his agony.

Within one of the books of that long, hot summer—I don't recall which—was an uplifting poem that had the power to elevate me out of that bleak little shack into a better place. It was titled "Salutation to The Dawn," by a popular 4th to early 5th century Indian poet and dramatist named Kalidasa. It was my first encounter with the "Power of Now" concept. I loved it so much I memorized it.

> Look to this day!
> For it is life, the very life of life.
> In its brief course lie all the verities
> and realities of your existence:
> The bliss of growth, The glory of action,
> The splendor of beauty—
> For yesterday is but a dream
> And tomorrow only a vision,
> But today well lived makes every yesterday
> a dream of happiness
> And every tomorrow a vision of hope.
> Look well, therefore, to this day!
> Such is the salutation of the dawn.

That poem was a real blessing because it brought with it a new way to look at the possibilities of each day beyond the cold, hard reality of the flea-bitten shoe-shine shack that was my physical home.

After a couple of weeks of life in that depressing match box, I was fortunate enough to find a nice little job at Woolworth's, a popular department store on the newly built Fulton Mall. I was happily bussing tables and washing mile-high stacks of dishes in their lunchtime café, replete with milkshakes and malts. Along with the minimum wage, I shared tips with the waitress, which made for a pretty good little income. I soon moved into a wonderful little one-room pad fit snugly over a garage in the comforting old City College community.

How to Leave a Lasting Impression

"You epitomize all I desire in this temporal world."
—Steve Santos' pick up line from the 12th grade …
Steve, it never worked!

Fresno Mall, Spring of '65. Her name was Beverly Novak—yes, like the then-popular film star Kim Novak and, though brunette rather than blond, she was every bit the beauty. Even Steve Santos, a connoisseur of these matters, agreed that she was a total fox.

She was a couple of years older than me, an old babe of 22 or so. We worked at Woolworth's department store on the downtown mall, in the diner area, she, the prestigious Head Hostess (she was the only hostess, but I do like the concept of *Head Hostess* … hmmm) and me, the dynamic, dashing young dishwasher—and, I might add, Head Busboy (of course I was the only busboy). Being just out of the Army, I thought I was pretty fuckin' cool, hot shit, as it were, swave and de-boner (that's suave and debonair in Okie talk.)

I would dream about Beverly, tall and glorious, and have wonderful fantasies about a romantic fling while listening to my Johnny Mathis albums in my little over-the-garage studio by City College. She always smiled at me and I took that alluring gesture to mean that she had the hots for this young Latin stallion. I finally got up the nerve to ask if she'd go to lunch with me and, to my immense pleasure, she nodded yes with that welcoming Head Hostess smile.

I had eaten a week earlier at a little restaurant a few blocks down the road. I remembered thinking at the time that the joint had class … after all, they had a French dish. What was it? … Oh, yeah, *Soupe du Jour.* Pretty good stuff, as I recalled, so, since I was out to impress her, that's where we headed for our late lunch.

The waiter was busy, so I led her to an empty table where I thought I'd have room to show off my romantic and culinary savoir faire. Smoothly taking control, I pulled her chair back to seat her and snapped my fingers for the waiter. With a phony Cary Grant accent, I masterfully directed: "We'll have this, uh, that and, oh, yes, waiter, we'll have the Soupe du Jour."

The waiter returned almost immediately with our soup. What the hell? "Waiter," I loudly complained, "Excuse me, but I was here a few days ago and I'm sorry, pal, but *this is not Soupe du Jour!"* How was I to know that *Soupe du Jour* was French for *Soup of the Day*? You know, she liked me anyway. The chick had class. You know, I'll put it this way: The lady helped me grow up a bit.

Note: Would you believe that Fresno was the first city in the U.S. to have a mall? … How 'bout that.

Further Note: Would you believe that Steve Santos was a guru by the time he was in the 10th grade? Only he could have uttered the deep and time-honored words, "Well, fuck it, man!"

Orlando in Phoboland

1964. Back at the Eagle Café … almost every weekend as my handful of high school chums sat having our Denver Omelets at two in the morning, all the while bemoaning the chicks we *almost* got over with at the ol' Rainbow, there would invariably be a snicker when a certain waiter/dishwasher came by our table. The guy's name was Orlando, a clean-cut average looking man who reminded me a little of Anthony Perkins of *Psycho* fame. He was really a soft-spoken dude in his late thirties I would guess, always wearing the well-pressed white shirt and black bow tie of his waiter's uniform.

Back in those days few of us had actually met a gay person, or more correctly, we were unaware that we had because it was such a hush-hush matter … It just wasn't part of our overall consciousness. So Orlando was a bit of a conversation piece for the anal-retentive gang, "Pssst, hey, see that guy? … He's a fuckin' queer!"

It was not uncommon for the poor man to have a noticeably black eye, a bruised face, or to walk with a limp because some quasi-Christian sadistic jerks had worked the guy over just 'cause. Yet to my amazement week after week, he returned. Like now, there weren't a hell of a lot of decent jobs in the valley for the under-educated, and Orlando, being a Latino with a slight accent, had probably had more than his share of the truly laborious work. The neatly pressed black slacks, black tie and white shirt probably felt pretty good.

So he came back again and again for his meager hourly wage and whatever tips he could muster. Like in most sizable cities of those years there was a hidden homosexual community, and I can only guess they'd show up periodically to support him. I'd like to think the guy finally said fuck it and moved to San Francisco or L.A. where there were whole neighborhoods of reasonably non-biased people. I'd like to think that you wouldn't have to move anywhere to be treated decently, whatever your make-up … or how messy it was.

That was about 50 years ago, and it's astounding that this kind of hostility still goes on—constantly—here and throughout the world. Sadly, you can actually find judgmental commentary about homosexuality within certain religions.

In the Still of the Night

Yosemite, the Summer of '65. We were both about 20. Her name was Loyva Archuleta … What a beautiful name and her name was a reflection of her own youthful beauty, glorious long black hair that fell, flowingly, all the way down her back. I met her when I was waiting tables for Camp Curry's Restaurant and Hotel in Yosemite National Park. She was a maid in the same hotel and, at that time, had yet to be made. I had a '57 Ford convertible, glossy black with white top, white wall tires, and sharp hubcaps … a very sexy ride, auto-erotic, you might say. The stage was set.

She agreed to go for a ride with me one moonlit night. I had a hard-on all week long and broke many a dish just thinking about the possibilities of that evening. Finally, the time came. We got off work and agreed to get together at sunset … there was a method to my madness, the privacy of the night. I drove by her cabin and picked her up. She was wearing pedal-pushers, a pair of pants cut just beneath the knees … very popular with chicks in those days. Pedal-fuckin'-pushers … Damn! I'd hoped for a nice, short skirt.

Anyway, I had taken the time earlier in the week to find a road in the boonies where I could safely drive and pull off the beaten path into a hidden grove. The thought plickens. I headed straight to our little love nest, with a six-pack of Hamm's (from the Land of Sky Blue Waters) for myself and a bottle of terribly sweet wine for her, a quasi-champagne called Cold Duck. I had the radio playing the very-happening doo-wop station out of L.A., the Wolfman Jack Show (in those days there were no tapes and certainly no CDs) ...In the still of the night, I remember ... I remember ... holding you tight, in the still ... in the still ... of the night ... wah-wah, wah-oooo.

Talk about the stage being set. I guzzled a couple of quick brewskies, and she daintily sipped the Cold Duck from a champagne glass I had stolen from the restaurant. This was not the White Theatre! Top down—the car top, that is—with a full moon out, the stars so close you could kiss them. Our lips met and, after original resistance— "Tommy, I've never done this before,"—gradually and slowly those damned peddle-pushers got down as far as her ankles.

"Are you ready?" says the male voice in lyrics of a song popular then; the girl responds, "Yes I'm ready, to kiss you, to hold you, to love you, yes I'm ready." We were ready. And then, and then ... and then we felt the car start to shake, moving up and down ... and it wasn't us doing the movin' and shakin'...What the hell? Earthquake? What?

We looked up and I'll be damned: there they were, three fuckin' bears looking down at us, two relatively small cubs, and one big-ass Mama Bear. Oh, shit, there went my woody, up came her peddle-pushers. I turned on the ignition, pounded down the gas pedal and screeched out of there. Talk about anti-climactic.

About a week later, I pleaded that we give it another shot, and she agreed. This time I found another site that I felt would not be as likely to have those furry fatheads screwing up the works. Pretty much the same dance proceeded. And no pesky peddle-pushers this time, just a nice pair of tight white shorts ... ah ha!

This time we went a little further. Just when the act was about to be consummated, I felt an excruciating pain shoot up the back of my leg, a "Charlie horse," a humongous cramp in the muscle of my thigh. Penis non-erectus. I let out a scream that I'm sure scared the hell out of her. I pulled up my pants, got out of the car and, groaning, stumbled around in the dark for a few minutes. That damned thing took forever to go away. Talk about cramping my style. I would not be surprised if Loyva Archuleta is still a virgin!

On the Steps of Saint Alphonsus

Fresno, '65. After mass at Saint Alphonsus, I dug cruisin' down Kearney Boulevard on a Sunday afternoon, top down with radio blaring oldies (which weren't oldies then) … As the Young Rascals had it, "There ain't a place I'd like to be instead of groovin' down a crowded avenue. (Check it out on YouTube … most mellow.)

On both Saturdays and Sundays there would be a dance at the Rainbow Ballroom for which we—The Boys—would put on our best sports coats, white shirts, ties, etcet (in my case my only sports outfit) and proceed to get a good beer buzz going while hanging out in Morris' little pad behind his parents' house, tuning up our dance steps a bit while listening to James Brown's newest album, "Live at The Apollo." All aboard … for the Night Train!

Now I hate to admit it, but we seldom "picked up" at these dances, that is scored a babe … but we did have a hell of a good time dancing, fast and slow. But when the final dance was over and we were left standing all alone, we'd head out babe-less opting for an early breakfast at the Eagle Café, generally around one to two o'clock. Denver omelet, please … a popular concoction with ham, bell peppers and onions.

On one particular after-dance trek I did indeed go to The Eagle, but still had most of a six-pack in my car … I ordered my traditional omelet and every few minutes I'd go out into the parking lot to refresh my buzz. About an hour later I had finished my breakfast as well as the beer. I headed across the tracks towards my shanty veiled in a West Fresno alley, the no-hundred block of Lemon Street.

For some reason I stupidly (it's called "drunk") took the path down a main drag, the well-lit thoroughfare Fresno Street, and then turned up Kearney Boulevard, a beautiful palm tree-lined four-lane road on which my church, Saint Alphonsus, was situated. (That's the church where a couple of years later I would ask the Father, a guy who had been there for many a year, why The Church always "talked down" to the folks … He said, in essence, that's just the way it is, my child. They are like sheep, and must be led. In essence, people just aren't smart enough to "get it." Hmmm.)

As I drove closer and closer to the church, it occurred to me that I needed to have a conversation with God, yep, a face-to-face with The Big Guy. There were maybe a dozen steps leading up to the door of the church, a wide opening to the four doors at the top and, at that time, no safety bars in the center. I made a direct right turn off of the boulevard and bumped my way up those steps to the doors. Good thing the car wasn't a low-rider. My top was down, and I sat there, discussing God-knows-what.

I really don't know how long it took—15 to 20 minutes—but sure as hell, there they were, two cops, red lights blinking in the squad car. The older one approaches me and says, "May I ask what you think you're doing?" I didn't have to think twice about it, I just told him point blank: "Talking with God."

The two of them stepped back and had a little conversation. About this time a couple of other police cars arrived. "OK, kid, let's back this thing down, and we'll follow you home." Can you imagine that? I had a little entourage behind me, like royalty of some sort. They followed me up to the little shack where I was then living in the wine-bottle-filled alley of Lemon Street in West Fresno.

You know, those cops were actually kind and respectful … There was a time …

Quickie Flashback: Back in high school a 45 record, a "single" came out titled "Devil or Angel." Part of the lyrics went, "Devil or angel, dear whichever you are, I love you." Good little tune to grind to, a slow dance getting the knee not so subtly between those legs in dimly lit corners of the purposely dark dance halls or living room parties, except for the lightly lit church gigs at the Magellan Club in the basement of St. Alphonsus Hall where the priests and nuns wanted to keep an eye on us … God works in mysterious ways.

Photo courtesy of my Church

Who made You?

Here's Saint Alphonsus Church on Kearney Boulevard, where I had absolutely no clue what the words of the Sunday mass meant in English and certainly not in Latin. As a teenager I confessed to fantasizing about things that *Hustler's* Larry Flynt would have classified as X-rated, then lit candles as penitence and dropped an extra quarter into the contribution box to cover any other trespasses I was probably guilty of.

Saint Alphonsus Ligouri, the Patron Saint of Confessors, had found a fitting home when a West Fresno church was first built in his honor in the Year of our Lord, 1914—and that certainly remains true to this day, a bona fide pillar of the community. There was something very pleasant about that particular cluster of buildings and the sweet human beings who inhabited them.

At no time did I attend a parochial school as a regular student, the boys with their tidy blue corduroy pants, white shirts, simple black ties and, we were led to believe, superior education. However, as a child I did partake of the mandatory rituals of Catholic inculcation: Baptism, Catechism, First Communion, and Confirmation. Holy Moley!

In fact, I made quite an impression as a seven-year-old kid in Catechism class when we learned to respond to the question, "Who made you?" The kids would squeal in unison, "God made me!" But then a question dawned on me and I made the mistake of asking the teacher, a nice enough nun, "If God made me, then who made God?" Threw her off a bit, but I still got my little certificate when all was said and done.

A Cross of Light

1966. The summer after working up at Yosemite, I was again hired to work in a national park; this time, however, I was to be in Sequoia National Park as the mailman for Camp Curry. Its owners managed the hotel, cabins, tents, gift shop, eateries, and its considerable staff throughout the park. (Who would've thought that my military occupation, my MO as a supply clerk, would so quickly pan out in civilian life?) I was issued a weathered gray '50 Chevy, a practical 4-door stick-shift that served its purpose but was hardly a babe magnet.

I was assigned to a spartan, two-bunk cabin where a Catholic renunciant might be comfortable, and I wasn't complaining. The job provided three hardy meals a day, and a decent wage. But here comes the rub: my roommate was the young minister for the worker-bees in that spectacular redwood forest, a pale White guy in his mid-20s. At first, I thought he'd cramp my style, and besides, I had already developed an anti-Christian bias. But in short time we'd talk a bit, he trying to explain his Christianity and me expressing my paganism and search for another route. He said that I was a good person in spite of it and it's really what you do in the world, with your life—that's what God cares about.

Now in the world of the flesh, despite my less-than-glamorous vehicle, I was still *the male clerk* in that little village, and as a consequence was thrown in bed, so to speak, with one of the maids on my route, a lovely hippy chick named Louise Gallup. A freckled brunette with long, straight hair and a non-stop smile, that's about all I remember about her looks. In that short span she became a real soul mate. We philosophized and laughed a lot, even when we were fucking (I just think some folks take themselves too damn seriously in this joyous animal act).

That was certainly my first time being so totally in tune with another person. She was a bit older, a very hip 21, and that summer she introduced me to haiku poetry, to simple meditation, and also taught me a form of radical fasting, which, after the second or third day of water and crackers—nary a spoon of solid food—my altered state was opening new "doors of perception" of which my linear mind was unaccustomed. My very first haiku up there in Yosemite went like this:

> Love, four-letter word,
> simply observe peanut-brained
> monkeys picking fleas.

This same fasting period also aided—was certainly a factor—in a profound synchronistic experience with God/Christ, a most beautiful memory unto itself. Many years later, it was to add to other events and spiritual readings (not necessarily Christian, mind you) that would eventually lead me to accept Jesus Christ as an enlightened soul sent to lighten our load and open our hearts. Yes, as an embodiment of God on Earth.

This conversion was not faith-based but, oddly enough, logic-based (which I shall discuss at a later time). But this is what I have come to believe in these latter days: that Jesus' very existence was blessed through and through; and that the incontrovertible truth, for me in any case, is that his life reflected an extraordinary abundance of pure love and that this love mirrored the divinity of its source.

The Door Opens. On the afternoon of my final day of fasting, I walked home to my one-room rectangular cabin, perhaps 20 feet wide by thirty feet deep. As I opened the door, I became quickly aware of the astounding synchronicity before me. It was in fact a matter of light, the sunshine coming through the one and only window on the left wall of that small dwelling and at the same time light was coming through the one doorway where I stood.

The light from both sources created a cross, a cross of light. The sunlight from the window on my left reflected directly across onto a picture of the torso of Jesus that my preacher-roommate had hung there ... *over my bed!* (I think he was trying to tell me something.) And the sunlight from behind me shot straight across to the perfectly centered mirror hanging on the wall opposite the doorway.

As I stood in that doorway, the afternoon light landed squarely on the mirror and my face was in that mirror. Difficult to imagine, but simultaneously the light from the little window was *also* squarely on the portrait of Jesus, being about the size and height of the window light from the setting sun. The light and reflection of all four items—light from doorway, light from the window, picture of Jesus, and the mirror—formed a cross beaming across the room, creating an effervescent Dali-esque *cross of light* floating in midair.

Confused enough? —admittedly, it was one of those you-had-to-be-there kind of experiences. It was not precise, it was ethereal. To what extent this may have been hallucinatory I can't really say, but I felt hyper-lucid. The words that come to mind are translucent, luminescence, a cross across and beyond time and space. The synchronicity was palpable.

When I shared this mystical event that evening with my evangelical roommate, he emphatically said that spiritual men like himself waited an entire lifetime for such an experience. At some level I knew there was something much more to the incident, that it certainly wasn't a pure coincidence. But I was by no means mature enough to give it the appreciation it deserved. The extreme fast was of course an influence on this exquisite moment, and my search, my openness to the Highest Self, may have played a part.

This profound vision was truly extraordinary, but it has taken a lifetime for it to sink into my ever-curious mind. It has allowed me to make my peace with a wavering belief in Christ as the manifestation of God on Earth, though I remain a doubting Thomas as to the entirety of the New Testament. I'm afraid that it's difficult for men as historians to avoid inserting bits of their own views, and in this case of not properly translating a transcendent view (as exhibited in the Gospel of Thomas, which was not allowed into the New Testament).

Whatever the cause, time and again the miraculous nature of synchronicity has brought me to the realization that there is something rich and beautiful and caring about the reality of a loving God, a spirit that chooses to interact with conscious beings, and that the eternal weave of things is composed of strings of light, starlight, sunlight, moonlight, light from behind our eyes which is God observing life.

The Midi Burger Recipe for medium-rare Sanity

1966. Back in the primordial ooze of non-conscious Fresburg there existed an island of sanity known as Café Midi. It survived in the old Tower District, not just because of the artist and artiste clientele, hardly so, as those very cool ones just sat, conversed, and drank coffee for hours on end. In those days a cup of a good quality java at the Midi was only 50¢; the cappuccinos and the like were a buck-an'-ah-quarter, very high for The Valley.

Nope, the place was a business success because the U.C. Berkeley educated owner, Mort Bennett, had one hell of a good menu, not only of superb coffee drinks but also truly delicious sandwiches: The Polish Sausage Sandwich, the Sword Fish Sandwich, and the king of them all, The French Burger. The place was always packed at lunchtime with business folks from The Tower District and beyond … that was the main source of income.

While a student at Fresno City College I desperately needed extra income and I found it there at that small café on the corner of Fern and Maroa. It was in an older building, late forties I'd guess. It soon became the hub of the fledgling bohemian-accented Tower District. It was the first espresso joint in Central California, a real oasis for the scattered number of intellectuals and artists throughout the region.

What in the hell a guy like Mort with his scholarly background was doing flipping burgers in Fresno I hadn't a clue, but I think from a business standpoint he'd figured it out: given nearby Fresno State and Fresno City College there had to be a market for the cappuccino and biscotti crowd who had experienced that ambiance in San Francisco, in Berkeley ... or for those who would like to take in a taste of it.

Mort was no doubt the real deal, a sharp little entrepreneur and quite the artiste himself. He was the perfect personality to launch that bona fide bohemian coffee house, replete with original art, poetry, jazz, and genuinely interesting conversation. I even learned to play chess there, where more often than not I'd get my clock cleaned.

There was a little head shop right next door owned by a cool hippy chick named Carol. Walking into that psychedelic scene you could smell the patchouli oil and pot, those scents co-mingling in the room along with the pipe smoke of wizard wannabes, all enhanced by the burning grease of Midi's fabulous burgers drifting in from next door.

These were really exciting times and Ché Guevara, Otis Redding, and the first Kennedy assassination were all part of the mix. I had a little pad above a garage just up the street on Van Ness, close to school and work—a perfectly comfortable place for a bachelor student-type, a one-roomer with a toilet, shower, a toaster, and an electric "hot plate" (microwaves didn't exist then). No TV—couldn't afford one—and no refrigerator. However, I did have a cooler, a plastic chest, in which I'd place a 5-pound bag of ice.

The spartan selection of munchies generally went something like this: a loaf of white bread (Rainbow, of course), a jar of mustard and small jar of mayonnaise, a package of sliced, pasteurized cheese and, yep, you guessed it, a pack of wienies. I'd fry 'em up, melt the cheese over 'em and have 'em with slices of toast, spread with mustard and mayo ... Mmm-mmm.

One day I got home late from school, 9-ish, with hotdogs on my mind. I went to the cooler and ... damn!!! ... the thing was filled with ants, hundreds of them. Those little bastards had discovered my stash. I emptied the cooler and put it in the shower to wash those little suckers out, while trying to salvage the dogs and cheese.

The next evening came and, needless to say, the results were the same. This called for ingenious action. So here was the plan: I took a small nail and hammered it into the center of the wood ceiling. I tied a string to the nail and tied a shopping bag filled with the goodies onto the string. Take that, you little fuck-heads!

The next evening came, and with confidence I walked home ready to chow down on a fried wienie sandwich. I walked through the studio door, flicked on the light switch and, to my amazement there they were, hundreds of 'em, in a busy line, up the side of the wall, across the ceiling and down the string. Flabbergasting!

Some folks of certain religious persuasions, such as Hindus, believe that people should not harm even the smallest creature, for all life is sacred. And besides which, it would screw up their karma. I concur… to an extent. (Those little fuck-heads!)

Little Ants with Kitchen Crumbs

They marched long miles,
they did not think,
little ants with little mouths,
to find my dirty sink.

The winter will be long this year,
the early autumn rain …
I came to wash the dishes
and there they were again!

Little ants with kitchen crumbs,
I washed them down the drain,
little ants with shock and fear,
I felt their little pain.

Little soldiers down the drain,
down the drain they went,
little ants with kitchen crumbs …
they don't pay the rent!

A Cozy College Cabin

In spite of the ants, I loved that little garret by City College—simple, clean, tastefully austere. Whoever built that snug cubbyhole put a lot of TLC into it. The walls and ceiling with a fine veneer of varnish over the redwood planks, an open A-frame in mini-form.

The older couple who rented to me were real mensches. They kept the rent down, 100 bucks a month or so, and always had the kindest of smiles, both of them. The loft was the kind of living space you couldn't help but think they had built for their son when he was in college.

I wrote the following poem years later, but it reminds me of that sweet little room I still long for:

Feng-shui says No Clutter

Heart bled Romance dead No dread
No clutter

Sky wet No sweat No debt
No clutter

Room flows Garden grows Heart knows
No clutter

Note. If the placement of physical items that you must live with and have around on a day-to-day basis is out of the natural flow, then of course your life becomes a bit fakakta. (Yiddish for someone or something that is completely crazy/fucked up. Example from the *Urban Dictionary*: "I can't believe your brother drank his own urine. That fakakta kid will do anything.")

The Full Catastrophe

> Basil: "Are you married?"
> Zorba: "Am I not a man? And is not a man stupid? I'm a man. So I am married. Wife, children, house, everything. The full catastrophe."
> —from the film *Zorba the Greek*, based on the book of the same name by novelist Nikos Kazantzakis.

Part One: *The Curve in the Road.* After a few months working up in the Sequoia forest, an envelope arrived that weighed heavily on my little wooden desk. Within it was a life-changing hand-written letter from my girl back in Fresno who was still in high school. She thoughtfully informed me that she was pregnant and suggested that her parents thought that an abortion should be considered. What, she asked, did I think?

One night soon after, a moonlit night, I drove up a curvy road to a massive boulder called *Moro Rock*. It is famous for its spectacular panoramic view down into the San Joaquin Valley. I jumped a small fence circling the rock, put there I'm sure to keep tourists from doing what I was about to do. I walked out to the furthermost edge of that monolith towering over Central California and then lowered myself onto its edge.

I sat there on the brink, even as my young life was now on the brink of a most significant move. I sat there, legs dangling down that steep, dangerous cliff, hundreds of feet to the bottom, seeking an answer, a sign. From there I could see the dim lights of nearby Visalia and the ever-so-faint light of Fresno, and I could imagine my girl sobbing in her room, lonely and worried.

The decision wasn't a difficult or complicated one. I would marry the young lady and do my best to be a good father and husband, though I had *worse than no experience* in these matters. All I had to work with as to marriage and parenting were the terrible memories I had, courtesy of my beyond-dysfunctional foster parents.

Part Two: ***A Decent Choice.*** I called M the next day and let her know my decision and she was overjoyed. I don't think her parents were. I gave notice to my employer the next day and said farewell to my preacher-man roommate, and my hippy girlfriend (who I think I was rapidly falling in love/lust with as she was with me). She was in so many ways a female version of me...poor thing. We just couldn't stop laughing at most everything, and that's a good thing.

As it turned out she herself was also pregnant thanks to a humongous doofus of a logger who walked like an ape with those big arms swinging like he was on his way to a barroom brawl. Whenever I saw him lumbering (yes, isn't that what loggers do?) up the road, I quickly walked the other way. I think that big sucker had some foolish notion that old Louise and I were gettin' it on ... ya think?

I returned to Fresno and, within a day, had a serious sit-down on the plastic covered couch of my in-laws-to-be. They wanted an abortion; we didn't. As an aside, I recall going to her parents' door during that period and her mom greeting me with a straight up, no nonsense statement, "We don't want a colored grandchild." I guess anyone with a tad of non-white is colored, whatever the hell that means. But I do give them credit for going along with our wish, as their "colored grandchild" turned out to be one of the more colorful people on the planet.

M and I got married in short time, with all the white folks up in front of the church and a handful of my Chicano buddies way in the back except, that is except for my best man, my dear friend Frank Quintana, bravely and drunkenly right up there by my side. I've recently looked at those old black and white pictures, literally black and white, her as white as a dove and me a Shinola brown ... indeed, "Guess who's comin' to dinner?"

Looking back, my in-laws did all they could to help us out: bought us a nice little car, rented an apartment, and her dad even found me a job in a warehouse where the rats were the size of small pigs. No, my in-laws were doing their best considering the uncomfortable position that M and I, with no forethought whatsoever, had put us all in.

At some point an older buddy, an exceptionally sweet man named O.C. Trotter, found me a great job with the State Department of Rehabilitation. (How ironic that I was the one who needed rehab the most.)

And like an idiot I topped that off by taking nine units at City College, three classes, one of which was about creating a successful marriage. Jesus! I was warned by a co-worker at the rehab center that with all this non-stop work, social activity, and marriage, I was cruisin' for a bruisin', achin' for a breakin', *breakdown* that is.

Part Three: *A Slap in the Face.* When I was about fourteen, I had learned that the only way to deal with the non-stop vile screaming of my drunken father John was to slap him and wrestle him down, then put my hand over his mouth so he'd just shut the fuck up. He just couldn't stop. Usually, even after covering his mouth, he'd just keep screaming until blood would come spurting from the sides of his mouth. He was such a tormented soul and the drinking surely brought out the worst. There was no therapy for his predicament, that being his castration by White society.

Little could I have known that such terrible conditioning would carry over to me as an adult. Throughout the few months of my marriage, my only marriage, I fell into a pattern: work throughout the day, drink with friends after work, and come home to a screaming wife. I am not pointing fingers (except at myself), just stating the facts.

One rainy night, after I'd had a few at the pub where I and my buds would gather, drink, laugh, drink, play pool and drink, we all headed out at pretty much the usual time, maybe 7-ish. On the drive home I was turning onto a neighborhood street not far from our apartment when the car skidded and rammed into a tree. There may have been a bit of whiplash—I mean though there were seatbelts, few people wore them then and there were no laws requiring people to do so.

When I arrived home, my wife was in an absolute tizzy, immediately screaming into my face what an unthoughtful bastard I was, oh, and that I was way-to-hell drunk. I can now certainly see her point. This was not the first night that I came home to this kind of reception, but this was the first time I reacted to it violently. I suspect I was flashing back to how I had dealt with my father's ceaseless yelling … I don't really know. I'm not a violent person so what was this all about?

That rainy night I slapped my wife, and when I did that I hit myself with the full fury of my entire past, with all the madness that had been my home since early childhood. When I slapped her, I slapped everything that was good and sane. And in instantly recognizing how I had lowered myself, how through this violent action I had allowed my foster parents into my new life, that night when I slapped her my whole world broke apart. I just stood there sobbing.

Then something happened … it was like a sharp electric shock running through my head. It was instant and it was horrendous! Everything was out of control; I could hardly think. I told her that I was not well, that in fact I thought that I had "gone insane." That is when I broke, when I mentally collapsed, when I became clinically mad. The word "breakdown" is quite accurate.

She said something to the effect of "Oh, silly, don't worry about it, you'll be okay in the morning." How I wish that had been the case.

Needless to say, it was a very short marriage, less than a year. It ended at the same time that then-Governor Ronald Reagan closed the program I was working for, the California State Multi-Service Center. It had been created to place the various State agencies that served the poor and marginalized under one roof in the ghetto so that people didn't have to bus all over town to piece together the support they needed. A group of us laid-off workers marched to the State Building in Fresno carrying a casket; we called the march "Death of a Service Center" (made the front page of the *Fresno Bee* as I recall, with me right there on the front line.)

So, on top of being fuckin' nuts, I was now unemployed. And then came the clincher—The Day the Earth Fell to Hell! When I walked through the door of our apartment late that afternoon to my shock everything was gone, wife, child, furniture, the works, thanks to my in-laws who were in the process of filing our divorce papers with the complaint being "mental cruelty."

Looking back, I should have divorced all of them on the same grounds. Entering that totally empty apartment without any notice whatsoever devastated me. I had no idea it was coming and, frankly, I hadn't realized how much my wife and child meant to me. I crawled on the floor and wept like a baby knowing what was lost. In retrospect, the relationship would never have worked, not for any meaningful period, and the in-laws were right in their anger but not necessarily for all the right reasons. There was no "Let's sit down and talk this over" period.

Part Four: ***A Crime of Passion.*** I was a terrible husband who had no idea of what I needed to do to "be there for her," and no notion of the hell she was going through, so young, often alone and confused. I still feel great guilt about that. The fact, though, is that our marriage could not have survived our differences, our immaturity, and my damnable upbringing.

Often, I'd come home with a nice little buzz and she'd go through the roof because I had downed a few drinks at a joint en route—Oh, and I admit, some nights it was more than "a few." In retrospect I can really see her position, just stuck there at home without a social life … terrible!

On certain days of the week, I'd arrive in the afternoon and more than once I was asked this question: "Are you promiscuous?" I was surprised she had that word in her arsenal. Am I promiscuous? Well, like most young dudes, married or not, and like President Jimmy Carter, I had to confess I had "lust in my heart" on seeing a cutie shaking her booty. But man, I had my hands full, and I was a happy camper on the home front … Nope, not an iota of promiscuity, I would reply.

She seemed particularly weird one afternoon after the obligatory promiscuity question, screaming about my pubic hairs, my hairs in the bathtub! Well, the questioning continued and I realized that she seemed to be on this particular warpath on the afternoons when she returned from her weekly visit to her gynecologist, the same doctor who had recently delivered our baby. What the …? Anyway, I'd shake it off with another cool beer and get ready for school or my coffee house job.

Within a few months our differences, our stress, my drinking, the involvement of my in-laws, and without question my slapping her, all added up to our divorce. (Again, she was under terrible stress and I wasn't helping matters by spending my leisure time hanging out with my buds.) She unceremoniously moved back with her parents and I found a little apartment close to my work at the coffee house and to my classes at City College.

Her parents and the court had placed a restraining order on me, meaning I could not come within a few miles of her house, and could only see the baby for "visitation rights"—only on specific and rare occasions. This really pissed me off, so I would have a few drinks and then drive over to her house anyway. Her parents would call the cops and I'd hit the road before they arrived ... cat and mouse shit. Embarrassing.

One day, a day that it was legal for me to visit, I showed up at her doorstep and her mom somewhat apologetically said, "Sorry, but she doesn't live here anymore."

"Well then, where does she live?" I inquired.

"Sorry, Tom, but I'm not to tell you." How fucked up is this, can't visit your own child, your only known blood relative in the world, a little baby for whom I had a natural loving bond?

I was obsessed about finding out where M now lived, partially because I still cared for her but most important, to be able to know where my daughter was, and frankly, under what circumstances was she was living in. I called a couple of acquaintances I had met as a consequence of our marriage, friends of hers and her family. No one seemed to know. Then it came.

I returned to the hospital where I had first met her when I was working as a Male Nursing Attendant and she was there after school as a volunteer of some sort, a candy-striper. She always had a good heart. I still had a handful of friends working there, and so I just walked around the familiar halls, hoping to find anyone who had a clue as to her whereabouts.

After several inquiries, bingo! A nurse with whom I had worked and befriended pulled me aside and said she knew but made me swear not to tell a soul where I got this information. Yes. Yes. So please tell me where she's at. She asked me to wait, she disappeared for a couple of minutes, came back and handed me a little note. And then she repeated her request that I keep her out of it.

The mystery boggled me, but I was excited and grateful. I left the building and walked out to my car. As I sat there, I nervously opened the note that gave an address that was on the "better side of town." And then I saw the name of a certain doctor that I immediately recognized. I knew Fresno but I couldn't place this specific street. I stopped at a service station (remember when they actually gave you service?) and bought a map (that was our GPS). Ah ha, there it is, a cul de sac.

As I drove towards the address, I started putting things together: "Are you promiscuous?" I remembered M hammering me with those words after her meetings with the doctor who had delivered our baby. The realization that she was now living with him was a blow that sunk deep into my gut—I was there in the delivery room and he, as our doctor, was of course also there as the baby arrived. (I chose to be there for this amazing moment though most macho guys back then weren't up for it.) I was actually the first to see my daughter as she pulled the rip-cord to parachute into this Wild West.)

So, I asked myself, "Did the good doctor, recognizing M's stress, purposely plant the seed of, 'Don't you think he's promiscuous?'" She was, after all, a very attractive young lady. Frankly, you'd have to be a full-blown idiot not to put those pieces together: This guy lusted after his patient, my wife, and calculatingly worked towards his goal. And how tempting for her—the guy was a bona fide doctor—and white at that. A white doctor in this country, like movie and television heroes of old, were all but gods.

Her parents, I thought, would certainly approve of her move into the arms of upward mobility. She had been in desperate straits, living with her middle class parents and a tiny baby, a "colored" baby at that. Now she was the mistress of a doctor, prestige (in her mind) and a degree of wealth (in her mind). This whole messy matter, unfortunately, was not *in my mind.*

I had a notebook in the car, and I took the time to pull aside and scribble a rambling note that went something like this: "I apologize to God and to all. This might hurt you, but I am going to kill Dr. So-n-so. He has seriously crossed the line and I am going to kill him with my own hands." I signed it and put it on the car seat.

I pulled up to the rather substantial home and sure as shit his name was on the mailbox. I hadn't been out of the Army for long, where I had won the annual "pushup contest" on the base and won the post's long-distance race, all of us wearing helmets and heavy packs on our backs, a two-mile trek. And after the Army I played a hell of a lot of basketball and worked schlepping heavy boxes as a supply clerk in a department store … In other words, I was in terrific shape.

Besides, when you have hatred and adrenaline feverishly pumping throughout your body, God help the person on the other end of that fiery energy. There was not an iota of doubt in my mind that by whatever means necessary, most likely by choking, I was going to murder this motherfucker (in this case the term was quite applicable.)

I rang the doorbell, but no answer. Again and again, no answer. But I knew he had a private practice, and so I went to a phone booth (phone what?) and looked up his address and number. I then called the number and his secretary answered. Shaking, I asked if he was there. I am now sure she picked up on my nervous vibes, my anger, and something I probably said. Originally, she had said yes, he was there, but changed her story in the next sentence.

I hung up and drove like a madman—which I was—toward that address. I jumped out of the car and went racing in, screaming, "Where is he, goddammit, where is he??" He had a couple of clients waiting so I was sure he was in his office. I asked his receptionist if I might speak with him. Now! She of course said no.

To her vehement disapproval, I slammed his office door open, praying that he was there. He wasn't. I stormed back out and asked where he was. She said she didn't know. I looked at the waiting patients, two or three of them, all female, and screamed to the receptionist something like, "Please advise the good doctor that he shouldn't fuck his patients—their husbands might just kill the son-of-a-bitch!" The waiting women sat there with mouths hanging open.

I headed to my favorite watering hole, Harry's Lamp Post, where good ol' Harry poured one hell of a cocktail for a buck and a quarter. As I thought about the whole matter again and again, playing out all kinds of scenarios, I concluded that my life was more important than his. This most certainly would have been a "crime of passion," but this wasn't Mexico where I might have been let off the hook or even given a medal. In the racist U.S., especially in those days, a Mexican kid who strangled a White doctor would probably have been executed, whatever his reasons. I remember reminding myself that I didn't want to go to prison and sure as hell didn't want to die.

Almost immediately, looking at all the factors I could piece together and deeply reacting to my own experiences, I developed a pure hatred for most White men and disdain for the White world in general. Over the years, as the radical '60s developed, I jumped deeply into "The Movement"—Chicano, Black, Asian, and my White, anti-war comrades—anything that I deemed to be for basic fairness. All of this fervent activity was fueled in part by my fierce hatred of this one man. Perhaps I should thank him.

This animosity towards Whites was short-lived in that half of my closest acquaintances and mentors were gringos. I would jokingly tell them, "Hey, some of my best friends are White." Nonetheless this all really opened my eyes to the history and, tragically, to the ever-present reality of racism in America. I am reminded of the line from the fine film *Little Big Man*, about a White boy raised by the Lakota, in which his wise adoptive grandfather explains the tribe's dilemma: "There is an endless supply of white men. There has always been a limited number of human beings."

PFSD: Post-Fresno Shit Disorder

I had had my first personal contact with bona fide insanity (other than when I was about six when my grandmother on my mother's side swung me around by my legs and bashed my head against a wall a couple of times—she ended up in the Stockton mental hospital for that one. In retrospect foster Mom Linn may have inherited some of her mom's madness, as she and hubby John had certainly created an existential looney bin as our daily habitat (that's both definitions of existential).

I still don't know the name for my schizy illness, but I was certainly out of my friggin' gourd. And that's exactly what it felt like at times, the precise sense of being literally *out of my mind*, no connection, out of my body. Over the years the term "dissociation" has been suggested, but the results of that break turned out to be far more than momentary madness. I had also lost contact with my work environment and my social world. I couldn't walk down the street or go to a market without freaking out, and sure couldn't sit still in a classroom for any period.

I was truly frightened that at any moment I'd fall back into that horrendous state. There was no easy treatment for my dilemma … but there was the quick fix of alcohol, gallons of it. The moment I picked up that bottle I immediately forgot my madness, and felt tremendously relieved. I really enjoyed—I mean I was ecstatic—with the entire process, except for the hangovers.

For many years drinking was my escape—you name it, I would gladly drink it. But over time alcohol became its own problem. Since I hadn't resolved my formative mental issues, now I had just added another layer … twin piles of mierda.

When I look over the circumstances I found myself in when I first cracked I am not surprised. As I mentioned before, the very night of my breakdown I had managed to plow my car head on into a tree. But the accident was nothing compared to the absolute mountain of pressure I was under: the wife and child, and me with no experience whatsoever in family matters; losing my job thanks to that insensitive, racist son-of-a-bitch Ronald Reagan; being increasingly aware of the plight of so many poor people because of the nature of my job with the Department of Rehabilitation; the recent violent death of my father at the hands of a demented gang of punks; and the imminent death of my mother who essentially drank herself to death. All of this turmoil, not to mention the extensive childhood trauma boiling beneath it all.

Looking back at my own past trespasses, back to whole decades of my thoroughly swacked and out of control life, I'm apologetic, appalled, and greatly embarrassed by some of my deranged and drunken behavior. A million mea culpas! The incredible confluence of negative influences all contributed to my having very little respect for the community at large and left me with smoldering anger.

Even the religion I had been raised in, dear old Catholicism, was fraught with contradictions, hypocrisy, brutality, and worse. I couldn't see the deeper good, and that was my split, dualistic (dual as in duel) mind at work. At some level, the sum total told me that it was okay to be such a reactionary, antisocial bastard. It really wasn't a matter of choice at this point of my life.

The worst part is that the overall effect of my catastrophic upbringing, my disastrous marriage, and the larger social-political forces at work significantly changed the course of my life and gave me carte blanche to behave as I saw fit—with anger, desire for revenge, and irreverence for societal mores—after all, I rationalized, that's the way life is, isn't it?

It is a terrible shame that I didn't realize, as self-help guru Wayne Dyer taught, "There are no justifiable resentments." None whatsoever. Resentments serve no positive purpose—in my case, they just festered and laid the groundwork for a bitter hatred of who I thought was the cause of my personal pain; and I detested those who had created the environment that had allowed this kind of suffering in me and in others. Truly, we must let go of this kind of reaction.

And even if others were responsible to whatever extent for corrupting my views and my behavior, it was a great error to give in to their influences. Others have their own sickness to deal with and their own karma—I needn't get caught up in it. For years my own inability to detach from certain emotions led to an out-and-out pissed-off reactionary response.

The fact is we can react in different ways, in positive ways. We can look back at all the negative, hurtful experiences in our life and say, "Thank you!" They themselves are blessed building blocks for the road back to wholeness. All I can say is thank God for good causes, thank God for good friends, and thank God for God.

About Domestically Caused PTSD

Now and then I look at photos I've kept over the years, photos of myself at home, in bars, on the street. One thing is common to all of them: I'm drunk on my ass and look like I've crawled out from a muddy hole in the ground. Shit, it even scares me!

So here I'm taking the liberty to quote an entire passage from Wikipedia because for me this subject is so integral, as it may be for some of you. First a definition, then a little info on its manifestations:

> Post traumatic stress disorder (PTSD) is a severe anxiety disorder that can develop after exposure *to any event* (my italics) that results in psychological trauma. This event may involve the threat of death to oneself or to someone else, or to one's own or someone else's physical, sexual, or psychological integrity, overwhelming the individual's ability to cope.
>
> Clinical findings indicate that a failure to provide adequate treatment to children after they suffer a traumatic experience, depending on their vulnerability and the severity of the trauma, will ultimately lead to PTSD symptoms in adulthood.

It goes a long way in giving me some idea what the hell happened to me, why I was always so damned angry, and what a relief alcohol has been to numb those effects. It's easy for me to write off my anger to things like corrupt politics, greed in the world, manipulation of the truth on a mass scale, etc., but these conditions are, to a great degree, surface matters. They are real, but not really at the source of my anger … nope, it's a bit deeper. Here's more:

"It has been shown that the intrusive memories, such as flashbacks, nightmares, and the memories themselves, are greater contributors to the biological and psychological dimensions of PTSD than the event itself." As if the events weren't enough. I still dream about those fucked-up foster parents and, believe me, those monstrous images are horrific.

So you see, my experiences in Fresno set the stage for a Cuckoo's Nest play. But I must say, as I headed up the road to the San Francisco Bay Area, it felt like I was removing several heavy layers of the suffocating social/political retardation that has become much of Central California. (Thank God for the then-liberal *Fresno Bee*, a bee-con of hope, and the island of hipness that was Café Midi.)

Fact is I couldn't deal with the overwhelming agony of my minute-to-minute insanity while living in that same valley environment, so I survived by finding an entirely new community, one where it was OK to be properly mad.

From Breakdown to Breakaway

After the divorce and mental breakdown, there was nothing left in Fresno, and even my buddies didn't fill the emptiness or cure the rage. I had to get the hell out of Dodge and so I abruptly quit my well-paying job with the Redevelopment Agency, drove to San Francisco late one night with only the one pair of Levi's I was wearing and the aging green blazer that I had graduated from high school in and worn during my stint in the Army. That was it, period, exclamation mark!

I do not remember a thing, not a second, from the time I left Fresno 'til the moment I arrived in The City 180 miles away. But I knew perfectly well where I was going and that was to the Haight-Ashbury that I had read and heard so much about at Café Midi, a place where I felt I might find a kindred spirit or two.

I drove my car—a sleek '60 Cougar with a bit of a dent on the front right bumper from that fateful drunken night in Fresno—to Buena Vista Park, just a couple of blocks from my destination. There I parked and purposely left the doors open and the keys in the ignition. This was by no stretch a drunken whim … I was literally leaving it all behind.

In the very early morning, sun not quite on the horizon, I walked into a coffeehouse/diner on Haight Street, a block or so before it crosses Ashbury. At a time in its earlier days the place must have been a drug store, because with a bit of irony, it was now called The Drug Store Café. Drugged was more like it.

I looked around at some of the characters sitting there that morning, all men, some bearded, all longhairs, reading the *Chronicle* or deep into a book, a couple guys just chatting near the window. I thought, yep, this is the place, these are my people: the world epicenter of wild-crazy mellow-yellow hip-trips. Without reservation, without question, I was home.

Incidentally, every now and then, I'd walk by my car, not really caring, oh, maybe a little curious. It just so happened that the adjacent park was where I and a newly found buddy would go to hang out and get stoned. One day I noticed that some fools had managed to steal the tires but never bothered to turn the key and just drive the whole damn thing away!

A Night at The Ritz

> "I find that principles have no real force except when one is well fed."—Mark Twain

It was 1966 and San Francisco's North Beach was still hopping, with barkers outside of Carol Doda's, and folks lined up at Enrico's (a hot late-night hang for the locals, the hip and the rich and/or the famous). Limos would pull up to the outdoor tables and who knows what set of legs would pop out.

I met Janis Joplin there, chatted her up for a few minutes until her way-protective manager butted in. Man, I thought I was getting somewhere … hey, that chick didn't have no ball and chain on those pale legs. Oddly enough, I saw her about a year later on stage. What's odd about it is that it was back in friggin' Fresno. Then again, that iconic venue—The Rainbow Ballroom—had over the decades been the backdrop for many busloads of hot bands.

Annnyway, back to Nortá Beachá … during that time there was an absolutely seductive dark and dingy bar just up the street and around the corner on Upper Grant. It's had different names over the years, Fresno Hotel Bar (because it was on Upper Grant and *Fresno Alley* … fitting), The 1232 Club and, simply, The Saloon.

It remains the oldest bar in The City with its swinging wooden doors, live blues and a mucho putrid downstairs pisser, downstairs like a place just down the road about a block on Broadway, Spec's, aka 12 Adler Place, and, get this, now 12 *William Saroyan* Avenue.

Fresno goes to Frisco, where one night I met an incognito Doris Day in that very cool, bohemian-to-the-bone joint ... or was it me that was incognito as Doris Day? Yeah, wearing a hat to cover most of that beautiful blond hair there she was standing right next to me. Then out of nowhere she asked one heck of a question, "What do men find attractive about ... Doris Day?" I was off my game and before I could answer she had moved on down the bar. Wish I'd had the quickness to say, "Sexy in a wholesome way."

But back to The Saloon. It occurs to me that it was the first San Fran bar that I had ever encountered back when as teenagers me and Danny V. fatefully stole that brand new '61 Chevy in Fresno and drove almost 200 miles to San Francisco, to which, like a swallow, I did and do return to swallow, suds that is, and find old buds ... trust me, many a doobie has been and is being puffed in that infamous alley next to The Saloon, Fresno Alley.

When I began frequenting that funky North Beach bar, '65-'66, the joint was filled with old Italian guys who would pop a dime into the Wurlitzer and play the Sicilian Tarantella (a death dirge on bennies, tarantella meaning tarantula, which was thought, I guess, to be deadly), jump up on the bar and whirl like a shot squirrel, dance that crazy jig like they were teenagers.

They'd knock over drinks and nobody gave a damn—in fact cheered them on. Especially Tony, the husky Italian bartender who took care of everyone—even obnoxious but brilliant Wally, an older guy with a long, white beard who verbally attacked everyone except Tony ... smart guy, that Wally. And Joe Malandra, the charismatic attorney who lived in his office above the bar, drove a motorcycle, and always supplied us with nice fat, well-rolled doobies, doo-bee-doo-bee-do (Malandra was from New York and sang the hell out of Sinatra!) ... Muchísimas gracias, José!

I was the youngest cat in the place and some of the older dudes appreciated the young blood, buying me a beer now and then ... maybe because I'd ask 'em to. One evening me and two or three others sat around a small coffee table in the back and played poker for nickels and dimes...just killing time as we drank. Then, as always, the "last call" hour hit, 2 o'clock, and all is closed. A fellow whose name I don't remember and I walked out the door together, both of us having lost our fortune in that high-stake card game.

No, I don't remember his name, but I do remember everything else about him: a good-looking fellow in his early 50s, short, scruffy beard and, most noticeably, wearing a sports coat with one arm missing. He had been a successful businessman, according to him, but like a lot of other Beats had "dropped out," as Timothy Leary later dubbed the process.

About this time the guy asks, hey, kid, yah hungry? Yeah, sure, sez I, knowing we're both flat broke. He sez, how about a nice chicken dinner with some pie for dessert? Yeah, sure, sez I, figurin' the guy is pulling my leg.

We stumble a few blocks up Upper Grant, make a turn here and there, and walk around behind a small Kentucky Fried Chicken take-out (now known as KFC to get away from the word "fried"). The place was closed for business, but there's a dumpster back there, and my no-name buddy flaps open the lid … Lo and behold! … The damned thing is filled to the brim with boxes of chicken, biscuits, gravy, apple pies, the works. We dive in, laughing and howling, taking one bite of this and one bite of that. Like opulent kings we tear into chunks of chicken and gleefully throw the rest every which way, a real hoot. Thanks, Colonel, fo' yo' Suthin' hospitality!

After that the guy asks, hey, kid, 'dyah like a drink o' somethin'? … tequila, bourbon, you name it, buddy. Yeah, sure, though now I'm starting to half-ass believe him. So, we walk back to an alley in the Broadway area where there are several bars in front, and, again, we hit the garbage cans. Bottles and bottles, empty I figure. 'Bout then he sez, here, buddy, have some tequila. He hands me a bottle and sure 'nuff there's a goodly little bit in the bottom, about a fourth of a shot, "corners," they call 'em. Hundreds of bottles in all those cans up that alley, a quarter shot per bottle … Dangeroso!

Then, staggering home to his pad, a tiny corner under a very small bridge in a Chinatown park he points out that there are no cats or dogs to be seen. Hmmm. His final shot that evening: "Hey, buddy … and they wonder why some of us become bums."

Tequila Sunrise

San Fran '66. I awakened one mornin' … I mean I awakened, became awake, woke. Not in bed but at a funky bar instead—and with nary a toke.

I was sittin' at the 1232 Club there on Upper Grant, that grand ol' joint—oldest damn bar in The City—with its swingin' doors and swayin' early morning denizens slow but cool there in foggy like my brain North Beach, ground zero for West Coast bohemia, maybe 9 or so, sippin' on my second tequila sunrise, orange juice and grenadine like a liquid grenade set off in my brain!

My head was buzzin' like I had dropped a tab of synthetic mescaline. I had pulled past my hangover dive and was climbin' at a rapid rate passed the Golden Gate higher than Mount Tamalpais and up above were stars in the middle of the morning, man was I high! ... and about this time it hit me, I mean like this stuff, tequila, ain't no normal fuckin' drink, I mean I'm high but the buzz is way open like I'm smellin' angel pubes so what's this all about, this gorgeous blast of orange-red good mornin' rays?

Flash! Tequila is from cactus like the mercurial mescal that old Mexicans with agave hearts would trip on, that and puffin' good ol' skunk weed the vatos would get high and discuss the virginity of Mary and see God in the worm at the bottom of the bottle and so the mescal connection must be a different trip, I figured, a higher high than plain ol' cerveza or even that gringo whiskey ...

Claro que si, I mean clear, my dear, the morning air feels like heaven and Frisco fog all wrapped up in the frisky pump of my eager heart ready to walk out of those swingin' doors and howl at the sleeping moon.

Note: As if to prove my point, a close friend named Debbie pointed out that PBS had recently aired a program where wild-eyed Mexican men loaded on Mescal, would get naked and ride horses without saddles all night long. Muy macho and/or very gay, Los Mescaleros, or just plain crazy on that loco weed & cactus bleed.

Louie, Me, and Mister Be kicked back with Augie Agave

Under the spreading Cactus Plant

Under the spreading cactus plant
a mellow fellow sits,
without scotch or tequila
or pills that'll kill ya
the Doobies still play the hits!

2020. That agave plant blew my mind this summer when the flower stock from its center suddenly shot up taller than the oak tree it grew next to—over 70 feet! In all these years I've lived here I didn't know that it was a famed "century plant" that have been known to live over 70 years and then send it seeds to the stars. It reminds me of me.

You know, I spent a lifetime trying to get here not knowing I already was.

Check, Mate

> "Give him two arms to cling to and something warm to come to. When nights are cold and lonely, stand by your man."—From the classic country tune by Tammy Wynette, "Stand by Your Man," 1968

Prelude to the Summer of Love, '66. I settled into my role of Senior Hippy—that's Señor Senior Hippy—in The Haight-Ashbury (Hell, I was an old 22 by this time and this enormous wave was heavily composed of youthful longhair runaways and/or Kerouac wannabes … 15 to 20.) I learned various means of getting over, survival skills like standing in line for free food and clothes from The Diggers, selling small amounts of pot (stuffed into small matchboxes) in the neighborhood or, better yet, sandwich bags filled with oregano to naïve tourists … pssssst, aye, ever tried this stuff?

Now, kicked back on some doorsteps off Haight, passing a doobie to a dude I hardly knew, I was rudely awakened to the fact that I had to make a buck or two, something, anything … I did have that thing called child support to pay. As Gorgeous George had once said to me, "Hey, kid, we all gotta make a living."

Well, I got busy and in a relatively short time found myself peddling a piddly stash of mediocre pot. It got a little cash flow going but, more important than that, it opened doors to the "action" … parties, babes, and interesting cats that were pretty deep … They had all immigrated to the hippy center of the cosmos, from across the nation, around the world, and no doubt from other planets!

But I never panhandled, no sir … no self-respecting hustler would do the "Spare change?" shuffle … but I did sleep many a night in Panhandle Park, just north of The Haight. As regards further means of urban survival, better yet and quite legally, I sold the underground papers, the two tabloid rags the *Berkeley Barb* and the *San Francisco Oracle.* That's how I caught my fish, the hippy-watchers, to wrap them up in a hot-off-the-press alternative mag.

I'd pick up 100 papers in the early morning, 7-ish, for about 10¢ apiece. The suggested sales price was 25¢, but with my acquired hawker skills I'd peddle them for a buck and have them sold to the massive number of tourists by one, two at the latest. The hustler skills I had learned back in Fresno peddling peanuts and Pepsies really came in handy. (Oh, and I'd offer a dazzling tour of the Haight-Ashbury for $5 or whatever they'd lay on me).

The Barb, as one might imagine, was heavily political (God-damned capitalist war-mongering pigs!) with lotsa freaky-sex classifieds; and *The Oracle* was an acid head/New Age/pro-community publication out of The Haight. The tourists preferred *The Oracle* because of the psychedelic-art covers (collectors' items, for sure … wish I'd saved a few), while the politics and sexuality of The Barb was just too much for them to handle.

By early afternoon I'd have quite a stash, at least fifty bucks or so (which was a helluva lot of money in those days). I'd then ceremonially head to the supermarket on Stanyan Street, right across from the main entrance to Golden Gate Park. In a daily ritual I'd buy a big loaf of French bread and a large jug of burgundy with the little "finger handle" on the neck so one could stand, Robin Hood-like, legs spread with one hand holding the bread and the other holding up the bottle for a deep swig.

Then into that park I'd go to share my good fortune, to hang out, puff weed, drink wine, and if fortunate score one of those hairy-legged patchouli-smelling hippy chicks whose armpit hair could be braided like Rapunzel's. (Interesting to note that patchouli oil is sometimes used as an insect repellant).

Every day and every night was dreamlike, filled with fresh new faces and open minds and endless sex. There were waves of idealistic humanity throughout the Haight and across Golden Gate Park whose positive vibes were palpable, could be literally felt penetrating the entire community. Kindness was contagious. We were an ongoing Woodstock with plentiful food, water, and, yes, toilets (though the trees and flowers in the park may have suffered a bit from shameless urination).

There was always dance and drums and free concerts, often with the great acid bands of that era. I don't know that there has ever been a time in history where so much innocence and goodness and hope was so deeply concentrated.

Late one afternoon on one of those bacchanalian forays, I spotted a lovely thing sitting by a pond, head down, not the happiest of creatures. "What's up with that un-smiley face," sez I. Turns out her ol' man, a mail carrier, had been committed—put into a nut house—for wigging out on some heavy drugs (I don't know what he took but I do know that psychedelics aren't for everyone).

Anyway, in a relatively short period, we decided to go to her pad and apply a bit of physical therapy—"sexual healing." I'll never forget it ... just one block up from Haight Street in one those familiar San Fran Victorians rebuilt after the great fire of '06. She and her postman hubby had a cozy but drab upstairs apartment with a small balcony overlooking the spectacle of the times, a parade of whoever could get the weirdest. I poured the burgundy and we sat at that little dinner table knowing full well what was about to happen.

Well, not quite. About this time, we hear steps, very heavy steps stomping up the stairway ... from my White Theatre movie days I envisioned the *Frankenstein* monster himself and I wasn't far off. There he was, standing in the doorway, *The Thing from Another World.* Her old man was the size of a football lineman with a frame built to pull a plow. He appeared to be in his early forties, clean and solid but with a forlorn, lost look that made you want to comfort him in some way.

Seeing his ol' lady having a glass of wine with this scheming scoundrel could not have been the best of sights, seeing that they had just let him out of whatever fruitcake facility. But, no, he looked at her and smiled and she jumped up and gave him a big ol' hug. He then even smiled at me and, after having shit in my pants, I too smiled with a sigh of relief.

I offered him a glass of wine and he accepted. Now we're getting somewhere. There was a chessboard on the coffee table, and I asked if he'd like to play a game. Why not? sez he. She stood behind him like a Tammy Wynette lyric and when I noticed a certain advantage, I moved a pawn to open the path to attack his queen.

At this point he stopped cold, stared at the board, and then looks up at me as tears begin to well up on that big, wide face. Stammering he begs, "Please don't take my queen."

God, that was heartbreaking. We didn't finish the game, I just made up a quick excuse to split, left my jug of congeniality and headed into the night.

Note. Back in Golden Gate Park during 1967, folks would get blown away on acid, mescaline, plentiful pot and loving thought, a whole city domed with good vibes that bounced for miles from smile to smile. They would dance through The Doors, the doors of perception, literally au naturel, naked as a jaybird. It was the right thing to do, but the cops didn't always seem to think so.

Man, what an amazing trip the whole Haight-Ashbury adventure was! It's like that blessedly beatific time and place was premeditatedly set up to heal me from the torment of my lingering Fresno nightmare. And it did, the best damn spa in the whole friggin' universe.

An Orgy of Sex and Drugs!

Living in The City, it would have been sacrilegious for me not to regularly hitch across the Oakland Bay Bridge to San Francisco's way-left counterpart, Berkeley. No doubt, the so-called radicals there were politically closer to my activist leanings than my hippity-hobbity San Fran pals. After all, UC Berkeley was where the fuckin' outrageous Free Speech Movement was launched in 1960, and the community continued with that fervor up until the People's Park protest of 1969, an event where the real violence came from the cops. Surprise!

While running for Governor back in '66, Ronald Reagan's public expressions of disgust at the supposedly scandalous behavior of Berkeley students were cleverly calculated to keep public indignation at the boiling point. (Same fear tactics as the racist and classist Republicans have always used, now ramped up to a pre-fascist state.) A notorious dance on the Berkeley campus conveniently occurred shortly after Ronnie declared his candidacy.

Police reports of the dance quite mysteriously made it to Reagan's campaign headquarters, most likely via the Alameda County District Attorney, one Edwin Meese (who eventually became Attorney General under the Ray-gun presidency … Surprise! Surprise!). Reagan claimed that the dance had turned into an orgy of sex and drugs and, as such, was evidence of the "leadership gap" at Berkeley. Wiki-quote:

> The hall was entirely dark except for the light from two movie screens. On these screens the nude torsos of men and women were portrayed, from time to time, in suggestive positions and movements. Three rock-and-roll bands played simultaneously. The smell of marijuana was thick throughout the hall. There were signs that some of those present had taken dope. There were indications of other happenings which cannot be mentioned.

Sounds like fun to me. In fact, when I arrived in Berserkely a couple of years later it was still every bit as beautifully pissed off and tuned in as ever. Flash forward: these were the parents and grandparents of the 99%-ers, the Me-too-ers, Black Lives Matter activists, and the Indivisible movement. Before there was Bernie there was Berkeley!

Dance of the Gypsy King

The dark stately hallways
brooding on Spanish soil,
filled with fountains, frogs and friends
and centuries of linen,
the dark stately hallways
whose walls demand reflection.

Here and there the statuettes,
the monolithic monarchs
chiseled from his childhood,
each form, the King of Gypsies,
each form, the King of Gypsies
in the hard stone of honor.

And here the Gypsies gather
with scarves of scars and passion,
here the Gypsies gather
to drink their youthful king;
black and white into the night
they dance with dogs and demons;

Intoxicating shadow boxing
whiffs of smoke and laughter,
they dance around the statuettes
crazed with mortal sweetness
lighting the dark, defiant walls
with silhouettes of brilliance.

The Man in the Gray Cadillac

1967, The Summer of Love. I made my living on the famed corner of Haight and Ashbury, the very heart of Hippiedom at its peak with over 100,000 furry freaks congregating, at times, within a frantic-frenetic one-mile radius.

Daily I was busily hawking my trippy tabloids, the *Barb* and the *Oracle*, and a little merry-jew-wanna on the side, stuffed into match boxes, five to ten bucks a pop depending on quality and the amount of stems and seeds. This particular day, as my work hours came to a close, noon-ish … hell, I'd been out there since eight … most hippies *did not work*—either they had bucks from home or did the "spare change" bit … What the heck was I gettin' to?

Oh, yeah, the man in the gray Caddy … He was in a shiny new luxury sedan, as gray as the hair of its driver. He slowly pulled up at the stop sign preparing to slowly turn right onto Haight. You really had no choice; you had to drive slowly because at any hour of the day the street was filled with both the local inhabitants, the homeless hippies, and the vast numbers of tourists from around the world filling the street with busloads of curious gawkers.

The Gentleman in the Gray Cadillac was sporting a matching gray suit and conservative striped tie. Likely his wingtip shoes were shined by some older black guy … shoeshine stands were common in those days. He waves for me to come around to his rolled-down window, and I think this has gotta be worth at least a five-spot. He says, "Hey, kid, let's see what you're selling." I show him a copy of each rag and he says, "I'll take both of them … How much." I tell him I'll give him a real bargain, two for five. Such a deal!

I normally charged a buck, a little steep but then they did have the pleasure of my tossing in my little touristy tidbits, like "Hey, and don't miss Golden Gate Park…that's where the real weirdos hang out." (In other words, that's where I'd be as soon as I finished selling my papers.)

As he handed me the money—and I'll never forget this—he said in all sincerity, "I know what you're trying to do out here, but you're going about it in the wrong way."

As I think about today's 99 Percenters, the Bernie Sanders backers, the Me Too Movement, and then back to those turbulent Sixties protests that I was part of, the anti-war marches, Black protests, and of course César Chavez's United Farm Workers activities, it is obvious that it is the mass of those who don't go along with The Program, and in their own ways, take to nonviolently protest, with the hope of this democracy's survival. I wish I had replied to The Man, "Sir, isn't it possible *you're* going the wrong way?"

Note. "Every movement creates its own media source, and the hippies of '67 San Francisco had a psychedelic one: *The San Francisco Oracle*. Published in 12 fantastic issues from 1966 to 1968, the *Oracle* is a fascinating artifact of the times. Hippies sold the *Oracle* on Bay Area streets to support themselves, and the newspaper made its way around the world by subscription. The editors estimated their circulation topped half a million when taking into account the number of people who shared each of them."—from PBS.Org.

Ken Kesey, on cover of the *Oracle*, the rag I used to peddle in the Haight-Ashbury back in '67. Little did I know that a decade later our paths would cross.

Lucy in the Sky

"Purple haze all in my brain, lately things just don't seem the same…actin' funny, but I don't know why, 'scuse me while I kiss the sky."—from *Purple Haze* by Jimi Hendrix

Part One: *Kissing the Sky.* It's been said that the Beatles wrote "Lucy in the Sky with Diamonds" based on the three primary initials … that is L…S…D. There's a pretty good chance that was the case. A minor note here is that Donald Johanson's 1978 discovery, a three-foot-tall, three-million-year-old ancestor of ours, the earliest found hominid at the time, a two-legged upright-walker, was named *Lucy* in honor of the Beatles' tune … Johanson may have been "dropping" more than a name.

Well, anyway, even before I arrived in the Haight-Ashbury many moons ago—slightly before Lucy—indeed I had smoked (but never inhaled) a bit of that wild wacky weed. At that time, however, not even the most potent of the stuff was remotely psychedelic. It made food more appealing—like major munchies—and sex for sure a little groovier, but we didn't see God or even yellow submarines, not even with a benny or two kicker.

In one of these soirées, I met this Chubby Checker chick who was quite the talker … I still remember those fat pink lips flapping a mile a minute. Part of her rap was how fuckin' mind-blowing (to use a term in vogue then) lysergic acid diethylamide was … Lysergic what? She and I got to yakking and she asks if I'd like to give it a shot; I say well it kind of scares me, you know reading about Art Linkletter's son jumping out of a window and all, but she sez all you need is a good "guide," you know, someone to be there with you that'll support you during that first experience. Hmmm, thinks I, this could be a good idea seeing that she had volunteered to be my guide, and of course I was thinking short term, those luscious flapping lips and all, like hey, let's go to your pad and discuss this a little further sez I, twiddling my mustache. (I think the chick invented the term "Let's get it on.")

She had a small house across the Bay, somewhere in Oakland … hey, that'll work. And it did. And it did. And … anyway, next thing I know I'm waking up the next morning, bit of a hangover but a good one. So, she sez, OK, today we're goin' over to Golden Gate Park, that's a good place to "drop."

We hung around, had a bit of breakfast, and went for a roll to get things rolling (so to speak). Finally, early in the afternoon we headed out. I dropped the acid tab just outside the park, downing it with a chug of cheap wine ... What a guy! We walked over to "Hippy Hill," where already there's a pretty good little crowd, the tribe, milling around, the rapturous smell of marijuana and the sounds of conga drums as hippy chicks with no panties dance, hands waving in the air to the God of Nature, twisting in circles like swirling dervishes ... Well, alright!

But even half an hour later, I still didn't feel a thing from the acid I had taken a hit of ... she said it was the real deal, 99% pure, from Kesey's buddy, Owsley (or, as The Dead had his handle, Bear). Then as she and I are sitting under a very large tree this big-ass black dude enters our sacred space, lights up a fat doobie, and starts drumming on a conga drum he's carrying. In record time my true love—*and my guide*—is flirting with this fool and I think fuck this, I'll just mosey down the road and, like Fritz the Cat, see what kind of shit I can get into.

Fritz the Cat, by the way, was a handle a close friend of mine—Sonny Madrid, the original creator and publisher of *Low Rider Magazine*—had laid on me about that time; somehow I reminded him of that feline comic strip character created by Robert Crumb of "Keep on truckin'" fame. (Thomas Albright, author of *Art in the San Francisco Bay Area*, describes Fritz as "a kind of updated Felix with overtones of Charlie Chaplin, Candide and Don Quixote." And Michael Barrier, comic book aficionado and mega-author on the topic, sees Fritz's personality as "glib, smooth and self-assured" ... well, alright!

Back to The Trip ... I recall very vividly thinking "So what's so hot about this LSD thing, I don't feel a damn thing." It was about this time—maybe an hour into it, hell I don't know—that I spotted a very beautiful tree about a block away. Out of hundreds of trees in Golden Gate Park, famous for its arboreal variety, I honed in on this one singular mushroom-shaped beauty, made an oblique right, and headed directly to its trunk. On one side of it was a considerable patch of moss, thick, deep engrossing moss; beneath a batch of small mushrooms, a bunch of tiny fairy stools. LSD, I would later learn, was originally fungus-based.

A delightful and rich conversation ensued (not one-way in any way by the way), mostly with the moss but the mushrooms did chime in with vim and vigor. We literally talked about such boring matters as where life began ... The moss said that its family tree, so to speak, was there in the beginning (on the north side, of course, here on Planet Earth anyway—charming patch of primordial ooze) and that, don't worry, it's all very groovy; God is everywhere, etc.

This went on for a considerable time; how long I have absolutely no clue, a fascinating three-way conversation. Those damned mushrooms were always butting in, but had cool notes and antidotes about the relation of psychedelics to spiritual consciousness. As I said farewell and headed back to Hippy Hill I thought, hey, so what's so hot about this LSD thing … I don't feel a thing.

Fungi Feature Flick: Today, July 30, 2022, fifty friggin' years later, I was emailed a reminder to watch a celebrated documentary titled *Fantastic Fungi.* As it turns out, my encounter with those little guys, the schrooms, in the park was not just a case of my being super-loaded on acid … There is an entire world, fascinating and wonderful, that we're just unaware of. I mean there is not only life-changing powers to be found and used, but possibly world-saving potential. "This powerful documentary dives into the mysterious and inspiring world of mushrooms, and reveals how they can be used to heal serious disease AND … to save the planet itself." —Nick Polizzi. For additional information see www.thesacredscience.com. Hey, in these dismal days of dogged disarray, this Critics Choice film is more than a breath of fresh air—it's a real ray of hope.

Part Two: *Guru for a Day.* Back to my ersatz "guide," it occurred to me that in a sense she had betrayed me … Her promise was that she'd be by my side during this journey into the unknown, that if things started getting freaky she'd be there for me. Just then I saw her walking toward me, hand in hand with yet another dude … gregarious gal, all smiles and flowers. As we passed each other down the walkway, I stopped the blissful couple and said directly to her, "Now I know who Judas was."

So much for my higher consciousness. What a strange thing to say, and to this day I regret having made that comment. But as this narrative continues, I hope to communicate as best I can from personal experience a bit of the effects when psychedelics cross over the line to integrate with spirituality.

As that day continued my high increased … I'm not sure if simultaneously smoking pot and swigging wine may not have enhanced or lessened it, who knows? I do know I was increasingly less conversational and more introspective. For some time, I laid on my stomach, looking into the grass at the swarming microcosm of tiny critters and miniscule plants or on my back, looking up at the wispy, swirling clouds …"Scuse me while I kiss the sky."

Or was it my mind that was swirling, swirling deeper, like a multi-colored whirlpool, all emanating from my mystical *Third Eye*, the pineal gland? There was no doubt whatsoever, as there is not this very moment, that it was this very area centered between my two eyes that was not only hyperactive but was a conduit for what at that time, in that moment, I knew to be a deep wisdom. (It is said that we generally only use a tiny fraction of our real brain potential, about 3%; on the other hand, on acid some have suggested that we're cranking at about 95% … in the case of some individuals, however, 95% of nothing is still nothing.)

It is not by chance that the Hindus mark that spot on their forehead with ashes and paint. Most, unfortunately, do not know the actual origin of that symbol, or just why it was located in the middle of the forehead. The truth is that this small area perhaps the size of a dime referred to as the Third Eye becomes activated it can lead to a very high level of consciousness—uncapturable beauty and wisdom without words.

What is referred to as the transcendent experience, which is reflected in the earliest Hindu philosophy of The Vedas, about 800 to 900 BCE, is based on experiences from the early Aryan immigrants to India. There is no relation here to Caucasians (as in Aryan Brotherhood) but more from the region now known as Iran (Iran … Ar-y-an), migrating into the vast Indus Valley … (Indus Valley, Indus River, Indus, Hindu … Hindu religion … As Mister Spock would say, "Seems logical to me, Captain.").

I have read that what they, the Aryans, brought with them was a psychedelic juice which they called soma, a concoction for ceremonial purposes, not unlike what is used by some indigenous peoples from up and down the Americas. Here however, soma is both an intoxicant and to those people a god itself. Knowing the psychedelic experience, I can see why that appeared to be the case.

In his book *Food of the Gods*, "Ethno-botanist Terence McKenna postulates that the most likely candidate for soma is the mushroom *Psilocybe cubensis*, a hallucinogenic mushroom that grows in cow dung in certain climates. In India … *Psilocybe cubensis* mushrooms are 'easily identified and gathered, and are effective.'" He went so far as to hypothesize, "The possible role of Stropharia cubensis growing in the dung of cattle in the lives of the lower orders remains to this day wholly unexplored. Is S. cubensis responsible for the elevation of the cow to a sacred status?"

Holy cow! I mean that: Holy cow! Wouldn't it make sense that cows are considered holy in India because folks were seeing God after eating mushrooms grown in those divine bovine droppings?

Meanwhile, back in The Park ... At a point everything was clear, beautiful and in harmony. I felt I knew everything there was to know, and it wasn't knowledge per se ... in fact "knowledge" would have gotten in the way. What it was a thorough feeling of consciousness, just being fully aware of all that is, not in harmony *with God*, but *as an essence of God,* God beyond ego, this, that, or any "other." Whether manipulated by a mushroom, a tab of transcendence, or deep meditation, there is a satisfaction in that state that is simply incomparable. It is an honorable goal to seek because the closest description is love.

As afternoon greeted evening my high continued, actually seemed to increase ... I was "peaking." I walked out of the park and onto Haight Street, heading toward the very hub of it all. As fate would have it, a religious parade of sorts was just finishing, right up the center of the street, probably Hare Krishna-ites by their ochre robes. They were all adorned with beautiful flower garlands and danced with chimes and incense sticks in hand.

A younger man, probably 19 or so, joined me and we chatted briefly as we moved to the epicenter of the busy crowd. The fellow had somehow taken me on as a sort of "guru" ... which, as I came to know, simply means "teacher." (The word suggests a transition from darkness (*gu*) to light (*ru*), meaning "that which dispels the darkness of ignorance.")

The kid was hungry, hungry for good old earthly chow; I was beyond hunger. In those days, some trashcans in The Haight were flat and square, placed on the corner of each block. For whatever strange reason I chose to sit cross-legged in lotus pose on top of one of them, right there on the famed corner of Haight and Ashbury. My youthful sidekick stood beside me. I began my little mantra, perhaps something I had seen in an old movie, perhaps a movie filmed centuries before this lifetime.

"Alms, alms," I repeated, not adding the traditional "for the poor." "Alms, alms." I was simple and sincere in my request. And then it started. First, a handful of coins placed on the garbage can right before me. Then a garland around my neck. Then more coins and then bills of various denominations. I told my young altar boy to take what money there was, go to the little grocery store across the street, and buy as much of the red wine and French bread as he could carry ... I specifically requested red wine, my Catholic heritage, I guess.

He returned and I told him to just pass the bread and wine to the folks who were beginning to hang around as they witnessed the street soiree building with bells, bangles, and bagels. At this point I was beyond requesting "alms;" I just sat in the lotus meditation stance as the stash at my feet was turning into a little mountain. I mean a sizable heap of candy, flowers, beads, you name it ... and a heckuva lot of money, mostly from the tourists. My little helper got busy and even got himself a helper ... we were emptying the wine and bread shelves of the mom-n-pop grocery stores up and down the street.

All this time I sat there, quiet, not because it was what I chose but because that was my state of being, blown out in a rich, deep way. Then I felt a presence; I couldn't see it, but I could feel it ... the "Blue Meanies." Not frightening at all, not good or bad, just another presence in this mini Mardi Gras. As it turned out there were two of them, a sergeant and his backup. The sergeant pushed the crowd aside and walked straight up in front of my little altar.

I bowed my head and kept it there. At the point that I felt the officer was about to say something I placed both my hands down into the sizable mound of gifts directly in front of me, scooped up as much as I could, and lifted this offering before his face as if to say, "Here, come, partake of God's bounty."

He looked at the colorful treasure trove before him. By this time, my head was straight up, as was my back in meditation form, and my eyes were focused on his eyes. He looked at me, looked around at the pleasant crowd, shook his head and walked away, not saying a thing.

As the night moved on, I began partaking of the ceremonial bread and wine, especially the wine. By midnight, I was right down there with the rest of the revelers, being a mundane nut, and howling at the moon ... again.

Psychedeletera: Kesey was right about a lot of things, about acid for sure. And in retrospect it was a damn good thing to promote. Why so? Because humanity needs a strong mental enema and that's what a dose of pure LSD does, cleans out the cranial caca. And if you don't believe me, "Go ask Alice ... I think she'll know." And just remember what the dormouse said, "Feed your head! Feeeed your head!"

As a whole we're just too damn out of touch as to deeper awareness. And I fear we as a species need all the brain power we can generate to achieve a level of consciousness where we aren't so damned greedy and violent.

In any case humanity itself needs a psychedelic experience; as individuals and as a worldwide society, we do need a resounding blast of mind-expansion that clearly lets us know that we are all truly brothers and sisters.

Here's recent material on the subject from the scientific view, a study out of the UK showing what happens to the brain on acid. I read about it in an article from a site subtly named *Wake Up World! It's time to Rise and Shine.* The LSD piece hit the racks on June 19, 2017 and is titled *Brain Scans Show Psychedelic Drugs Really do Spark Heightened States of Consciousness.* No shit.

In fact, jumping way forward to October of 2022, I read of an international online symposium, headlined by the Who's who in the brainiac category—it was called *The Psychedelic-Assisted Therapy Global Summit*, produced by the Heart Mind Institute.

It's important to note that though these kinds of drugs have been known to momentarily open the mystical Third Eye, they are but a peek into supraconsciousness. The old and lasting method is by applying the venerable practice of meditation and focusing on walking the pathless path.

Forty-one Stories

> "And therefore as a stranger give it welcome. There are more things in heaven and earth, Horatio, than are dreamt of in your philosophy."—*Hamlet*, Act 1, scene 5

Forty-One Stories are not actually forty-one stories, that is forty-one individual tales; *they are stories about the number 41* and its synchronistic interactions throughout my life. In all actuality there have probably been at least 41 of these incidents, strangely at just the right time popping up on a street sign, a movie, here and there again and again … Twilight Zone stuff. But here are three of the more poignant ones. (Hey, and it continues to happen!)

Story Number One: *The Great K-Mart Heist*

1965-ish. My first run-in with Forty-One was when I was about 20 years old, just out of the Army. I had applied for a job as a "Male Nursing Attendant" (a slight step up from orderly) at the Fresno County Hospital and been accepted. This was mid-week, and I was to show up the following Monday morning in a certain attire: pressed blue shirt with short sleeves, clean white T-shirt beneath, and pressed white pants.

Of these items I had one, the T-shirt and it wasn't clean. I was flat broke and couldn't figure out how to get the pants and shirts I needed. In desperation I read the *Fresno Bee* Help Wanted section and lo and behold there it was: "Part-Time Help. New Department Store wants young man to assist Customers." This was a brand-new K-Mart out on Blackstone Boulevard, then a reasonably fashionable area (less fashionable with K-Mart there ... Good morning, K-Mart shoppers). I applied and got that job, a real no-brainer. I just stood by the check-out counter and waited for the older customers to pay for their merchandise; I would then push their carts out to their cars, put their bags in, and off they went. No brainer.

Turned out this was only a three-day gig, Friday through Sunday. I had to go to work at the hospital Monday morning. I knew that I would probably earn enough for one set of clothes, but I figured I'd need at least two sets, and was doubtful I could earn that much in such a short period at $1.25 an hour.

Sunday afternoon, around 3 p.m. or so, they laid me off and gave me my check in an envelope that I didn't even open. I stuck the envelope in my back pocket, because regardless of the amount, I had a plan, a brainstorm, a real doozy: Since no one on the floor really knew that I had just been terminated (or so I thought), I'd get myself a pushcart, fill it up with the white pants and blue shirts I needed, and then push it up around the front cashiers. Then I'd wait there for a little old lady (Herb Caen used to refer to 'em as LOLs), chat with her as she was about to leave so that the checkers would think I was about to push *her* cart out to the parking lot, but oh so cleverly push my own.

Well, I did just that. In fact, I had been rather greedy with that cart: besides my pants and shirts, I had included a James Brown album, a Johnny Mathis album, some nice cologne, and a few other oddball items. I was almost to my car when I felt a large hand on my shoulder. It was the store cop. They didn't have overhead cameras in those days, but they weren't *that* stupid ... so much for my lame-ass brainstorm.

In a few minutes I was handcuffed and off to the local pokey. When I arrived, I was told I could get out temporarily if I had 10% of the bail, and that the best bondsman in town was a certain Mr. Torres. So, with my one phone call out, I rang old Emil, Emil Torres that is. He showed up at my cell and said, "Well, let's see what we have here ... Hmmm ... $410 bail (a lot of money at the time). At 10%, Tom, that'll be forty-one dollars ... got forty-one dollars?"

I told him I had no cash but had a small check from K-Mart for the work I had done for them that weekend. I pulled the unopened envelope out of my pocket, opened it and looked at the amount of the check: *exactly forty-one dollars!* He looked at it, shook his head in disbelief, and then a strange look came over his face. He said, "Hey, will yah look at this? It says right here on your arrest papers that you live at *41 East Lemon* and you were arrested on *Highway 41* … how 'bout that?" That was the beginning of a lifetime of unfathomable encounters with "My Number."

By the way, I spoke with Mr. Stevenson, my wonderful mentor from the Boys Club that afternoon because I knew I would need help when this went to court. He asked, "Did you learn anything?" I responded with an absolutely sociopathic "Yeah, don't get caught." I could see immediately that this hurt him, and so I went on with a little excuse about stealing just not being right. That helped a little.

Someone—I think it was Ed Perez—loaned me the money to get those pants and shirts for Monday's appointment. It was there at the Fresno County Hospital where I was to meet my first and only wife. After that fiasco I swore I'd never marry again. Thanks a lot, Ed … I think.

Story Number Two: *A Blessed Cup of Water*

This synchronicity blast happened shortly after the Fakakta K-Mart Kaper. As had become customary over the years, Eddie P. and I would dude up a bit and head a mile or so into town (almost always walking for lack of wheels) to take in a movie or two, often with the fantasy that we'd get lucky. On this particular occasion, right after my fateful arrest at K-Mart (and still blown-out from the Forty-One blast), I asked Ed if he wanted to break away from his old lady and check out a classic flick that was showing at The Crest, then a handsome theatre on the corner of Fresno and Broadway. He declined, citing the simple fact that his wife's bad-ass brothers were on his case and that it would probably be a good idea to stay home with her and their kid. So I headed out solo.

What was showing on the then-impressive Cinemascope screen was a re-release of the Academy-Award winning epic *Ben-Hur: A Tale of The Christ.* (This first hit the screen in '59, but few of us kids back then—not from our side of the tracks, in any case—could afford the high-ticket price of 50¢.) As per the American movie ritual, I bought the wine (Pepsi) and body (popcorn) of the ceremony, and headed to my seat.

What I was about to take in was nothing like I expected, not the hokey Roman sword fights and mythical gods swatting the local townsfolk with demons and thunderstorms. This movie was indeed majestic, and so much more than I could have dreamed of, bigger than that Cinemascope screen itself. It was history, romance, treachery, wrath, revenge and glorious salvation, all wrapped in two hours of celluloid. "Spectacular" actually applies here. The historicity of it was and is irrelevant because movies, for the most part, are meant to be experienced as sensation, not documentation.

As the tale evolved I, like most everyone else in that theater, felt the suffering of the hero, and sadness for his plight, his loss of family, and his fate to become a galley slave on a Roman war ship. In a scene while headed to board the ship, a shackled Ben-Hur, a Jewish prince, observes a man being beaten by Roman soldiers. He has the compassion, at his own risk, to fetch the wretch a cup of water ... What a scene. Needless to say, without Ben-Hur's knowing, that person was Jesus Christ Himself.

When Ben-Hur finally arrives on the ship, he is handcuffed in the galley and, like his fellow prisoner-slaves, is forced by whip and threats to row or die. He, having the dignity of a prince, an honorable man of deep faith, never submits to what would appear to be his destiny: a lifetime of drudgery and then meaningless death.

At this very moment, for some reason I thought of my recent fate—on the infinitesimally smaller and certainly less glamorized level of K-Mart rather than a Roman war ship—of being rescued and given a second chance. I had found a good little job and was enjoying my life, thanks to a little paycheck with the number Forty-One on it.

On screen at that moment, the ship's master, the Captain of the entire Roman Fleet tells Ben-Hur, "You, *Number Forty-One*, row well and you will live another day ..." There are times when a person knows when he or she is in a state of grace and, to my knowledge, there is no real way to communicate that to another soul. It is a private conversation, one that I had back then and that I'm trying to share with you now.

After decades of this sort of astounding synchronicity, I haven't had a significant Forty-One Encounter for over thirty years, not since that time when a group of whales beached themselves up in Seattle.

Story Number Three: ***Forty-One Whales***

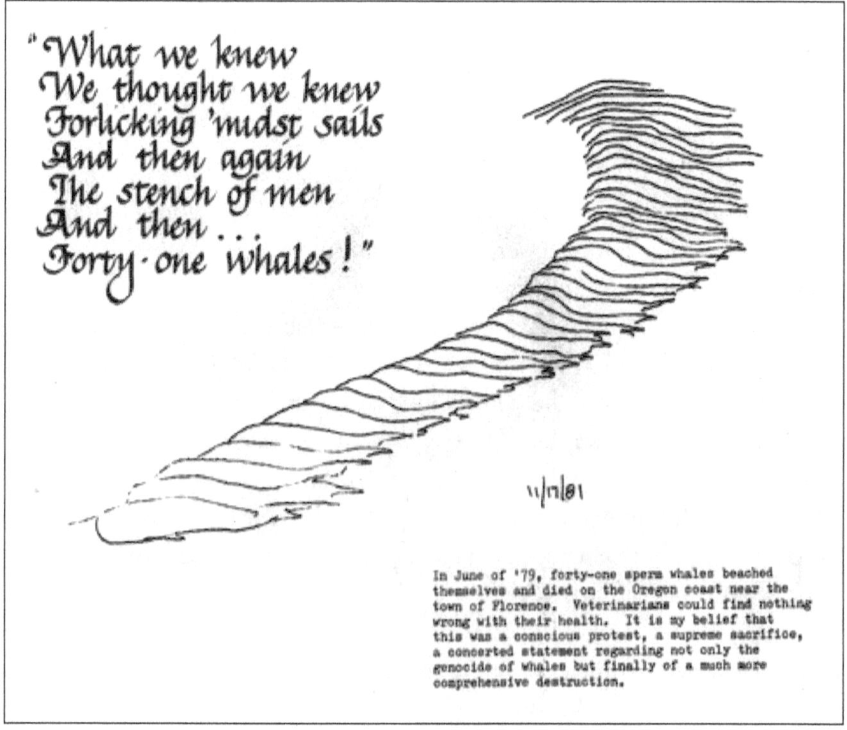

> Here's the small print above: In June of '79, forty-one sperm whales beached themselves and died on the Oregon coast near the town of Florence. Veterinarians could find nothing wrong with them. It is my belief that this was a conscious protest, a supreme sacrifice, a concerted statement regarding not only the genocide against whales but finally of a much more comprehensive destruction.

The above sketch, including the accompanying poem and footnote, was rapidly scribbled first on a paper placemat in a dark bar in Seattle, then later typed onto with a big ol' manual clunker of a typewriter. If you count them, you will find 41 bodies lined up at the beach. Because the number 41 is my synchronistic connection with The Great Spirit, the event struck me deeply—I felt strongly that there was something very profound about this strange phenomenon.

A note on the note: The article I had just read that morning of 1981 had to do with a handful of whales who had just beached themselves on a Northwest coast. It made mention of an event from a couple of years earlier. The earlier story was that forty-one sperm whales had beached themselves and died on the Oregon coast near the town of Florence. *Veterinarians could find nothing wrong with their health.*

Lucky Number: I feel exceptionally blessed, I know I am. Blessed for having had the incredible fortune of experiencing so much undeniable and ongoing contact with the Great Spirit.

And how many times have I dodged the bullet, near death, yet somehow been protected from beyond and within? At least a dozen times hospitalized with deadly pancreatitis and ketoacidosis ... or just thoroughly drunk, driving down the wrong way on a freeway. So many very dangerous situations throughout my life ... and I'm sure some that I'm not even aware of.

I don't think much about all of that, I just count my blessings. I mean for God's sake, how many folks have their very own synchronistic number? Dear ol' 41, that is. The wonderful fact is that 41 ... *For One* ... is *our* lucky number, I mean for all of us. "All for one and one for all" was the call of the Musketeers. Synchronicity is an ethereal contact to be respected as a sacred language and so the next time you get zapped by one of those eye-opening co-inky-dinks take a second and rejoice in the Source.

The word agape means wide open with surprise and wonder, and the Greek word agápe is love of family and, reciprocally, love of God. For those who are receptively "wide open," forty-one is a little note from your Dad from the Upper Pad that you can tack on your fridge that says, "God loves me."

Ho'! Ho'! Ho'! (A Christmas Tail)

Xmas, '67. Hustling in the Haight with a modicum of success allowed me to finally scrape together a couple hundred bucks to pay on my child support. I recall that for me it was a pretty hefty sum, and I felt good about getting ready to take the trip back to Fresno, seeing my little daughter, and dropping The Ex off some much-needed cash. It was literally the day before Christmas and the mice were certainly stirring.

I figured while in Fresno I might as well do a little business, so I wrapped a few lids of pot and other sundry articles and prepared for the trip. At the time I drove a cool, older (1959) bright blue Volkswagen bus that came with the license plate 000 WEE (as in ooo-wee, baby, I wanna take you on a scenic cruise). I took the Frisco to San Josie to Pacheco Pass route … big mistake! I got stopped in every little piece-of-shit redneck town on the way down … local cops, Highway Patrol, sheriffs. A long-haired Mexican hippy wearing a colorful African dashiki in a funky VW bus was easy pickin' in those days. But I was conscious of this likelihood and was especially careful in hiding the stash … thank God they never spotted it or had a pot sniffin' hound because at that time peddling—even possessing—marijuana was a serious penitentiary rap.

Anyway, I got to Fresno late that afternoon and called The Ex. She says come on over but give her a little time to freshen up … hmmm … she was still a fox. I show up, knock on the door, walk in, give her a little hug, see my little daughter crawling on the floor and … within a couple of glowing moments comes another knock on the door. She answers and … it's the cops! Child support. My loving wife called the fuckin' cops while I was trying to pay my dues.

I'm handcuffed, not behind like nowadays, but in front. I guess I wasn't considered that much of a threat. One cop plops me in the back seat of the squad car, driver side, and he jumps in front to drive me down to book me; the other leaves in a separate car. During this time, I'm Houdini-like trying to get a couple of doobies out of the inside pocket of my peacoat. (As I said, in those days getting caught with even a joint was to do serious time.) Simultaneously I'm rapping with the officer, letting him know that one of my mentors is a sheriff—good ol' Uncle Lou—and that it's sure fucked-up going to jail on Christmas eve, especially when I was just trying to do the right thing.

By this time, I've managed to get the two doobies—real fatties—out and am anxiously looking for a place in the back seat to hide them. Man, there's thick, clear plastic covering everything—not unlike my in-laws' furniture—with literally no place to conceal anything. Shit! I fling them to the floor opposite me, using my feet to push the sticks as far away as I can. We get to the jail and the cop comes back and opens the door. The overhead light goes on and, blam, there's those two fat joints, popping out like a couple of neon footballs. He looks at them, looks down at me, and … get this …says, "Merry Christmas." He didn't bust me and to this second, I am *very* grateful. (I do have a sneaky suspicion he probably had a very merry Christmas as well, chomping doughnuts while puffing on my stash.)

Within a few minutes I found myself in the holding tank with a young man with whom I had gone to high school, Robert Vinson—Bobbay—the younger brother of a classmate, Joe. "Wazzup, Bobbaaay," sez I, and he proceeds to let me know what his beef is and how pissed off he is to have to spend Christmas in the pokey. I concurred.

He asks, "Wazzup wit' you?" and I proceed to tell him, A, that I'll be bailing myself out early that morning; and, B, about San Fran, how cool it is, and how I'm making a buck or two peddling lids and a bit of acid here and there. He livens up, gets all animated. "Hey, you know, man" sez he, "Like I done tol' yah, Tommy, I be ah pimp. Won't be getting' out fo' a day o' two *afta'* Christmas—thaz when Mr. Toe-rez, the Bail Bond dude, take care of my black ass. But I gots my main girl I needs to take care o', you know what I means, man? … Tell you what, I still gots my call t' make … I'll tell my lady you be droppin' off somethin' fo' Christmas … Know what I mean? She be havin' cash."

I knew fo' sho' what he meant. So, I get the phone number of his girl, and let him know I'll drop by her house early the next morning. Upon release, I catch a cab out to my van. I then place his order in a small brown paper bag … hmmm, let's see now: two lids, a roll of bennies and two tabs of acid. That'll be … hmmm … make it a hundred even. A lid of Mexican pot in those days was only about ten to fifteen bucks.

Being a reliable and conscientious businessman, like clockwork I head out for my delivery early the next morning. The infamous San Joaquin Valley tule fog, known for the annual deaths of so many drivers from surrounding farm towns, was just lifting and again it was Happy Harold's sunny West Side. I drive up to a funky little pad, a duplex, on the outskirts of West Fresno … can you say get-toe? I knock and the door opens … Man, this chick is hot, and decked out, well, like a Vegas hooker, pretty fancy, scanty sexy look, you know what I mean? I have my little brown bag, neatly folded—it looks like I'm carrying sandwiches to high school—and I say, "Well, shall we take care of this now?"

"Here, now??? You cray-zay? Let's get in yo' cah, we find us a good place." What the …? I drive down the street a bit and there's St. Alphonsus Church, where I received First Communion. "How about in the parking lot?" "You cray-zay?" sez she, "By da chutch? … You gots to be cray-zay! We gonna us find a moe-tel!" Hmmm.

We pull into the first place on old Motel Row, along Highway 99 just south of the city. The average rent then in these rat-holes was about five bucks a day. She says she wants to see the room—but there's no radio. Nope, that won't do. She insisted on a radio but most places in those days didn't have one because everyone always ripped them off. She also insisted on a bottle of champagne. Hmmm. Well, I finds me a lickah stoe, gets the 'ho some wham-bam sham-pain, and gets me some o' da hawd stuff, Jack Daniels black-ass label … I be ready, Teddy.

Finally, after a half dozen or so hole-in-the-wall motels we find one that suits her fancy. I get some ice and pop the bubbly for her and swig a deep shot of whiskey, no chaser—Get back, Jack! She turns on the radio to the Blues station—old faithful: *Happy Harold's House of Blues*—and then she starts dancing, gyrating and slowly removing those sexy-ass garments. I kick back on the bed, take a sip, light a doobie, and enjoy the show.

But wait, there's more! In a tasteful, methodical routine, after her arousing dance of Salome (make that salami) she proceeds to do me every which-away. What the …? Upon finishing she looks up at me, rolls those big brown eyes, and sez, "How you likes that, Mistah Toe-rezz?" Mistah Toe-rezz? Turns out ol' Torres, the bail bondsman, had a business appointment with her as well that morning. "You mean you ain't Mistah Toe-rezz?"

Given the free ride, she tried to get the price down on my merchandise. Hey, it was Christmas, so I gave her a discount and did my best to weasel another freebee.

A Taste of Honey

> "Yours was the kiss that awoke my heart, there lingers still, 'though we're far apart, that taste of honey, tasting much sweeter than wine."
> —from "A Taste of Honey," vocal version first recorded by Lenny Welch in '62.

1967. Me and a hippy buddy sat that afternoon on the sidewalk of Haight Street, sharing a bottle of burgundy and a batch of fish and chips that had been wrapped in newspaper. It was an unusually warm summer weekend—certainly for San Francisco—with a lot of girls, especially the tourists, wearing bellbottoms with phony patches, trying to look the part. All in all, for the young folks going through their rite of passage from Lawrence Welk/Stepford Wife parents to sheer freedom, I doubt there was a better spot on the planet.

And for me, it was a similar graduation: the scars of Fresno were gradually being replaced with jazz bars and acid-rock stars. Most people were not uptight racist assholes. Pot, wine, and free love! Free food! Free puppies! Free concerts in the park with some of the greatest bands in the world … "Got to believe it's getting bettah, it's getting bettah all the time," so buzzed The Beatles. Well, it just couldn't get much better. But it did.

They say even a blind squirrel eventually finds a nut … Well, I got my mother-of-all-nuts this particular day. I spotted her a block away, heading up our way. Out of a dream, with an hour-glass figure that knew what time it was. Think Rachel Welch, Gina Lollobrigida, Sophia Loren, all wrapped in a tight T-shirt and tighter shorts. She had a lovely face and a full head of dark hair, cut in the mod look of the day. And she was older than the runaways and community hippy chicks—late twenties, I'd guess—and, though she was glancing in the store windows she didn't have the shopping-for-something-freaky tourist look.

The closer she came, the clearer I became as to my approach: smile and say exactly what I was thinking … well, almost. I stood up, brushed off the food residue and, using my hands, brushed back my long, curly hair. "Excuse me, but damn, you're excruciatingly beautiful!" … or something to that effect. Whatever I said, it seemed to work … truth is, whatever you say, they gotta dig the cut of your jib.

I tossed out a pretty specific and ballsy proposal, "Hey, it's pretty hot out here … care for a cocktail?" I have to admit I was amazed that with little hesitation she said yes. My buddy was still on his ass, observing with his mouth hanging open, pieces of greasy French fries drooling onto the sidewalk. He made out OK though, scoring what was left of the wine and fish.

Just a little note here: It's not just that I've been lucky babe-wise, it's that I've always had a healthy heaping of chutzpah. The great slugger Babe Ruth was the home run champ of his time, but guess what? … He was also the strike-out king. Storal of the morey? You'll never knock a home run if you don't keep swingin'!

Speaking of striking … It struck me that she was not only strikingly lovely, but also tall, taller than me, anyway … 5'11" or so, and thoroughly confident. *She* was unquestionably in control of the scene. "There's a nice little place close by," she offered, "… let's go there." I sure as hell wasn't arguing. We turned onto a side street and headed east a couple of blocks. There it was, an unusually clean little establishment with a handful of tables towards the back and against the side wall. As we walked through, it appeared that everyone knew who she was, with a nod and a raised eyebrow or two as to my being with her.

It didn't take long for me to see that there wasn't a guy in the place … women, women and more women. I thought I had died and gone to horny toad heaven … but nooo. I was a young dude, just 22, and still pretty unsophisticated but it didn't take a friggin' genius to figure this one out. And to top it off, as it turned out, she was The Queen Bee, with drinks coming our way every few minutes. Can't say I blamed that crowd, she was a traffic stopper who didn't need to say a word, didn't have to.

We chit-chatted, my yakking a bit about how I arrived in San Francisco, my horrid marriage, being an orderly and wanting to kill a certain white doctor. She startled me by asking, "Would you kill me?" She said this whole story was a bit of a coincidence because she was about to become an M.D., graduating from a school right there in The City. She said she liked the idea that we had a little something in common, a passion for the human and humanitarian aspect of the hospital environment.

Within an hour, she grabbed me by the hand and said, "Would you like to see my place … it has a great view." Shit, *she* was the great view. Her vehicle was parked close by, an older Brit sports job, an Austin-Healey, top down. We jumped in and she sped around the hills, upward to her pad. It was a two-story apartment, fairly modern, with a nice deck. As she had promised, one hell of a view of the bay. She got us a couple of drinks and we sat on the veranda as the sun set.

Soon, as the drinks glossed over any inhibitions we might have had, there was a good slobbery kiss or two. As it became darker, she said that I'd probably feel better if I took a nice, hot shower. This was not a subtle request; this was a demand, and I was too drunk and horny to be insulted. Well hell yes … the fact is I probably hadn't showered in a couple of weeks.

She brought in my drink, fresh towels, a razor and a new bar of soap. She made mention that I should come into the living room when I was through, but never mind putting my clothes back on. They were pretty filthy, but that had little to do with what was in process … Hmmm.

I was going nuts in that shower, fantasizing about the possibilities. I didn't waste much time getting dry, wrapping a towel around my waist and heading straight to her. And here's the kicker: There she lay in all her glory, spread eagle ... *on a gurney*! Yep, a hospital gurney, with a fresh sheet across the bottom ... and a bright light above. Sur-fuckin'-real!

Not so much as a small towel covering the gorgeous mounds and valleys of her beckoning body. It struck me that she had mentioned she was an intern, with only a few months to get her medical degree. Maybe this was some bizarre experiment as part of her studies, maybe she was going to kill me ... what a way to go! I didn't know and I sure as hell didn't care.

She looked like a transfigured Dali painting, full and rich and bright, limply spread across that canvas of de light. I walked up to the gurney, wheels already locked, and just stood there in awe. Her eyes were closed, her legs welcoming. There was a bit of foreplay on my part—lips to lips, to breasts, full and firm, to vagina, wet and warm. I could have spent more time in this massage mode, but I didn't want to get off before I got on.

What an ambrosial gift, the Goddess of the Gurney, mellifluous, a taste of honey. It didn't take long for her to climax, not long at all. She had meticulously planned the whole blessed thing. When we were done there was no talk of romance or tomorrow. With me on the verge of full-blown love/lust, she methodically and matter-of-factly got up and left the room. She returned in a few minutes, clothes on, almost indifferent to what had just transpired. She did have a subtly satisfied smile, or so I imagined. But she was clear that I really needed to go now because she had to get to work early that very morning.

As we drove down the hill back towards the Haight I asked if I might see her again. She said sure and gave me her number, which I quickly scribbled down and shoved into my wallet. I have no idea what became of that number or, for that matter, of that woman. I'm not even sure if she gave me her real number. Was this all a dopamine morphine-mushroom mind-meld? Had this really happened? ...Yeah, it did.

For me, the Haight-Ashbury was a youthful Mecca for summer love and every day was joyously explosive, a super nova of heaven on earth.

A Frantic Romantic

> "And think not you can direct the course of love,
> for love, if it finds you worthy, directs your course."
> —from *The Prophet*, by Kahlil Gibran

In spite of my perilous and oft-pathetic pursuits of romance, and the real pain that came from much of it, I never gave up on the prospect of the idealized cornball mush that I had come to fall for again and again. A shame I never really applied the wise lyrics from the *Nature Boy* song ... "The greatest thing you'll ever learn is just to love and be loved in return." I really didn't know how to give love, not fully, not nearly. Nonetheless, if I wasn't "in love" then I was looking for "Her." Damn those corny old movies!

The point here is that on this mundane plane, I'm still a full-blown Valentine's Day dripping-with-sap romantic. (I once kiddingly commented that the definition of a Latin lover is a fuckin' Mexican...I resemble that remark.) Yes, as a Buddhist I know it's all an illusion, a source of confusion, an impetuous intrusion, but you know, I wouldn't trade it for all the wine in France, no, not at all. What a lovely dance, this thing romance.

Here I offer three of my more sentimental soliloquies ... May we all find someone to take walks with.

Someone to Take Walks With

Oh, I suppose a dog might do or a fairy tale friend
—someone to take walks with toward the road's dear end.
And we would talk of things amiss and ponder things afar,
perhaps of Christmas time in June, or the distance to that star,
We'd kick a can and throw a rock and traverse a verse or two
—alas, my dog or fairy friend has not the hands of you.
We'd briskly bounce across a bridge that holds two worlds apart
—alas, my dog or fairy friend has not your fervid heart.
We'd speak of heroes, gods and men and of the muse's charms
—alas, my dog or fairy friend has not your waiting arms.

A Portrait Waiting

A portrait waiting to be painted,
never captured, almost sainted,
with the morning mist abating
on the park bench a portrait waiting,
in the dawn she sits untainted.

Through the morning haze comes seeping
a cup of beauty, slowly steeping,
her sunlit shadow thaws the picture
of sweetness is this misty mixture
of forest nymph and goddess sleeping.

Like nature naked she purely poses
for the art my heart composes,
for my brush to blush her lips
and my pen to stroke her hips
and plant the garden of her roses.

But as the sun burns through the cover
she fades away as I discover
my painting blurred with tears depleted
by the portrait not completed
of my one and only lover.

If I told You

If I told you of the hanging moss
On a distant, beckoning beach,
If I told you of the sea-swept caves,
Gods hidden in the verdant rocks
Beyond our mortal reach ...

If I told you of the whales
Glistening in the bay,
Mythic gods riding turquoise waves,
Arriving in their perfect time,
A masterpiece at play ...

If I told you of the fairy's trail
Out of a misty dream,
A path of clover, fern and phlox,
A bridal path to heaven's gate
Lit by Cupid's beam …

If I told you of two lovers
On a perfect day,
Of a kiss beyond mere bliss …
You'd say it's just a poem,
You'd say it's not that way.

Wanderlust

> "Oh, I met him there in a border town/he vowed we'd never part/Though he tried his best to settle down/I'm now alone with a broken heart."
> —"The Wayward Wind," Gogi Grant, 1956.

Wanderlust. What a grand word. It might also have been spelled *wonder*lust. Story of my life, at least two-thirds of it. I could've been living with Sophia Loren in a mansion on The Riviera but, sooner or later, up the road I'd go. What the hell's up with that? Try *wanderlust*, an insatiable desire to scoot onward, new people, new sights, new intoxicating smells … women do smell different, each and every one of them like scented snowflakes. How strange and wonderful that forty years later you can still remember a person's smell, kind of relive the passion.

From the time I was very young I've contemplated the contemplative life, that of a monk or priest or just a hermit in the woods with a simple, clean shack to settle into. I've even tried it but my alcoholust and my lunacy always got in the way. History is filled with the graves of those who have been driven to destroy themselves one way or the other.

There is a line from a major figure in the history of Haiku verse, Matsuo Basho (1644-1694) that seems to sum up my travels: "I seemed to be possessed by the spirits of wanderlust, and they all but deprived me of my senses. The guardian spirits of the road beckoned, and I could not settle down to work."

Perhaps one of the most telling of my wandering tales occurred around the time I was 24, a first-year student at San José State. When I found out about the loose and super-hip town of Santa Cruz being right over the hill, well, you know where I spent my weekends. That first spring "over the hill" I was befriended by a fellow at the old Catalyst, a coffeehouse/bar/concert hall combo, which could well have inspired *The Magical Mystery Tour.*

There was still a renaissance going on in the Bay Area, for sure, but the Haight-Ashbury and Telegraph Ave in Berkeley had cooled down a bit. By the '70s the runaways, mostly White youngsters who fancied themselves rebels, had stuck their unwashed tails between their born-to-be-bourgeoisie legs and headed back to daddy, to become doctors, dentists, and developers. They cut their dirty, long hair and went from Walden Pond to stocks and bonds, though many of their kids were branded with monikers like Sunrise, Moonbeam, Rainbow, Karma, and of course Peace ... actually cool.

And it's also true many of those kids went home and became creative and compassionate pillars-of-society, did, in fact, make this a better world. And in Santa Cruz, like Berkeley, the stimulus of the '60s translated into a thoughtful, politically liberal scene, pre-Starbucks, still alive with activism and hope.

Now, back to the old "Cat," The Catalyst and the older cat I met there ... I don't remember the gent's name, just that he was tall and slim with wisps of grey in his long hair and beard—early fifties, I'd say.

I was sitting by the indoor fountain that was central to the establishment, having my morning mug of cappuccino. Sitting near me was that kindly fellow with the sensitive, soft face and a comforting smile. What really stood out, as I recall, is that the guy had unusually large hazel-green eyes that were all but mesmerizing. As it turned out, he ran a meditation retreat in the nearby Santa Cruz Mountains, truly a misty fairyland. That got my interest and I asked him if he had a reduced fee for minorities ... I've always felt that genius was a minority.

The guy gave me a break on my class cost for the coming weekend, a three-day stint way to hell and gone up in the SC mountains. He said bring a toothbrush and a change of shorts. Was he hinting at something? Oh, and a sleeping bag. Seeing that he noticed that I was already a bit tipsy by mid-morning, he also requested that I lay low on the booze the night before ... Schuuuur, I schlurred. Anyway, I obliged him (for the most part) and was there early the next weekend, slight hangover and all. The ride up there was the courtesy of a Latin lovely with whom I'd spent the night—the sister of a

Chicano professor-friend, who wouldn't have been that much of a friend if he knew I was boinging his seester.

The one thing the good guru didn't fill me in on was how sparse … not sparse, but Spartan … the whole weekend would be. Hell, I was a San José Spartan, so I could handle it (or so I thought). There I was at six in the morning, toothbrush, *clean* shorts, and a ready-Teddy attitude. The Guru, my buddy from The Catalyst, had transformed from Gandalf the Grey to Gandalf the off-White, with a humble cotton robe and Hindu beads.

Off with the shoes and into the sizable living room. A clean beige carpet covered the entire floor, with pillows scattered here and there, the scent of incense in the air. Sizable pictures of Indian gurus around the walls, sequenced in the order of their time here on this planet, some who were, I was later told, the incarnation of the previous one. Hey, well all-righty then, I can dig it, I mean some of those cats had that way-out look I could so identify with.

Then came the first lesson: a brief history of our leader's beliefs and the lineage of his gurus. Followed by the importance of meditation, the mantra and then the proper cross-legged meditation stance. There were large windows with views of the redwood forest and the hills behind. As the sun rose, I wanted to be out there, just walking, sitting by a stream, breathing the clean mountain air, that's all.

Mantra time. We were to slowly repeat the two-syllable mantra he'd given us, silently and slowly. A foreign-sounding utterance that had no meaning, no language equivalent. Breathe in, first half of the mantra; breathe out, the second half. This went on for fifteen to twenty minutes, just silence and then a question from the guru to the small class, about a dozen of us all in all, "How do you feel?" Groovy, man!

It doesn't take long for time to pass when meditating, not for me anyway … like the snap of a finger and you're back here, back to this reality. How was I to know back then that this reality *is* that reality if we want it to be … and even if we don't. Anyway, the reality I was thinking about at about that time was food and drink, and lunch was fast approaching. Lunch? I could hardly wait. The plate: an apple, a small slice of cheese and a bottle of water … What the …?

Well, the meditation exercise followed by question-and-answer process pretty much went on for the rest of the day, breathe in, breathe out. I had noticed that there was a cutie of a hippy chick, a young, curvaceous creature that kept giving me the all-knowing eye … I think she was reading my mind. That evening as we sat around the fireplace, I kept glancing across at that hungry young thing, both of us fully knowing each other's desires. Desires!—the antithesis of why we were in this very special environment.

The next day one of our exercises, after a morning of meditation, was to sit on the floor in the full lotus posture (cross-legged position) across from a partner, and ask of the other, "Tell me who you are." I'll give you one guess who my partner was. (Hint: it wasn't the guru, or the old guy who had been eyeballing *me*.) Yep, the hippy chick. So she sits across from me, legs widely crossed, short skirt with bulging panties pulsating sweet peach prayers and says, "Tell me who you are."

This was supposed to be a profound moment, finally seeing my Eternal Self and all ... Damn! Who the hell am I? Shit, I was really losing my cool, I stuttered a bit as a bead of sweat slithered down my forehead ... and I swear there was a subtle smile on her face. (Now we know what Mona Lisa was thinking and what position the rest of her body was in.) Yep, she socked it to me without saying a word. I have no idea what my verbal response was, but when this exercise was over, I asked my guru-bud if I might have a word with him outside. We put on our shoes and walked onto the front porch.

Listen, I said, I am most grateful for this opportunity and I think I got quite a bit out of it, but, honestly, I just don't think I'm quite ready yet, please accept my apologies, and again, my gratefulness. He said, hey, that's cool, whenever I want just let him know, the door's always open. In record time I was hitching down the hill to The Catalyst, with beer, Rubenesque women, and a thick Reuben sandwich on my wicked fleshy mind ... double the corned beef!

Now, this is a very long-winded way of my saying that my style wasn't exactly meant for the contemplative life, certainly not at that age. It was about the time in my life that I became aware that my deep desire was to be settled down with a good woman, a garden, and the smell of home-cooked soup. A veritable quandary indeed, in that I was crazy as hell and couldn't have lasted with any mate, no matter how wonderful she may have been. My dick was my compass and it kept pointing North. Yep, she was up there somewhere.

Slightly related note: All of the men and women in that meditation group were White. Throughout my life I have found this to be basically true in similar meditational settings, be they of the Hindu or Buddhist tradition. The same is pretty much the same as to the lack of "people of color" participating in the environmental and personal growth fields.

So many factors are at the base of this under-representation: lack of higher education, a Christian influence that disses meditation, and poverty in general. Hell, when you need to hustle to pay the rent or get food—just basic survival—the likes of mindfulness and transcendence appear as vacuous luxuries, distant and foreign. What an absolute shame because the calm and conscious space that meditation leads to is just the mental/emotional place that helps liberate the bonds of lack.

The Tide Pools of Tomorrow

While residing in Santa Cruz back in the early seventies, I was most blessed to live in the pleasant home of my lover there on Cliff Drive, just a few yards from the ocean (sometimes we don't know what we have until we lose it, and that applies more to people than to things).

There was no beach to speak of, a few feet at the most, but one could climb down the cliff ten feet or so and be there alone at the water's edge. There you would actually be standing on, or in, or next to, any one of numerous tiny tide pools—most of them a mere foot or two in diameter, none larger than a living room aquarium.

In those pools one would find fittingly miniscule fish and other infinitesimal salt-water inhabitants, like mini-crabs, shellfish, anemones, sea stars, sponges, and always the clinging algae and seaweed gently flowing back and forth along with the numerous near-microscopic wigglers, all looking just the right size for those aquatic habitats like babies in their cribs.

When the waves came in, larger and larger until the grand finale seventh wave hit, following each surge were always dozens of miniature waterfalls flowing downward from the highest pool to the next lower, and the next, cascading down and back into the waiting ocean, each chute indescribably intoxicating. Each wave would wash away some of my newfound friends, sadly, but then new ones would come with the next rippling swell.

Usually the sun would break through the morning fog, an excruciatingly lovely interactive system whereas you, the little sea creatures and the process of the moon-swayed waves coming in and going out were indeed all one in that perfect permeating second. When the light hit the minute falls flowing back into the sea so as to create a turquoise translucence, and I knew there was not a more beautiful total experience of sight, smell, and sound in the world.

But then I would feel so badly when the water rushed away, or the sun began to change its position, or a cloud darkened the clearness of those micro-ponds, obscuring my little rapids, dozens of very private miniature Niagaras.

I never wanted them to end, and I would lament the loss of each tiny waterfall with its unique Lilliputian marine community. It still brings a tinge of chagrin to think of all the experiences I forever lost as I foolishly tried to capture the moment, that fleeting paradise, worrying about never seeing the specific sight or never feeling that particular rush again. Had I only known to sit quietly and simply enjoy the present gifts.

Man-Wolf Metamorphosis

Splitting from the merry-go-ride,
Said Dr. Jekyll, "There's nothing to Hyde."
—So said me, Sept. 1, 1981

Dr. Jekyll and Mr. Hernandez

For years I dabbled in ditties I called "napkin poems," basically little pieces of paper, almost anything I could get my hands on in a bar—business cards, little pads that some bartenders had handy, and when all else failed, good old napkins. The following zinger was one of them, musing on what was indeed my own split-personality:

> Jumping off the merry-go-ride,
> said Dr. Jekyll, "There's nothing to Hyde!"

Sometimes I'd manage to get these generally crumbled wads home and make a little sense of the poems and drawings (more often than not, horrid renderings of women I was trying to pick up … what a horrible thought that some of these sketches were accurate.) Many of these pieces were so terribly incoherent and illegible that I'd wonder who the fuck wrote or drew that crazy shit. Thanks to the unconstrained forms of "modern art," the sketches made a little more sense … just a little. I've included a handful of those bizarre scratchings here and there in this memoir.

Now, as to the Dr. Jekyll piece, there's a bit more here than meets the eye. Essentially, it's this: when an addict manages to remove himself from the downward cycle of his addiction, the monster disappears. Poof, just like that … Amazing!

The monster is the habit, compulsion, or drug of choice and the subsequent misbehavior that the addict chooses. (Most people, I believe, fall into these addictions as part of what is seemingly normal … we drink, for example, because it's social and takes off a bit of stress. It loosens those endorphins and can be a lot of plain old fun.)

But there is a point when excessive anything can wreck our lives and that's when we must choose to remain a victim and harm others in the process or have the balls to get off of that hellacious cycle, the "merry-go-ride." Tough love.

I personally hang in there, as the Beatles have it, "with a little help from my friends," a very serious commitment to stay sober, along with professional counseling … and even then, I fall like a two-year-old learning to walk when a trauma or tragedy occurs. The deeper we're in the tougher it is to get out … So don't be afraid or ashamed to ask for help.

Persona non Grata

(The Mortifying Self-Portrait of a Manic Maniac)

This was my persona, bone fide: I had a picture of an alcoholic in my mind, a Latin lover with a jug of wine, the staggering but sensitive escritor, not a bore but a scoundrel and a whore. The embodiment of a Beat bodhisattva, Hemingway and Lorca in Mallorca, a Quixotic, chaotic thief of fire, a stallion, stud, a potent sire, the entire macho bit … God, was I ever full of it!

I didn't know how sick I was, what a dick I was, it's true. Yep, that's who I thought I was, especially when I had a buzz, but as mi muy culto curandero muttered, "Tomás, mi amigo, I do not stutter! It is clear to teach (not a reach in any sense, a winning bet by any stretch) that we wee ones tend to be attached to an image of our self as a giant not an elf, and that's why we are small."

Hey, and that's not all. Books are filled with the rise and fall of maniacs like moi. Oh, I could blame it on my pa (my whole past sticks in my craw!), but, my dear, I fear that when the story's fully told and when the rubber hits the road, the brakes must stop on the spot were I ever to find the gold.

So when all is said and done it stacks up to the things I've done when in deed I was not one, when the light was mostly off in me peewee lot. A runaway train with no stop in sight, all those beings that I am not—what a frightful thought!

Until the time that I can see that those characters are not me, nope not hardly one of them, alas I must ask again, "Who is me?" "Who is me?," asks me pee-wee brain. Am I the mind I seem to find watching from the room behind, a field, a force, an eternal source of peanut butter and jam?

Or frankly, my dear, it might just be that I don't give a damn.

My Take on Politricks (Think '69)

I call it *Politricks*, "poli" meaning many and "tricks" as in "Trick or Treat" or as in a "John," a "trick," a fellow who partakes of a prostitute's under-wheres, appropriate these days for more politicians than we care to know … poli-tricks.

Back in the year '69, a writer buddy of mine, a character named Jerry Kamstra who wrote *The Frisco Kid*, had painted and printed a colorful political poster celebrating the year '69. The art told it like it is about our two political parties. He ended up peddling them in a handful of bookstores and novelty shops in The Haight and in North Beach to make a little cash for his habits … like eating.

The gist of it was quite simple: it portrayed the sexual position of a donkey and an elephant in, shall we say, the act of mutual and simultaneous cunnilingus—not to be confused with "cunning linguist." (Being a biography, I suspect that this is as good a time as any to admit that this Tomcat has coughed up his share of hair-balls.)

Meeting…kind of…Herb Caen

> "Oh but you can't help that. Everyone here's mad. *I'm* mad. *You're* mad. There's probably a chance and careful planning if you're not!"
> —The Cheshire Cat, from *Alice in Wonderland*

For years I've had a fondness for what that wonderful San Francisco columnist Herb Caen was famous for: his "3-dot journalism" … dropping an ellipsis with three pricks of a pen. Ellipsis is three consecutive periods … bloody good! … designating the author's attempt to change or drop the subject or just inject a new or different thought … and it's the way some of us old potheads think anyway.

Speaking of Caen, it was he who insisted that only the "lame out-of-towners" called San Francisco "Frisco." Personally, I'm OK with Frisco, San Francisco, San Fran, or The City … Hey, like a lovely lady, just love 'er.

Pee here now. And speaking of SF, many moons ago I was taking a piss at Vesuvio's, that piece of Beat history that's still there on Columbus and Jack Kerouac Alley, with the lyrics to "Lush Life" under the veneer of one of its tables. That wonderful joint won't let us forget that there was once a time …

It was maybe 11-ish or so, evening that is, and the two-story place was, as usual, packed to the rafters, upstairs and down. And at a point I was the only one in the men's head, a winding basement level pissoir that you gotta be half sober to navigate down to.

Waiting for me at a table near the entrance was blessedly silent Bob Kaufman and his wife Eileen, sippin' 'em down ever so slowly, oh, and there was yet a fourth party at our table, a lady from across the bay, Berkeley way, whose name but not butt I have long forgotten.

Anyway, back to the toilet (where my mind tends to be) … I don't know where the hell this came from, nor do I care … the fact is, it did. I pulled out my trusty pen and drew a cartoon on the wall of what I imagined to be a fat Cheshire cat, humongous grin and all, with a bubble above him that said, "Better to be Cat-atonic than Dog-matic."

Following my graffiti, I drew the same image on a sheet of paper. I amaze myself that I've carried these scratchy, scrunched-up notes around all these years … I've lost my mind many times, but still managed not to lose these strange things.

I was very pleased with my little quip, but immediately forgot it and returned to my carousing. The next morning, true to form, I faithfully got my wretched ass up, wobbled down to … actually it was *up to* … Café Trieste (still there, on Upper Grant), grabbed a left-behind copy of the *Chronicle*, ordered my cappuccino, and proceeded to chat with a familiar face or two. George Tsongas, the poet, and Jerry Kamstra, the novelist, were usually on hand for the banter. How very pleasant the times were.

In those days my favorite light-reading delight was the Herb Caen column (it wasn't that I really cared who was doing who, or which politician was the most corrupt, but that the cat was swift, I mean on top of his game and, to my punny satisfaction, always brought a smile to my face.) That particular Sunday I opened the paper and I'll be damned, there it was in Caen's section,

"Found on a North Beach toilet wall: *Better to be Cat-atonic than Dog-matic.* That friggin' soon … Didn't the guy ever sleep?

When puns are outlawed only outlaws will have puns. At the time of scribbling the "cat-atonic" line I was still a student at San José State, and when I returned home I shot off a letter to Caen thanking him for using my little late night nibble (As a pseudonym I used the name of the cat as the author, Barnabus W. Butterball … the "W" of course standing for .)

Within a few days my girl of the time—a fellow student, super-sensitive, too-lovely lady named Janet Morgan—picked up the mail, and again I'll be damned, there it was in his own handwriting, a cool little note that thanked me for my post, said what a pleasure it was to have received my notoriously off the wall letter, and that he himself was damned tired of all the "dog-mail"—meaning dogma-mail, I guess, or "for the dogs"—that he received on a regular basis. The entire letter, like his column that previous Sunday, was nothing but a series of dog and cat puns, separated by ellipses … Caen-fetti!

Looking back, there was more to this riff—the catatonic bit—than met the eye, unless we're talking about the "Third Eye," the pineal gland which some say is the portal to supraconsciousness. And that's the real point of it: In India, folks who are in fact catatonic-like are considered saintly, that is, their dedication to just sitting and being honed in on The Grand Void, aka Brahman, is revered. Makes sense to me and, in meditation, I can really understand why this is the case … better than being dogmatic, yes?

About Mulattos on the Moon

"Should I chew my fingernails down to the wrist?
Perhaps it is better to blow eternal jazz."
—Bob Kaufman, the quintessential Beatnik

Bob, Bob, no wonder you flew like out, man, for your winter,
Checked out, did you, Abomunist bodhisattva,
Leaving Nixon in his checkered cab and most of us lost in sanity.

Pacing North Beach with kamikaze karma
Like a thoroughbred with no race to run,
Walking through the walls of museums,
Your house, fresh painted, a color only you knew,
Pacing North Beach with Benzedrine eyes
And be-bop blasts only you could hear.

Alas, we now know The Smithsonian turned down your beret
For fear of anarchism amongst the relics,
And the F.B.I. stored your Cross of Silence with the Kennedy files.

Lorca was buried in an unmarked grave, Bob,
But for you, North Beach, her walls still alive
With Abomunist propaganda and burgundy laughter.

Nortá Beachá (Italian for North Beach)

By the mid-'50's North Beach had become famous for its bohemian ambiance, enhanced by the considerable influx of lefty politicos and artistic pioneers, some immigrants from the clamor of New York's Greenwich Village, the only other major sanctuary of sanity in America. Certainly the "cool cats" were not the caricatures I saw in cartoons as a kid and watched on TV—like the fumbling, dopey Maynard G. Krebs of *Dobie Gillis* fame but real people who, like the gays, migrated from all over the country to one of the few communities solidly for "their kind."

It was the *San Francisco Chronicle* columnist Herb Caen who coined the term *beatnik*. In '57 those damned Russkis had put up the first satellite, *Sputnik*. During those repressive McCarthy-era years Caen in his punny peculiarity meant that The Beats, with their religion of non-conformity and a degree of communalism (easily mistaken for communism) were considered un-American—hence *beat-nik*.

Beat Generation was a handle that writer Jack Kerouac and others had brought into the American scene, beat being, like, beat up, man, but maybe closer to the real meaning was Kerouac's vision, as beatific, you know, spiritually mellow, a straight shot of heaven, no chaser. There is a case for both.

Catholic saints are beatified and Kerouac at heart was both catholic and Catholic, for a time an enthusiastic proponent of the hipness of Buddhism, a chum with The Dharma Bums, and a crony with the stonies. That said, the man was no doubt a tortured soul who just flat-ass drank himself to death. (Oh, God, I remember sitting in a bar up Seattle way seriously saying to the guy next to me, "I'd rather die than stop drinking!" … Hello?)

A glimpse of Kerowackyism in the early '50s is reflected in a rare book written by an acquaintance of mine, Jack Micheline, titled "*Letter to Kerouac in Heaven*." Micheline had the deserved fortune to have hung out for a time with Kerouac and Ginsberg and Burroughs (hardly KGB) when they were first together in the gritty, black-and-white noir streets of New York, a brilliant synergy about to crack the back of the straight line, that dynamic trio of Jack & Allen & Bill—some say the three of 'em hit the rack in Hackensack as they were about to unknowingly launch the Beat thing and in so doing change the course of her or his story.

So Micheline's flow came with the know. When I say that book is rare, well it has to be. It was written both in long hand and also on a typewriter that was built like a Panzer tank (a clunky manual Burroughs, manufactured by the Fortune 500 Burroughs Corporation, of which oddly enough dope-addict/beat de-generation writer William Burroughs II, fascinating Harvard-educated reprobate, was a bit of an heir to (essentially he was provided scootability with a decent monthly stipend from his parents for most of his life, a kind of millionaire's welfare check that supported his debauchery—the good news for the Berth of the Beats is that he chipped in more than his share of rent and running money for these three amigos; and second being that his demented, drug-driven dive set him off on one hell of a writing spree. Met the man a couple of times, and there was just something jagged about his demeanor. Hung out a taste with his son, Bill Junior, who was a born mess and died way too early thanks to his dad's shenanigans.

My buddy Jack was a pioneer of self-publishing, well kind of … he made copies of his Kerouac manuscript by having them Xeroxed somewhere in pre-Kinko's San Fran and then personally bound each one with a plastic spine. I consider my signed copy, probably one of only a few dozen, a real treasure … Will donate it to The Beat Museum in North Beach one of these days, or maybe sell it for rent money and a lottery ticket.

There's a certain irony in that simultaneous to the Beat's landing in their sought-after niche—not utopia, just a little bit of peace, camaraderie and reason in everyday life beyond the contradictions, hypocrisy, cruelty, racism, and the permeating materialism of this society (Did I miss anything?)—was that for so many the ever-present edge of the volcano, that Vesuvius blast of madness, drugs and/or booze, would ultimately impact their health and longevity.

Yeah, a great relief and agonizing joy at the same time, the stuff that junkies are made of. Prevalent in this subculture, beatniks and their black counterparts in the jazz world, was the sad inheritance of a lifestyle driven by the vehicles of "the high"—a self-medication ball of bennies, heroin, pot, and a hell of a lot of booze. (There are certainly no statistics on the subject, and this thought-line is just my sense of it from what I've read and witnessed.)

San Francisco at the time, besides being pretty damned beautiful and wide open was—and this is key—affordable. You could rent a flat, a studio, or share a house for a hundred bucks a month. You could live in a doorway or in the park *free.* The Beats, in my opinion, in spite of their anti-establishment angst, invigorated—brought more verve—to a community that already had a great history of being on the dynamic, creative, and wild side of things, all the way back to the Barbary Coast days.

To this moment I ache to have lived in Paris in the 20s with its earthy literary and impressionistic art renaissance—Gertrude Stein, Gauguin, Hemingway, Dali, et al. Like the main character of the film *Midnight in Paris,* I deeply long for that magnificent milieu. I know I've romanticized it but I am absolutely enamored with the time, place, and most significantly the artists who walked those cobblestone streets at all hours.

But San Francisco in the '50s and early sixties had a pretty similar atmosphere—a modern jazz scene, a unique brand of poetry, insurrectionary art, classic concerts and opera in the park; a flamenco dance club off of Upper Grant, and espresso haunts sprinkled here and there long before they reached anywhere west of the Rockies.

I arrived on the tail end of that, but the tit-ular Carol Doda, the Grand Brassiere of Broadway, still danced at The Condor Club, and many a roaring raving rhymester (well, sometimes they rhymed) could still read poetry at the Coffee Gallery (the first place I ever did). Artists were still living in their VW vans parked on Potrero Hill or in their cheap-rent not-so-lofty lofts, like those of early Project Artaud out in The Mission. And, if you look real hard, some of the old cats still come sniffin' around in those alleys as alley cats will do, beatified as in a groove.

P.S. The Beat Museum, you gotta see'em, no fluff/good stuff from wall to wall: 540 Broadway, San Francisco, CA 94133.
Try www.kerouac.com or 1-800-KER-OUAC for a yak.

Beat Attitudes

(De Gig in da Hall)

Now when de Main Man,
De hippest o' dem all,
He say, "De house be jammed,
No room in de whole dang hall!"

He den go backstage
An' He say, "Wowzee!
Ain't no room
Fo even a lil' ol' mouzee!"

He say to all da groupies,
"Dis gig be on me …
I will lay it out like a big ol' bird
up in a big ol' tree."

Blezzed be de bongos beatin' on de patio.
Blezzed be de cool, fo' dey shall be called Daddy-o.

Blezzed be de babies, fo' dey shall be most huggable.
Blezzed be de Holy Wine, fo' it shall be most chuggable.

Blezzed be de cold, cold hearts fo' dey shall be unshivered.
Blezzed be de pizza guys, fo' dey shall be delivered.

Blezzed be doze who meditate, fo' dey shall give no lip.
Blezzed be de pranksters, fo' dey shall share de trip.

Blezzed be de kats & kittens from Grenitch to Norta' Beacha'
Ginzy, Kaufman, 'Ghetti, Hoffman, an' all de wild creacha.

Blezzed be de Salvation Army, fo' dey shall spread de bread.
Blezzed be Ben and Jerry and de Grateful Dead.

And den He say, "Rejoice, yah'l, rejoice an' be glad
fo' dey be room to party hardy up in my Daddy's pad."

A Prescient Poetry Piece

> The Grizzly Bear is huge and wild.
> It has devoured the little child.
> The little child is unaware
> It has been eaten by the bear.
> —A. E. Housman

In the seminal, history-altering Allen Ginsberg poem, *Howl* (1955), the author empathizes with an asylum inmate, Carl Solomon (to whom he dedicates the piece) because in part he sees in him the brilliant but obliterated, psychologically dismembered human being that at least acts out against the machine that is the cause of his afflictions, the self-righteous power of a heartless conglomerate reeking of religiosity, pomposity, an arrogant monstrosity of mainstream miscreants that labels profane the fucking truth! Yes, Ginsberg sees himself:

> I saw the best minds of my generation
> destroyed by madness, starving hysterical naked,
> dragging themselves through the negro streets at dawn
> looking for an angry fix,
> angelheaded hipsters
> burning for the ancient heavenly connection
> to the starry dynamo in the machinery of night …

The "best minds" that he refers to were the terribly tender and angry and explorative and mind-blown running-naked dreamsters being asphyxiated by the McCarthy era, bogged and boggled by those with an allegiance to the flagellation, flag-elation of normal American creeps-du-jour; those who knew the contradictions and felt the oppression of a strange blend of pseudo-Christianity, authoritarianism, and hyper-capitalism, felt it personally in so many ways, experienced overwhelming pressure with nowhere to go except to flat-out explode and/or implode. Many were institutionalized, died of drugs or, if lucky, pioneered their way to small artist communities where they could find solace with kindred spirits. Many who made their way to North Beach and Greenwich Village fell under the media-enamored brand known as beatniks and, once-labeled, lost their anonymity virginity and/or became closet-normal.

Howl is a litany of all that was and is wrong with society and consequently what breaks down many of us who give a damn. Sometimes it is the subconscious morass of a painful upbringing combined with the pressures of our everyday lunacy that become the proverbial "straw that broke the camel's back," more like a bale of horse shit dropped on your head from the top of the Empire State Building.

But in being able, difficult as it is, to identify this mountain of pure unfiltered mierda that smothers us, Ginsberg is able to see a little light and becomes unknowingly one of the heroes of later generations of unbridled coffeehouse crazies and liberated gays, in time even becomes a force in the Meditation Nation.

Ginsberg was way-the-fuck crazier than what many of us ever dreamed of and fortunately for us he lived to write about it. More importantly, he lived to grow beyond his own lunacy and rage, mostly through his abiding commitment to a highly conscious, non-addictive lifestyle, in the practice of Tibetan Buddhism. Buddhism, after all, is primarily a therapy for the madness and pain caused by delusional thinking and way-reactionary behavior.

The neo-bohemian culture of the '50s began at that time in America when one had to search for a tiny oasis of sanity. We are so blessed now to have sane psychologists, doctors, and whole communities of "angel-headed hipsters" who haven't succumbed to either joining the minions of the walking dread or being broken away, falling into the pits of criminal activity, all-consuming addictions, and a wide variety of mental masturbation ... and/or all of the above.

FIRST OF A SERIES

A New Paradise For Beatniks

By MICHAEL FALLON

Five untroubled young "hippies," sprawled on floor mattresses and slouched in an armchair retrieved from a debris box, flipped cigaret ashes at a seashell in their Waller Street flat and pondered their next move.

It was 5 in the evening. Dinner was not yet on the stove; the makings for dinner were nowhere in sight.

No one appeared worried, though. Or even interested.

The same apathy controlled the discusson of their next pad, a move forced on them by a police marijuana and drinking party raid the week before. "Maybe we'll move to the Fillmore," said Jeff, 21, the oldest. The proposal drew loud snickers and seemed doomed.

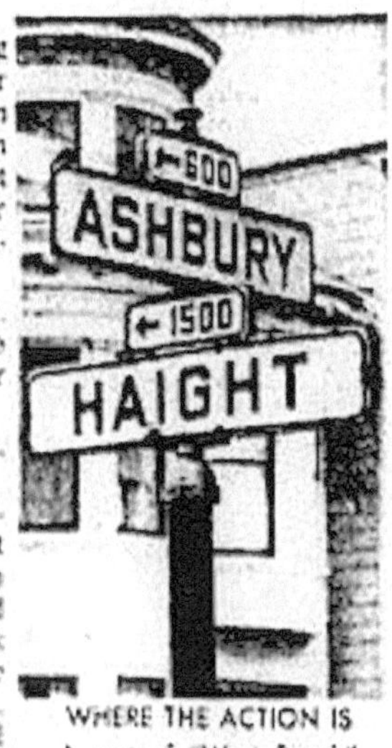

WHERE THE ACTION IS
A sort of "West Beach"

A New Paradise for Beatniks

Above is part of the *San Francisco Examiner* article/series by Michael Fallon about the new hippy movement (September, '65). It was one of the first times the H-word was used in print. What's important about this writing is that it links the Beats to the Hippies, the Hiparama-to-Nirvana transition.

You know, I run into so many young people these days who tell me they wish they could have lived in those days, and I truly hope they can find ways to revive the spirit of that hopeful time. I can tell you firsthand it was an astounding and magical tour—the hills were alive with the sound of mushrooms.

A Thousand Years Ago

I lived in the wilds of the city lights
when madmen howled throughout the nights
wrote naked poems on Vesuvio's walls
protested in the Berkeley halls
painted old buses with neon blasts
synaptic zaps on tie-dye grass
I hitchhiked to heaven and left my past
a thousand years ago.

Buddha blew a be-bop mantra
hippy chicks practiced their tantra
on subterranean cable cars
we reached the moon and kissed the stars
behind the swirls of Van Gogh
I found my tribe of kindred souls
when life was all aglow
a thousand years ago.

There were some folks strict and straight
with knife and fork they ate
I preferred the chopstick way
the curves of jazz the Latin sway
the hotel smell of sex and squalor
white men washed starch from their collar
a rose replaced the mighty dollar
a thousand years ago.

Through freeway sounds and clashing words
we still heard the songs of birds
a robin's chirr, a meadowlark
warbling in the golden park
across the bridge a white crane flew
but now there are so very few
oh, when life was fresh and new
a thousand years ago.

I met a man who was just plain mean
laughed at me from his limousine
with smug tight lips what he had to say
was that I was going the wrong way
I told him I was of peasant stock
and asked if he would please not mock
the dance I did to my own beat
where space-time travelers chance to meet.

When I moved all else moved too
I saw it through a Third Eye view
up my chakras the spirit flew
Nirvana was my aim it's true
a glimpse of paradise in purple haze
but even in heaven the rent was raised
the I Ching says go with the flow
nothing stays the same you know.

I lived in the wilds could not be tamed
by the gravity of the game
but all things go and nothing stays
oh I do long for those days
when we raved against the machine
when there was hope and dope was clean
when fake was fake and the scene was green
a thousand years ago.

Chicano Power!

> "We cannot seek achievement for ourselves and forget about progress and prosperity for our community ... Our ambitions must be broad enough to include the aspirations and needs of others, for their sakes and for our own."
> —César Chavez

1968 - 1971. I was never able to recapture those days at San José State, not even close. I certainly couldn't reproduce being in my amped-up twenties, full of questions, full of fire, and some would argue full of shit.

Nowhere since could I find the impassioned camaraderie of the Chicano Student Movement, of the Black and Asian friends of the same ilk, of the White kids who stood up side by side, foregoing their privilege; nowhere could I find the companionship, the alma of a close knit group who were artists and activists of all persuasions. San José State, *mi alma mater.* Every single day was alive with intelligent discourse, passionate politics, and/or outrageously hilarious stunts.

Earlier, when I lived in San Francisco, I hung with an intimate but scattered circle of bohemian crazies—artists, singers, and more poets than should be legal. What glorious memories of boarding a streetcar from Ivo Buddeke's pad at 41st and Geary by Golden Gate Park and getting off at Market and Powell, then the sheer exhilaration of jumping onto the side of a cable car headed to my beloved North Beach! Always hung on the pole, too excited to sit, God, the conductors were cool! Clang! Clang! Clang!

Years later I had one hell of an exciting and rich life in Santa Cruz, surrounded by natural beauty—the ocean, the forest and rivers—and just living day to day in that quaint town, and, oh, the truly loving people I found—or who found me—that to this day I adore. But still not the dynamic familia from my Chicano student days.

I had tidbits of it in the late '70s/early '80s up in the Great Northwest, in Old Town Portland with its jazz clubs and coffeehouses that actually had bookshelves with books on them ... books? Art Barfield, a soul bro from back in Fresno who had moved up to Portland ... Movin' on up!—and I tore that town up, no doubt about it. Same up in Seattle, right there in the University District, Jazz on The Ave, the Blue Moon Saloon and the life of Riley, that's Dennis Riley and his wild buddies.

But no, it was never the same. I kept looking but never found that marvelous mix of creative and caring souls that was San José State in the sixties. Maybe it was the time in history that threw us into a cauldron of hot activism—Vietnam, Bobby Kennedy, Martin Luther King, César Chavez, Chicano Power, Black Power, Women's Rights. No, it was even more than that.

We came from all over the state and country, even other countries, urban kids, rural kids, and mentors of all races, all passionately involved with The Cause—¡Que viva la causa! By our actions there was never a question as to our commitment to social change. Without being aware of it we had become a family. There was truly a richness and beauty about us.

During those college days, a couple of buddies and I wrote an agit-prop play. The term "agit-prop" is a condensation of "agitation and propaganda" which originated in Russia during their revolution, then spread to France, England, and Germany with the plays of Bertold Brecht; when imported to the U.S., it was embodied by the San Francisco Mime Troupe, which was headed by R.G. Davis who taught me how to use chop sticks in San Fran, even as Luís Valdez studied under him. Valdez, with deep commitment to the betterment of U.S. farm workers, developed what became known as *Teatro Campesino*, a dedicated group that directly brought important information to the farm workers of Central California using music, jokes and political pokes ... agit-prop. It was an educational *platform*—quite literally—because it was often performed on the mobile platform of a flatbed truck. This powerful mode of propaganda was an important arm of the United Farm Workers Union of Cesár Chavez. The little group I named and was a co-creator of—Teatro Urbano—became a tiny spinoff ... whew. Where was I?

Oh, yeah, the play, boss, the play ... we students (Tino Esparza, Ben Ybarra and myself) wrote a little one-act play—an agit-prop piece—with a few contributions from fellow students Ed Flores and Rosalinda Martinez, and most of us ended up performing in it. It's about some young Chicano students who get into college and manage to forget their roots, become "sell-outs."

It was eventually taken throughout the Bay Area and to cities throughout California (there's a video of it somewhere). It was titled *Chicano Commencement* and was originally written and performed as part of the first major college graduation ceremony "walk-out" in history.

That event highlighted the disproportionate number of Latino students in colleges across the U.S., with a focus on our own community, San José. When I say disproportionate, I mean that the Latino community in San José was then about 33% of the general population, whereas the number of Latino students graduating from San José State that year was about 3% … Hello?

At the beginning of this decades-old celebration of graduation (San José State had been an institution since 1871, the oldest of all California State Colleges), all of the young Latino men and women graduating that year—about a dozen of them—stood up during the beginning of the traditional ceremony at Spartan stadium, as did many of the professors. (Actually, there was one graduate who didn't join us because it was so important to his parents to proudly witness him graduate *traditionally*, that is with all the White kids. I can really understand that, and in all likelihood the parents had sacrificed for that very day and didn't understand the significance of our activist statement.)

To the cheers of our many supporters up in the stands, the graduating Chicano students and sympathetic professors, wearing their own graduation gowns and hats, stood up at the beginning of the ceremony and walked out, leaving the remaining audience wondering "What the hell was that?"

We then proceeded to march to the Mexican melodies of our home-grown band—Rudy Madrid, Ben Cadena and a few others—over to a smaller venue, the track field, where we had a modest but intimate celebration which just happened to include a lot of national media and a celebrity or two.

Unbeknownst to us writers/actors at that very first performance of the *Chicano Commencement* play was the fact that this activist alternative would be played out in several colleges across the Southwest for the next fifty years. The little I knew about the art of agit-prop and took with me to San José, I'd learned from Luís Valdez at his tiny center in Del Rey, a small town about 20 miles out of Fresno. It was certainly an education that went beyond that experience.

Note from www.artsopolis.com:

> The first Chicano Commencement was established in 1970 as a celebration for Mexican-Americans graduating from San José State College. Its roots can be traced from the 1968 and 1969 walkouts and protests by Chicano students and Chicano community members against the San José State Administration. During the era of the Civil Rights Movement, Chicano students felt misrepresented by the

college. When demands for change were refused, Chicano students and community members walked out of the college's annual commencement ceremony held at Spartan Stadium and as a result, decided to hold their own commencement, a Chicano Commencement.

The San José State Gang

"Our gang … I've heard the same refrain: Isn't it a shame it takes someone passing away to get us together again."
—my words at Rudy Madrid's funeral

We weren't exactly in lockstep, not like the Nazis and Repugnicans, but in spite of our tremendous differences we had a common goal: to get more Mexican kids into college and then into respectable, decent-paying jobs. At that time, the number of Latinos in colleges and universities was dismal at best, so very far below ethnic proportionality no one could actually argue against our anger and consequent activity. No one sane.

We called ourselves "MASC," which was really an acronym for the Mexican-American Student Confederation—you know, mask, as in Zorro. We were a predecessor of what is now called MECHA, replete with buttons and banners … but I'll tell you one thing: we could not have been more serious about opening those academic doors. We were the primary organizers of *Chicano Commencement*, the history-making walk-out which celebrated its 45th birthday in 2015.

Several of us spent a hell of a lot more time as dedicated activists than nose-in-the-book students (Thank God for our liberal gabacho professors, Doctors Tansey and Newman, Bob Freimark, and many others who supported us as we marched). Within our group we had our own diversity, ranging in color, size and political propensity.

For example there was tall, handsome Ed Flores, a bit of a nationalist who actually felt that the concept of Aztlán, the Aztec nation that spread at one time from the southern tip of Mexico all the way into the Southwest of the U.S., could take hold again (in some ways it has) … He also owned his own little Tex-Mex café, which I dubbed Edwierdo's Speakeasy because at two in the morning he'd just close the doors and pull the shades down as we continued to guzzle our beer, philosophize (aka talk shit), and mastermind our next activist pendejada.

Every group needs a leader, and ours was our cocky, charismatic field general, Dañiel Hernandez, a sharp-as-they-come properly pissed-off Chicano from Arizona, the reincarnation of Pancho Villa himself. He was ably assisted (sometimes ably) by his side-kick sergeant, Ben Ybarra, who constantly got us into shit because of *his* demands of the college administration (e.g., "replace the sandwiches in the cafeteria with burritos! ... You have one week or face the wrath of MASK!").

There was Dean Hartline, a very talented, burly sometimes surly half-Mex who could pass for a straight-up White dude, but was Mex-I-Can to the bone, and the Lostaunau brothers, Charlie and Loco from Bakersfield ... "Lost, and how!," quipped Arnold Bojorquez, who I almost got into a fight with for his using the N-word one eve over many a beer. We left the popular bar we were in, the Red Ram, with a little entourage of half-ass friends who were spoiling to see some good blows thrown. We walked across the street and into the parking lot behind the corner store of 14th and Williams, stood in each other's face, screamed a bit, turned around and returned to our beer ... now that's *real* machismo. I think our blood-thirsty buddies were disappointed with our faint-hearted flaunting of phony fisticuffs, but shit, I'd rather drink than fight. Apparently, Arnold agreed.

And then there were the young'uns, like theatrical Andreas "Red" Vargas; the calm and collected Antonio Chavez; the organized and thoroughly dedicated writer-to-be, Humberto Garza; and the wide-eyed John Garcia. (*Doctor* Juan Garcia to us peasants, now a bona fide shrink ... ay, John, I need an appointment.)

And what movement could survive without its artists? There was Malaquias Montoya, part of that great family who developed the Royal Chicano Air Force; The Soto sisters, Graciela and Rosie (Rosie later became Rosanna DeSoto, a TV and Movie actress. "Reee-cheee!" was her somewhat famous scream who, as the mother of rock legend Richie Valens learns of his tragic death in Luis Valdez' movie *La Bamba* ... You know, kind of like Marlon Brando's "Stel-lahhhh!" but with a Latina flair.) And the Madrid brothers, Rudy and Sunny ... Sunny Madrid was the consummate entrepreneur who, with a little black and white camera and a lot of huevos, created and developed *Lowrider* magazine, which can still be found on magazine racks everywheres (yes, that's "everywheres," plural.)

And Rudy, Rudy—God bless that boy!—him and his warm-ass Miller beer. Rudy, day after day, year after year, entertained us all as the total troubadour. He was always there, at rallies, for quinceñeras and funerals, in cantinas and restaurants, on street corners, and, with raspy voice, strumming away in our pads 'til the midnight hour. He became a well-recorded guitarist and singer who wrote a lot of his own stuff; and he had an uncanny knack for instantly learning the music and lyrics to damn near anything … rock 'n' roll, rhythm 'n' blues, and of, course, all things Mexican: corridos, rancheras, salsa, and the songs that make you wanna cry … ¡Aiyyyy-yi—yi!

Rudy y La Familia, he called his band, Rudy y La Familia—and the family was all of us. For many of our gang those were the best years of our lives. I include myself in that bunch of bananas.

Note: All in all, there were maybe thirty in that core group, too many to mention here, including students like the Madrid brothers, Norma Fierro, Rosalinda Martinez, Jess Amaro, his wife-to-be Rosamaria, and others who were equally dedicated. And there were older folks from the community and the faculty who were our mentors, powerhouses like Sophie Mendoza, José Carrasco, and Eliju Carranza. Sophie was very central to this all and deserves a book of her own! Rudy, sad to say, passed away January 30, 2010 … God bless that boy. Ay, Rudy, The Saints won the Super Bowl right after you kicked … how apropos.

The Garret at San José State

1969. I was a student in my second year working my way through, you might say. I received a few bucks from the G.I. Bill for having been in the service and I was a bit of an entrepreneur on the side. In spite of my navy pea coat, bell bottoms, and Che Guevara beard, in contrast was my dark leather businessman's briefcase filled with neatly packed lids of marijuana, tightly rolled doobies, a couple of bags of synthetic mescaline in gel capsules, and little vials filled with LSD tabs. A New Age hustler.

I figured that the briefcase was so overtly straight no one would dream of the contents. And they never did, with the exception, of course, of my clients, close buddies and a chick or two that I was hitting on.

I lived in the upstairs, the attic, of a run-down house a couple of blocks from the campus near 8th Street and Santa Clara. The space was separated into four tiny rooms, with walls so thin you could hear the guy next door snoring or jacking off. You could actually hear the Doobie Brothers practicing just up the street and you could hear one of my garret-mates ("Trash Gordon" was his handle) strumming away night and day, a classical guitar player.

The other two roomies were Uncle Lou, an older Portuguese man who, by day, was a part-time addiction counselor at Stanford U. in spite of the fact that by nightfall he was drunk on his ass; and then there was Eduardo, a handsome Romeo of a Latin who arrived one weekend after I had made mention at a Chicano student meeting of an empty room available in the house where I lived. When you're a student cheap is good.

Everyone at the pad knew that the landlord's rule was one person per room, no exceptions. For 35 bucks a month, you damn well stick to the rules. Eduardo, however, had his own premeditated plan.

Within a day or two his pregnant wife, Minerva, arrived. Shortly thereafter came his little son, Papiro. Then, a grubby, molting parrot that only spoke Spanish, "Chinga tú madre! Chinga tú madre!" Finally, his yapping little mutt arrived, aptly named Shorty—or, in Spanish, Chorty.

Well, not quite finally … a couple of weeks later Ed capped it all by bringing a fuckin' goat into the back yard, where he tied him to a tree with a rope. I bitched a bit about it, but a couple of weeks later after the barbeque (courtesy of the goat) I changed my mind. It was about this time I scribbled the following meritless ditty:

Hey, Eduardo

Rent is due, usual space
Something masochistic about my pace,
Traffic warrants, child support
Very difficult holding the fort,
Teeth are rotting, got the flu,
Ulcers, migraines, hemorrhoids too,
Athlete's foot and got the clap
And crabs and warts and other crap,
Other than that, everything's fine …
Hey Eduardo, pass the wine!

This, mind you, was written when I was about 25 … As of this writing I'm closer to 75, and reluctantly add these lines:

Hair is falling, got arthritis,
Diabetes and pancreatitis,
Knees are shot down to the bone
Medicare! Right on! Right on!

A Not-so-Virgin Sacrifice: That very same Eduardo Flores of birria fame, as it turned out, was quite the back-to-Mexico, Atzlán fanatic. (In his defense, we were all fanatic about something in those days.) He'd tower over his fellow Chicano students with his considerable height and sound on them as to how to be a *real* Mexican.

One day after we both had graduated from the garret scene, we were barbequing and pounding the brewskies out in his back yard. Again the subject of the greatness of the Aztecs came up, with Ed waving the bloody painting of the grieving warrior prince holding his beautiful dead lover in his arms, that ubiquitous piece we see on calendars hanging in Mexican restaurants, barbershops, and toilets. I said, "Hey, Ed, they weren't all that great; in fact, they were a bunch of imperialistic rip-offs who stole their culture from the Toltecs and performed a lot of unnecessary sacrifices, mostly dudes on the losing end of their battles and innocent virgin maidens. What a waste!"

"Parále, parále," he would scream in that thick Mexican accent, "You just don't understand!" "Don't understand what, Ed?"

"Understand the significance of sacrifice!!! You just don't understand!!!"

"OK, dude," I said as I grabbed a knife on a cutting board next to his Weber grill, "Let me cut that big head of yours off and throw it on the barbeque. Would you understand that?"

"Pinche Tomás, you just don't understand!!!"

Note: Señor Flores has in his later years become quite the sophisticate, spending considerable time listening to classical music and visiting fine art museums that transcend any sort of nationalism. But he's still passionate about the permeating injustice that is still with us … Mi muy macho amigo, Eduardo de Brownsville Flores.

San José Foot Notes

In my junior and senior years at Edison High School back in Fresburg, I was the assistant (aka water boy and general flunky) to track coach Frank Fletcher and our exceptional track & field team. I'd schlep along the equipment and go on the bus with the superb athletes who were otherwise my classmates to the various track meets each season.

But when they were on that track, they became my heroes, beautifully passing the baton or flying over those hurdles. What a pleasure watching these strong, graceful kids, my buddies for years, out run, out jump and out throw most every other m-f-ing team in the region—and that they did, twice in a row *California State Champs* ... from a funky little high school of about 400 students versus every other school in this enormous state! Young'uns like Alvin Mann, John Moore, John Davis, and Stanley McDonald.

It was during that time that I had the unfortunate fortune of watching a certain Tommie Smith, an exceptionally talented kid from nearby farm-grown Lemoore High School, leave our Edison Tiger asses in the dust of those dirt tracks. As a team we kicked butt, but as an individual Mr. Smith was the undeniable front-runner, quite literally.

May I note that just a few years later in his life, Smith held 11 World Records. In 1984 he had the distinct honor of being asked to carry the Olympic Torch at the 1984 Olympiad in Los Angeles. It is no wonder that when we raced against him the outcome was preordained. It was by no simple coincidence that Smith, like myself, was born in de year of de Lode, nine-teen foe-tee foe, the auspicious year of superb athletic stars ... Have I mentioned my medals from the '69 Olympics?

As it turned out, I also had the fortune of attending San José State when it had the best men's track team in the nation ... make that in the world ... Speed City! Two of their runners at the time (1968) became internationally famous immediately after winning their Gold and Bronze medals for the 200 meter race at the Olympics in Mexico City. They were none other than Tommie Smith—that Tommie Smith—and his teammate John Carlos (of Cuban descent from Harlem...the cat was always within inches of Smith!). Their other mate, record-setting Lee Evans was also from the Fresno region, born next door in the quiet town of Madera. The dude was hardly a slouch, winning two Gold medals and setting world records at those same '68 Olympics. Needless to say, he shared the political sentiments of his teammates, once wearing a black beret in imitation of the Black Panther Party while receiving his medals. By the way, the cat was a Fulbright scholar.

But what Smith & Carlos did as they stood on the victor's podium as the world watched—like a precise and powerful Smith & Wesson—was to shoot straight into the hearts and minds of America and most of the world: "... they wore gloves to represent black America and removed their shoes and wore black socks to symbolize the poverty of the American black community. Smith wore a scarf and Carlos a bead necklace, recalling lynching. Both Americans wore the badge of the *Olympic Project for Human Rights*, and they planned to raise their gloved fists, which according to Smith at the time 'stood for the power in black America'"—article in *The Guardian*, by Simon Burton.

Because of this bold, defiant act, both Smith and Carlos were ostracized from mainstream America, contracts were cancelled, they lost their jobs, and both of them and their families received death threats. They were slammed by most of the American press, including the wimpy pig-of-a-broadcaster Brent Musburger, who responded like he had personally been slapped by one of those gloves. He should've been.

The next day this little asshole wrote, "One gets a little tired of having the United States run down by athletes who are enjoying themselves at the expense of their country." Musburger then infamously called Smith and Carlos "a pair of black-skinned storm troopers." To add to this all, then International Olympic Committee President Avery Brundage, an anti-Semite, white supremacist, and Nazi sympathizer (whom the athletes preferred to call "Slavery Avery") did what he could to damage their reputation and their future.

One of few voices of support from White America came from Robert Clark, the enlightened president of San José State, who praised them as "honorable young men dedicated to the cause of justice for the Black people in our society." (I know that Clark was a conscious fellow from the meetings he held with a handful of us Chicano student leaders back then regarding our demands to open doors for more Latino students at that very White school.)

Amazing after all these years we have come full cycle with our social movements—Women's marches, Gay Pride, Colin Kaepernick protest, and Black Lives Matter, and the new anti-gun groups of courageous kids formed after the mass shootings of Sandy Hook, Stoneman Douglas, and elsewhere.

Flashback '68: SJ Prez Clark really lost his cool once when our fiery young leader Dañiel Hernandez ranted in his face, at one point asking if the old dude would care to "step outside." I have to admit, in spite of my allegiance to our Chicano students, I had respect for Clark's response. When Dan physically challenged him (which is fucking ridiculous to begin with), the old guy reflected a little, then stood up and said, "Hey, if you wanna go, let's go!" The ol' vato had huevos! How could Dan possibly win that one? Great theatre.

Finally, on October 17, 2005, a 20-foot-high statue was unveiled at SJ State, showing former students Smith and Carlos frozen, fists aloft, just as they had stood exactly 37 years earlier on the Olympic podium in Mexico City. "Tommie Smith and John Carlos stood for justice, dignity, equality and peace," reads the inscription. "Hereby the university and associated students commemorate their legacy." San José State, right place, right time … Power to the People! … right on!

Photo courtesy of San José State University Athletics

Feet accompli: San José State University Commemorative Statue. Here's the statue depicting runners Tommie Smith (left) and John Carlos (right) showing the Black Power salute in the 1968 Summer Olympics.

What to me is rather miraculous is that *just after* I put the finishing touches on the above vignette about the famed San José track team, I found the above photo in this morning's *Sacramento Bee –this morning's paper!* That photo is of the very statue I spoke of in my vignette … In this day's news, November 22, 2013, 50 years after Kennedy's assassination … Syn-chron-icity City!

The protestors in the photo might well have been us back in the '60s, except there are a heck of a lot more Blacks and Hispanics in the mix. I would like to think that our own protests back in the day had a little impact. Yeah, they did. (… and if any young folks are reading this now, *your protests* will also better the future.)

Also in the News: There's an accompanying article today about the contemptible racist treatment of a black student by four of his white class-mates, who hung swastikas and photos of Hitler on the wall and commented about a black person being only a "fraction" of a real human being. Made national news. Right here at SJ State, forty-some fuckin' years later! Who'd have thought that three years after this tidy little mess we'd have Nazis in the White House?

The Corner of 6th & Williams

> "Life is just another scene in this old world of broken dreams/Oh, the night life, it ain't no good life but it's my life."—From "Night Life," as sung by Willie Nelson, Ray Price, and other night crawlers

'69 or so. Well, it seems only fitting that I should jump into this sordid soliloquy, pen and pad in one hand and brandy in the other, my pain subdued, dude, by banal banter, a jivey jutebox, and a cool bartendress who's been known to have a shot or two with the rest of us lushes. I scribble my notes and stick quarters in the box.

Looking back, it blows my mind how many hours, days, months and years I wasted away in honky-tonks like this one, and houses with mounds of smelly beer bottles and cigarette butts. Looking back, I've got to say, man, of all my stretches of time, I loved those college days in San Josie and the wonderful folks I was blessed to hang out with, professors, community activists, and students alike.

At one point, three or four of us rented breakout apartments in the same rundown two-story house on the corner of Sixth and Williams, close to the college where we were sporadically enrolled, studious to a degree, but not about one … I mean most of us didn't give a damn if we graduated or not.

Indeed, our real study was of the morsels, the fawn-eyed, short-skirted denizens of delight, damsels who generously fed our imaginations as they strutted past our dilapidated porch where we were wont to sit, whistling and making lewd but creative comments. "Ah-oooooo!" said the wolf to Little Red Riding Hood.

We were all quite over the average age of your basic college freshman, mid-twenties to early thirties, most having first served in the Armed Services. We were a little community of guys who loved the collegiate atmosphere, creative types of all persuasions and ethnicities—Blacks, Chicanos, Asians, you name it … and our token gabacho all-American dude, just to keep our quota proper. We called him Brooster, Bruce Crane, a handsome square-jawed boozer who looked like Bruce Wayne of Batman fame, a petty thief who gambled the way we all drank.

At one point or another, it seemed like every crazy in the cosmos lived in that two-story wonder … It was as if the way-trippy Chicano artists of the entire San Joaquin Valley had been abducted and dropped down onto that spacey corner … there is no doubt the local cops considered us as aliens.

This hodge-podge of characters included Sam Parraz, the mad (as in pissed off) painter who would bang the hell out of his old-ass missing-keys piano and sound almost as if he knew what he was doing); Marco Sajkovic, the mad Yugo-slob (as in mad at his father for booting him out of the crib back in Massachusetts because Marco was just a wild and crazy guy); Tino, the smooth mover, shaker and heart breaker, my friend and mentor; Eduardo Flores, Casanova (in his mind) reincarnated, and proud owner of a greasy spoon called El Cachito del Terre (meaning "a little piece of land"... very humble, though I dubbed it Ed-Wierdo's Speakeasy or El Cachito del Terror).

Other cool cats from that very hip scene were Skip Pyles, a brother with all the talent in the world, true definition of hip, jazz aficionado, who has a superior book to write; Ishmael "Zeke" Navarette, a top-notch sax playin' fool (played with the avant-garde trumpeter Eddie Gale for a few years); oh, and even Luís Valdez, the now-famous writer and producer of *Zoot Suit* and *La Bamba* (the biography of Richie Valenzuela, aka rock'n'roller Richie Valens, and other culturally rich pieces ... Reee-cheee!)

By the way, Luís had moved out long before I got there and, from what I recall from spending time with him one summer at his Teatro Campesino center back in the tiny valley town of Del Rey, he was hardly a lush like most of my buds. Well, maybe a beer or two in the eve when we'd philosophize on non-violent activism, the grape boycott, Chicanismo, and the place of us grape-pickers in the Greater Mocosmos. If Luís did have an addiction it was his passion for his people, well exhibited throughout his life.

Now what did the rest of us have in common? Hmmm, let's see. This might give a little insight: Sam worked as a butcher and periodic clerk at the M&J market, right across the street from our mutual pad. The store was owned by Milt and Joe—as in M&J—a couple of middle-aged Italians who themselves were lightweight mafiosos, so we felt no guilt when we ripped them off for wine and cigarettes. At night when the owners would leave Sam in charge, we'd hit the place wearing long jackets (even in the summertime), always leaving with a bottle or two hidden under our arms. We'd guzzle that shit 'til the wee, wee hours.

Well, for most of us, booze, bullshit, and being reasonably hip was our common denominator. With that of course came modern art, be-bop and re-bop, straight-ahead and outer-edge jazz, and the Mary-jew-wanna we were wont to toke in the sauna of summer or the mild rains of winter, chip-chipping away at what was left of our hick upbringing. That being said, the reality is that most of us were right out of the bumpkin patch, transplants from funky little Valley towns like Fresno, Bakersfield, Visalia, Corcoran and the likes … and at the same time we really did, when all was said and done, have a lot in common besides the pretty-damn-creative bit.

At one point or another, we had all worked our butts off in the blazing hot fields and orchards back in The Valley and, whether in the fields or in the city, had experienced racism firsthand. This led to the lot of us becoming, in our own way, sincere activists either by in-your-face protests or with statements within our art.

Este Pequeño Boceto

This little sketch is by Esteban Villa, an original founder of the famed *Royal Chicano Air Force* (some have said *Farce* and there was no shortage of surrealism nor absurdity … Chicano Air Force, indeed!) Dr. Villa was also a muralist, printmaker, and a dedicated activist for Cesar Chavez' United Farm Workers Union. What a nice little gift from this wonderful man as we sat reminiscing about political art, beautiful women, and the old days in The Valley. He was from Tulare, a stone's throw from Fresburg.

Cause du Jour

> "Picket lines and picket signs, don't punish me with brutality. Talk to me, so you can see, Oh, what's going on, what's going on."—Lyrics from "What's Going On," by Marvin Gaye … Nailed the Sixties, still relevant today.

The late Sixties and early Seventies were both meaningful and exciting for us activists, a real cornucopia of causes. On any given day there was a rally for some damned thing: Chicano, Black or Women's liberation; anti-war, specifically Vietnam; anti-capitalism and its unholy, undemocratic push, globalization; pro-environment (at the time mostly a white thang … minorities had more pressing matters); and the ever-important voter registration. And let's not forget the tidily tucked away subject of overpopulation (a cause washed over by the wishy-washiness of politicians … don't piss off the Catholics, or Christians in general, if you want to get elected).

This is not to mention the overall loss of nature to crowds of zombie beef eaters, I'm talkin' land … "Give me land, lots of land, under starry skies above," but that ain't hardly possible because sitting on every nook and cranny of decent land is a cookie-cutter franchise like McDonald's or Taco Bell, or an ostentatious ticky-tack tract home. Taking a dim view of that 40% of Trump voters, it seems the only things sustainable are greed and idiocy and overpopulation. Amen.

Yet in spite of all of these challenges, in a very real way my college years were full of goodness, friendship, and hope. This was because this particular time in history brought us young activists all together, those of us who gave a damn enough to get off of our butts and get out into the streets. (Could be why the hackers and backers of the right-wing are constantly trying their best to destroy real education.)

We truly believed we were accomplishing something, including bringing consciousness to the powers-that-be and opening doors for the oppressed. Perhaps we did leave a little dent, but we were naïve about the depth, power, and viciousness of The Man. Witness the rip-off elections by George W. Bush and Company with the help of the Supreme Court; witness the combined conniving and business brutality of Wall Street and the banking and oil magnates that damn near sank the ship.

The comradery of our groups was enhanced by the in-the-trenches activities, being out there with picket signs and periodically getting our asses kicked and thrown in jail. The non-violent approach was and is the only way to get the message heard, but a lot of cops and ultra-right thugs don't give a damn about Mahatma Gandhi. Hey, but the sex was sizzling, what with the great push for sexual liberation and all. Even sign-of-the-cross cross-their-legs Latinas were into it... Ai, Chihuahua, going to hell for sure. We got more nookie in those days than any time before or since; prostitutes couldn't give it away.

Stop the War! Chicano Power! Que viva La Huelga! Make mine with cheese, please. Right on, my brother, right on!

Sweet Jesus!

March 1969. There was a comfortable old Asian café in North Beach—nothing special, from the '40s it felt. It was called The Bamboo Hut, located off Broadway on Sansome Street—hell, I don't know, around the corner from Enrico's. The food was fair-to-middlin' but I dug the ambiance and cheap drinks, it being so near the touristy-therefore-pricey Broadway bars. That little two-block stretch was pretty notorious, as I recall, for peep-shows and kinky shit ("How would you possibly know that?" you may ask.) Dismissing that segue, I share this little detail so what you're about to read won't come as much of a surprise.

I was still in the midst of my Chicano Power days when there was some sort of political pendejada going on most every day. We of course were tight with the other lefty groups, our Black, Asian, and White counterparts. It was not a time to take shit from any racist assholes or from any of our own raza that we felt were sell-outs.

Well, I'm not sure how this all came about, but back in San José my best friend was a cat named Tino Esparza, a very hip and dapper dude who was about ten years my senior. He knew a great deal about jazz, even had his own nightclub back in Texas before landing in Central California, and then settling in San José.

About that time Tino was hitting on a lady by the name of Alejandrina Espinoza, aka Alex—a wonderful, woke woman who taught Spinach at SJ City College, and that was a real plus. Tino's Spanish was almost as *horrible* (pronounced orrr-eee-blay) as my own.

Well, one Saturday I convinced Tino and Alex to come on an impromptu jaunt to The City with me and my gal, a perky Chicana whose name I've somehow forgotten and/or don't wish to remember … hmmm. So that evening we took in a little jazz on Upper Grant, followed by a visit to a club on Broadway, then went back to our car which just happened to be parked in front of … The Bamboo Hut. Hello.

But of course we went in for a nightcap before our SJ drive home. As it turned out we had a window seat and as we drank and rapped, every few minutes we'd catch the knockout shapes of the naughty ladies slinking by. Even in that outrageous neighborhood their glitter stood out, as well as everything else.

We were about ready to leave when I noticed a tall cat lurking in the shadow of a doorway directly across the street. I mean this dude with his flashy red Pachuco brim and rings the size of brass knuckles would make Superfly look like one of the super-straight bankers in the TransAmerica building that was just a block away.

I really hate to cop to it but I was quite full of righteousness about my politics and anyone who I thought was counter-revolutionary was fair game for my verbal assaults. So I told my friends to hang on for a minute, I'd be right back.

With all the force of Emiliano Zapata, Che Guevara, and Huey Newton all wrapped up in one bad and very drunk hombre, I then marched directly across the street (all five-foot eight, 170 pounds of me) and looked up into the face of this big, not-to-be-fucked-with gangsta.

Poking my finger up into his chest I said, "Listen, man! What you doin' ain't right! The Rev-o-lution will not tolerate this kind of bullshit; I mean get it togethah, punk!" (Well, no, I didn't call him a punk, that was Eastwood.)

No difference … the guy was flabbergasted; I mean in shock. He knew I had people in the café, he had to see it through the window, and he probably thought there was someone else out there with a gun aimed just a tad below that pimp-ass hat he was wearing. And with my Fidel beard and kamikaze attitude I wasn't quite what he was used to. He just kind of nodded his head and scanned the scene as I ranted.

About this time, fortunate for me, my friend Tino came through the door with a howling, joyous grito—you know, that voice, that scream you hear on Mexican Independence Day or when a bunch of crazy-ass Chicanos have reached the bottom of the tequila bottle.

Tino yelled to me, "Ay, Tomás, Alex an' me are getting' hitched and you're the best man!" I smiled, then turned to this character I was intimidating, put my finger in his chest, and said something to the effect of, "Remembah what I said, suckah, the rev-o-lution be watchin' yo' ass!"

I went back across the street to find that not only had Tino and Alex agreed to marry, they were doing it that night, Reno style. Reno, it turns out, is only about four hours east of Frisco, and real early that morning, maybe 4 or 5, the happy couple said, "I do" and gave the preacher man their fifty bucks, or whatever the price was then.

And I had learned in the course of that long, winding drive that I too had something to celebrate … just being alive! Turns out the character I was messin' with was the most notorious pimp in San Francisco.

Tino, "Man, do you know who that man was, do you have any idea?" Well, no, but I'm sure you're gonna tell me. Tino filled me in. Turns out the dude was the pimp-daddy for the entire region, went by the handle Sweet Jesus. Certainly not a person to piss off! "Fuck it," sez I, "I'll never see that fool again." We went on to have one hell of a weekend, even found some mariachis in one of the casinos. For some reason I drank more than usual, and that is an impossibility.

Mack Daddy of Monterey. I was very fortunate to live in the Bay Area a handful of years when the annual Monterey Jazz Festival was held in the early fall. God was it beautiful, "a setting beyond forgetting." The music, the people, the exhilarating smell of an ocean breeze.

And it was sexy as hell. As the days turned to night all these elements combined to produce some very memorable trysts … on two occasions I was even there with the same woman, a White chick who lived up around Palo Alto. She had a nice little sports car, only saw her twice and both times it was at this very special event. I think she had a beau, maybe a husband, but those weekends were ours. And when the final notes were blown we'd head to our motel room, spend the night, and head out the next morning. She'd drop me off in San José and head her way up to the bay.

But I do digress before I've even started. Yeah, *that cat.* I recall going up on one of those Monterey adventures with a couple of friends, instructors at SJ State, Carlos and Sally Iraheta. When we got there, being as sophisticated as they were, they of course like most everyone else went up to the ticket booth and paid for their admission. I told them I'd meet them inside in a little while, close to the front of the main stage.

I had a different kind of ticket that I was given as a kid back in Fresno. Often when a small group of us teenagers, three or four of us, wanted to play basketball but the outside court was closed, well, we'd just jump the fence. We don' need no stinkin' tickets! So I don't wish to lead anyone else astray but in those cocky young years it was kind of my responsibility not to pay. Besides, it's not like I had an extra fifty bucks on me.

Well, anyway, once over the fence I set out to meet my pals. The crowd was already pretty thick, like at the old county fairs. As I moved along I recall looking to my left, and there, propped up against a building wall was a familiar face. Jesus! It was him … yep, Sweet Jesus. That was about the last man I wanted to see, being both alone and relatively sober.

My dress at the time may have popped out a little, but frankly that was just the place for your glad rags. As I recall I was wearing my "special occasion" white bellbottoms and a colorful African dashiki … just friggin' cool. Oh, yeah, and I was carrying a bota bag strapped over my shoulder, filled with a half decent red wine. Well, buddy, seeing Sweet Jesus I was ready to guzzle that sucker.

When I got a little further along, I dared look back on The Mack, who I'm glad to say had other fish to fry that fine day. Soon I was with my friends in seats they had found up close to the front stage … damn, it just don't get no betta'. That afternoon I recall hearing Sly and the Family, stoned, Joe Zawenal and all, with Cannonball Adderley sounding like MLK on a saxophone … Mercy! Mercy! Mercy! Great sets, good friends, and not to be sacrilegious, but no fuckin' Sweet Jesus!

Elementary, My Dear Watson

My grades in elementary school were exemplary and the reason for this was quite simple: I was not dependent upon my crazy-ass parents for a friggin' thing. Just my own raw creativity and innate ability … and no damned homework. What with the unceasing chaos on the home front—and by unceasing, I mean just that, night and day, seven days a week of full-blown knock-down drag-out warfare—there is no way I could have produced a page of anything in those run-down shacks on E Street. E, I guess, for Excessive E-nebriation.

In spite of it all, in elementary I was the only kid from the entire West Side who was sent to art school "across the tracks" in the 5th and 6th grades, and I was already scribbling dippy ditties. This all changed dramatically when I reached Junior High. Suddenly and increasingly, we were asked to do homework ... home what? That singular word remains emblazoned on my mind because it altered my life significantly.

Going from A's to C's and D's—even a sporadic F—does something at some level to a kid. I can't say that it hurt on a conscious level—it didn't—but it took its toll over my six years in Junior and Senior High at Edison. Simply said, wherever there was the need for homework, I failed, clear and simple. Even where there was no need for homework, I was ill-prepared for anything scholastic, zilch encouragement. Only once in grade school do I remember my parents going to a parent-teacher meeting ... drunk on their ass, to my considerable embarrassment.

I just kind of stumbled along in high school, except for the few classes I had interest in, such as art, band (God bless that trombone), and typing (God bless June Lujano for unknowingly motivating me to take those classes!)

This of course carried through to college. I have dreamed all of my adult life about not completing my college degree, pretty nasty fantasies on the verge of nightmares, like not having the answers when being asked by a professor, not the proper academic answers. When all was said and done, though, I was simply not cut out for academia because I wasn't trained for it. I couldn't do homework in high school because of my emotion-laden home life: no desk, no space, no silence. In college I just didn't and wouldn't because I hadn't developed the habit, the routine, for study.

But there was even more to it than that: I could never bring myself to study subjects for which I had no interest, grades be damned. Kerouac, in *On The Road*, writes about the William Burroughs character: "... The things he learned were what he considered to be and called 'the facts of life,' which he learned not only out of necessity but because he wanted to." (Ironic, in that later in my life I had conversations with said Burroughs and lived briefly with his writer son, William, Jr.)

I just flat-ass wouldn't do homework, and for the most part, wouldn't attend classes. Some of the subjects, to top it off, I considered totally useless. All that, combined with my lack of study-savvy, accounted for some pretty mediocre grades throughout most of my college years.

Now, as to the exalted altar of academia, The Almighty Degree ... It's never been an overriding desire but more a nagging matter of pride. The pride of completion, a subliminal ache to finish what I started. I shoulda' picked up one of those damned things, a diploma...in psychology, sociology, anthropology, art, music or, for God's sake, creative writing. And I admit to being proud of my ol' buds—The Boys—for having toughed it out to pick up their diplomas.

But by the time I got to college I was already quite mad, I mean literally stark-raving lunatic-level fuckin' crazy! I couldn't sit in a classroom for any period of time—it was absolutely suffocating, I felt nervously closed in, we're talkin' class-trophobia! And I was still feeling the effects of my marriage-related breakdown, which in retrospect was just one more blow in a lifetime of PTSD.

The good news here regards unrelated factors contributing to my academic failure: to begin with, I was too busy participating in—being submerged in—the intoxicating whirlwind of the late sixties, booze, drugs, jazz, poetry, and The Revolution, right on, right on. Oh, and short skirts. For me, the enshrined sheepskin turned out to be more of a reference to prophylactics. My choice was to be a scoundrel rather than a scholar. My choice was elementary, my dear Watson, elementary.

Alan Watts meets Che Guevara

'69-ish. "May your bowels rot in hell for eternity!" roared the Reverend John Jones, who looked and sounded every bit like the middle-aged, defrocked minister played by Richard Burton in the movie *The Night of the Iguana*. I had never set eyes on this fellow until I heard that cavernous bellow aimed at me as I walked one mid-afternoon into the Interlude Bar & Grill in downtown San José.

At the time I was a student at San José State where I majored in Community Rabble Rousing and minored in Advanced Debauchery. As it turned out Reverend John Jones was the minister for the entire university, having been removed from the same position at the very radical San Francisco State College the previous year. The man did drink a mite and that may have played into his transfer; I never found out … but let's just say it would be a good bet.

He and I hit it off right off the bat because upon first hearing his outrageously jocular scream, I had no doubt I'd buy the man a drink—decades apart in years but soul brothers in so many ways. On one occasion I mentioned that the distinguished author and philosopher Alan Watts was the guest lecturer one year, and that though I'd had the opportunity on several occasions to attend his classes I chose not to.

Fact is I was so madly immersed in the Chicano Movement and the overall activism of that time and place a seemingly distant philosophy was hardly a priority. As it turned out Reverend Jones knew Reverend Watts very well, Bay Area boys with similar backgrounds and interests, including a penchant for a nip or two … or three.

Even before landing in San Francisco's famed Haight-Ashbury district, I was aware of Alan Watts as a guru of Taoism, Vedanta, and Buddhism. So when I reached my new home in The Haight, Mister Watts was way ubiquitous, I mean you couldn't drop into a coffee house or crash pad without someone sitting there paging through one of his Greatest Hits, like *The Supreme Identity*, *The Way of Zen*, *The Joyous Cosmology*, *The Book on the Taboo against Knowing who you are*, or *Psychotherapy East and West* … the audacity of those titles!

Turns out he was an ex-Episcopal priest, resigning it seems due to an extramarital affair—shades of *The Night of the Iguana* and *The Sandpiper*. In spite of it all, Watts evolved into a messenger of transcendental thought and practice. With his refusal to accept orthodox religions, he was a perfect fit for the hordes of young seekers across this and other Western countries.

The guy even had his own radio program on the still popular people's radio, KPFA, out of Berkeley. Still available are dozens of hours of audio that are in part captured in the *Out of Your Mind* series. And you can still "attend" his lectures on old videos, YouTube, and elsewhere; you can still get his ever-enlightening philosophy on CDs, DVDs, and of course in the 25 books he wrote.

The first book of his I ever read was in a funky little hippy haunt, an espresso house in The Haight. It was titled *This is It* … Hey, if *This is It* then why read anything else? Well, so it was that his teachings of The Way blended perfectly with what I was experiencing in real time.

But sadly I was pissed off because Watts' views seemed insensitive to my deeply passionate dedication to The Peoples' Struggle. How ignorant and shallow. I still kick myself in the ass for not attending his classes, but my heart just wasn't there at the time. I didn't have the spaciousness for consciousness … how friggin' lame is that? For me the "happening" was in the street, with the rallies, the placards, the picketing, and the perpetual petitions. I only attended one of his talks and walked out in the middle of it.

About a year later I had grown up a tad, was back to reading my Hesse and Jung materials, and was back on track with my pursuit of transcendent matters, for which my Chicano chums would chime in, "Tomás is in a universal bag." In other words, I wasn't totally towing the company line. Most of them respected me for my consistent activism but didn't appreciate this other "out there" aspect of my studies and direction. Oddly enough that was the best thing that I could have been doing for my various causes—raising my own internal awareness.

One day I was reading the local daily, the *San José Mercury News.* I noticed that a jazz musician that I appreciated, a smooth Brazilian guitarist named Bola Sete, was appearing in Sausalito at an upscale joint called the Trident. What a great environment, an intimate venue built to look like a landlocked Mississippi riverboat, just hanging over the water, offering terrific food and entertainment on a constant basis.

That very pleasant fall afternoon I filled the gas tank of my thumb and hit the freeway with nothing but a shoulder bag filled with a notebook and a small bottle of handy-dandy brandy. With my white bellbottoms, navy peacoat, and black beret, that fifty-mile stretch up to The City was always easy hitching but it was a bear getting to and across the Golden Gate Bridge to Sausalito. There was no easy pick-up stop for the racing traffic.

Nonetheless, "I made it to the church on time," time for the first set of Bola Sete, maybe eightish. There was a small cover charge, and of course you were expected to buy a drink or two, no problemo. My drink of choice (when I could afford it) was Courvoisier cognac, a high-end brandy, drunk from a snifter but of course ... ah, the very hip and smooth sounds of jazz

When the set was over, I was quickly out of there, one because the place was filled with couples, not a single babe in the place, and two, the drinks were too damned expensive. Oh, and three, because I really wanted to float about this intoxicating town, bopping from bar to bar along the waterfront. I had heard of Paterson's and the kicked-back No Name Bar, with a little patio for live jazz in the back (cool, huh?), and so I scooted up the main street, Bridgeway, to take in these inviting pubs. First the No Name, with an ambiance that fit its name, intimate and mellow, like the cognac I'd been sipping back at The Trident.

Then Paterson's, no jazz but a hell of a juke box and good conversation. Well, I must say, I was delighted but not totally surprised to find a certain buddy of mine, Reverend John Jones, loudly pontificating at the bar's end. Turns out that this was his regular haunt when not preaching and counseling at SJ State. He had lived there a few years earlier and still maintained a room somewhere within sauntering distance. Offered me a floor to crash on. Can you say propitious?

It didn't take us long to get into the thick of it. And somehow the conversation got around to my confession that I had really fucked up by not taking in the enlightening classes of Alan Watts the previous year at SJ State. John sez not to worry, how would I like to meet him, that he was a personal friend, and that Alan lived close by. I say sure, but when and where? Just about a mile up the road, he lives in a houseboat, sez the Rev. I'll give you the directions. Well hell yes!, sez I. John sez make sure to take a bottle of wine, the guy loves his vino. Right up my alley, the alleys of the valley being my mode.

This all happened, mind you, 'round midnight. So, I bid John adieu, grabbed a cab, stopped at a liquor store, snagged a couple bottles of decent vino, one white and one red. I tell the cabbie where I'm headed and he sez sure, I know the place, I'll take you right there. Within moments we're pulling up to a string of houseboats. I tip the cabbie, grab my gifts, and head up the rickety ramp of the designated houseboat—where I was soon to meet my mentor, or so I thought.

I rap on the door of this swaying home and guess what? The door slowly opens and what do I see? A fuckin' two-barrel shotgun aimed directly at my face. How enlightening is that? Yeah, like a hole in my head, ready to enter The Great Void. The guy asks what the fuck I want at this hour of the morning and I say, hey, hold on buddy, I was told my old friend Alan Watts lives here. Sez he, Nah, you got the wrong boat, he's the next one over. Slams the door shut. Nice guy.

By this time, I'm sure I needed to change my shorts, but hell, I was already there. So I open my backpack, pull out the brandy, and take a really strong snort, I mean I was severely rattled. I then compose myself and by this point, being brazenly blasted, stagger up the plank—maybe three feet wide—leading to the back of Watts' pad (which was in fact a converted ferry, the *S.S. Vallejo*). I'm so ripped I manage to slip off the side of the ramp and fall into the shallow water a couple of feet below. I am somehow able to land on my feet, though, hanging onto the ramp's side. I'm soaked up to my knees but still holding those two bottles. What a guy!

Try it again, Sam. This time I reach the door and loudly knock, but no one answers. However, within a couple of minutes I hear a voice, a recognizable voice, coming across like a gentle Wizard of Oz. Turns out the man has some sort of speaker set-up. He can see me it seems, but I can't see him.

He naturally asks who I am and what am I doing there. I tell him the whole story in condensed form, being a friend of his friend, the Most Reverend John Jones, almost getting my head blown off next door, falling off his plank but still hanging onto the bottles of wine I'm bringing to him as gifts, one white and one red. Oh, yeah, and because he's into raising folks' consciousness maybe he can help me with a plan I'm developing to turn people on … without drugs.

His response? The guy, after patiently listening to my ordeal, informs me in a manner befitting a great philosopher and spiritual guru, "Young man, your pro-cess is ceremonial and ritualistic." Not prah-cess, but pro-cess. Ceremonial. Ritualistic. Huh?

He then, in robe and slippers, greets me at the doorway with the clear stipulation that our little chat will only be for a moment or two. And that was about it. He quite cordially thanks me for the cordials. We converse oh so briefly and then he graciously boots me out … with a handshake and a mild smile, mind you.

In that brief span, I did have the opportunity to mention my idea of a portable venue that I called "The Om Dome," a high-tech acid hit without the drug, just mind-enhancing visuals with commentary and meditation education using the portability of Bucky Fuller's easier-than-a circus-tent geodesic structure.

That said, he does give me his home number and says call him sometime about my project, that he has some contacts that might be very interested in being supportive. I did call—ceremonially and ritualistically, of course—and he gave me the names and numbers of a couple of contacts that might be supportive, like the Hog Farm Commune. I excitedly jotted the information down in my little black book.

That afternoon I went back across the bridge to North Beach and got smashed in one of my favorite watering holes … or was it all of them? Before the night was over, along with losing my mind I also lost that little black book-of-amazing-characters. This loss of things of value, including people, was a pattern and a natural consequence of my voluntary obliteration. Lord, what fools we alkies be.

Lessons from The Glass Bead Game

1970, downtown SJ. That summer, playing chess and drinking the sweet Yugoslavian plum brandy known as Slivovitz with Marco Sajkovic, it occurred to me that just maybe college wasn't all it was cut out to be, not for me anyway.

I wasn't interested in "making it" in the traditional sense and my beatnik/ hippy values told me that, all in all, the priority of the educational system wasn't necessarily preparing me to find the holy grails of Truth, Wisdom, and

Art, but rather to hone "my little grey cells" to fit into the establishment. I was wrong. That was my simplistic, anarchistic brain at work and, truth be told, I was way off base as to my disparaging view of academia. It is what you make of it, and the opportunities are immense. Besides, the fact is I was not mentally stable enough to take advantage of this golden doorway.

Academentia. When I was a student at San José State's "New College" (an alternative curriculum for hyped-up and/or terribly creative students who didn't quite fit) I read a fair amount, but much of what I studied was not "required reading." I read what I was interested in and periodically reported to my professors, generally a synopsis of and speculation about what I found to have meaning and value for a more thoughtful and less materialistic life.

By and large I did not read novels because I simply had little interest, and frankly had little patience with such lengthy, intricate tales. I foolishly wanted to experience the "real things of life"—carefree joy, rich friendships, and even the angst and agony of everyday reality. (Not much of a reason not to read novels, the great ones, and take in the profundity, creativity, majesty, and beauty of those creations. I sometimes marvel at my ignorance and pray that I still have time to take in some of those great works.)

But I was drawn to certain fields—philosophy, psychology, sociology, astronomy, oh, and organic gardening—and I would periodically peruse books (both meanings of peruse) on those topics. I was fascinated with both the challenge and the promise of these branches of knowledge but just didn't have it in me to get a degree in any of them—that would have taken patience and focus, neither of which I possessed.

I did, however, read a few books within those categories. At the same time, I clearly decided not to educate myself via the traditional approach, that is I didn't force-read, certainly didn't study, in order to regurgitate answers to get good grades. Besides, it's tough sitting to read anything when one is either heavily intoxicated or recovering with a doozey of a hangover—oh, and still reeling from one hell of a life up to that point. To top it all off, my penchant was to be "on the road," the place where my destiny was to ultimately lead me.

But in that early period, I did somehow manage to read some of the works of the radical sociologists and the East-meets-West philosophers, like Alan Watts, and bits and pieces of the psychologist Carl Jung, a healer who looked beyond the sheerly scientific to unravel the mystery of our mind. (As was often the case, books like those of Jung and certain spiritually abstruse works were simply beyond my capacity to understand—I would have needed one of those darned intellekshul professors.)

And of course there was the Steppenwolf himself, Herman Hesse. I read damn near everything the man wrote. Novels, yes, but because of his Eastern bent I felt drawn to, at once spiritually, philosophically, and aesthetically magnetic. He wrote in a fashion that made complex ideas palatable, like in *Siddartha*, a somewhat fictionalized tale of the Buddha. The richest and deepest of his gems is, in my opinion, the voluminous, brooding *Magister Ludi: The Glass Bead Game.*

Magister Ludi translates from the Latin to "Master of The Game." (The stem "lud" means both "school" and "game," which in this case is significant in both senses). Who is The Master, why is he The Master, and what is the game? Intriguing, no? Unfortunately for the impatient reader, the introductory chapters of this futuristic novel kind of drag along about life in Castalia, the fictional European province that is home to an austere order of intellectuals … yawn. But Hesse was just setting us up.

I started reading it during a humdrum summer as boring as the book's first pages, a season highlighted by nothing, not deserving of a single exclamation point. Thank God for Marco's Yugoslavian stuffed bell peppers and plum brandy … Ziveli!

But then at an abrupt turn in the book there's a cosmological shift, suddenly in his summer of life our hero Joseph Knecht (Knecht, by no coincidence, is German for servant) reluctantly comes to life in his quiet, introspective way, starts questioning the very foundation of the system of which he has been appointed the leader.

After a lifetime of focused ambition and academic prowess he decides not to be a milquetoast mouwess; after being crowned by his peers as Magister Ludi he suddenly realizes that, having attained the highest position from which to teach matters of culture, philosophy, and art, he himself is still unsure of the ultimate value, integrity, and veracity of "the game" and so has the nagging suspicion that his own tidy ritual might just be missing something ultimately of equal or even more importance than he finds in his academic perch.

He is steeped in Western intellectualism but is a virgin in the world beyond its rigid doors, beyond the *study* of life, an innocent in the direct experience of it all. He makes his break and seeks wisdom in deeper pools where he is to meet his fate. It is that font of transcendent knowledge that I have long sought, and Magister Ludi helped me crystallize my Eastward trek.

ClariTea

Sit and sip it quietly
Sans angst or anxiety
(Calmate' y callete'!),
With you, my friend, I share

A cup of soothing ClariTea,
It's good for all disparity,
Without attachment, charity,
Like fresh, clean mountain air.

I swear in all sincerity,
Sup a cup of ClariTea
(In this day and age a rarity
From New Zealand to Zaire).

It's up beyond sobriety
(No boring apple piety!),
A veritable variety
Of conscious savoir faire.

A splendid spot of ClariTea!
A piping pot of ClariTea!
Forsooth, I share this verity:
There's nothing to compare!

January 2, 2000

Cocktails and Food at the Interlude

"Modesty is for people who have something to be modest about."—So said Professor Louis Mangani with a somewhat snide snicker.

While still a student at San José State I would systematically find myself late each afternoon at a tasteful little downtown cocktail lounge and supper club called The Interlude (which we fondly dubbed The Inner Tube), a friendly getaway filled with witty repartee, a respite from the pervasive pressure of collegiate measure and the rigmarole of the teacher's role.

This conversational salon was replete with drunken professors, philosophers, and cats who just fell in from the street, often quite literally. With comfortable dark leather seating against the wall in the rear of the establishment, its large dinner tables provided the setting for "a moveable feast" of mostly imported teachers, artists, writers, and bon vivants who, following each evening's mini soirée at The 'Lude, would move on to yet another bar or to someone's home where the whole dance would go on into the wee hours, jazz, more cocktails, and personal dramas. (Lou Mangani, we miss you!)

There was no shortage of top-notch academicians and wise elders hanging in that bar. San José, among other things, had become a mecca for serious art students and, not by chance, the fellow who held court every night at The Tube was the head of the Art Department, Dr. Richard Tansey (who, along with his co-author, Horst de la Croix, wrote what was then arguably *the book* on art history, a tome titled *Art through the Ages*).

Tansey, incidentally, had a martini named after him—a *Tansey,* but of course. I once asked him what made this any different from a regular martini and he pointed out that it did not have an olive. "Imagine how much gin will have been displaced over the years with that damned olive!" Makes sense to me.

One of his closest chums was the aforementioned Professor Louis Mangani, aka Lou, who was a lovable little man, eccentric thoroughbred, full-blown intellectual lush who, with his vodka drink held daintily in one hand and forefinger pontifically circling on the other, would sit amongst us just waiting to share his terribly insightful comments about most everything.

The man was a hell of a teacher, a dynamo of a cook (but always leaving the kitchen looking as if a tornado had hit), and a giant amongst neurotics. When he broke the lens on one side of his thick reading glasses he just put scotch tape across the crack and wore them like that for months.

When I told Lou that he not only looked like Ratso Rizzo of *Midnight Cowboy* fame but sounded like and behaved like the guy, he admitted that he went to see the flick but had to abruptly walk out of the theatre because the similarity was "too damn scary."

And there was Henry O. Johnson, deadly handsome English instructor from City College who dressed and looked like a young Mark Twain. Henry, with a soft smile and a glimmer in his eyes, always had one of two remarks to make when anyone said anything about anything, "I think you're on to something" or "You can do no wrong" … I think he was on to something.

Rounding out the regulars was an attractive couple, Professors Carlos and Sally Iraheta (Carlos and his parents, who were Hispanic, were nonetheless rounded up to be sent to an American concentration camp—euphemistically called "internment camps"—during the Second World War because their last name *sounded* Japanese); gourmand Sam Trolongo, a sweet, relatively silent dude who knew a hell of a lot but would wisely just sit and listen; and Lou Vierra, a guy in his early 50s who was an addiction counselor at Stanford yet still drank like a fish. He was a gay dude who, as he got increasingly plastered, would tell the same story again and again about the love of his life. He spoke with a lisp but since he was Portuguese that provided a little cover for certain swishy words.

The anecdote of Lou's went something like this (without the lithp): "There we were, a small group of us in a taxi headed up the road for a night in San Francisco. My guy was sitting on my lap because the car was soooo full. We stopped at a red light and it simply seemed *like foreverrrr* because even after the light changed our driver just sat there. My guy soooo cutely says, 'Hey, driver, that's the only shade of green they have.'" Lou, it was kind of funny the first time.

On one particular afternoon at The 'Lude (I'd usually hit it about five or so) the place was damn-near empty. I found a stool at the bar and within minutes this middle-aged Black guy blows in and sits a couple of seats down. I, donning my usual bar-talk mask, ask, "Hey, there, how yah doin'?" We introduce ourselves—Eddie was his name—and we start yakkin'. Like many an exchange, here comes his story that sounded like an old blues tune: "My baby done left me …"

It went like this: He and his ol' lady had a great little business back somewhere in the deep South—I never found out exactly where. His best friend schemed on his lady and the two of them somehow hooked up, grabbed what they could from the business—money, files, even pots and pans—and split. Cold-blooded! The man had tears in his eyes and either he was one hell of an actor or this shit was true.

By this time I was well aware of the synchronistic nature of my meeting various significant "Eddies" along my path, starting with my foster brother. So I inherently wanted to help the guy. "Well, Eddie," I asked, "what exactly did you folks do?"

"We had us ah bah-bee-que," said he in that familiar southern Black accent that I had grown up with, "We was doin' good."

"Eddie," I offered, "I think I can hook you up for some bucks for your business." Basically, it was funding for small businesses that had been set up for minority entrepreneurs, even with a very little background check … that's the way it was back in the day. I gave him an address and phone number and said to mention my name. Shortly thereafter he thanked me and split the scene.

About two months later I was walking a couple of blocks from the campus and there, across from the M & J market at 7th and Williams, in a building that once housed a barber shop in its downstairs space (think *Cheers,* the bar in the TV program), I noticed a freshly painted sign in the window: "Eddie's Fast Chili Dogs." Could it be?

He had chosen the name to attract the college students. Fast and cheap was the suggestion but, as it turned out, his menu was much more than a quickie hot dog … it was a full-blown barbeque joint, with callah' greens, links, ribs, and suthin' fried chicken.

He welcomed me with open arms, pulled out a couple of Miller High Life beers—the choice of brothers back in the day—and said, "Brutha' Tom, this be yo' table." The table it turned out was right next to a window where I could look up and check out the legs of the pedestrians, most of them en route to class. Short skirts were in vogue. Near a college campus. Get the picture?

I managed to get fucked-up in record time and, looking up at those shapely gams, I had a most wicked thought: How come all the charts, the profile images of prehistoric people—our ancestors—were only profiles of men? Never once did I see a nice side shot of a Neanderthal, Cro-Magnon, or Australopithecine *woman*, butts and tits proudly busting out. Which, in my spacey mind, indirectly—I don't know how—led me to scribbling the following ditty on a greasy napkin: An anthro-apology, a dig, if you will, titled

Australopithecus, Yo' Daddy or My Robe is from Nairobi

Doctor Leaky's slightly stocky knuckle-walking clue,
Eddie's fast chili dogs and bad-ass bar-bee-que,
There is no missing link, there is no missing link,
Always was and always is, *I am* therefore I think.
(Descartes before de horse?)

Anyway, I ate and drank free for many a day and remain forever grateful for the little table at Eddie's Fast Chili Dogs where I had the rare opportunity while looking up through that wide wonderful window to have observed beavers in their natural habitat.

A Doctorate in Drunkology

Back at The Interlude saloon/salon, a gathering of the going and gone, an extension course for extra-curricular carousers and collegiate hangers-on, an old professor, his elbow slipping off the side of the bar, shared this most insightful observation as regards the levels of academic achievement: "Well, guys," he schaid schlurring, "there are three levels of college schertificates:

1. B.S.—Bull Shit
2. M.S.—More Shit, and
3. Ph.D.—Pile High Deep

Well, Buddy, I think I've hit Numero Tres, the deep stuff, and deserve that piece of papyrus—no doubt I'm way full of it. And I should be given that certificate if for no other reason than hitting more pubs on the West Coast, mostly while hitchhiking from San Diego to Vancouver, than any other fool on the planet. (There is, incidentally, a Vancouver, Washington, right across the bridge from Portland, Oregon, and I even had a cocktail or two there, in a jazz haunt where I grooved during a fabulous Ray Charles set).

Limer-Hicks

In college I was introduced to a form of raunchy poetry called the limerick. Here's a somewhat academic take on the subject: Gershon Legman (no relation to Foghorn Leghorn), compiled the largest, most scholarly anthology on the topic.

He held that "The true limerick as a folk form is always obscene, and cites similar opinions by Arnold Bennett and George Bernard Shaw, describing the clean limerick as an object of magazine contests, rarely rising above mediocrity … the form is essentially transgressive; violation of taboo is part of its function." A-ha! No wonder I loved the stuff.

But the truth is that these days, given late night yucking and online fucking, the limerick is mild and even archaic. With that in mind, please allow me to offer a handful of spontaneous attempts at this risqué form of litter-ature, all written after one properly debauched night. It's four in the morning and, as you will observe, I should go back to bed:

There was a gay hick from the sticks
who hitched with some biker chicks,
so on this rally of bikes
(Harleys and the likes)
he mistakenly thought dikes meant dicks.

There was a young lady from France,
who had ants in her pants,
Came an exterminator named Arnold
who was so darn old
he pissed down his leg while she danced.

There was an old lady named Myrtle
too slow to run, jump, or hurdle,
On the path to her mail
she was humped by a snail
Then mounted by an old turtle.
(It all happened so fast.)

There was a young lady from Fresno
whose sex you couldn't guess, no!
In a car, on a bench
be it dude, be it wench,
you can bet the lady never sez no.

You try rhyming with Fresno, dammit. Go back to bed, Tommy! ... hey, you know, maybe Shakespeare did write all of his own stuff.

Buddying up with the Mayor of San Francisco

San José to Santa Cruz. I'll never forget my first day up that wicked, winding Highway 17, a dangerous 32 mile drive even when sober. I had made the near fatal mistake of letting my Slivovitz-guzzling buddy, Marco Sajkovic, drive my car because I was way too loaded to get behind that wheel. Little did I know *he didn't know how to drive at all!* By the time we got to the then-little coastal town, less than an hour away, I was dead sober (at least not dead) and desperately in need of a brew or two.

We pulled into the first saloon we spotted, right there where all the roads intersect: Highway 17, Highway 1, Highway 9, the winding road from Ben Lomond, and the roads from downtown, Front Street and Pacific. It was a funky little joint, beer and wine only, great burgers and a pool table … I forget the name. It didn't take long to get juiced and begin taking in the local color.

Marco sat starry-eyed with his new girlfriend that he had dragged along and I focused on the pool table. I chatted with a fellow shark—well, I was more of a porpoise—to frolic with.

Then someone walked in and turned on the television set—the fucking television set! —a sizable black and white '50s sci-fi looking thing with rabbit ears that was rigged up on a table in one of the corners. I always felt that there was something insidious about those damned things, and I sure as hell didn't think an up-and-coming hippy bar was a suitable atmosphere for such a capitalist-spewing monstrosity.

With little effort and no restraint, I picked up my pool cue and, using the heavy end, sent it hurling into the TV screen. The little crowd in there probably figured I was a violent nut and didn't want to fuck with me (I could hardly blame them).

I knew I had screwed up and went up to the owner—a fellow long-hair—with an offer to pay for the set and, to soften it a bit, explained my anti-materialistic logic. He stared intensely at me for a second—I thought oh, shit, here come the pigs! But no, instead he smiled and bought me and the house a beer! Such things happened back then, when long hair meant something.

Afternoon became evening, and at one point I found myself in the head, pissing next to a grubby-bearded character who called himself The Archbishop Prince Jesus Christ Satan, with his dirty, once-white Bible-style robe, sloppy lipstick job, runny mascara, and more makeup than Tammy Faye Bakker ever dreamed of. He had been in the saloon during my outburst, and so apparently I had passed his test. Scary. He looked over at me and remarked, "You know, it takes a lot of work being this fuckin' crazy!" Yep, I concurred, it ain't easy being sleazy. I found out later that he had run for Mayor of San Francisco and actually got quite a few votes … I think he would have done a swell job.

Barroom Bards

During my travels I did pick up some bits and pieces of real brilliance from those shithole sonnets, enduring masterpieces, many of which could be found on the walls of raunchy restrooms reeking with timeless classics like:

> Here I sit broken hearted …
> Tried to shit but only farted.

Oh, and classier yet, found in the Ladies Room of a Portland pub (Man, some of those chicks can be every bit as gross as foulmouthed men … gender equality!) So what was I doing in the women's head, you ask? Looking for wisdom, but of course:

> Here I sit amidst the vapor …
> Who's the bitch who stole the paper?

Now how can you top that? Well, I gave it a shot…and though theoretically intriguing, it's a little too … hmmm … head-y:

> The universe in itself doesn't fit…
> Aren't you glad you took a shit?

Well it doesn't, it just doesn't … that's why the Big Wheel keeps on turnin'. The whole *is more* than the sum of its parts. Do not be misguided … There is always something new under the sun.

Catalystic Synergy

Santa Cruz, The Holy Cross. The original Catalyst coffeehouse and nightclub back in the mid-'60s was just that, a catalyst, perhaps the greatest gathering place for mad artists, hot musicians, and long-haired intellectuals of all shades from Portland to The Netherlands. This coastal-non-postal establishment was all that, *hot* and *cool* at the same time.

The Catalyst was located on the first floor of an historic hotel, the St. George, lavishly re-built after the original burned down in the Great Fire of 1894. The owner then was San Francisco millionaire Anson P. Hotaling, who named his new hotel after St. George, the knight who conquered the fire-breathing dragon... Ironic that it was fire yet again that burned it down in 1990, an absolute loss of unrecapturable ambience.

That marvelous pre-Art Deco environment was the most glorious combination of funky hotel, bar, coffee house, restaurant, music hall, meditation room, dope exchange, and pissoir this side of Paris in the '20s, perhaps the only establishment with all of this going on under one roof. Right there by the ocean and boardwalk and redwoods and rivers, the very epicenter, it was without debate the coolest hang on the West Coast, and that's sayin' a lot.

The entire place was a living Hieronymus Bosch canvas, just oozing creative character. I found myself transported back in time to the dreamlike setting in Fresno I so loved as a child, the White Theatre—built in 1914—with its stylish opera balconies and ornate ceiling ... except here I played with grown-ups acting like kids.

The Catalyst, built partially in the livery stable of that once opulent hotel, did not suffer from the fact that its new owner was Randall Crane, an ex-dean of the San Francisco Art Institute, who purchased and developed the venue.

Of Which the Angelic Doth Sing

The voices cannot help themselves,
They are not quiet in matters of beauty,
impressions of divinity,
and they are not quiet
in matters of degenerate souls.

The voices speak in raindrops,
at times comforting
with veils of opium and chocolate.
They sing from the cliffs
over a stormy winter ocean
pounding wayward travelers
with haunting choruses,
full and glorious choirs,
distinct and devastating.

They warn of the jagged rocks below,
of unspeakable and terrifying fates,
They warn of the dark intervals
between the old and the new moon
when demons masquerade as joy.

The voices cannot help themselves of duty,
They bless us with exalting guidance,
They transmute irony to gold
and tragedy to wings.

O Praise these celestial choirs and the heavens
from whence they doth come,
Praise each voice and each note
and each sacred breath,
and praise beyond all song and all poetry
The beloved composer
of which the angelic doth sing.

A Healthy Helping of High-Ku

In spite of my frequent lack of the necessary reflection of nature and her seasons within the traditional haiku form, here are a handful of my less-than-formal contributions to those inscrutably screwy seventeen-syllable sketches (hsssss!) of impenetrable profundity:

Internet cut off,
without smart phone or TV …
time to sip my tea.

Politics be damned!
Nothing to get hung about …
Strawberry fields.

Landlord will not wait!
Diarrhea will not wait!
Nature will not wait!

Again, without doubt,
morning brings a ray of light—
something to crow about.

A single red rose
heavy from the drenching rain
warms my wintry heart.

That lovely grey moth,
lovelier than butterflies,
ate my fucking coat!

Note: Little did I know that my life-long love of this enigmatic form, haiku, would help keep me on the path of my quest, always wondering about the Japanese adoration of a simple nature poem. But it was within this very form that I later fully appreciated the "oh!" and the "ah!" of it, within this and the equally mystifying koan.

Paradise on the Precipice

(Written on the Fourth of July, 2020)

Flash Backward and Forward. "The mind is its own place, and of itself can make a heaven of hell, a hell of heaven." In 1667, when Milton first published his epic poem *Paradise Lost*, newspapers did not exist, radio did not exist, television did not exist, and social media was beyond science fiction, which also did not exist.

We still have that heaven-or-hell option, but time and again we tend to make the latter choice. Why is that? We could simplify and say, "poor decisions," but I'm afraid it's not that simple. Then you must ask, "Why do we make poor decisions?" As we drill down and look around in the caverns and taverns of our mind, in the dark places, there is an odd and almost evil attraction to the alluring things we find. And that is precisely the word … *things.*

So many of us are so captured by heightened sensations of the senses that we are ignorant of the cause. What does our obsession really mean and what does it do to each one of us and to the world in general? Is this attraction to things bad, is it immoral? Is it even unnatural? The short answer is no. After all, we are clothed, housed, fed, and entertained with things; our sexual attractions are certainly of the senses. But when we cling to anything—*any thing*—we are no longer in control; we have become imprisoned by that object.

And for that reason we are vulnerable to the manipulation of others; for that reason we self-destruct. Whether this "pull" is from a political environment, that of dictators, oligarchs, and capitalists, whether from the domination of a given religion, from the motives of family and social relationships, or from the primordial pull of sex, we are swayed by circumstances that most of the time we are not even aware of.

Frequently we have been indoctrinated by what Vance Packard in his 1957 classic termed *The Hidden Persuaders*. "A brisk, authoritative and frightening report on how manufacturers, fundraisers and politicians are attempting to turn the American mind into a kind of catatonic dough that will buy, give or vote at their command."—*The New Yorker.*

Packard's worry has for decades unfortunately come to be the case. Using the sophisticated psychological techniques of the advertising industry our craving for possessions and flimsy power have become the breeding ground of a pandemic of obsessions and addictions. Even our daily life is greatly molded by the apparatus that has manipulated us to Buy! Buy! Buy! or think this way or that. The multitudinous "hidden" factors that influence our daily lives is layered beyond immediate calculation, especially now with the algorithms of social media.

But the fact is *we do have a choice* and we needn't live in a mental prison (and often a real one) because of our passion for material objects and our acceptance of fragmented and destructive thought.

In spite of the sick and premeditated propaganda of all types of media, old and new—yes, that old term "brain washing" still applies—most of us still possess the power to break the bonds of our addictions in all of its forms and not submit to what we inherently know is wrong. By clearing our minds we can spot the hucksters, mucksters, and shucksters.

In my poem *Existential Soufflé* I wrote, "Though thought is treasured this meal is measured by the things we do." Yes, ideas have consequences but making the right choice is only the first step … it is what we do then that "stirs the existential roux."

Existential Soufflé

Our dish shall start with Jean-Paul Sartre,
a dash of Albert Camus,
then scramble a ramble of Kierkegaard
for our experiential roux—
Though thought is treasured
this meal is measured by the things we do.

"If the doors of perception
were cleansed daily," reckoned Billy Blake,
"then man could see quite clearly."
Well, kind of, almost, nearly,
well, maybe, give or take.

When Huxley dropped his Owsley tab
the doors did open widely,
and the mushrooms spoke to that blown-out bloke
who puffed his grass so idly;

When Morrison lit his fire on the spire by the sea
he became a rider on the storm of LSD.
Again the doors came open
and the truth shall set you free.

Saints Aquinas and Augustine
drank from Saint Bernard's barrel,
breaking bread, hearing The Dead,
while the Gentiles ran feral;
The High Priests fretted, had John beheaded,
then sung a Christmas carol.

Reading The Gita with a chimp named Chitta
The Buddha begged to dine;
His bowl was filled but his mind was stilled
while Chitta-vritti drank his wine.

Chuang Tzu paddled his bamboo boat
on The Yellow River, rowing
without oars he floated his craft
into the Cloud of the Unknowing;
bowing to the Tao Te Ching he kept his tai chi flowing.

Han Shan was an uncarved block
aside the road less taken,
he lived away from society's sway
preferring beans to bacon,
without desire he put out the fire,
his silence stirred, not shaken.
Above the fights and skirmishes
of the brutal sheiks of gloom
swirling, swirling swerved the dervishes
as the poet Rumi bloomed,
but like wasabi was the hot Wahhabi
who threw him to his doom.

Meister Eckhart softly, secular,
spoke in the vernacular, "Power to the people!"
The Inquisitors looked down with a firm frown
and hung him from the steeple.

Into the fire, burning,
is where the mystics were tossed,
their dance was their undoing
and The Church, their final cross.
It is the cheek turning
that churns the secret sauce.

In Praise of the Invincible

1940. When Nazi Germany invaded and after Paris fell, French philosopher Albert Camus had an epiphany: "In the depth of winter I finally learned that within me lay an invincible summer." Though an atheist he felt that, if nothing else, life itself is quite worth living and fighting for. Politically an anti-communist leftist he may not have believed in a distant heaven but kept alive the hope that humanity was capable of building a harmonious society in this world.

2020. Now, in the middle of a certainly historic summer that is testing our invincibility, we are all bombarded by an avalanche of horrific news and death is literally a breath away. The climate crisis remains out of control, with wildfires and ferocious tumult on land and sea; scientists point to man-made sources that have stoked this devastation.

A consequence of the parallel pandemics of Covid and climate change is the deafening terror of those who live day-to-day, not sure if they will have a home tomorrow or even a meal. Addictions of all sorts and other mental health issues have dramatically risen as therapy sources are more difficult to find or afford. The viciousness of global, national, and local politics has dramatically increased our anxiety with unbridled social media to spike polarization among the people.

And to add to this is the unleashing of the far-right fascist/racist movement in America that have caused alarm for democracies around the world. The frightening reality is that Donald Trump remains in office and is overt about his intention to stay in power, democracy be damned. He has built a fence to keep civility out.

Fascism, Nazism, Authoritarianism, call it what you will, has coalesced its followers here and abroad reminding us of mankind's horrific history of oppression and worse, like the genocide of the Jews and Armenians. The Second World War had its own dictators in the formidable forms of Adolf Hitler, Benito Mussolini, and Joseph Stalin. These people represent present-day archetypes of a latent darkness lurking in the primitive brain.

In 1776, Enlightenment philosopher Thomas Paine wrote a series of inspiring pamphlets aptly titled *The American Crisis* to bolster a fledgling revolutionary army. This writing was so stirring that General George Washington, full knowing the dream of a free country was at stake during that pivotal winter in Valley Forge, ordered Paine's initial pamphlet to be memorized by his officers and read to their troops. Its very first line is one with which we are all familiar, "These are the times that try men's souls."

With so many destructive forces all about it is difficult to find personal peace, let alone even contemplate universal peace. The work of conscious and compassionate people is an enormous task but I maintain that truth and goodness will ultimately win out, will be victorious. This steadfast conviction is not based on prayer or faith alone but on the synergistic power of unceasing non-violent social activism, conscious media, and the potential of exponential change. I do not underestimate the astounding power of human creativity and dedication, and the ability of most people, at some point, to come to their senses. Everything is possible.

All of this said, I need to stress that when weaponized by social media these "hidden persuaders" are nothing less than *the manipulation of our biology.* This is the point of the 2021 Nobel Peace Prize recipient Maria Ressa of the Philippines. In a most insidiously calculated manner, we are bombarded with the repetition of lies ... like Trump's Big Lie. Say it enough times and, for the gullible, it becomes true.

Over time, the following of this folly becomes an addiction. Gullible people are first snagged by their deepest emotions of fear and hatred; then with increasing repetition of the same lies they're drawn in deeper and deeper to the point that some are capable of the worst of crimes. The infamous attack of January 6th and ethnically motivated, multiple mass shootings are a clear result.

The best defense on this aggressive attack on our mind is to be aware of how this all works, and that there are viciously calculating people behind the scene who wish to control us for any number of reasons. When we understand what is going on, when we develop our consciousness, we can soon spot the efforts of these social media sociopaths and recover from our downward spiral.

Jeta's Grove

In the old park called Jeta's Grove
magpies repeated empty words,
picked at fallen mangoes
left by other birds;

On the virescent path in Jeta's Grove
a priest stumbled in the mist
while trying to carve eternity,
eternity in his fist.

In the open field of Jeta's Grove
came merchants, monks, and kings
seeking the lost knowledge,
the knowledge of all things.

In the forest theatre called Jeta's Grove
came the music heard by none,
sweet music of The Dharma
that no one heard—not one.

Note: Jeta's Grove is a park in Northern India where the enlightened Prince Siddhartha Gautama, The Buddha, gave most of his earliest sermons and discourses. Known as Jetavana, it is located just outside the old city of Savatthi. It exists now as a gated archeological site and a sacred mecca for Buddhist pilgrims.

Above photo and design by *moi*, taken circa 1995 while living in exile in Fresno, California. It was during that time when I took a 16-week Vipassana meditation course and came to discover my Original Face.

The Concrete Buddha

Just being on my no-holds-barred karmic quest, hardly heroic but neither stoic, I have been so blessed as to have found a path so vast in beauty and love I can hardly contain the mention of. But then this tranquil joy, though calm, is not to be contained as is the universe itself ordained.

The path continues to ground me in gratefulness and inner comfort; it is this way of meditation, along with reverent prayer and contact with Spirit that anchors me in this tumultuous sea.

This elevated state of being, however, is not without considerable flux, and matters of the world and daily needs tend to tug at my activities, such as earning a living, oh, and eating—yes, like so many seniors I still have to crack the monthly nut.

Fortunately for me I have my Concrete Buddha. I've carried him with me for over forty years now, living in my gardens and sometimes in the house (but he must remove his flip-flops). He teaches me a lesson now and then, patience being one of them—I do so wish he'd hurry! And when I have to move him, about 50 pounds of solid cement, I just say, "He's not heavy, he's my Buddha."

Following is a series of nine consecutive Haikuesque poems with, as you will see, a common theme.

Shrine of the Concrete Buddha

The concrete Buddha
quiet in my busy mind
sits just sits and sits.

The concrete Buddha
scent of roses in full bloom
sits just sits and sits.

The concrete Buddha
sounds of city in his ears
spiders spin their webs.

The concrete Buddha
I wash the sparrow droppings
he just sits and sits.

The concrete Buddha
wet and cold the moss grows old
at his lotus feet.

The concrete Buddha
of Nagasaki's furnace
utters not a sound.

The concrete Buddha
hands in lap, no hands, no lap
cross-legged without legs.

The concrete Buddha
unattached to black or white
rainbows from his eyes.

The concrete Buddha
unattached to this or that
ah, the universe.

And so ends Book One of *Zen Matador*, the memoir of the drunk-as-a-skunk monk Tomás Chavez, also humbly known as The Great Tomasso, or formally Tomás Jesús Chavez de la Fuente de Juveniles Perrenes y Prostitutas Benditas (Tommy Jesus Chavez of the Fountain of Perennial Juveniles and Blessed Prostitutes).

Comin' up next … I'll be darned if there ain't even a few synchronistic epiphanies, symphonies of the soul, and a whole slew of truly incredible characters I've had intercourse with (intellectual, that is, and sometimes not), many of them you might have heard of if you're over forty, like Della Reese (*Touched by an Angel* … and she was!), sassy songstress Sarah Vaughn, poet Allen Ginsberg, Country Joe McDonald, and *Cuckoo's Nest* novelist Ken Kesey.

And did I mention Lawrence Ferlinghetti, William Burroughs, Charles Bukowski, "The Laureate of Low Life," and a drink with Bill Murray who wasn't in a hurry? How 'bout Sir George Shearing (good on the hearing!), Rev Jesse Jackson for social action, oh, and was it Cheech and Chong and who knows who with whom I had a toke or two? Yep, dinner and doobies with those two … make it three. Well, it all happened, yessiree, fine, just truckin' down ol' 99.

Can you say, "name dropper?" Will adventures with the fascinating characters I've chanced to encounter help my book ring up at the counter? … Oh, Lord, won't you buy me a Mercedeeez-Benz? … Yep, a krew of Krazy Frenz … an' Janis too, late one night right out of the blue! … mustn't forget The Smothers Brothers and a bunch of kooky others. Shameless, you say. Capitalist pig, you say. No comments.

So you might want to take a break, go pee, grab some popcorn and peanuts and Pepsi … oh, my! … and come on back to your seat for the riveting **Book Two** of this breathtaking Double Creature Feature!

Book Two

THE FOUNTAIN OF YOU

From an Oddball Odyssey
to finally find Om, Sweet Om

(1971 to 2024)

Intro to Book Two

This portion of my memoir by and large covers my final years of collegiate carnality con mis carnales at San José State (1971-73); *The Lost Years* (1980 through 2000—though one might rightly argue they were all lost); and finally, close to the present, *Return of The Cool* (2001-2024).

Here the author finds himself in seclusion within a cloistered monastery in a remote region of Tibet … Would you believe on a pilgrimage to a whorehouse in Reno? It moves from subterranean slime to prime sublime, with little in between. If there's a point then maybe it's that life, in spite of ourselves, is a bit o' alright—or, like the Volkswagen bumper-sticker has it, Fukengrüven.

And with all of my kidding about my birthplace, Fresno, isn't it obvious that happiness and peace is really within you, no matter how funky your home may have been? Oh, Auntie Em, I'll never leave Fresno again—yeah, right. In an old western classic, *The Man from Laramie*, actor James Stewart is asked where he's from. He says in that distinctive, soft-spoken voice, "Well, I figure my home is wherever I'm at at the time."

Veritable Quandaries. When I first sat down to write this book I was filled with major contradictions and philosophical conundrums (use the lubricated ones), and a sense of real need for reconciliation in certain matters, e.g., What the hell drove me nuts to begin with? Is there an effective therapy for all forms of madness, or do we just grin and bear it? And, of course, on the macro scale, "Why doesn't God involve Itself with the man-made atrocities that kill so many innocent people?"

I do my best to tackle these Big Questions while living in this temporal space, with all of its hiccups, kerfuffles, and most trivial of trifles—that's the trouble with tribbles! I've done so first and foremost for myself. I've done so while darting and dodging within the daunting gauntlet of unresolved nightmares. I've done so by studying, yes, but mostly by cogitating on the compelling and perplexing experiences of my own life, trying to make sense of the surreal yet very real things that have happened to me.

In this volume I try to share highlights, lowlights, and the ever-severing no-lights, as in lights out, blitzed, blasted. After all I've learned about the terrible consequences of such extreme consumption, I still fall off that wagon now and then, and bash my hard head on the indifferent cement—addiction is a bitch!

But more important, I demonstrate how it's possible to get it together no matter how deep the hole one has dug. Can you dig it?

Now ... envision yourself seated for a late evening show in the back row of a reeeally old movie theatre (as in reel-y), with the silhouette of the audience in front of you. Teenagers smooching, little kids stuffing candy into their fat cheeks, and a tall guy sitting where he shouldn't be. The lights dim, and you can hear the whirrrrr of the film projector ... the second feature begins.

The Blob goes to a Midnight Horror Show

Introducing my bulbous bud, *The Blob.* Made in 1958, this original was to become a classic and it was the creature's leading role debut. There have been three re-makes since but none as feel-good hokey as the first. And, to be fair, it was also Steve McQueen's debut as a movie star.

Script-wise the flick sucked big time but was a great make-out show ... it even had a sequel, *Son of Blob.* Hey, and what a catchy little theme song, composed by Burt Bacharach, no less, and sung by a one-hit-wonder group who called themselves The Five Blobs (real creative dudes).

In spite of mediocre lyrics, the tune made it onto the hit list ... "Beware of the blob, it creeps and leaps and glides and slides across the floor, all around the wall, a splotch, a blotch ... Be careful of The Blob!" Scary shit! You'll get a kick out of this one: just search "The Blob theme song" on YouTube.

Escape from Freedom

> "Keep you doped with religion and sex and TV
> and you think you're so clever and classless and free,
> but you're still fucking peasants as far as I can see,
> a working-class hero is something to be."—John Lennon

1971. As mentioned, after struggling in "normal" college at San José State, I requested transfer to its so-called "New College," where we could pretty much call our own shots. The school had been set up for us creative crazies, wired kids who would have had a tough time in a conventional class. (These days they'd give our condition a fancy name like "attention-deficit–hyperactivity disorder" and shoot us up with pills.) The Montessori-esque figuring was that we could go further if we were allowed to spread our neurotic little wings with very little supervision (this is my oversimplification, but that seemed to be the gist of it). It probably worked for some of the more disciplined students but for characters like me it was a great excuse to simply do whatever I wanted.

What I wanted was to be an activist, chase girls and drink … not necessarily in that order. However, there were some very conscious professors in the group who taught at State's New College, and they encouraged us to "follow our bliss," as Joseph Campbell would say.

And so in letting them know of my desire to study "political activism" I gathered a valuable list of books to read and report upon. These included *Conquest of Violence*, about Satyagraha, the Gandhian term for the use of non-violent confrontations; *Rules for Radicals*, by Saul Alinsky, theories and methods of organizing that have influenced both Martin Luther King, César Chavez, and President Barrack Obama; and *Escape from Freedom*, by Eric Fromm, about the nature of the authoritarian mind which comes in so many forms under different regimes, such as Fascism, Nazism, Communism, and even good old oligarchic Capitalism.

Yes, there are folks of all stripes who have repressive leanings and believe the false equivalent that claims "there are fine people on both sides"… but the very nature of White Power, etc. is inherently dangerous, often blatantly violent, and corrupt to the core. For decades it was just a fringe notion, yet in the 2020 presidential election almost half of the voting public—74 million people—went for a man with all those leanings.

The idea that most struck me about Fromm's concept was that we, the human race, are always on the brink of falling into this state, of giving in to the Viking deity Wotan (aka Odin), the Nazi god of fear and opting for the security of an all-powerful state … hence, "escape from freedom."

As I've indicated, that "state" applies to *all oppressive systems* of government, any overriding mechanism that under a propped up flag is in fact exploiting our energy and resources, claiming to free us while in fact doing quite the opposite. Sadly, convoluted reactionary thinkers feel that the solution is turning over democracy to a singular power, as in Russia, North Korea, China, The Philippines, Brazil, and now even to Italy with a female Mussolini. And sadly a huge chunk of right-wing America—40% or so—would be okay with a White-knight dictator.

New College was certainly allowing me to escape, escape from what to me was the boredom of normal college snore-riculum. Looking that period over, I think that in spite of my anarchistic party-mode I managed to learn a little. The truth is we—this entire society—need those open-minded professors more than ever.

Meditate, don't medicate. In other words, many mental health professionals have often taken the easy (and profitable) route of prescribing a wide variety of quick-fix medications, like opioids or less invasive calm-you-downers like Valium. These have their place, I suppose, but lasting solutions involve getting to the real roots of complex mental problems, including the resulting physiological pains and pressures. In knowing their causes, we are more capable of breaking away from their repercussions.

So even if we aren't able to fully recover from the factors that have so controlled us, there are relatively simple things we can do that are really helpful, even life-saving. The two that are the most obvious (and least expensive) are meditation and prayer …Ask God for help and shut the heck up. It works, my friend.

Gavíota Ghost Stop

There was a young man from the coast
who had an affair with a ghost;
At the height of orgasm
the she-ectoplasm
said, "I can feel it … almost."
—Limerick heard at a bar in Seattle

1971. Gaviota, California is a tad of a town—if it can even be considered a town—on the coast a little north of UC Santa Barbara, a genuinely nowhere place. Or so it was back in the '70s; even now it has a population of about 30 … Can you imagine that? I was still attending San José State but was dating a young lady who had transferred from SJ State to UCSB to get her teaching credential … perky girl named Adrienne, at that time really on the naïve side of things and, frankly, that was refreshing.

Bagel-ly Familiar. Which reminds me, during my own hot and heavy Tiger Woods/Charlie Sheen Period (Yeah, right, I had more dates with my hand than mates I could land) … anyway, there was a point back then when I was dating three Jewish jewels, sensuous Sephardics … *simultaneously.* Oy! Count 'em, three, all from L.A. but going to school at San José State. Their names were Amy, Andrea and Adrienne, all smart, sexy and funny … must've had good genes … uh, make that Levi's (hey, no one can say I'm anti-semantic!)

I had convinced myself that they didn't know about one another because even as opened-minded as they were they wouldn't have put up with another chick on the stick, let alone three on the bone. Would you believe that within a year or so I had traveled with two of them to meet their parents in L.A.? Really nice liberal folks!

Well, back to my zaftig harem (zaftig meaning juicy or succulent). Things often got strange in the middle of getting it on, "Ohhhh, Amy-y-y-y … uh, I mean Ahhhn-drayyy-ahhh …"

Go, Van Gogh! I digress, as usual. Anyway, being an artistic sort, and of good hippy stock, I of course owned a VW bus, early '60s model, gutless wonder, yes, but damned good on gas, repairs, and at being a portable, cheap motel. I'd periodically fill'er up and head down south to visit Andrea … uh, I mean Adrienne. After all, *she* was my Main Squeeze. (I still dream about that chick, Adrienne, a real winner … too bad I was such a jerk, but I did love 'er when I loved 'er).

This particular clear, warm October weekend I headed south to visit her in Isla Vista, a.k.a. I.V., right next to the UCSB campus where there had just been one hell of a commotion … seems some of those damned radicals had burned down the local Bank of America branch … oh, my!

I took Highway 101 all the way down from San José, a delightful drive anytime of the year, through Garlic-y Gilroy, Steinbeckian Salinas, San Luis Obispo (a.k.a. Slo-Town), that strange little chachka-packed faux Danish burg called Solvang, and on. As I neared Isla Vista, I could almost smell Adrienne's sweet nothingness.

After a considerable stretch of unpopulated nature, it suddenly appeared out of nowhere. Running along the ocean Gaviota was one of those don't-blink towns. I had never heard of such a place. In fact, when I was there I still didn't know I was there, which in a way is a wonderful thing.

What there was of Gaviota, unbeknownst to me, was mostly on the eastern, foothill side of the highway, not visible from the road. There was not a house to be seen. On the ocean side was just a sliver of sandy land with high, dry wild grass, maybe a half-block deep, separating the highway from the ocean.

At one point I noticed what appeared to be a large, round oil tank right at the brink of the sea, surrounded by a few trees. And standing close by were a handful of dilapidated shacks encircled by a small grove of eucalyptus trees. Mustard yellow shacks out of the '40s, just like the ones I grew up in back in Fresno when my dad worked for the railroad.

The little kid in me who wanted to go home and play took over. I pulled the van aside, got out and looked across that empty field—nothing but dried weeds, all fenced in by barbed wire that was clearly posted "No Trespassing." The tug of those shacks was unbearable, an irresistible force and I sure as hell was not an immovable object. Without reservation, I jumped the fence and headed toward the beach, toward those haunting shacks, toward touching the wings of angels.

How thoroughly absorbing it all was, there alone overlooking the ocean with a handful of those long-abandoned homes identical to the ones I clearly remembered from my childhood. Not a soul, not a soul was there, just the soft, warm wind stirring the clear ocean air.

I then noticed the old railroad tracks clinging to the precipice of the bluff with the ocean far below, old tracks like those whose rails I had rapidly walked upon time and again as a child, thinking I was quite good at my fantasized tight-rope balancing act.

Now, as I stood in the ocean breeze, I noticed there were four small cabins, each identical, and a central storage shed with the same architecture. And in the heart of this long-evacuated mini-community, this camp, was a sizable trellis, a kind of gazebo, held together by a few 4-by-4's, tall enough to walk under. There remained unattended grapevines that still had fruit growing after all those years. How delicious in their solitude!

All the doors to the buildings were wide open, just barely hanging on the hinges. I walked into each one of them, unimaginably excited with this discovery. There was very, very little in terms of "things" left in these two-bedroom shanties, yet I could feel—sense—the presence of those who once lived and loved in those very rooms. This space was truly enchanted.

And then, in a closet of one of the rooms, I found a crumpled letter posted back in the fifties. It was written in clear English from Carmen to Lydia, two young Mexican women who were, I gathered, close friends (I surmise Mexican by their first names, and the fact that a great number of Latinos were hired back then as workers on the western railroads. And there was just something about the letter and the feel of the place that let me know.)

Carmen, by the return address, lived in the "big city" of Santa Barbara about thirty miles down the highway (in those years maybe 5,000 population or so) and she was sharing her joy of getting a brand-new clothesline … Wow, a brand new clothesline!

After taking in this faint feel of family, this touch of earthiness, I meandered out to the tracks and looked down at the turquoise ocean softly caressing the beach. I thought, you know, these workers may well have had an idyllic life without even knowing it … a home with a panoramic ocean view, a vegetable garden, a grape trellis, decent work, a loving family. What more, what more?

Meeting Madam Butterfly. About this time, within a block or so south of this point, I noticed a cluster of spots moving low in the air, coming along the coast in my direction. And then the first one, the second, third … then dozens, hundreds, thousands of these "spots." Suddenly I was standing there in the midst of millions of migrating Monarchs!

Everywhere, everywhere, so many you could touch them in the air. Such lovely, lovely creatures, the royalty of butterflies, there at the ocean, the place of my ancestors, with the history of this lifetime's past being washed away by this truly magical moment.

I basked in the beauty of timelessness, a sensation beyond description, the whole experience excruciatingly beautiful. Yes, I remember joyfully walking on those rusty railroad tracks, balancing on the rails as I did as a kid.

Oddly enough, at that time it crossed my mind that if you tracked those very rails in Gaviota far enough, somewhere a few hundred miles away they would eventually connect with the Southern Pacific in Fresno where my dad had worked and where I did my original balancing act as a six-year-old.

What a joy it was to get up on those rails again, but now with the company of countless little fairies. I was a kid again! I honestly don't know how long I was there, but in a sense it was eternal. I truly wish everyone could have at least one experience like this, especially kids from the city. The mountains, the forests, the ocean—it's transformative.

There is something grand in this natural spectacle, not unlike the migration of birds—as in the film, *Winged Migration*, the impressively massive annual journeys of ducks, geese, swallows and other birds—something that brings us down to earth and at the same time transports us quite beyond all worldly things. A recent article in *Psychology Today* (05/10/17) is lucid as to the value of these transcendent experiences that nature provides. It's titled

"The Power of Awe Images," by Christoper Berland. Here's an insight gleaned from that piece:

> First, in May 2015, a study, "Awe, the Small Self, and Prosocial Behavior," led by Paul Piff of University of California, Irvine was published in the *Journal of Personality and Social Psychology*. Piff and colleagues found that the power of awe experienced in nature (i.e., visiting the Giant Redwoods in the Sequoia Forest) can promote altruistic prosocial behavior and puts our individual lives in perspective by helping people realize that there is something much bigger than yourself in the universe.

May I add that gazing at the stars, the heavens, can do that. Smog and all, just find one single star in the heavens and contemplate the vast distance of these celestial objects, the closest being the tri-star system of Alpha Centauri, that group being nearly four-and-a-half light years away, that's light that travels at 186,000 miles per second—per second! And then think for a second about the staggering number of stars in the Milky Way galaxy alone, this being but one of hundreds of billions of galaxies in the visible universe. And how many more universes might exist? Astounding, amazing, marvelous, and pretty darned cool.

I finally returned to my car to continue my journey southward. Within a few blocks I noticed a very old and weathered wooden sign on the corner of a dirt road leading up into the hills. It said, "Mariposa Reina," which in English is "Queen Butterfly," a reference to that very same Monarch family that was likely observed by early Spanish explorers at this very spot two centuries earlier. Perhaps I was there.

And then, within a moment or two, comes a train, a long freight train chugging up the tracks toward me... It hadn't dawned on me that those rusty old rails were still functioning! As I drove on toward Isla Vista, I couldn't help but think of what a wonderful time it must have been, to be excited about a new clothesline to dry your garments on.

A Tad of History for a Tyke of a Town. "Explorer Gaspar de Portolá led his party through the pass in 1769. Expedition diarist Father Juan Crespi dubbed the coastline here San Luis in honor of the King of France. However, Portolá's soldiers figured that La Gaviota, Spanish for seagull, was more appropriate." —from www.parks.ca.gov

> From mid-October through February each year, Monarch butterflies sleep in California's coastal eucalyptus groves. In early morning, visitors watch the trees like a crowd of expectant theatre-goers. Basketball-sized clusters of what at first appear to be brown leaves rustle and stir. The air fills with orange and black wings, and a monarch butterfly parade begins. —From about.com

Persevering and tenacious, most migrate over 500 miles every year, some much further than that, from Central America all the way to Canada. But my little guys and gals are more local … in fact they're called Western Monarchs. Their route is along the California coast, from Mendocino down to Baja California, cruising a little over 600 miles over land and ocean! So the next time you see one just think of what a heroic little critter he or she is. Take that, Amelia Earhart!

There is a magic about these gentle travelers. The late Wayne Dyer shared an incredible story about himself and his very special friend, a monarch butterfly who Dyer named Jack after the recent death of a dear friend of his. Seemingly out of nowhere the butterfly landed on Dyer's finger one day—and stayed there for hours!

The darned thing actually left for a little while, flitted above him, then returned, landing on that same finger. Could this be … Jack? Mr. Dyer says it is the "signature story of my life," a spiritual and synchronistic event that is so striking the source is unmistakable. Check it out by Googling or You-tubing "Wayne Dyer's amazing butterfly story." Amazing indeed, as was the wonderful Mister Dyer.

Birth of an Impresario

'71ish. *Alleys of the Valley* was a concert/poetry bash at Glide Memorial Church in San Francisco. It was the first event I ever produced. Renowned poets, artists and musicians from—get this—Central California performing in San Francisco!

It was a pretty creative concept, bringing Fresno artists to The City, and the very hip Reverend Cecil Williams thought it was a cool idea and so let me use that now-iconic church.

The darned thing sold out and was one hell of a show with great entertainment from folks I had known for years or had met back in Fresno, including songstress Jeannie Tracy (my high school classmate), poet Omar Salinas (Crazy Gypsy), and Philip Levine, the Poetry Bard of Fresno State and to-be Poet Laureate of the United States.

I also invited a couple of artist friends and jazz buddies from SJ State who were also from the Central Valley. All these fine performers loved coming to The City and on that very kicked-back evening The City loved them. *Fresno's Got Talent!*

The show was a hit and by producing that modest event I had inadvertently found myself a nice little profession—event production—which has kept me afloat in my little boat of pub crawling and hardy howling for all these years.

From it was born an original flicker of the Santa Cruz Poetry Festival that featured Lawrence Ferlinghetti, Ken Kesey, Gary Snyder, and dozens of the biggest and brightest literary stars, to quote Allen Ginsberg, "... burning for the ancient heavenly connection to the starry dynamo in the machinery of night."

Over the coming decades I produced several other notable West Coast fairs, festivals, and expos. Around 1968 I attended an event called the *Whole Earth Expo* in San Francisco's Brooks Hall. It had been inspired by the amazing-for-its-time counterculture book, the *Whole Earth Catalog.* That breakthrough, over-sized publication was created by Steward Brand and it appeared in a series of updated editions over the years.

At one point I had collected all of those old catalogs, and from them I learned the lingo of holistic thought ... Holy Geodesic, Bucky Fuller! I was duly impressed with the messages within and of that groundbreaking exposition, the *Whole Earth Expo*, regarding the environment, natural foods, self-sufficiency, and holistic thinking. The show was truly avant-garde.

So with the blessing of the producers of the SF event who warned me that such an undertaking wasn't a piece of cake, organic or otherwise, the next year I took a version of it to the Portland Coliseum where I co-produced my first show with this theme and then produced it solo the next year up in Seattle.

Those became wonderful life-changing events for many people, with 200 to 300 exhibitors at each one and a paid attendance of over 15,000 people per show. During my time in Seattle, my *Environmental Faire* at the Seattle Center was the nation's largest event of its kind with many well-known speakers, authors, and authorities on matters of ecology and human consciousness. The term "green" had yet to be popularized.

Above is the ticket art for an event I produced light years ago. The work is by Antonio Perales, a Fresno artist now living somewhere in San Francisco. That's a pretty darned good image of what some of those old alleys looked like back in West Fresno when I was a kid—the only things missing are a scrawny cat and a couple of winos sitting in a thin slice of shade with their back to the wall.

2013 Photo Courtesy of Stacey Lewis, City Light Books

261 Columbus Avenue. Lawrence (Don't call him Larry!) in front of his world-renowned bookstore and publishing pad, notorious for its network of those conforming to non-conformity.

Ferlinghetti's Fat Nude

Back in the mid-seventies I was honored to have him read at three of my large poetry events, two in Santa Cruz and one in Hermosa Beach. So, as it turned out, I had the opportunity of having dinner with him after the Hermosa Poetry & Art Festival I had produced that day. He, I, and a dear friend of mine from that quaint little beach town, Maggie Moir, ended up that evening chowing down in a pleasant seafront bistro and bar called The Mermaid.

Lawrence came to the event not just to read on stage as a poet, but also to showcase his art, and that evening he brought his portfolio with him, maybe half a dozen or so drawings of, among other subjects, fat nudes. Certainly got mini-me's attention. I shared with him my attraction to the Rubenesque and by the end of that mellow evening he most generously gave me one of his sumi-e-esque drawings of a chubby nude. Very cool. Here's some of his art found at www.artnet.com/artists/lawrence-ferlinghetti/

So here's a terribly embarrassing scenario that I'd much rather forget: One very drunk night a few weeks later I jumped into a cab going somewhere with that Ferlinghetti art in tow. As fate would have it, the taxi driver was a bonafide chubbette who looked a hell of a lot like the model in the Ferlinghetti drawing.

So genius that I am, I gave that wonderful piece of art to the cabbie, not just being a good guy, no, not at all, but rather for a possible rollicking romp which, incidentally, got absolutely nowhere other than a coquettish thanks. Can you say, "Idiot."

The Grand Plot: Cultivating a Sense of Humus

When I moved to Santa Cruz I was in my mid-twenties. This was in the early '70s, don't remember the exact year. As it turned out I went back to my roots (quite literally), bending over, working in the fields (I'm the guy shoveling, wearing white pants, left center, no hat). But this was a field planned for our yield and I was organically orgasmic ... my first community garden.

In 1974 the old Hotaling Building was leveled there on the prime corner on the Pacific Garden Mall in downtown Santa Cruz. The bare lot was a real eye-sore ... and that ain't cool in this heavily visited tourist mecca. I approached a small non-profit group for a little funding, the very progressive William James Foundation.

They had previously chipped in to finance the historic SC Poetry Festivals I was co-producing—biggest and bestest darned poetry slams in the nation—and now they were donating a few bucks and helping me get a permit to plant a garden on the then-empty lot where the winos (including myself) would hang out at night, litter, and pee on the wall … The Chamber of Commerce was not pleased.

I proposed to beautify the spot (a little ironic, huh?) and simultaneously made a statement about organically "growing your own." At the time, U.C. Santa Cruz was teeming with those learning to become "French Intensive" gardeners (French Intensive … how sexy is that?), made popular by the well-known English gardener Alan Chadwick. He had been recruited by UCSC to establish an organic gardening research, teaching, and training facility. It's still there, bigger, better and more important than ever. That's what Dr. Paul Lee tells me, and he should know … he was instrumental from the get-go.

After learning a bit about this fruitful method (It's absolutely amazing how much more yield you get if you plant in this fashion), I planted my own garden on that dynamic corner with the support of Drs. Page Smith and Paul Lee, as well as the use of an old-ass pickup truck driven by my bud, the Most Irreverent HL Moore, and Frank and Judy Foreman, the owners and baristas of the far left, far out Café Pergolesi (then located behind Bookstore Santa Cruz, right next to the above mural. Now where the hell was I? Oh, yeah … the City Fathers gave the plan a big, fat O.K.

When we first started turning the soil, the ground was hard as a rock and had many rocks in it, not to mention being filled with chunks of cement left from the wrecking ball. Setting aside the rocks and concrete, in order to prepare the soil (never say "dirt," sayeth Master Gardener Chadwick—in fact, with his great reverence for the soil, he went so far as to say it should never even be walked on.)

We had to break every lump of the hard material beneath, first by pick and shovel, then by hand, crumble it into smaller and yet smaller pieces, eventually into fine grains of earth. At that point we'd bring in loads of horseshit from the nearby farm towns, like Watsonville and Gilroy, and gallons of fish emulsion from leftovers down at the pier … pyu-wee! This was all done by a couple of volunteers using their personal tools and pick-ups, like that clunker of HL's.

By the way, the beautiful mural in the background was painted shortly before I began planting the garden. It was painstakingly created by a small crew of exceptional artists living in S.C. They called themselves P-38 Graphics—Don Cochrane, Dennis Marx, and Bob Shaw.

Ecotopia Revisited. About this same time, a fellow up in Berkeley named Ernest "Chick" Callenbach had written a well-received novel titled *Ecotopia*, again on the subjects of organic gardening and alternative energy.

I met the guy on a few occasions, hung out with him in friendly get-togethers in Berkeley, and brought him in as a speaker at major events I was producing and co-producing up in The Great Northwest, like the New World Expo in the Portland Coliseum and the Environmental Faire in the Seattle Center … both of these were pioneering efforts on the subject of environmentally-sound lifestyle long before the term "green" had come into the mainstream.

Chick was well aware of the "Two Americas" way back then, and he yearned for a culture that was both culturally sane and self-sustainable, nourished by small, intensively-cared-for plots of land and powered by alternative energy vehicles (think bicycle!), windmills and ocean-power. He called it Ecotopia.

In his book the progressive types on the West Coast had somehow gotten hold of a bomb—the Big One—and with that threat had managed to secede from The Union … yep, Washington, Oregon and California turned totally green. Those three States, properly governed, bio-dynamically farmed, planted and lived by their very conscious population was indeed a utopia, with balanced budgets, an abundance of healthy, wholesome food which they were able to export, and very little crime. Everyone had meaningful work. The Earth as a living, loving organism … what a concept.

Now this might be a pipe dream, but it is something to really consider. No, not seceding, but large numbers of people saying screw it, we're growing our own, converting lawns to gardens, recycling every damn thing imaginable, and sharing with one another using a barter system similar to those still popular in Europe.

By the way, it's good to know that there is great work being done to get folks to grow their own veggies (and other stuff). I recently saw a late-night show that featured Zooey Deschanel, the co-founder of a considerably successful program called *The Farm Project*—it empowers initiatives that reconnect people with food. Please do check it out at www.thefarmproject.com. Can you dig it?

Frank, Judy, and Café Pergolesi

1972-ish. Many moons ago I met a couple who have meant so very much to me over the decades—Frank and Judy Foreman. (Judy's claim to fame, besides just being Judy, is that she was perhaps the major source in popularizing the term "random acts of kindness." Tells you something about these folks, doesn't it?)

They were the middle-aged owners of the way-comfortable coffee house in downtown Santa Cruz, Café Pergolesi, long before a barista was a bore-ista. There the weekly classes of The Penny University were held, and Sunday Gregorian chants were faithfully sung by a small group of atheists, agnostics, and maybe even a Catholic or two (Frank was of the former group, but as I've often told him, "If there were more atheists like you, we wouldn't need churches.")

It was Frank or Judy—don't remember which—who in a hot tub one star-lit night asked, "Have you ever watched 'CBS Sunday Morning?'" This was in reference to the marvelously uplifting 90-minute long-form news and culture TV show which has been running since '79. Well, I hadn't, but I did from that point on, still do (though it ain't quite what it used to be after Charles Osgood and Charles Kuralt ... but then neither am I). It's an educational and entertaining sampling of the best of America—writers, singers, activists, artists, musicians, actors, sensitive and stirring stories of all sorts ... a beautiful montage of the America that is truly loveable. So here's to Frank & Judy:

Feast of Sunday Mornings

Of olives and capers and bright Sunday papers,
DaVinci's, DeMilos, Deniros,
Of gandy dancers and high-stepping prancers,
Of quiet home-town heroes;

Of valleys of vino and frothy cappuccino,
Biscotti, calamari and shallots,
Of snappy old tunes and bouncing buffoons,
Of Banana Republic ballots;

Of colorful cliffs and jazzy horn riffs
With Louie and Dizzy to blow it,
With Sarah so sassy and folks oh so classy
You'd never ever know it;

Of books and bells and gourmet smells,
A platter of chatter replete
With old friends, flowers and steamy hot showers,
Of thoughts we've yet to meet;

Of an uncensored quirk and a satisfied smirk
Not waiting, not walking, not working,
Of a romp in the hay (Let's not get risqué!)
While the coffee just keeps on perking.

Meeting Tommy Smothers... Smart, Very Smart

"Greed, like a fire, is more a process than a thing. It is the state of combustion, the activity of consumption, the procedure by means of which organic resources are quickly reduced to a heap of ash.

It is insatiable by nature, since the moment one desire is gratified another flares up, demanding also to be sated."
—Andrew Olendzki, "Burning Alive"

Santa Cruz, 1974. The Cooper House was both a local hang and a tasteful tourist trap owned by impresario Max Walden, a good-natured soul whose heart was as big as his stomach. Each afternoon marimba player Don McKlesson's little band Warmth would set up in the sunny patio in front of "The House" and lay out some smooth jazz sounds for the regulars and the passers-by. Day after day, I'd request *Green Dolphin Street*—"Green Dolphin Street supplied the setting, the setting for nights beyond forgetting."

Each day in this for-real paradise I'd kick back in my cushy chair and dandily adjust my Panama hat; I'd kid with my fellow-mellows as to what the poor people might be doing that particular day. We were all broke as hell but always had some little hustle going ... in the right town at the right time in history ... you don't need to be a millionaire to live like one.

One evening I was leaning on the bar in the Oak Room Saloon, located in the first story right across from the gift shop and, not surprising, there was the comedian/musician Tommy Smothers standing next to me, having a cold one and conversing with the bartender. I say not surprising because he and his brother Dickie were living in Santa Cruz at the time and, though famous as hell, were really just one, or two, of the guys.

I knew that he had attended San José State a few years before me, and I used that as an opener ... go Spartans! He was a genuinely friendly and accessible guy, not reluctant to chat about whatever. It was easy enough to get to the subject of television, he and his brother having one of the hottest shows of the time, *The Smothers Brothers Comedy Hour.*

Their humor was laugh-out-loud funny, at the same time the brothers, being very conscious of what was cooking politically, were not afraid to make their minds known. "They were going to speak truth to power and they were not compromising," a line I overheard while cooking and *listening* to television, in this case a documentary called "The Sixties." I don't know who said it, but "speaking truth to power" is a Quaker phrase from the '50s.

I wanted to hear about their TV program, how it came together, the controversy regarding their politics, particularly as they related to the Vietnam War, and why they got shut down. All this, mind you, in a 30-minute bull session in a Santa Cruz bar. He shared a little but then segued to the matter of advertising.

"Tomás," says he, "look at the ads, man, that's where the power is, and the real creativity. They put more money into those ads than they pay to produce the entire show. And don't underestimate the intelligence that goes into some of those things, for better or worse." That was over 50 years ago!

This was bothersome enough but it never really hit me until about 15 years later when a buddy, Frank Foreman, mailed (as in snailed) me an article about the public relations pioneer Edward Bernays. Among other hustles, Bernays was a consultant to American millionaires and presidents. Turns out he had been heavily influenced by a handful of European psychologists—most notably his uncle, Sigmund Freud, as well a couple of fellow shrinks, Gustave Le Bon and Wilfred Trotter. Both Le Bon and Trotter had similar ideas regarding the use of propaganda to control the masses and what they referred to as "herd mentality."

It isn't surprising that "the fascist theories of leadership that emerged during the 1920s owed much to Le Bon's theories of crowd psychology."—Wiki. Indeed, Adolf Hitler's *Mein Kampf* drew largely on the propaganda techniques proposed in Le Bon's 1895 book, *The Crowd: a Study of the Popular Mind.* In addition, the fascist Benito Mussolini made a careful study of the book, apparently keeping it by his bedside.

And during his presidency wanna-be dictator Donald Trump mistakenly made a Covid reference to "herd mentality" when he was trying to say, "herd immunity." (Freudian slip?) Nonetheless it is obvious that Trump has been guided early on by the condescending, calculating views proposed by Bernays & Company's authoritarian notions.

In his famous work *Propaganda,* Bernays declared that a major feature of democracy was the manipulation of the mass mind by media and advertising specifically. Flash forward, 2010: TV special on Coca Cola's grip on us malleable schmucks that keep drinking that over-priced, hopped-up sugar water; or back to 2004, when the infamously vicious and false "swift boat ads" were used to torpedo John Kerry's run for the presidency. And I don't even know where to start with Trump's campaign in 2024 … hemorrhoids on steroids!

FYI: There's a lot of info out there about Bernays and Company, and their overall tragic impact … For example, there's a 4-part BBC special called *The Century of The Self* that goes into grand detail. Check it out on YouTube.

By the way, I saw Tommy Smothers several years later, only this time he was on television. In fact, he was *selling television sets…* "Magnavox—smart, very smart."

Life-long Love Affair

The very first bar I set foot in was a pretty clean place called *Jerry's* on Fresno and E Street, kitty corner from the firehouse which was then brand-new. Most of the bar's customers were Mexican-American, guys who worked various jobs throughout Fresno who came in after five to have a few before heading home. Some were fortunate enough to work for some agency—state, county, city, hell, dogcatchers—but most were working under the thumb of agriculture one way or another.

There in Jerry's is where I heard my very first jukebox, with Perez Prado doing the very popular "Cherry Pink and Apple Blossom White" ... that trumpet solo got my attention even then. I was maybe nine, and I vividly recall coming in late one afternoon from some orchard or field with my brother and my old man. For me the experience was quite wondrous; there was something magical about the lights of the old Wurlitzer with the 45 rpm records, the large mirror behind the bar that made the place look twice its size, and the sound of men sharing gripes and laughter.

Over the years there were literally hundreds of joints up and down the West Coast that I was to frequent, holes-in-the-wall, like the very Black hang outs on Highway 41 on the outskirts of Fresno, in places like Jericho; elegant bistros in downtown Portland on the Willamette River; or The Blue Moon Saloon in Seattle's University District, mostly cool hippy types and a few derelict professors. A Mexican cat named Fernando was interviewed back in the '80s by a local TV station and asked what made the Blue Moon establishment so popular. He was quick to reply in his thick Latino accent, "It's a place where lonely intellectuals go to seek companionship."

In a sense I was always looking for that, the warmth of a home where "everybody knows your name." In my early blitzed-krieg days I wasn't much of a sit-at-home-and-get-shit-faced kind of guy; it was the folks, the drama, that sucked me to the center of these whirling cesspools of banal banter, and now and then a blast of utter brilliance from some wasted maniac. Oh, yeah, and of course the remote possibility of getting laid.

But booze has a way of slinking in and next thing you know it's less the charm of human interaction but in fact an alluring love affair with the sugar-pumped high of alcohol itself surging through an ever-addicted system. By my mid-thirties I would find myself sitting at home into the late night hours, brandy in one hand and a phone in the other, cleverly—I thought—yakking with others as lonely and loaded as I.

Reality Check

> "I'm proud to be an Okie from Muskogee,
> a place where even squares can have a ball.
> We still wave Old Glory down at the courthouse,
> and white lightnin's still the biggest thrill of all."
> —from "Okie from Muskogee" by Merle Haggard (who years later acknowledged somewhere that the piece was the stupidest crap he ever wrote).

Santa Cruz '76-ish. Some of my best friends are boozers … correction: *most* of my best friends. Some recovering, most not. Of those who are not in recovery, most will not acknowledge a problem … that's the nature of the beast.

Several have seen their kids going to prison and worse because of booze-related crap, their own jobs in jeopardy, their relations in shambles, but they still will not admit that they have a problem with fuckin' alcohol, and they will not openly discuss it. At our dinosaur-ass age, they still won't admit it!

Most have been "functional alcoholics," and frankly I would if I could—and that's in spite of how much I know about the sickness. How insidious this devil is, how controlling. But even as a functional alkie, there's still the devastating effects: ill health, strained relations, and an occasional drunk driving charge … about $5,000 these days, not to mention loss of work, many mandatory rehab sessions and weekly AA meetings (trust me, I know).

In those early years I certainly never admitted my alcoholism … *for-ev-er* never admitted it. The comradery, the memories, are strong things to let go of. And that warm, fuzzy buzz … damn I loved that stuff! At a certain point, one's entire being craves it, aches for it.

When I was about thirty, I was already heading into smelly barrooms the moment they opened at six in the morn. I remember when I was a younger man hearing about guys like me, sitting there with a couple of bucks in their pocket, nervously waiting for that first drink. And I know I was that man, so nervous I couldn't hold my drink without spilling half of it, "the shakes" they call it.

Finally, I'd get the second half of what was left in the glass down, and then quickly order another one, ashamed that the bartender might have seen my hands uncontrollably shaking … as if he hadn't seen that action a million times. After a couple more I'd finally settle down, start playing the jutebox, bullshit a little with whoever was around at the time, redneck or revolutionary, I didn't care, my buds of the bottle, bozos on booze.

I had a penchant for finding the most degenerate holes-in-the-wall; I never really understood why, though in retrospect I was simply *going home.* Black, White, Latino, I really didn't care. I would have to admit, though, that my least favorites were the redneck bars, where I could never hang for long—a result I'm sure of my politics, cross-wiring country music with bigotry. In those hillbilly hangouts, invariably I'd hear the "N" word ... well, they couldn't help themselves and I couldn't help but tell them to go fuck themselves.

Ironically, though, I would often find myself in those very same joints, sobbing in my beer about that redhead mother of mine who was long dead and who I had never really loved. Woe, woe, woe. Every now and then, I'd get into belligerent situations because of my left-wing ways ... I'd rather drink piss than white lightnin' (serious barf-a-rama!) and I *was not* proud to be an *Okie from Muskogee.* I still have a missing tooth to prove it.

How many times have I walked into those peckerwood pissholes, just praying that someone had a fraction of a brain! It ain't that they ain't smart people, it just that so many look at things through shit-covered, red, white, and brew glasses. Don't get me wrong, ain't no shortage of Blacks and Mexicans with the same fucked-up views. You know, there's a real common thread between Middle East terrorists and local grown haters.

Now where the heck was I goin' with all this? Oh, yeah ... smelly barroom, six in the morning, I still remember that foggy morning, standing outside a little coffee house, Café Pergolesi, right behind Bookshop Santa Cruz. I'd go there to visit Frank and Judy, and down a shot or two of espresso (after I had had my first handful of brandy shots—kind of a get sober so I can drink longer strategy).

My girlfriend of the time showed up in the parking lot. She pretty much knew I would be there, and her presence may have had something to do with the fact that I had kept her car a few days longer than she had offered.

After a few paragraphs of choice expletives—fill in the blanks—she looked me up and down, wobbling there in the doorway, reeking of smoke and a dozen different kinds of alcohol from consecutive days of debauchery. She asked me a simple question that no one had ever even suggested. She was kind enough to ask it in a soft, considerate fashion, but it had as much punch as if she had hit me upside the head with a shovel. She looked me square in the eye and asked, "Do you think you might be ... an alcoholic?"

I had been drinking since I was sixteen, heavily since I was twenty, and it had never once crossed my groggy little mind that I might have a problem. Needless to say, I resisted. Pardon the cliché, but "Denial is not a river in Egypt."

Alkie Notes:

- It's kind of spooky when you wake up at 7 and you don't know if it's a.m. or p.m.
- It's kind of spooky when you accidentally swallow your mouthwash thinking it's a shot of tequila.
- It's kind of spooky when you wake up and the digital clock reads 6:66.
- It's kind of spooky when you wake up and brush your teeth with Preparation H … we're talkin' puckered!

A Naked Lunch with William Burroughs…Junior

Mid '70s. I shared a very old and tiny condo with the son of the infamous bohemian writer William Burroughs. He was William Burroughs, Jr., no less. He'd experienced modest success as a writer but was a bitter disaster as a "normal person." (I almost hate to admit it but there've been a handful of times when I've actually wished that I might find a little piece of "normal"… but there was a certain vibrancy in being crazy as hell, not knowing what's coming next, a delicious addiction.)

That compact little space with an old-fashioned bunk bed that I shared with Junior was fitting for our lifestyle at the time: damn-near broke, night-n-day drunk, and way wild. And, hey, it was in Santa Cruz-at-the-Beach.

Romance at the Last Resort. So Billy and I had found this cheap bungalow style set-up, a mini condo with one other unit attached next door. An elderly couple lived there, but we seldom saw them during the day but certainly heard them throughout much of the night. I'm not sure which was worse, their creaking bedsprings whose squeaks permeated our room on and off during the night as the old guy got on and got off, or the sound of their cracking bones as they huffed and puffed, wheezing their way to their ultimate nut … Ughhh! This was before Viagra, mind you … wonder what that old coot was usin'?

Anyway, Junior was a real work, God bless his severely sauced soul, a strange dude in his early thirties who'd had the Angel of Death hanging over him since he was born, just walked and talked in a broken way. Talk about a real work! ... His dad, a notorious hipster druggie, *Naked Lunch* incarnate, blew Junior's mom's head off with a pistol, supposedly by accident while pulling a William Tell stunt down Mexico way ... He missed the fuckin' apple balanced on her head ... ooops!

So Junior, who went by the name of Billy, and I would do whatever was needed to be done to pay the weekly rent and self-medicate, i.e., get fucked up in some fashion. He got some sort of stipend from the State for being a nut, which wasn't a hell of a lot, and a periodic check from his still wild and modestly wealthy dad. He may have had other more expensive habits than I, though supposedly he had left heroin in his past.

I met him through a great little chick, a bleach-blond Marilyn-style shorty named Kathy ... Cute chick with a chipped front tooth who preferred women but to my satisfaction said that I was an exception and gave it up now and then. Anyway she introduced us, me an' Bill, and that was cool because the three of us had a helluva good time getting high and howling at the moon, going down to the beach with a conga drum and a jug of Red Mountain to bring up the sun which of course would never have risen but for our frequent indigenous ceremonies.

After a few months of this, Billy and I headed our separate ways. We were buddies but never deep friends. He was a sweet guy, but to me was so terribly tormented and often distant—what agony! But thrown together we made the most of our sordid circumstances in that seedy motel.

I was down at the old Catalyst a few months later when I heard news that didn't shock me one iota. Billy had done himself in—from cirrhosis of the liver. Fact is the cat was never able to overcome the giant shadow of his dad.

In some ways he and I had things in common, which causes me to shudder—we were walkin' talkin' PTSD. Fuckin' Burroughs Senior—brilliant, strange, sinister—whom I had met a couple of times at large poetry events that I produced, was idolized by many a beat-wannabee, half-baked hedonistic poet. He amazingly lived yet another thirty years while most of his famous buddies kicked the bucket. Go figure.

Notes: Junior had managed in his 33 years on this planet to write three novels, the third titled *Cursed from Birth* ... got that right! He underwent a liver transplant in 1976 then kept on guzzling ... I know the story well because

I have lived it with pancreas matters. He died in 1981 from a destined liver failure. He appears briefly in the 1983 documentary *Burroughs*, about his father, in which he, Junior, discusses his childhood, his liver problems, and his relationship with his family. In the documentary, John Giorno calls him "the last beatnik." Pish posh, I say, there's still a few of us kickin'.

A Not-so International Poetry Reading

1972. I was living in a comfortable pad at the ocean in Santa Cruz when I heard about a literary event taking place in San Francisco. It was on a weekend in Golden Gate Park's Hall of Flowers and was billed as an "international book fair."

When I arrived, I was handed a program for the afternoon's poetry reading and, as I recall, there were four prominent readers, all famous from the beatnik era. I was very politically active at the time and so a certain detail caught my eye: all four were male and all four were white. White. Males. No minorities. And to add insult to injury, no women of *any* color ... So what's international about this line-up?

The more I thought about it, the more pissed off I became. So without a second thought I finagled my way backstage and confronted the Master of Ceremonies with my beef. He responded, in essence, well that's just the way it is ... Wrong! The next-to-final reader had just finished, and before the headliner could be introduced, I stomped out, grabbed the microphone, and made my case to the audience. I bitched about the fact that there were no so-called minorities and asked if I could read a couple of short pieces. About this time the stage manager rushed onto the stage and let me know I shouldn't be up there. Nothing rough—after all, this was a book fair, not a boxing match. But the audience booed him away with chants of "Let him read! Let him read!" Good old liberal San Francisco.

And so, with a glow of satisfaction, I recited two pieces that I had memorized. I was hardly a great poet, but the stuff was honest, with the degree of politics young men are supposed to have. The first was a thing I'd written a few years prior, when I was about 20, working as a busboy up in Yosemite National Park. My cabinmate was a kid about my age named Lincoln, a lanky Indian lad—I know, *Native American*—with sullen, sunken eyes who already drank too damned much and had the smell of death about him. The poem went like this:

Yosemite Bus Boy

Yosemite California is crowded on the Fourth of July;
The dining halls are packed with cheerful faces,
Fresh summer faces.
And there are fireworks off of mountain cliffs
That must qualify as spectacular;
Yosemite California is America on the Fourth of July.

By the rockets' red glare
Lincoln, Indian boy/man, red lean boy/man
Serving laced tables of laughing hyenas,
Lincoln, a great American name, out of time, his time,
Time to dive for pearls and swine,

Dumping more meat than his two families eat,
Lincoln, the doggie bag,
Lincoln, the broken glass,
Lincoln for tips and all you can eat
But don't let your eyes
Get bigger than your stomach (Ha! Ha!)

Lincoln, whose name is un-man,
Whose eyes are without smiles,
You can make it if you die!
Where was what lost
Who lost what war
Chin up for tips and all you can eat.

I followed this with the "Hey, Eduardo" poem that ends with "Hey, Eduardo, pass the wine." Then, swaggering and staggering down the middle aisle came a hulk of a man looking like a mad Russian Cossack. The guy walked right up to the podium and handed me a large jug of red wine. With a rascally grin he looked back at the audience, raised his arms triumphantly, and yelled "I am Eduardo!"

The fellow's name was Ivo Buddeke, a true beatnik who had given up a very comfortable life to *just be*, just be himself without the overt contradictions of America in those days. As I was to find, he was also a Second World

War Air Force hero who had received several medals and citations, a bomber pilot as I recall. He and I became great friends and lived together for several months. He taught me the ropes as far as the Bay Area bohemian quarters went, into nooks and crannies that I would not likely have found.

After the International White Dude's Book Fair, we went to an Allen Ginsberg reading in a sizable hall, just where I don't recall. We got to watch him beat off behind the podium while reading a poem about his sexual fantasies (talk about live theatre!); left 11-ish, stole some wine and steaks from the nearby market. (Ivo actually opened a package of meat in the store and bit a chunk off of that raw-ass steak—Steak Tartare à la Safeway! Holding that large, blood-dripping choice filet in one hand, he pushed it to my face and grunted in a deep, purposely peasant-like voice, "This way eat steak! You Eat! Eat!")

That night we ended up jumping on a bus and heading out to his pad just off Geary on 31st, right across from Golden Gate Park. It was a pretty rundown wooden shack-in-the-back, looked like it had never been painted. It sat behind a two-story house that had been converted to apartments.

We drank the jug of wine we had liberated and cooked the stolen steak … just fried it up in a classic black cast iron skillet, a splash of soy, a slosh of burgundy, cut it up and devoured it right out of the pan standing there at the old gas stove. Don't get no better.

Ivo was in his late fifties by that time and still in damned good shape. After finishing off that steak we tossed his basketball back and forth in the small kitchen, and after my prodding—calling him an old fart and telling him I'd kick his ass on any court—he challenged me to a game … me, the outstanding center for the West Fresno Boys Club. You old goat, you want some of this?

He then led me to the nearby middle school, where we jumped the wire fence and played ball until five in the morning … in the dark, in the cold, in the rain and, since we were soaking wet anyway, in the nude. Dude! (Good thing we got out of there while it was still dark … we'd still be in jail. That by the way was one of the best times of my life and I think even God got a kick out of it.)

Unbeknown to me, there was another character in the audience the afternoon of the book fair. His name was Ken Kesey; he was the author of *One Flew Over the Cuckoo's Nest.* I met him the next day at the book fair's exhibit hall where he was manning his booth to market his latest endeavor, a periodically published magazine called *Spit in the Ocean.* Apparently he had witnessed my backstage/onstage shenanigans and that turned out to be quite propitious, for me anyway. In fact, according to him, there was more mention about me than him in some morning paper. Years later his buddy, Ken Babbs, told me that after reading that article and hearing that I had some poetry creds Kesey thought that I myself was a bit famous ... infamous maybe, but that's fuckin' crazy!

When Ken was sitting in his booth he was playing cards on a little fold-up table, not by chance a game called "Spit in the Ocean." He welcomed me to have a sit-down and I guess I was just lucky that day. We were playing for nickels and dimes, and I just knew when to hold 'em and when to fold 'em. Cleaned him out. Couple of weeks later I received a letter welcoming me to his home up in Oregon, which he fondly referred to as "The Swamp."

Ivo Buddeke, circa 1944. Here was a dashing and heroic young Second World War bomber pilot who could not possibly have dreamed he would someday become quite the bohemian in San Francisco twenty years later.

And here's a note from Ivo's son—May 12, 2019 (48 years later!):

> Thanks Tomás, I enjoyed reading your vignette about "Big Ivo" as he was known in my youth. I was of course "Little Ivo" after expressing to my siblings that I no longer wished to be called "Bappit" (short for Baby Pee Butt). I also recall walking into Safeway with "Big Ivo" wearing a rather large over-coat and watching him walk out with a slab of beef beneath both arms.

A Morning at the Swamp

"A little learning is a dang'rous thing;
Drink deep, or taste not the Pierian Spring."
—from Alexander Pope's *An Essay on Criticism*, 1709

1972-ish. Kesey had for some time, at least since Frisco's 1967 "Summer of Love," been the poster boy for the new "counterculture," aka "hippy movement." And already his *One Flew Over the Cuckoo's Nest* had hit it big as a book and as a play, so the guy was poppin' up all over the media. Reporters would end up at his home for an interview and from the little I saw of it the man was gracious, generous with his time, and straight-up genuine.

One morning during my earliest visit to "The Swamp," hanging with Ken Babbs, David Butkovich, and a handful of their fellow trippers, came the ritual *I Ching* reading at the dinner table, a large discarded wooden electric wire spool Ken had snagged somewhere.

Along with the coffee and a hearty country breakfast prepared by his dedicated wife, his high school sweetheart Faye, came a separate menu of sorts offering beer, marijuana, and sometimes more than that. In fact, one of the handles of their loose-knit group was "ITSART," an acronym for *Intrepid Trips Society for Aesthetic Revolutionary Training.*

At a point, Kesey sez, "Hey, Toe-moss, check out the library." Upstairs in that wonderful old barn that he and his family had converted to a way comfortable, kicked-back pad was a sizable library, a few rows of books from every-damn-where. I started poking through and for whatever reason a certain book leaped out, you know, just screamed "Read me!"

It was a tome called *The Urantia Book*, a thick and heavy thing (in more ways than one), and as I paged through it, I thought, man, this is fascinating and amazing if true. Ken was reading something a few feet down and so I took the book over, showed it to him, and asked, "Is there really something to this thing?"

About this time one of his dogs, a spaniel mutt named Stewart (as in Stewart Brand), nudges up to us with a ball in her drooling mouth, a rubber ball that he drops at our feet. The ball was manufactured so as to have the appearance of Planet Earth. Earth being dropped at our feet by a let's-go-play drooling dog. That damned ball fell *slow motion* out of his mouth and just bounced and bounced ever so slowly at our feet. We looked at each other and nodded our heads … slowly.

I believe that whether it's within *The Urantia Book*, *A Course in Miracles*, *The I Ching*, whether it's reading tea leaves, yarrow sticks or runes, the truth of it is that these practices and items can be sacred tools to help us understand and recognize that there is a level of reality existing beyond and even within our mundane lives. These tools are not necessarily for divination but for introspection, and they present an opportunity to acknowledge synchronicity and to give synchronicity a chance to acknowledge us.

We needn't take every word literally or a shake of the dice as fatefully fatal. Rather we should use these little miracles to acknowledge that which is our gift: pure being, pure spirit, now and always. Think about it: every time a synchronistic event happens to you it means that God has moved time and space to let you know that He exists and that He cares about you.

Note. The Pierian Spring from Greek mythology is the metaphorical source of knowledge about art and science. Pieria was a region of ancient Macedonia, the location of Mount Olympus, believed to be the home and the seat of worship of Orpheus and the Muses.

For the Benefit of Mister K

Part One: ***A good ol' Country Boy.*** Back in the very early '70s I went to see Woodstock's Country Joe McDonald—"One, two, three, What are we fightin' for?"—at one of his little barroom gigs on the West Coast, somewhere in Monterey or Carmel. I'd met him before—in those days there were top-flight rock/blues/folk concerts everywhere all the time in the Bay Area, including the great free events in Golden Gate Park.

And so, with a bit of familiarity, we yakked outside during the band's merry-jew-wanna and imbibition break. Joe was not only accessible but I think just loved people and hanging out. Reminds me of another cat I had the privilege of meeting a time or two in San José, the third Blues Brother, harmonica playin' Charlie Musselwhite. The man had been an absolute lush but at a point said fuck it to booze and went on to live a long and productive life.

But back to Country Joe: I mentioned that I'd met Kesey recently and had been up to visit him. His comment to me regarding Ken was, "Oh, he's just a good ol' country boy." Maybe so, but that country boy was pretty damned sophisticated as far as I could tell. I got to know Ken fairly well over the next few years, hanging out at his home or at poetry festivals I was producing, via drunken phone calls, and long rides up and down the West Coast.

We'd truck along in those big old convertibles of his, Buicks and Pontiacs and Olds, oh my! They were funky, unwashed early '60s boats. Sometimes with Babbs and Bucko (David Butkovich) and sometimes just him and me, top down, floating down the highway. In the few times I ran with him, he was a mentor of sorts, nine years my senior, but ninety-nine in worldly and other-worldly experience. For whatever reason, he generously shared bits and pieces of his life, and a little bit of advice now and then.

Part Two: *Inside The Demon Box.* Another night in the shack-in-the-back of his barn-turned-home, just K and I partaking of his up, down and sideways refreshments, just yakkin' into the night. At a point of this particular evening the subject of that seemingly perennial dichotomy "God versus The Devil" came up. By this time in my life I was pretty steeped in Eastern philosophy and holistic thought and, frankly, was closed minded as regards archetypal Christian concepts—really quite ignorant, in retrospect.

Nonetheless, I shared a couple of my own chilling alcohol and/or drug-induced experiences with what I perceived as The Devil. The Catholic Church and sweeping big screen Cinemascoooope film pageants had early on imbedded this satanic image deep in my subconscious … e.g., *The Greatest Story Ever Told*, *King of Kings*, etc. This does not include the massive television and movie imprints like *Rosemary's Baby*, *The Exorcist,* and who can argue that Boris Badenov wasn't the very incarnation of you-know-who? What does the church say? "Give me a child for his first eight years and he'll be a Catholic for his lifetime." And that includes the subliminal vision of evil personified.

At one point I told him how I'd look into the eyes of someone—usually when I was on pot and God-knows-what-else—and see that guy's face change, not so much a contortion, but a view *beneath* the surface, a look into the actual character, or so I felt, of the person with whom I was speaking … scary as hell when it turns out to be an Evil One, I mean an aura of pure malice. I put it to him: "Ken, tell me, have you ever had an encounter with *The Devil.* I mean the Real Deal?"

His answer, with a little pondering as if to bring back an unpleasant memory, was "Yes, yes, I have." He shared the following encounter: During the well-documented period that he spent running from the cops and landing in a Bay Area jail, he recalled that he was originally housed in a cell with a big, muscular Black prisoner. Ken was no wimp, being a northwest wrestling champion and all, but according to him, this guy was not only a bad-ass but had the guns (arm muscles) and attitude to prove it. It was mutual hate at first sight … this is significant in that Ken was hardly a hateful person, quite the opposite.

Sadly, I don't recall the details of it all … pretty loaded, I was. But the gist of it, yes. They conversed, briefly, his cellmate going out of his way to *mentally* fuck with him (many of these low-lifes in city jails are ex-cons or cons-to-be, fully capable of the worst of crimes, and as is suggested, not to be bent-over before.) Ken said this was not a *normal* encounter, but that there was much more to it, a diabolical thing.

It all centered on the deep-seated hatred on the part of his cellmate … Too many men are like that, straight-up sociopaths. Ken had to live with him until their jail cells were changed a few days later. He said that he hardly slept during those nights. You can pretty much tell when a guy is bullshitting, and he certainly wasn't. He was clear when he said that this cat was *The Devil Incarnate*. You know it when it happens to you.

Footnote. Kesey was arrested in 1965 and 1966 for possession of marijuana … just getting popped with a joint or two back then was a serious rap, often prison time. So the cat fled to Mexico to avoid prosecution. When he returned to the U.S. some months later, he was apprehended and sentenced to six months in jail. It was during this time that the above encounter with Mister K's demon took place.

Part Three: *In Motion to the Ocean.* On one occasion Ken invited me to truck along with him to a cabin he owned at the Oregon beachside, maybe a hundred miles or so from his home in the Eugene area.

While cruisin' along that wild, winding Siuslaw River, Ken pointed to a little shack that was nestled close to its shore. He said that he had once lived in that old cabin where he had first conjured up the brainstorm that was to become his other great novel, *Sometimes a Great Notion*. He asked, without expecting an answer, if I had any idea where he got the notion for *Notion*. Nope, not I sir.

A little further along that riverside road he shared where the title of his book came from. It was from a line of an old folk tune titled (not *en*titled!) "Good Night Irene." I'd heard this song hundreds of times—literally—on the radio when I was a little kid. It was right there on the old Hit Parade for quite a while (even reached #1, by The Weavers in 1950). Lines in the lyrics went:

Sometimes I live in the country, sometimes I live in the town,
Sometimes I have a great notion to jump in the river and drown.

Incidentally, it was the pioneering blues singer Huddie Ledbetter, known in the world of folk music as Lead Belly, who originally popularized "Goodnight Irene" as early as 1908 and first recorded it much later when he got out of the pen in '32. You can find him on YouTube, pluckin' his beat-up gee-tar while singing "Goodnight Irene."

By sheer chance and having little to do with anything, I later met Lead Belly's great grandson … grand-something … Les Ledbetter. As it turned out Les was a feature-story writer and editor for the *New York Times*, and not by chance he was with Kesey and his clan as we all watched the glamour and glitz on TV during the Academy Awards in which *Cuckoo's Nest* made quite the sweep.

Les was a great guy I chanced into a year or so later in North Beach. We drank and bullshitted, often with attorney Joe Malandra, one hell of a character himself. I'm told Les died of good old alcoholism a few years later. Too young, too talented, too good.

"Les Ledbetter, a former reporter and editor for *The New York Times*, was found dead Monday in his apartment in San Francisco. He was 44 years old. Among the articles he wrote was the front-page account of the killing of John Lennon. He left The Times in December 1983."—August 1, 1985, *New York Times*

Part Four: ***A Banger in Topanga.***

> "As I've often told Ginsberg, you can't blame the president for the state of the country; it's always the poets' fault. You can't expect politicians to come up with a vision, they don't have it in them. Poets have to come up with the vision and they have to turn it on so it sparks and catches hold."—Ken Kesey, 1989

We drove down old 99 from Oregon to Southern Cal one summer with Ken at the wheel of one of his big ol' convertible boats, don't recall the details … I wonder why. It wasn't an acid trip, but a trip focused on something that involved a great deal of money and legal shit about *Cuckoo's Nest* movie rights, his being ripped off, it appeared, by Michael Douglas, Saul Zaentz, and company. Quite a story, that.

Anyway, once we got to the City of Angels (yeah, right) we headed straight to the UCLA Campus, and that I do remember, us meeting up with Allen Ginsberg and sometime during that little on-campus get-together my mentioning that I was aware that, quite by chance, Dick Gregory was giving a talk at one of the lecture halls close by, just about that time of the day.

They were of course fully aware of who Gregory was, but Ken had never heard the man perform or met him in person. I had had that good fortune on a handful of occasions—his being a speaker at a couple of my big shows, several phone conversations, and once driving him around L.A. in my beat-up VW hatchback—so I said, hey, this is a cool opportunity, he's right around the corner, let's go check him out.

And that's what happened. We walked over and I finagled our seats (as I've always been able to somehow do, not always legally). The speaking hall was packed and so we sat in back row seats and took it all in … Taking it all in means watching Gregory pace back and forth without a podium, just a chair and a mike, hammering away at the political/social/economic bullshit going on that particular day, a pithy black Jon Stewart of sorts, but decades before him.

Gregory, then in his fifties, was in fine fettle, yakking a mile a minute in his famous style about the most recent scandal or conspiracy. As serious as these matters were, he was a very funny man and kept us howling and pissed off at the same time. When the talk was over, with Ken's OK, I went up to the stage, shook hands with Dick and said there were a couple of very interesting folks in the audience who would be delighted to say hello. I then went back and brought Ken and Allen up to stage. I have no idea what they said to one another but there was a lot of head nodding and hand shaking.

Later that afternoon Ken mentioned that there was a private little party that night up in Topanga Canyon, L.A.'s equivalent to the Bay Area's Palo Alto Hills, filled with pot, patchouli, and good vibes. We show up that night and Ginzy is there with a small group of hangers-on, listening with bated breath to each guru-esque uttering.

And speaking of canyons, earlier that afternoon while on the UCLA campus I'd managed to snag a hefty heifer, just my style, Sarah somebody. So snatch-urally I invited her to the little happening in Topanga that night. In like Flynn … or so I thought.

Ken and I arrived fashionably early, taking advantage of a nice spread of hors d'oeuvres, mostly non-meat munchies. And speaking of spread, the woman I'd invited that afternoon soon arrived with a female friend (yep, in like Flynn, maybe even my fantasy of a ménage à trois … hmmmm).

As the evening went on folks would poke their way into one little corner or another, listening and jumping in, a tasteful gathering of professorial types, writers, and God-knows-who-the-hell.

Which leads me to what this vignette is really all about. What could possibly trump it all, Ken and Allen, Sarah Somebody, Mary Juana, and a tasty offering of whores' divorce. And the answer is? … And the answer is? … God. Yep. God. Ken and Allen were in the thick of it, jabbing and jabbering, and looking back at the beliefs of those two I could see why.

Ken at a certain level was a spiritual man, certainly not a religious one, but for sure a believer in The Big Guy, or something like Him. I know this from our one-on-ones here and there. And I think it shows, not blatantly, but there, in some of his work are subtle innuendoes. Like *Cuckoo's Nest*, which others have pointed out has touches of religious symbolism, not the least being *the other hero's*—McMurphy's—lobotomy where he's strapped, arms spread, like Christ on the cross.

Ginsberg, on the other hand, was a guy who had early on broken from Judaism and gradually found himself in the heart of Tibetan Buddhism, studying and teaching at the Naropa Institute in Colorado (The Tibetan school, unlike mainstream Mahayana and the more conservative Theravada, does believe in divine beings, gods and demons, but doesn't deviate from the concept of anatta, or no Soul, Self, Ego, or the Hindu concept of Atman. It does not believe in an unchanging substance at work behind the scene.)

Over time, the man became a full-blown bead-wearing, Om-chanting devotee of Lord Buddha who, as was the case with Buddha himself, never considered himself lord of anything. Perhaps because Buddha thought any form of ego, including attachment to a belief in God, is a hindrance to clarity. Actually, on the subject of God, the Buddha chose to remain silent. which in itself makes a point (don't worry, I'm just being inscrutable).

Anyway, Ken and Allen got into this matter of God's existence … way too blurry to recall the details. Besides, I was far more interested in de tail, as in the young lady I'd invited to the gathering … Sarah Somebody … some body!

Well, to my great disappointment, Sarah had mysteriously disappeared into the night as did Mr. K. Not surprisingly, as the eve came to an end, Ginsberg put the hit on me. I think my feelings would have been hurt if he hadn't. I mean the guy was notorious for it and this ain't exactly chopped chorizo. "Well, thank you, sir, but it just ain't my thing." The next day Ken said he owed me one. Que Sarah, Sarah.

A Late Letter to Ken

November 12, 2001

Dear Ken,

Sorry I missed getting this letter to you before you moved on up. There are a handful of things I'd like to have shared, things I've meant to tell you all these years. But the times we were together, I was certainly and gratefully the listener. Man, you turned me on to a great notion or two, like your integrity of not ever seeing the multiple Academy Award winning flick, your own story … *Cuckoo's Nest*. You said this is because of how those bastards, Michael Douglas and Saul Zaentz, tried to rip you off … Amazing! Besides ripping you off, you told me that they really fucked up the whole concept, that indeed it was the big Indian who was the hero … typical racist shit.

Thanks for dragging me along when you sued the shit out of them down in L.A. … and won.

Annnyways … that note you sent so long ago welcoming me to "The Swamp," well, it turned into one hell of an adventure. It thoroughly changed my life and that of my sidekick, Jimmy Dalessandro, who I invited to tag along with me to your home in Pleasant Hill. As you might recall, Jim spent the evening sleeping out in the grassy field where that rusty old bus *Further* had been retired … but not re-tired.

Right off the bat Joanna Leary was flying around the room on a vroom-schtick (Tim Leary's old lady who changed her last name to Leary but wasn't really married to him … little suspicious for sure). She was hanging out there for a week or so, that strange creature who could drop acid without flinching … I still don't think that made her hip, just incredibly in control, as assholes can be.

I once told her that I thought she was an elitist, and about a day later she smugly acknowledged, "Yes, Tomás, I am an elitist." I then wrote her a little riff titled "Bzzzz" that said, "De Queen Bee don't be no queen bee 'les she don't know she don't be no queen bee!" So close to the truth it buzzed right over her head, broom and all.

You know, on one trip with her to visit Tim in Folsom Prison where he had free rent for a few years, she said that we—she and I—should consider busting him out. "What do you think about a helicopter," she asked, "just dropping onto the grounds there and snapping him up." I told her it was an insane idea. In retrospect, I'm glad I was unimaginative on that one, I'd have ended up in there with him.

As you and others later informed me, the wench was an international agent of some sort, Interpol type shit, getting the goods on major trippers. That's why she was fucking Leary—in more ways than one—and that's why she was at your place. I guess *thinking* is a real threat … no doubt about it.

Jim and I, as you know, stayed up there on your farm-of-sorts a few days, you throwing the *I Ching* every morning and some of us partaking of an early buzz with a variety of good old mota, lotsa beer, a shot or two, and/or all of the above.

At one point you wanted to produce an event, a fund-raiser for your bud, Mister Leary, the *Captain of The Team* as you put it. It was not only to bring in a buck or two, but more importantly to bring attention to his plight in the pen for espousing the benefits of dropping psychedelics and dropping out.

This was about the time of Comet Kohoutek. First sighted on March 7, 1973 by Czechoslovakian astronomer Luboš Kohoutek, it was a bust, never got close to Earth, and Herb Caen accurately dubbed it *Kohoutek, the Cancelled Czech*. Before it fizzled, I suggested that we capitalize on the comet's notoriety, do a big show in San Francisco, maybe at the already famous-for-fuzzy-wuzziness Fillmore West, and call that event *Comethon*. The comet fizzled as did my idea. Cometh-on?

As you I'm sure recall, we did end up producing a large event anyway but chose Santa Cruz where Jim and I lived and had great contacts. From the list you gave me we invited several of your famous friends, including Lawrence Ferlinghetti, Ginsberg, and a host of others. I'm sure you made a few calls because there was no shortage of headliners. It was primarily your energy and the outstanding list of your famous buddies who made this at all possible. And then the very hip community of Santa Cruz, banana slugs and all, leaped on board and history was made … As one local rag headlined, "Biggest Poetry event in the Nation right here in River City!" … or something to that effect.

After the show was over I remember Joanna Leary grabbing the money out of my hands—I mean snatched!—and doing God knows what with it. At only three bucks per ticket, the purse was about $6,000 and that was quite a bit back then.

In retrospect the Santa Cruz Poetry Festival changed a lot of people's lives, heavily, impressively. Certainly, my own and Jim's ... He and I co-produced the first two shows, I produced the third annual event solo, and Jim produced the final fourth show. Didn't make any money but had great times with great people. Can't ask for much more than that.

When I think about the presenters, it's obvious why those mega poetry fests became the nation's largest and most exciting literary events of their time ... probably changed how poetry was to be presented in America. I mean among other things the festivals were one hell of a weekend party! Lineups of American bohemian Who's Who filled the stage: yourself, Ginsberg, Snyder, Ferlinghetti, McClure, Burroughs, Bukowski, DiPrima, Corso, Krassner, etcet, etcet. ... not to mention phenomenal music and entertainment: Ali Akbar Khan, Charles Lloyd, Country Joe McDonald, Teatro Campesino, Wavy Gravy, old Tom Scribner, the saw-playing commie with his twinkling eyes and bowler hat, and a busload of other creative souls. Oh yeah, and the comedy juggling team who called themselves The Flying Karamazov Brothers, and who you called The Kara-matzo Bothers ... very funny Jewish guys who, while juggling bowling pins and torches back and forth, would zing us with outrageous one-liners like, "Time flies like an arrow; fruit flies like a banana." Made it into the movies, did they.

One evening, just prior to the second poetry festival, I was boozing and schmoozing in the old 1232 Club, the Fresno Hotel Bar on SF's Upper Grant Street. Sitting at the bar on those old wooden stools were the same characters I'd gotten to know after years of damn near living in that intoxicating atmosphere. But this particular evening I found myself sitting next to a fellow I'd only seen a handful of times—usually I'd spot him nervously pacing the North Beach streets, turning, and twitching.

At that time I'd only heard of him, but being aware he was a well-known poet I bought him a beer (which I was wont to do anyway) and began my usual chatter with the idea of inviting him to our big poetry soirée, a potpourri of many of the best damn writers in the country.

Of course I dropped a name or two and of course he was fully aware of these writers seeing that—unbeknownst to me at the time—he was an icon amongst icons. East Coast, West Coast, super popular in France, Bob Kaufman, the man in the black beret, epitomized the word *beatnik*.

I'd been told that he had taken an oath of silence in protest of the Vietnam War, and so as we sat there he would listen and nod now and then but uttered not a peep. As you've probably gathered by now, I'm pretty straight-forward and don't mind asking anyone anything ... So I just said I'd be really honored if he'd come on down and read with us fellow crazies in Santa Cruz. That meant he would be reading in public after years of being totally out of the scene.

Well, everyone in the bar was amazed that he had said even a single word—but that was *the* magical word and that word was *yes!* After his well-received performance in Santa Cruz, he went on to read in public for the rest of his life, five years or so from that point on, and the audiences adored him.

And you know, you were right on about Leary being "Captain of The Ship." And by that, I mean "Turn on, tune in, and drop out" was far deeper and more socially significant than I realized at the time. Turn on (go deeply inside the doors of perception and see things as they really are); tune in (be aware of what's going on around us and within us—spiritually, politically, socially—how we're being manipulated ... and hone in on the alternatives); and finally, drop out, out of the system that is. That one I'd change, however. I'd change it to, "...and help out."

I told you once on one of our drunken/loaded marathon runs, when I was totally shit-faced, "Ken, man, don't get this wrong, but I love you, man." You responded kindly, simply saying "Same here." Well, I have just over two years of total sobriety as of this writing ... shocking, huh? ... and I have something I'd like to tell you: I love you, man!

Yer amigo, Tomás

P.S. Thanks for your response back then when Joanna questioned "Who's Tomás?" Without a second thought your cool reply was, "Tomás? ... he's a beatnik." That was big ol' hash marks on the left sleeve of my fraying Navy P-coast.

Borrowed from Wiki:

> Kenneth Elton "Ken" Kesey (September 17, 1935 – November 10, 2001) was an American author, best known for his novel *One Flew Over the Cuckoo's Nest* (1962). But his popularity soared as a counter-cultural icon who considered himself a link between the Beat Generation of the 1950s and the hippies of the 1960s." In a 1999 interview with Robert K. Elder, Kesey said, "I was too young to be a beatnik and too old to be a hippie." Yep, remember him sayin' that more than once.

Lunch with the Munchie Bunch

'74-ish, Capitola. I was invited to dine with an old friend I knew from Fresno, of all places, Carol of Head Shop fame. She, like myself, had gotten the hell out of Fresburg, and in our case landed in Santa Cruz. The soirée-of-four was held in her laid back pad on the outskirts of Santa Cruz, Capitola-by-the-Sea. Just as in Fresno, Carol was the hostess with the mostest—I'm talkin' cannabis.

Which brings me to her guests that particular evening, none other than the up-in-smoke duo, Cheech and Chong. Those cats, the original Doobie Bros, were just like the movies I'd seen them in. Man, they were fu-ucked-up, same-o-same-o.

At a point I myself was so loaded I thought I was in one of their trippy-ass, munchie-mania movies. Trust me, there wasn't a crumb or a leaf left of that very generous spread.

The Best They Can

A friend of mine once said,
"You know, people really do the best they can."
And I could not believe him
—But then I look at weeds and winning roses,
Nishiki Koi and common carp.

I watch their often courageous struggles,
These creatures, each and every,
I watch them send their leaves to heaven
And their roots as deep as is deep,
I watch them hustle like so many
Poor boy peanut vendors
Scrambling to crack their nut.

And I for the likes of me,
Finally thinking each and every,
cannot help but believe
   Finally! Finally! —
That criminals and carpenters,
koi and common carp,
With precious and ancient maps
Travel ever onward
Doing the best they can.

Three Gentlemen of The East

Part One. It was backstage at a major literary event, the Santa Cruz Poetry Festival, where I was privileged to mingle with *whoever*. Seeing that I was the event's original Executive Producer, meaning I called the shots, I could pretty much do as I pleased, and I pleased to drink and bullshit with the terrific poets and artists backstage. I wasn't earning one red cent on the deal but meeting some of those amazingly talented folks was a real pleasure and one hell of a learning experience.

In this case, the guy's name was Ali Akbar Khan. He was a top flight musician, a bit of a guru, and a virtuoso on the sarod—a stringed musical instrument similar to the sitar—who often played along with sitar maestro Ravi Shankar, the father of contemporary singer/piano player Norah Jones. I hired him because I thought it was a nice fit with the poetry, what with that touch of Eastern spirituality that the Beats had been known to introduce, going back to Kerouac's *Dharma Bums* and Ginsberg's Tibetan Buddhist bent.

For some foolish reason, based on the style of music Khan and Shankar played (so much of it is steeped in ancient Hinduism), I had figured these guys had to be exceptionally spiritual people ... and maybe they were. For me this had to do with the whole Eastern mystique that had throughout the years been magnified in my biased mind.

At one point, me and ol' Ali found ourselves pissing next to each other in the Head for the Stars, whoop-dee-doo. He knew I was the producer and so, his dick in one hand and a drink of some sort in the other, asks without pause, "You know, I just finished my set ... got my money?" How spiritual is that?

Part Two. Which brings me to the Yogesh Kothari Gandhi Affair, the center of which is yet another talented personality of The East. In this case Mr. Gandhi's claim to fame was that he was the grand-nephew of you-know-who. You guessed it, the Mahatma guy. Yogesh—pronounced like it's spelled, yo-gesh—would get on the New Age speaking circuit, do his "I'm the grand-nephew of Mahatma Gandhi" schtick and would get folks to pay a pretty hefty ticket to kiss his ring.

But Mr. Gandhi was quite the moral opposite of another gent of the East, Tulshi Sen, an Indian fellow I became acquainted with and worked with a few years later. Tulshi's father was a prominent spiritual teacher in the old country and had told him, "Guru very good business." Tulshi, after a lifetime of entrepreneurial ventures (and adventures) in the U.S., Canada, and throughout much of Asia, has of late combined the two fields of spirituality and business success with an insightful book titled *Ancient Secrets of Success.*

In the case of Yogesh, the star-starved airy-fairy types often paid through the nose just to hang out with a distant relative of Mr. Gandhi. Tulshi, on the other hand, was most amiable and had something tangible to offer, a real opportunity to get into a profitable business, and minimally to have a pleasant and memorable journey to China and elsewhere in the Far East to learn about the import business.

At one point Yogesh was hanging out at my rather spacious rental down in Hermosa Beach, him and his dirty-blond dirty blond girlfriend. I don't know why—I sure as hell ain't no angel—but it surprised and even bothered me to find them unabashedly drinking, smoking, and fucking at all hours … him especially, as he was fronting himself off as the "Chosen One." The last I heard of him he was being chased by a notorious Japanese mafioso—in Japan known as *yakuza*—for some scam of his.

Note: Here's Wikipedia's take on Mr. Gandhi:

> In March of 1999, Yogesh Kothari Gandhi was charged by the United States Department of Justice with tax evasion, mail and wire fraud and perjury. Prior to the charges, Gandhi had presented Bill Clinton with the 'Gandhi Peace Award' accompanied by a bust of Mohandas Gandhi, and had his picture taken with the president.
>
> In 1987, Gandhi gave an award to Ryochi Sasakawa, an individual the United States Senate investigation referred to as 'a controversial, wealthy Japanese businessman who has been accused of links to organized crime and extreme rightists.' A year after Sasakawa received the Gandhi award he donated $500,000 to the Gandhi Memorial International Foundation." —Wiki

Guru very good business indeed. Whatever happened to the man? Well, I'd venture to say, Yo-gesh is as good as mine. In likelihood he's Gandhi with the wind.

Part Three: 1987-ish. Tulshi Sen was a bit of a guru and a shrewd businessman. Wilma was a wise woman and didn't know shit about business. I was a budding Buddhist and a drunkard who produced large events. The three of us went together one day to a business seminar somewhere near Torrance, California.

Wilma was driving her comfortable Mercedes and Tulshi was in the back seat. The subject of angels came up. I was quite the skeptic, "We don't need no stinkin' angels!" However, when I asked Tulshi, the man whose father was a revered guru back in India, if he believed in angels his succinct reply surprised me, "Oh, yes. Yes."

Perplexed, I asked again, "Do you really believe in angels, wings and all?" "Oh, yes," said he with his comforting all-knowing East Indian accent. To add to that Wilma, whom I respected as a clearheaded person, chimed in, "Yes, yes, no doubt."

Over the years I've done my best to be open to all possibilities and I've grown a bit, metafizzically speaking. And with that receptiveness I've come to my own belief that one of the ways that God interacts and communicates with us is by the extension of "beams" of His sacred energy, a filtered and often subtle energy that is specific to and for the spiritual growth of each conscious being when the time is right, the energy that connects us all to "Indra's net."

By the way, I don't believe that each animal is in need of these ethereal forms, as animals are by nature "in tune." We human critters, on the other hand, have managed in our hubristic fury to fall out of nature, to lose touch with The Divine, and so need these loving hand-me-downs.

And so these days if I'm asked if I believe in angels I'm prone to reply, "Oh, yes. ... wings and all." Well, if that's how you like your angel food cake, the Master Chef will bake it to your delight.

An Important Dream

In the United States, Muktananda was a little-heard-of guru. Came to America in the seventies, it seems, spent a lot of time around Oakland, California, could have easily passed for one of the "brothers," with his dark shades, dapper hat and Afro-looking hair. He passed away in 1982.

My only real recollection of him was from a little pamphlet I found lying in an otherwise empty country field about 45 years ago that, upon reading, had brought me to tears. What a surreal fluke, standing there alone in a barren field on the outskirts of Watsonville, just south of Santa Cruz on a windy day, nothing but an old horse and a rusted plow. But there it was, right under my feet. How the heck did it get there?

This was at a time when a Transcendental Meditation course was selling for about $300. Well worth it, I know, because I was trained years ago and it saved my crazy ass on more than one occasion! The course now runs for over $1,500, as does a similar one marketed by Deepak Chopra. I believe this instruction fee is reasonable because the Chopra group, and especially the TM folks, are having a positive impact on the planet in so many ways … see TM.org for insight on the subject. Also see a segment on the OWN (Oprah Winfrey Network) channel titled "America's Most Unusual Town," with Oprah doing what she does best … bringing wisdom and kindness to all of us.

But as regards the fee to learn meditation, old Mookie said in his little pamphlet that, as a rose is a rose, a mantra is a mantra. He believed that basic meditation education should be made available to everyone … *absolutely free* with basic instructions to anyone who wished to apply it.

So he offered a generic and ancient brand mantra: *So'ham.* Here is the meaning according to *Yogapedia*:

> *So'ham,* or *So'hum,* is a Hindu mantra pronounced as so-hum that can be translated as 'I am He/That.' It is a universal and natural mantra because it is present within everybody as the breath, with the sound of 'so' during inhalation and 'hum' during exhalation. As such, So'hum is a mantra that is chanted just by concentrating on the breath because the breath chants it naturally.

So in Muktananda's loving little pamphlet, he included, along with the mantra, the essential meditation instructions (mind set, breathing, posture, etcetera), free to anyone who wished to apply it. This in my opinion was bona fide goodness. He was sharing perhaps the most profound realization conceivable, and that is that we are one with "That." He was sharing how we each may commune with That.

To fulfill John Lennon's "Imagine" dream, we'd need a planet filled with conscious people, of people with raised awareness, mindfulness that transcends all that holds us back. *Transcendental … Meditation.*

1997. My dream this morning is now vague to me, but I do remember that in it I was speaking with a dear friend of mine, a poet named Schyleen Qualls, a bit of a guru in her own right. And somehow during this conversation a door opened and there stood Muktananda, very alive and very focused. Communication took place most clearly, but without verbal conversation.

The guru said in a straightforward manner that I should *teach meditation and give it away, no strings attached … free.* From this dream it became absolutely clear to me that I needed to pursue this path, first to meditate regularly, to learn from the meditational experience, and then to do my best to communicate its lessons freely.

On an even more personal level it tells me that my own therapy should come from an enlightened posture which is the result, in part, of meditation. Anything short of that keeps me trapped in *maya*, illusion and its countless seductions. (In my case they have been primarily that of sex and alcohol. Old age, thank God, has settled one of those battles and fear of death the other. Hardly heroic, though therapy and unending effort to "do the right thing" and achieve higher consciousness have for many years altered who I am now.)

Most of us live in consistent illusion, which includes false and limiting views of who and what we are, and what greatness we are capable of. The "Earthy Mysticism" hermit Father William McNamara's definition of contemplation is "a long loving look at the real." So with *applied* transcendental consciousness, in-tune-ness with all existence, comes the strength to deal with most obstacles, addictions and even pain.

I believe that this consciousness only comes from a dedicated and prolonged humility and openness which, if we are fortunate, results in growing and glowing rays of grace, and to be enveloped in this light is the most one could possibly wish for. For me, Old Mookie was—and is—one of those rays.

Meeting Sarah Vaughn, aka The Divine One, aka Sassy

1980-ish, Toluca Lake, CA. Basking in the glow of my brief but for-real exchange with Miles Davis (referred to by fellow musicians as The Prince of Darkness, pinned on him because of his salty, sullen moods), I'm reminded of an interlude with an equally talented musical wonder I chanced to sit next to at a night club down in Toluca Lake, an older yet tasteful joint called The Money Tree.

Straight out of the '50s, maybe older. It wasn't an elite place at all, no cover charge for the music, but a great steak house with an Italian flair, intimate and classy with its thick red-leather booths and polished baby grand. There were tall, padded stools, maybe six or seven, surrounding the piano where you could literally rub elbows with the who's who musicians of the Big Band heyday, cats who would sit in to play most evenings.

By the way, the club was located smack in the middle of the Disney/ Warner Brothers/Universal studios triangle, and late night shows à la Johnny Carson were just up the road in "beautiful downtown Burbank." So because of the proximity to this swath of top musical talents and the known quality of the piano man, a jazz buff like me was in absolute heaven! The Tree was indeed the perfect ambiance to take in the old pros who still jammed with their renditions of the Great American Songbook, guys who were top studio musicians as well as some very special guests now and then … God, does a place like this exist anywhere in the world? Did it ever? I pray that such environments emerge for the next generation of jazz lovers to be immersed in.

That particular night the person sitting next to me just happened to be Sarah Vaughn, the world-renowned jazz and pop singer—"Sassy" they called her in her heyday. She was well into her years now, mid-sixties I'm guessing, and sassy she wasn't, just super mellow.

Like most of America, for decades I was certainly aware of who Ms. Vaughn was, but in that dark and smoky setting I really didn't recognize her until the piano player asked her to do a tune or two, and that turned into a wonderful mini concert, maybe a half-hour or so.

At the end of her set, I scribbled a quick poem on a napkin (which I was wont to do in those days, you know, like some artists do sketches or caricatures). When she returned to her seat, I slipped it to her, the note that is.

A few days after this memorable encounter, I met her at yet another jazz hang just up the street there on Riverside, a joint called Alphonse's where Frank Sinatra, Jr. and friends frequently played. I asked what she thought about my little poem; her response, with a nod and a nice little smile, was "Man, that was heavy." Wow, wish I could remember what the heck I wrote.

I still kick back after a nice meal, throw on one of her CDs and listen to her rendition of "Misty." Yep, I fall in love all over again with a voice that flies me to the moon.

P.S. Here's a video of Sarah in a late-night spot. Just listening you'll get a good feel for the ambiance of a jazz club from my time. Kicked back, cozy, smoky, and okie-dokey. What's not to dig? And do take in the righteous range of The Divine One. Sarah Vaughan, Misty (Live from Sweden) Mercury Records 1964. 3.8 million YouTube views!

The following series of vignettes are grouped together even though the various dates are spread across a forty-year span. As you read this tale of fateful friendship you will see why I needed to put them all in one bag.

The Art Piece

"Romance is mush, stifling those who strive,
so I'll live a lush life in some small dive,
and there I'll be while I rot with the rest
of those whose lives are lonely too."

—Lyrics from *Lush Life*. This generously morose piece was composed by a 16-year-old musical genius, Billy Strayhorn, while he was with Duke Ellington's band. I loved those lyrics, combined with the bittersweet, languorous flavor of a melody that tempted me to madness. Check out Sarah Vaughn's devastating version on YouTube.

Part One. ***King Arthur of the Bar Table***

I'd like to introduce you to a dear buddy with whom I've had a lifelong friendship—in fact it has gone on for over four decades, close to five. It all started in a smoky club in West Fresno back in sixty-five.

That's where I first met, really met, Arthur Barfield. I had seen him and his younger brother Tommy earlier in high school—'58-'59—but they were two or three years older than I and, as it goes with the strata, you just don't fraternize with the younger, un-cool kids. I recall meeting him once in all that time, a hardly memorable encounter in the school lunchroom. This skinny, bespectacled yet blind as a bat color-of-purple kid was hitting on some chubby white chick, but despite all his jive-talkin' he was getting nowhere fast. This was a scene to be repeated time and again … yet, I must admit, he did score every now and then.

As it turned out, during my brief Army stint at Schofield Barracks, Hawaii, I had been introduced to jazz by a couple of older black soldiers who I had befriended and vice-versa. They were from back East, New York City, the nexus, the hub, the womb from whom the jazz was brung, so cool, so hip, intoxicating orchestration with syncopation, straight-ahead sophistication, be-bop and beyond. Uh-huh!

We all have our personal taste, but for me something marvelous happened when jazz first entered my bumpkin brain. I was swept away with this fusion of breakaway brilliance, brought home by the absolute geniuses that came together to deliver a juxtapositioned baby, a C-section on the A Train. For me, in spite of the newness of its offbeat sense, contemporary jazz was flat beautiful, deeply imbedded in the very being of those creative cats, deliberate while simultaneously rivetingly spontaneous. How can that possibly be, blending A flat with don't B square?

And so it was that when I was just out of this man's Army on a sweltering Fresno night, 'round midnight I found myself still wearing my silk Hawaiian shirt from my Waikiki days, thick sweat running down from my armpits. I was sitting in the small, dimly lit bar in the Greyhound bus depot, a seedy place with velour paintings of clowns with tears running down their cheeks … how apropos.

I was there because of a sharp little jazz trio that played on weekends. In those days, most places like this didn't have a cover charge, just "pass the hat" by the players and maybe they made a buck or two from the bar. As the night came to an end and the overhead lights annoyingly flicked on, I looked across the room and there he was: black on black. Man, in the thick of a sizzling summer the cat was wearing a black suit, black shirt, black tie, and black sunglasses, hip personified. Come to find he was stone blind but wore those dark-ass sunglasses just to be cool.

What the fuck. I got up, went over, and introduced myself. It was Art Barfield, King Arthur, all kicked back and mellow (the snifters of Courvoisier may have had a little to do with it … Art was a tightwad, but not when it came to his liquor). He was exceptionally cordial with his cordials, with one of those ear-to-ear winning grins and loud, contagious laughter that I came to know and love.

He was a relatively short, skinny dude who normally wore large, thick reading glasses that gave him a studious look … what he was normally studying was the butt of the nearest chick. The two of us, both being young jazz buffs and horny hound dogs (not necessarily in that order), immediately hit it off.

And since the bar was now closed we decided to bop on over to his pad where he was still living with his mom. Nonetheless, his room was in the very back of the house, and so we had a degree of privacy to banter and blast the sounds. He poured us both a glass of brandy and pulled out some choice albums from his considerable jazz collection (vinyl, dude).

He also brought out a beat-up relic of a trumpet, which he proceeded to play along with the album's music. Good thing I was drunk because in spite of the fact that Art couldn't hit a fuckin' note, I snapped my fingers, nodded my head up and down, and expressed, "Yeah, Bru-tha', yeah!" The cat did have a taste of rhythm and a feast of soul. We palled around for a couple of years, and then the man just flat-ass disappeared.

Part Two: *"Do you know the way to San José?"*

I had no possible idea that this was to be one in a series of "coincidental" encounters with Arthur that would span the West Coast over a forty-year period! These most pleasant albeit head-scratching happenings kicked into gear when I moved to San José, about three years after that fateful meeting in a Fresno night spot. No, I hadn't seen Art nor made contact with him in quite a stretch.

Seeking jazz joints was now in my blood, and when I moved north to go to college in San José I took no time finding the most happening haunt. It was, as was often the case, an intimate little setting with a jazz trio. And who just happened to be sitting there taking in the sounds? … You guessed it, Mister Arthur Barfield. Turns out he had found a gig at the big IBM plant there in San Josey.

And it happened again a couple of years later when I was spending a lot of time in the City, San Francisco … Yeah, just scootin' 'round North Beach where there was a handful of really hot nightclubs—places like The Black Hawk, Keystone Korner, and others along Broadway and Upper Grant; and of course there was the in-the know 'Mo (The Fillmore) Both/And Club. Every night of the week you could get your fix—lot of excellent local groups, yes, but also the headliners, the icons, coming out from the East Coast.

City nights were rich and alive with avant-garde sound and the finger-snappin' aficionados that caught it and got it. And yep, there he was on one of those marvelous eves, my man Arturo, black shirt, skinny black tie, and endless smile.

Part Three: *The Grrrreat Northwest.*

When Art and I were hangin' in San Francisco he mentioned studying to become a city planner. Said it was a decent paying occupation, all comfy with lots of perks, as in perky secretaries. The guy was still married but a real womanizer, addicted to his dick. Seriously, that satisfaction always came first, before holidays, before family, just the way he was. And I get it … it's like a leash attached above your balls, leading you wherever and whenever it wants. I get it.

And you may ask, "And so where is all this leading?" Well, somehow Art got accepted into grad school at the University of Oregon to get his City Planner degree. In no time he and his little family packed their few possessions and headed northward.

But let me back up a little. Turns out that while I was living in Santa Cruz I got a mighty tempting letter from *Cuckoo's Nest* author and counter culture hero Ken Kesey. I had met him at a large poetry bash in The City, and we hit it off pretty well. So one day, quite out of the blue, I get this "Come on up to the Swamp" letter. Long story short, I damn sure took him up on it.

Turns out Ken and his family lived on a small ranch in the tiny community of Pleasant Hill, Oregon, a few miles from the university. So I ended up visiting Mister K for a few days, but spent much of my evening time scootin' 'round Eugene to check out the booze and the babes … oh, and of course the jazz scene. Didn't take long for me to find a mellow establishment, this place featuring white players in the Dave Brubeck mode (Did you know that *Take Five* is the best-selling jazz single of all time?)

By now I'm sure you know what (or who) is coming. Once again there sat Mr. Barfield, snappin' his fingers, lookin' cool. So that was the fourth "encounter," as in *Encounters of the Third Kind.* This was getting trippy! Ok, so let's count'em: Fresno, San José, San Francisco, and now friggin' Eugene! Four kooky co-inky-dinks! Hey, I'm starting to hear the music from Twilight Zone.

Part Four: *Portland, Origami*

Again I headed north, *as in "North to Alaska."* But that's another story. This time I only got as far as Portland, with the beautiful Willamette River flowing through it. What a pleasant, kicked back town, clean as the snow on the nearby mountain range, the magnificent Cascades.

Not knowing a soul on the first day I drove in, I decided to scout around and check out the scene. In those years, Portland was yet to be built up, but the powers that be definitely had plans. Too bad, because it was absolutely perfect as it was.

So I'm parked and walking down one of the main streets along the river and notice a nice little shop with big glass windows. They are selling frozen yogurt, a novelty at the time. And behind the counter—you might say counter *culture*—is a vivacious creature, just bursting with the goodness of one of her scoops. Turns out Andrea was the owner of this hot little frozen biz, quite the entrepreneur. Little could I have known that she was all over that town, owning the yogurt shop as well as co-owning the very popular Saturday Market Place that took place weekly along the river. That was a very cool event, with hundreds of exhibitors peddling their art, their food, and their music—and dear Andrea was getting her share.

And there was yet another gig in Andrea's bag of goodies—she was a city planner. Yes, that very first day upon meeting her we sat at a small table near her store window and got to know each other. For whatever reason I happened to mention that I was originally from ... *Fresno.* I still can't believe it! Her eyes lit up and she asked, "You wouldn't happen to know a man named...*Art Barfield*?" Turns out she was a mucky-muck for The City and Art somehow worked with her!

With this rather amazing three-person connection I was immediately in like Flynn, as in classic film star Errol Flynn; in with the voluptuous Andrea, a Jewish goddess in the land of milk and honey. We ended up living together for a year or so, yep, it was 1977, the year that the Portland Trailblazers won the NBA championship ... that little town had never partied so hardy!

Needless to say, Art and I further cemented our friendship many a night over jazz and cocktails.

Part Five: ***Los Angeleeze, if you pleaze.***

1983-ish. A couple of years later I found myself up in Seattle, Washington, producing large events at the Seattle Center and now rooting for the Seattle Supersonics (with my support, they of course won the 1979 NBA title). And I was commuting by Amtrak regularly to Portland—almost a three-hour trek—to hang out with Art and take in the sounds. This went on for a few years, five or so.

There came a time, however, when things in my life just kind of fell apart, went south. And that's exactly where I headed … south. All I had was a hope and a prayer of selling one of my do-gooder TV scripts to the Big Guys. Talk about a long shot!

I was in my late 40s, no spring chicken, so it was now or never. I grabbed a ride with my long haul, truck drivin' buddy, Dennis Riley, and headed down to Los Angeles, down to Wilshire Boulevard where the TV honchos sat behind their big desks and made decisions that could change your life with a nod. Well, I did get as far as meeting those fellows. Thank God for the L.A. Lakers, the time of Jabbar and Scott and Magic, when again in 1985 I helped a team win the NBA championship.

Truth be told, L.A. was just too damn overwhelming for this country boy. This was the last place I wanted to be in the world, struck with panic attacks while stuck in perennial traffic jams! I went down there using every red cent I had, trying to peddle those TV concepts I just knew would sell … yeah, right.

As you can well imagine, the scripts were never picked up and I was soon stuck there, like the dinosaurs in the city's famed La Brea Tar Pits. Still, in little time I was working wherever I could to make a buck, doing shitty little telemarketing jobs just to keep the proverbial wolf from the door. And then I returned to my bread-and-butter occupation of producing events with a couple of fairly successful Art & Poetry Festivals. I hung out at a joint called Residuals in North Hollywood (residuals, as in what you receive from a successful script), still thinking I might chance into someone interested in my film and TV ideas.

And as usual, I sought out the nearest jazz club. It was called The Money Tree in Toluca Lake, a you-had-to-be-in-the-know intimate little nightclub with one of those rare-these-days piano bars. People would sit around in the evenings, many of them recognizable by their first name … like Frank (Sinatra), Tony (Bennett), and Sarah (as in Vaughn), and several big band stars. After all, The Tree was in the Triangle of the major movie studios, and there were stars galore who were into jazz.)

One evening I enjoyed a date with an older but still gorgeous singer-actress named Barbara McNair, whom I had met earlier at "The Tree." That chick had one helluva story—one of the first black women to have her own TV show, Bill Cosby's girl in the *I Spy* TV series, oh, and the first black centerfold of *Playboy.* She was single at the time, so lucky me. I would really like to have pursued a relationship with her, but frankly I was having a hard time buying my own damn drinks.

I recall asking her one evening what type of music she sang, and her answer was "pop." Pop, I take it, for popular. I was surprised. I said that so much of it, with the smooth piano, standup bass, and usually light drum brushes, sounded a heck of a lot like mellow jazz to me.

She explained yes, that's true, but originally most of these were tunes that were big hits in their day, the '40s, '30s and even '20s, the romantic harmonies and lyrics by the likes of Hammerstein, Hart, Cole Porter, even recently by folks like Burt Bacharach and Carol King. I had to pull the straw out of the gap of my front teeth on being so oblivious to that obvious tidbit. Boston *Pop* Orchestra … duh.

Anyway, we were sitting there that evening—fourteen million people in the megalopolis of Greater Los Angeles—and again I hear that most pleasantly identifiable, thoroughly joyous laugh. I turn around and … damn! … there's Art, Art-fuckin'-Barfield!

Of all the jazz joints in all the towns in all the world, he walks into mine. Yep, it was him alright, wearing his signature black-on-black suit, shirt, tie—hell, that cat probably wore black underwear! I mean the guy shows up out of no-fuckin'-where in the heart of Los Angeles!

"Hey, buddy," sez I, "you gotta admit this is outta this friggin' world!"… and in a sense it was. *Six times* our paths had serendipitously crossed in six different cities in three different states, us never having a clue that these meetings were to occur … Fresno, San José, San Francisco, Eugene, Portland, and now down L.A. way.

Turns out he had gotten divorced, split from Portland, found a planning gig down in Inglewood, and like a homing pigeon naturally flew to one of the most happening jazz sets in the region. Art, I sez a few days later, there's obviously more to this than meets the eye. I told him that maybe we didn't have to read too much into it, that maybe it was just God saying hello, again, again, and again … and that's one heck of a blessing. In the truest sense, Art is my soul brother.

Blue Note Love Note. Down L.A. way one totally sober day Arthur and I were hanging out, just kicking back in my living room, listening to the great Los Angeles jazz and shooting the shit. I was in the midst of my usual metaphysical mumbling when, out of nowhere, Art sez, "Damn, Tomás, I wish you were a woman … I'd marry you."

A compliment, I guess … I'd venture to say we got along better than most couples. We were both night owls who spoke of metaphysics and madness, music and the muses. But nonetheless I was compelled to respond to the off-the-wall marriage proposal, "Art, if you were a woman with yo' skinny black ass, I wouldn't let you suck my dick!" Art thought that was fuckin' hilarious. But to soften the letdown a bit I added, "Well, maybe if you gained a few pounds and put on a shitload of lipstick."

A Happening Set with Miles Davis

Flashback from The City, Circa '68. I'd meet up now and then with my old buddy from Fresno, Art Barfield, the guy who turned me on to Miles Davis. Davis was his hero, defiant, moody, deep … a very intense man who took his brilliance to soaring heights, and still delights with Sketches of Spain in the brain. Art literally loved Miles and would go for miles to see him in the flesh.

We were living in San Francisco at the time, he with his new wife and child, Tanya (who became a fabulous playwright and performer—I'm sure Art's creativity had a bit to do with that). At the same time I was living nearby in the Mission District. Art and I had agreed to go out one evening to take in some sounds but the cat never showed up. You might say he was plying his trade, but I'd say plowing. When he would "catch"—meaning score a lady, marriage be damned—everything else went by the wayside, Christmas dinner, a graduation ceremony, whatever. The chick could be ugly as sin, old as dirt, didn't make no no-how—if she still had a heartbeat he was on it. That's what happened that night, as he copped to a few days later.

It was close to midnight and I didn't want to miss the final set of the group that was playing in The Fillmore in a joint known as the Both/And Club. Figuring that Art was up to his usual shenanigans, I caught a cab and headed out. When I got to the club there was still a line, albeit a short one, outside the door. I honestly don't recall the name of the group but they were definitely kickin'. When I finally got in I found the place was packed with hardly a corner to even stand in.

And yet, dead center of the whole place was a sizable table that could seat at least six, with only one very suave cat sitting there. What the …? Since my Army days I've always had a taste of swagger (more often stagger), moxie, whatever you want to call it, and this was not about to be an exception. Needless to say, I headed straight to that essentially empty table and, with a brief appeal, asked if I might join the man's table. He looked me over and, for whatever reason, he just nodded with a finger pointing to the chair next to him.

Now I have mentioned that the dude was dapper, but it was in a conservative way, dark suit, sharp silk tie … immaculately sophisticated in appearance and demeanor is probably the best way to describe him. The rest of the brothers, true to the threads of the time, had bellbottom slacks, long sleeve shirts with large collars flaring … the wider, the hipper. The band had been on break and was just returning. Piece by piece the music crescendoed as did my groove.

I am personally used to bopping my head, snapping my fingers, and making guttural sounds consistent with the blackness of a jazz joint … yeah, uh-huh, yeah man, etc. But not this audience, who were 99% black but had jacked up their cooler-than-thou condescension in a kind of slow-motion. "I'm such a hip muthahfuckah, prove to me that you are worthy of my praise" attitude. Mind you, these idiots knew the idiom.

They just sat there in front of the stage like fuckin' zombies, legs stretched, one foot over the other, heads slightly down staring up over their thin pimp shades meticulously placed near the end of their noses. Apparently, the fad du jour had become not to applaud but just sit there, quasi-sophisticated, with only the slightest nod if a musician was really cookin'.

"Fuck this shit," sez I to my table host, "These motherfuckers don't know shit … A musician, like all of us, appreciates a little acknowledgement. Lot of fuckin' work … can you dig it?" For decades the sign of approval in a jazz set was a healthy applause after *each* solo … sax, trumpet, piano, drums, bass fiddle … Yeah, brutha!

So, like a fool, I stood up solo and after each musician's riff I applauded. Uh-huh! Finally, after a couple of these scenes, with everyone in the joint staring at me like I was from … well … Fresno, the dapper cat actually stood up with me and applauded, not as loud as my country-ass self, but still he applauded, his bottom left hand stable and open, and the other softly slapping the palm. The band definitely took notice.

Eventually a few others in that hall took our lead. My courteous host split before the set was completed, with a finger pointed at me and a "catch you later, my man" farewell. It didn't take a second for a handful of brothers to swarm in on *my table* with questions for me.

The main one was, "How long you been knowin' him?" Knowing who? "How long you been knowin' Miles." "Shhheeeit!" thinks I, "For a while now, for a while," I replied as to mean "quite a while." That "while" was all of

20 minutes when I had the unusual honor of taking in a set with Art's hero, Miles Davis.

Blue Note. One of Miles' nicknames was "The Prince of Darkness." He was dark skinned and more often than not dressed in black attire (which finally explains Art Barfield's choice of rags), but add to that his fiercely serious looks and no-nonsense attitude, and the moniker is spot on. Turning his back to the audience as he soloed only added to this persona.

Owed to Art

Yesterday is here today, a rhapsody in blues,
snapping your fingers in smoky haunts of reminiscent hues.
No quarter note is left unheard with eternal jazz to dope us,
a foggy night in Portland town up Burnside to Jazz de Opus.

A cognac snifter Shearing sips, the Vine Street Bar & Grill,
fingers glide the baby grand, my lady pays the bill.
The Both/And Club in ol' San Fran drips notes of silv'ry rain
like Billy Strayhorn's lush lament burning in my brain.

Again I hear the West Coast riffs from the Lighthouse Café—
Mulligan, Mann, and MJQ sweep the night away.
The salty air drifts through the door, Tjader and Brubeck play,
Chet Baker proposes "Let's get lost" —They too are here today.

I still hear your joyous laugh, embrace your endless smiles,
your old trumpet tucked away with memories of Miles.

A Fool for Beauty

Here and there throughout my life, I've found myself rather astounded to find a tear welling up for no apparent reason. I recall stumbling home one very drunk morning by the Santa Cruz beach. I noticed a broken green wine bottle in the gutter. I recognized the cheapness of the brand. It was probably thrown out of a car window the previous night as rowdy out-of-towners headed back to their humdrum lives. I stopped and stared at this piece of splattered art with its droplets of dew glimmering in the morning mist, the glass fragments creating a crystal rainbow onto the moist cement. I stood there like the village idiot as tears rolled down my face.

At one point back in the eighties I had purchased a large old Pontiac for a song. When I say "for a song" I mean that, yes, it was super-cheap, maybe 500 bucks, but also that the thing had a hell of speaker system already installed—Blaupunkt—which alone was worth more than that boat of a car. As I headed to Fresno one morning from my home down in Redondo Beach, I listened to a classical station that I had picked up as I crossed over The Grapevine, that steep stretch of highway where many a vehicle has met its demise. I truly wish I could remember the specific piece, but all I recall is that it was an overture played by a full orchestra and had a sizable choir in the background; the mode was full, fast and lively—prestissimo!

The whole experience just flat overcame me. At first, I simply allowed the music to engulf me, but then, so touched by its beauty and power I became awed by the fact that human beings were playing those instruments, and human beings created the harmony in those voices, and that some brilliant, sensitive soul sat sometime, somewhere hearing that music in his head and generously took the time to write out each note, each chord, each nuance from his amazing mind.

The mere thought that individual human beings were capable of creating and executing this complex masterpiece—that they themselves had *to feel* in order to convey—that we earthly creatures could as a group produce such absolute beauty, thoroughly floored me. The tears poured yet again, a deluge, so much so that I had to pull off the road and just sit there and listen until the final notes went silent.

When it was over I drove back onto the highway. Even though the name of the orchestra and title of the piece was transmitted, in my overwhelmed state I simply wasn't receiving. I was blown out by beauty. This experience has occurred a handful of times in my life, in an opera setting, driving home from a class reunion, and just sitting alone in a forest, but it was never again so thorough and all encompassing. I think of the word *rapture.*

The Love Supreme

"Let the different faiths exist; let them flourish; and let the glory of God be sung in all the languages and in a variety of tunes. That should be the ideal."—Sri Sathya Sai Baba

1985. Jazz great John Coltrane, once anointed "Saint Coltrane," first penetrated my shallow senses when I was hanging out with Art B., whom you've heard a lot about. Coltrane conquered his addictive demons and went on to compose and play some of the most creative, avant-garde, and strikingly devotional music in the jazz idiom … for me, some of the most beautiful, period. "A Love Supreme" was his paean to the Spirit who brought him back from the depths of addiction.

A deep monotone voice in the background of that spiritually driven piece slowly repeats, "A Love Supreme, A Love Supreme …" The voice is that of Coltrane himself.

The tenor saxophonist Pharoah Sanders, who played with Coltrane's group (circa '65-'66), wrote and played his own salute to Coltrane's song which he titled, "The Creator has a Master Plan." In his composition the vocalist Leon Thomas repeats the refrain, "The Creator has a Master Plan, peace and happiness for every man." I've often thought that some very worthy musician should put the two pieces together … "Master Plan of The Love Supreme."

After one lengthy and deliciously dangerous dive into thoroughly (not Thoreau-ly) premeditated debauchery, I found myself sedated and close to death in a Los Angeles hospital. This happened on my 41st birthday, the very day. There it is: Number 41. For years I actually thought I would die on my 41st … Well, I was sure trying.

My condition was caused by yet another bout of alcohol-induced pancreatitis. The nurse working with me was a middle-aged man, a soft-spoken African-American gentleman who was well traveled and educated. Over the weeks while I lay there on the edge of The Big Sleep, he and I spent a fair amount of time casually rapping about most everything. However, when it came to the subject of jazz he really lit up. As it turned out he was also a jazz buff and a Coltrane devotee, *quite literally*. That is to say he was a devotee in more ways than one: he was an ardent John Coltrane fan but he was also a dedicated practitioner of the Vedanta school of Hinduism. Who was his guru? Well of course … Alice Coltrane.

Alice Coltrane, John's remarkable wife who herself was an accomplished classical and jazz pianist, an artist who had played in Carnegie Hall, had gone on to become a bona fide guru. (She was a *swamini*—a female swami, a "spiritual director.") She had an ashram (a Hindu center and place of worship) close by in Woodland Hills, on the west end of the San Fernando Valley. Her teacher, in turn, was the famous Indian master Sathya Sai Baba, an elevated personage who had millions of followers and who, I have read, performed miracles. He also had over the years opened great hospitals and schools throughout India and elsewhere.

After about a month of care for my illness, I was finally discharged from that V.A. hospital, once again an agonizing ordeal and a close call. I had learned over the years that when I went in with this particular malady there was a very good chance that I'd never come out ... For some reason this greatly enhanced my sense of humor. I guess there was some kind of cosmic irony in the fact that I had ended up on a near-death bed as a gift for my 41st birthday. I had thought for years that, due to my astounding experiences with the number *forty-one* throughout my life, there was a very good chance that I would die on this particular day. But nooo, I was just in great agony and dangerously close to the other side. I've since decided to double my number, making it 82, at which time I'll double it again).

When dismissed from the hospital I found a phone number on a small piece of paper in my pocket. On it was also a familiar name, the name of the fellow, the very hip nurse, the devotee of Alice Coltrane, who had turned me on to Alice's ashram, Alice's ashram, Alice's ashram ... Ommmmm. He had earlier suggested that I visit someday and that someday was to occur within a week after my discharge. I called him and made an appointment.

Alice Coltrane's guru had given her the name Turiyasangitananda, which beautifully translates to *The Transcendental Lord's highest song of bliss.* Apparently my new friend, the nurse, had mentioned to her that I would be visiting and she graciously took the time to greet me in private following the afternoon teaching and meditation.

In this tradition, when a person is in the presence of a divine teacher, he is to first lay prostrate before him (or, in this case, her), that is to "make obeisance." I don't think she expected me to lay before her as I was not a devotee, but honestly, I was not hesitant to do just that if it had been appropriate.

There were just the three of us, my friend the nurse, Alice and myself. We spoke briefly and in that span I mentioned to her that my dear friend Tino Esparza, who was a tremendous John Coltrane fan, was rapidly passing away from cancer. She took a moment and then considerately replied, "There are times when it is time."

Her husband John had passed away at a relatively young age, just 40, but in his lifetime he had touched millions with his warm ballads and soulfully lilting salutes to God. "Over the course of his career, Coltrane's music took on an increasingly spiritual dimension, as exemplified on his most acclaimed albums *A Love Supreme* (1965) and *Ascension* (1966). He remains one of the most influential saxophonists in music history."—from Wikipedia.

Alice Coltrane offered to speak to my dying friend, Tino, and so I gave her his number. I found out soon from him that indeed she had called and that he had very much enjoyed the conversation. I loved that man a great deal, being the best man at his wedding, being together in the thick of the Chicano Student Movement, and consuming our share of jazz and cocktails. I confess to wishing that I had heard what was said.

In preparing to leave that sacred, quiet village, a dozen or so small huts surrounded by a eucalyptus grove where the devotees lived, my friend the nurse walked with me up to my car. He said that he had never seen his teacher, his guru, respond to a person quite so warmly, if that is the right term, and that it was a very positive thing for me that she did so. I didn't quite know what to say. I've only now discovered that her guru, Sathya Sai Baba, and I were born on the same day of the year. She could not have known that. Happy Birthday, Sathya!

A Young Lady of the Oldest Profession

San Francisco, early 70s. Seeing that most of my life I've had this understanding that there was a great chance my "real mom" was a prostitute, and that I've always felt that prostitution should be legalized, it was hardly surprising that as I matured (well, kind of) I found myself being somewhat attracted to the Women of the Night. Never paid for it, that wasn't what it was about at all … though in my younger years I certainly considered it. It was about finding them fascinating, yes, and enjoying their company.

In fact, I periodically hung out at an old bar not far from the Tenderloin District … typical dark joint, pool table, jukebox, no TV—which was uncommon even then. The majority of the clients were "working girls," and this was their hang, you know, kind of like a cop bar in reverse. They would just sit around during the day, drinking, smoking and BS-ing much like the guys who worked the docks. Sometimes they'd be bad-rapping their tricks—"The asshole wanted to pay with fuckin' food stamps!"—or sexually scheming on one another, though the majority were pretty straight.

Loved to watch'em shoot pool with those mini-miniskirts, stretching for the long shots, their big asses spread across the table like a Viking feast. I never saw a pimp in the joint, but periodically the cop on the beat would poke his head in the door, make some sort of wisecrack, and move on. They all knew him by his first name, probably had a little barter thang goin' on.

So it wasn't that unusual when I fell quite in love/lust with a stunning young woman, a wavy-haired brunette in her mid-twenties, who was doing tricks in The City. She was flying solo with no mack-daddy attached. Parking cars for an elite older hotel, the famed Mark Hopkins, she met more than her share of tipsy johns who would stagger out most evenings quite ready for "a date." According to her they were generally moneyed and weren't the least bit chintzy. I agree with them—she was damn well worth it!

I first met her at a wild and woolly Winter Solstice pagan party with hippies, Hells Angels, and a motley gathering of freaks somewhere in the East Bay. We hit it off right on the spot—that's the way it usually works if something hot is about to pop. She lived in Berkeley and I at the time had a small studio apartment across the bay in The City, so we'd go back and forth periodically but mostly stayed in her flat, an upbeat pad with a large, framed Maxfield Parrish-ish poster hanging above her bedroom wall—you know, nymphs frolicking in the forest with a drunken Sagittarian satyr chasing them about...It's like someone fuckin' painted me in my primal romp. Can't a guy have a little privacy?

We hung out for about three months and at a point, get this, she offered to take care of me, I mean in style ... that was a new one! But I've been a terribly jealous cat all of my life and somehow her profession—and I ain't talking about parking cars!—was starting to get to me.

After a good roll in the hay, we'd light up and she, with a look of satisfaction, would say things like, "Lot of girls say they don't like it, ain't really there, just do it for the money. But, you know, I love it! Getting paid big time for enjoying myself, imagine that." Well, to my dismay, I did imagine that.

She said I was funny and a keeper. At one point we even touched on marriage—and that's when it got to me: too many jokers had played at that poker table, and she was the pokee. Even though I tried to say fuck it, man, ain't no big thing, that was a lie because of all the big things that had tapped that sweet, sweet spot.

Wish I'd have been more open-minded, able to get over my own pettiness and insecurity, but man, the whole idea was just too much for a guy who had his own sexual fears and fucked-up-ness. Forgive the cliché, but I think it's a fact that true love is hard to find, and this chick really dug me. She of course let me know there was no real intimacy with her playmates.

I felt a loss going our own ways but the truth of it was I just couldn't handle the idea of her getting it on with all these other dudes. More nights of jazz and cock tales, that was the ticket.

Playing Pool with the Chief of Alcatraz

'70-ish. He was Richard Oakes, a Mohawk Indian born in '42 on a reservation in New York State. He was a short, handsome guy with a full head of hair and a half-decent stick … as in pool stick. They called him "The Chief of Alcatraz," or just "Chief" for short, and that he was. Proud, brave, charismatic.

At the time, the so-called Indians—originally 14 Native-American activists who came from various tribes across the U.S.—had "occupied" the infamous tiny island of Alcatraz for the purpose of bringing attention to their plight, and in order to create a university there for Native-American kids. But, as it turned out, taking over "The Rock" was a tougher nut to crack than they thought. It was nonetheless a powerful symbolic gesture that got massive publicity and in the long run accomplished a great deal towards the ends they sought. (The fact that Dee Brown's excellent book *Bury My Heart at Wounded Knee: An Indian History of the American West*, had just hit the best-seller list, only stoked the flames.)

I'd meet Oakes and a handful of other activist-crazies over beers and games of pool at an old saloon down on a corner by Potrero Hill. That joint had been there since the '30s, a mecca for every stripe of lefty—wobblies, socialists, commies, even a common Democrat or two.

As I recall, someone whispered in my ear one day that Richard had a steel plate in his head, a result of being beaten senseless with a pool stick by some violent rightwing asshole. It took an immense will for him to just live day to day, and a great amount of dedicated energy from a medicine man who had danced and chanted and prayed for him to pull out of the coma caused by his beating. Not long after we had met, he just kind of disappeared from the scene.

I read in the *Chronicle* one morning that he had been shot to death by yet another idiot with the same m.o. as the cat who hit him with the pool cue.

The Chief of Alcatraz

There on Isla de Las Alcatraces,
Island of the Pelicans, Turtle Island,
14 stood taller than any statue,
taller than The Lady herself,
proud as the faces of granite
in those South Dakota Hills
now occupied by the ghosts of Wounded Knee.

Richard Oakes, Chief of The Pelicans,
rose like a big bird from a night
on the cold cement floor of the local slammer,
combed back his long, black hair,
"Drunk and belligerent? Drunk and belligerent?
Well, fuck you and the horse you rode in on!"

The jailer, while kicking the man's foot
to trip him as he walked out of his cell,
couldn't help but let him know,
"You'll be back, Chief, you'll be back!"

As the barred doors swung open
at six in the morn,
out into the misty San Francisco air
walked The Chief of Alcatraz,
the city still delicious in every direction...
coffee smells, bacon smells, and even pussy smells
lingering from the loose and easy night before.

The smell of freedom,
only minutes from a cold one,
a game of pool and talk of
General Custer's well-deserved vacation
to the Great Hunting Grounds.

Charles Bukowski and the Nurse

1974. I spent a couple of days with Charles, big guy with an alcoholic's nose, pocked, bulbous and red. Unattractive and pretty unkempt, at least on the few times I met him. Though I'm not a "big guy" like him it was still like looking into a fucking mirror after a year-long bender. He was arguably more infamous than famous. Had written quite a column down L.A. way for an underground weekly rag, the *Los Angeles Free Press*, a very smart dude with a lot to say in an entertaining, albeit dark, way.

He was a prolific writer, wrote hundreds of books and short stories and poems with titles like *Notes from a Dirty Old Man*, *Play the Piano Drunk Like a Percussion Instrument Until the Fingers Begin to Bleed a Bit*, and *Erections, Ejaculations, Exhibitions, and General Tales of Ordinary Madness.*

But his real claim to fame—or I should say, what really made him famous—was the movie they made *about* him and written primarily by him, a semi-autobiography starring Mickey Rourke and Faye Dunaway. It was called ... are you ready? ... *Barfly*. Gee-ma-neee! You gotta be quite a lush for an honor like that. It gets better: In 1986 *Time* called Bukowski a "laureate of American lowlife." I'm envious.

Anyway, I met him in Santa Cruz and had the pleasure of popping a few shots with the guy, salutes to God-knows-who-or-what, any excuse will do. I found out that he had been married-of-sorts, divorced, etc., and had had his share of wild and crazy broads, marriages made in Hell with him holding the pitchfork.

But now he was dating a very healthy and, I noted, relatively young and attractive nurse ... Hmmm. I asked him if that meant that he was straightening up, getting his alcoholic act together and maybe even contemplating marriage. He explained that there was a method to his horniness. "Marriage, no, but *healthier*, yes. She'll help me get healthier so I can fuck up longer." Good strategy.

Meanwhile, Back in Portlandia

During my brief stint in Portland, I drank a lot of port and spent quite a bit of time with my jazz bud, Art Barfield. He turned me onto the hot spots when I first got there, really wonderful environments to kick back and take in the real deal, I mean seriously cool jazz from marvelous musicians who had found a getaway in the Great Northwest, and periodically famous cats, like Art Blakey, Ben Webster, and Ahmad Jamal, who would do a gig in Portland and then scoot on up to Seattle and Vancouver.

As it turned out, my squeeze du jour, Andrea of Frozen Yogurt fame, was exceptionally well-connected, working at a high level in the mayor's office. So when I said I wanted to produce a large ecology expo similar to the one I had attended months earlier in San Francisco, she just pulled a string or two, and voila, I had dates at the Portland Coliseum, home of the Portland Trailblazers, to co-produce a mega environmental expo. "Build the field and they will come." Turns out a couple of her associates wished to produce a similar event, so we ended up working together. Synergy ... what a powerful force.

This was the first event on a large scale that I had ever attempted. As it turned out, the two-day show, produced about six grueling months after we first secured the venue, turned into quite a success, about 15,000 in attendance! But in spite of a rewarding production, behind the scene, I was busily leading my other life, the late-night howl-at-the-moon jazz-poet thing, brutally burning the candle at both ends. When you're young you can get away with shit like that ... or at least you think you do.

Well, after co-producing that event, my time in Portland came to a grinding halt when I started getting shit from Andrea about my midnight shenanigans, I mean damn near living at the Jazz de Opus with its opium den/funky furniture ambiance. I got to know the owner pretty well, and more than once found myself crashed overnight on one of those well-sunk lounge couches.

Andrea had always been miffed with my extra-curricular night-owl life—it was just too much for her Jewish-American Princess pride to countenance. That and the fact that one very drunk night I got jealous about some stupid thing and in a rage slapped her. Horribly sick behavior I had learned from my warring parents...but really there's never an excuse for it.

So she flat-ass kicked my brown butt out, I mean like with little adieu, you're out-ta here! (She was too civilized to be crude but in a calm tone she let me know it was time to move on). This break, combined with a scary encounter with some mafia maniacs—real "Wise Guys"—gave me good reason to scoot on up the road.

I had heard good things about the beauty of a green-minded Seattle, a perfect wave to catch on the environmental scene, and so I jumped into my trusty little Volvo and made my way northward with about 200 bucks in my pocket.

One of the best damn things I ever did, because Seattle, back in the '70s, was happening in spite of the fact you had to drive to fuckin' Tacoma to find a good bowl of menudo.

P.S. During lunch hour in New York a couple of years later, with zillions of folks squished together on the sidewalks like a bowl of gefilte fish scrunched into a tiny can, I was about to cross one of the mega-avenues and I spotted a familiar face across the street. It wasn't exactly the love scene from West Side Story, but I still couldn't believe it ... Andrea, Andrea of Portlandia fame! I got her attention, and she too was genuinely stunned. Three thousand miles away, ten million people ... What are the chances of that?

We walked to the first deli we could find and sat pleasantly yakking for a few minutes. Seems she was working for a high-level planner who had an office in Manhattan, I don't recall the details. I mean the chick just had class and smarts and the world was her erster.

Unfortunately, Andrea also remembered the negative incidents from back in Portland, and so in spite of this remarkable meeting we ended up having a brief cup of coffee. She had to move on with her day and I needed a stiff drink.

The Three Wise Guys

> "I shot a man in Reno, just to watch him die."
> —from "Folsom Prison Blues," by Johnny Cash. The prison crowd went wild when he sang those lyrics in a live concert there in The Joint ... Psycho-City!

In my travels I've run into men who were just plain evil, no doubt about it. No conscience. Capable of the worst of crimes, rip your heart out for a dime—or worse yet, for the sheer fun of it. These guys were genuinely scary. I often wonder what could possibly cause a human being to become so devoid of feelings for others.

I've been quite mad and done some pretty fucked up things—but I've always felt guilty as hell for it. And I ain't killed nobody though I admit to thinking that if certain persons were to leave this planet I wouldn't cry a lot.

I've had meetings with men in what turned out to be frightening metaphysical settings quite apart from their mundane locations, who have done their best to let me know just who they were and what evil entity they were the servants of. Some of the best lessons, it seems, are learned from the worst of experiences.

At one point while living in Portland I fell in with a very sharp fellow, a Puerto Rican New Yorker named Fernando. This smooth dude had all the charm of a refined gentlemen, a tall, unusually handsome, muscular man, early thirties, whose skills were such that he had been both a pro football and pro basketball player, as well as a bit of an actor. He could've been most anything; he could've been a contender, but instead he chose the route of crime, joined the Mafia and killed a guy in the process. When I asked him if he had left that life behind, he shook his head and said, "Once you're in, they never let you out."

In spite of knowing that I ran with him for a couple of months, taking in the jazz joints and the honky-tonks. This big guy always opened the door for me and daintily drank his cocktails, always with a straw. He was afraid of germs—go figure.

One evening we were driving to an intimate little hang, the Jazz de Opus in Old Town, warm, dark and comfortable. It featured mostly West Coast musicians and periodically the biggies from the East Coast, like Dexter Gordon, Ben Webster, and Art Blakey and the Jazz Messengers.

At a point I noticed that we were being tailed by a glossy silver Lincoln Continental—the damned thing looked like a shark. In the rear view mirror I could make out the silhouettes of three men.

I was in my little '66 Volvo, a stick shift sports sedan. I knew that sucker could jam because I had taken it *to the max* on a couple of occasions, once in a midnight race with a new Cadillac the entire way, about forty miles from Santa Cruz to Monterey. I had no idea who the other driver was, we just got into this thing because earlier on he went flying dangerously by me when I first got on that swerving old Highway One. Ultimately the guy couldn't keep up, although we did go back and forth. I recall beeping my horn as I was the first to turn off, and he beeped back saying he too had a hell of good time.

But now it was my heart that was racing, and I decided I sure as hell didn't want these thugs on my tail. The chase began with them in close pursuit. I shot through alleys, across parking lots, zipping one way and then another … I thought I was Steve McQueen in *Bullitt* … left'em in the dust!

That's when Fernando told me who these guys were … The Three Wise Guys. According to him, these men wouldn't just let him be, and stop being part of their activities. He then had the nerve to ask if I had ever considered "buying a politician," you know, finding one that is greedy and gullible (no shortage of those characters) and setting him up with favors of money and women. I looked at him like he was fuckin' nuts and he dropped the subject. He was a fascinating cat but I didn't fully know just who I was hanging out with.

The following evening I was sitting in another smoke-filled jazz joint, a mellow place featuring a crooner/sax player who had a mean version of "The Days of Wine and Roses." I happened to be wearing a favorite shirt, a somewhat unusual long-sleeve garment with a green paisley design. I went to the head as always—liquid in, liquid out. I looked over to the stall next to me and I'll be damned—there it was: my exact shirt, same everything, even size. Just hanging there. Oh well, says I, but to be honest it gave me the creeps because by this time I had a sense of The Twilight Zone and this was starting to have the makings.

I went back to my seat close to the small stage and sipped my brandy as the performer came out. About this time in walked three sharply tailored dudes, very East Coast and clearly out of place in this setting. It was pretty dark in there, but I made them out to be surely sinister, wearing their dark duds—suits, ties, the woiks—in the middle of the friggin' summer.

At one point I went up to the bar to buy a drink, and to do that I had to walk right up to the spot where these bad boys were sitting. I nodded to them, but they didn't budge, just stared, all three of them just stared. Upon closer examination it became obvious that these guys weren't friendly music buffs, though they were way buffed out—prison will do that.

One was Black, one Latino, and one a greasy-haired Italian, right out of *The Godfather*. Hmmm. Turns out these were the same maniacs tailing us the night before. I overheard the Black dude saying to the others, "This *is* paradise," with a real emphasis on 'is' … "This *is* paradise," he repeated. As opposed to what, I wondered. The fucking joint? Or maybe hell itself.

As I'm picking up my drink, I can't help but feel those cold, staring eyes from all three of them—wicked motherfuckers! Then the Black dude stands up and walks over next to me. Oh shit! He pulls out his wallet and removes a card. He doesn't give it to me but just shows it. It had fancy large letters across the center. It said something like "El Diaboloix." Strange spelling but I knew what the fuck it meant. The guy says, "You know, we really dug your driving."

Then he points to the card again and repeats, "Do you know what this means?" Rattled, I remembered a Hawaiian encounter with a fellow named Richard, a merchant marine, who I thought was the Evil One himself. Now this monster was letting me know upfront that he was an emissary of that dimension. I nodded soberly, "Yeah, I know what it means." That seemed to satisfy him for the moment, and he sat back down with the other gunsels.

The rest of my evening was totally fucked! I could hardly enjoy the music—every friggin' time I glanced in their direction the three of 'em would just stare at me. I mean with no break, not even conversation between them. They had decided to give me The Evil Eye. I sure as hell didn't dare stare back.

At one point two of them stood up and abruptly walked out. I figured they were going to their car to wait for me, the other one, the big black cat, was posted to follow behind me when I left (or so I believed, and I wasn't about to find out if I could help it). I strongly felt they were planning on either trying to recruit me, or more likely, just kill me. Perhaps they thought I knew too much.

It was almost midnight when the music finished. I was genuinely afraid to leave the place on my own. Over the last few weeks, I'd become buddies with the singer/band leader, so I waited for him to start packing his gear and followed him off stage and into the back room set up for musicians. I told him about the spot I was in, and he said, "Don't worry, I'm parked behind the club, we'll go out the back door."

And that we did. The entertainer was originally from New Orleans and as he drove me home, he said that it sounded to him like they were hexing me. He used a Cajun term that I don't remember. But I do remember those three slick suckers. All I can say is God bless 'em—they sobered my drunk ass up for a day or two.

About five years later, I found myself at a soirée in the Hollywood Hills home of the actor/football legend Jim Brown. It was a small gathering for his group called the Amer-I-can Foundation, set up to help black youth. As I recall, there were a handful of Who's Who from the African-American social activist set. I ended up sitting at a table with the singer Dionne Warwick (but I didn't ask her if she knew the way to San José). As it turned out there were a couple of empty chairs, and an attractive couple approached and asked if they might join us.

As it turned out the man was my old acquaintance, Fernando! He sat across the table, sipping his drink from a straw as usual. Either he didn't recognize me, or he acted like he didn't. Maybe he was trying to turn over a new leaf. I don't know what the hell he was doing there and frankly, my dear, I *still* don't want to know.

Trav'lin' Light

"No one to see, I'm free as the breeze,
no one but me and my memories
Some lucky night he may come back again,
but until then I'm trav'lin' light."
—Lyrics by Johnny Mercer; originally performed by Billie Holiday.

Post-Portland, 1980-something. There's something to say about not having attachments. And I'm not necessarily talking about the arduous path of non-attachment in the Buddhist sense, no, I mean being as free as a bird without a bunch of stuff to drag around, hit the road, Jack, at the drop of a hat. That would be me back then, in my twenties, thirties, and even into my early forties.

Hitchhiking was the preferred modus operandi, nothin' but the pack on yer back, and half the time not even that. And when I had a buck or two, I'd pick up a good ol' VW van, run the damn thing until it blew up … Oil? What's oil? … What an idiot!

Crazy adventures, most cool, some fucked. The liquor laden nooks and crannies of the West Coast, I hit 'em all, from San Diego to Vancouver, BC, the cities and tiny burgs, the alleys of The Valley … You likes colored girls? How come you likes colored girls? The countless tempting names of all those dingy bars, like The Lime Lite, The Lamp Post, The High Hat, Mecca Club, Midnight Hideout, Siete Mares, Monte Carlo, and of course Cheers.

I guess the reality is, any low-life neon name attached to a funky dive is tempting to guys like me. (How many times have I walked into those piece-of-shit bars, just lookin' for a pop of brandy in the cool nights or a cold vodka drink during the summer. I always sought out the older parts of whatever town I was in, something good about the nostalgic feel, someone to talk to, and an occasional quicky from a divorcee who would take me home and send me down the road the next morning.

Those travels landed me in Seattle one bleak winter, with $200 in my pocket. That's when I met Dennis Riley and flopped on his couch until I could afford a pad of my own. That's when I met Barbara Temple, my squeeze du jour, and scraped up the bucks to produce The Environmental Faire at the Seattle Center.

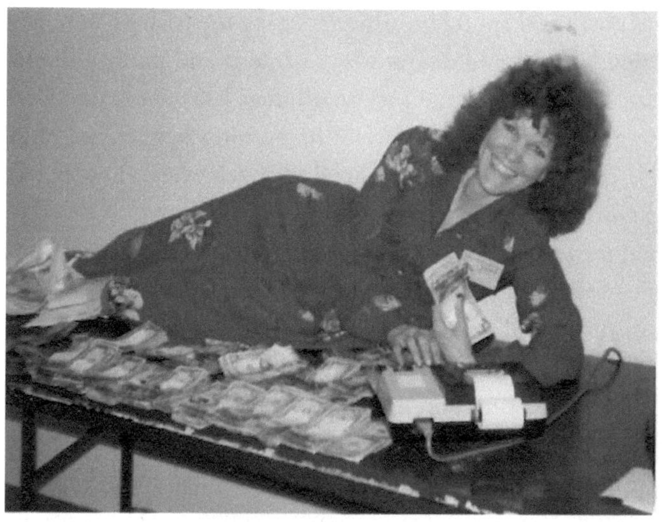

Barbara Temple, my "significant other" back in the early '80s, counting the massive moolah we made from the first Environmental Faire. It was an historic avant-garde 3-day expo at the Seattle Center, right next to the landmark Space Needle. Over 300 exhibits, 12 seminar rooms, and 15,000 paid attendance. Best damned show I ever produced, largest environmental symposium in the U.S. at the time. Got loaded with Kesey the second night of the event, just a six-pack and a toke or two. Yep, right there in the parking lot while hippies in the show stripped off their clothes and jumped bare-naked into the hot tubs on display. I about shit when I heard this on my walkie-talkie. I could already see the headlines in the Sunday morning paper: "Naked Hippies at The Environmental Faire!"

It was a Cold and Drunken Night...

I was driving home in Barbara's red VW van, a relatively new one with all the bells and whistles: refrigerator, pull-out awning, a little port-a-potty and a great fold-out bed ... the friggin' Waldorf. The bars had closed, and the rain was coming down lightly as I sped along the road through the tree-lined Queen Anne district, a street that was a showcase of large, still-prestigious mansions, many Victorian.

Out of nowhere I spotted a critter crossing my path … hell, between the rain and my drooped eyelids from lack of sleep and many a brandy glass, I couldn't see for shit … a large cat? Small dog? I hit the brakes but my reaction time was way the hell too slow. Whatever it was, there was a substantial bump and a quick second one—front wheel, back wheel. That poor thing got clobbered twice in a matter of seconds.

I pulled the car aside and got out, only to see "it" drag itself into the large yard of one of those mansions, into the yard like it knew where it was going, and then up a very tall tree, a tree that shot straight up like a redwood. That poor crushed critter had been driven up that tree in the rain. My fault, my fault. I went into the yard and up to the side of the tree.

I've been aware for many years that there is consciousness in everything, yes, everything. Consciousness in me, though limited from drink; consciousness in that huge tree, and for sure in that agonizing creature up there somewhere. I so wanted to capture her—I don't know why, but I *felt* it was female, go figure—to somehow get a hold of her and one way or another get her to a veterinarian to possibly save her life.

I walked right up to the tree and—to this second, I'm not sure where this action came from—began pounding on the side of the tree with both of my hands simultaneously, pounding as hard as I could. Arms stretched full out, slowly, methodically, in three very distinct, slow hits, one-two-three, one-two-three, as hard as I could, again and again. And along with those thumps were three words, silent but loud in feeling: *I-love-you, I-love-you, I-love-you.*

A very primitive message from the depth of my soul, yes, I-love-you, again and again. The idea was to use the tree as a medium, the conduit, the telephone line if you will. And I thought that the continuity and the deep, deep passionate message I was conveying might somehow reach this little being. Conveying on the most basic level that I cared and wanted to help.

I stood there in the rain, in the glow of a streetlight, looking up and pounding, pounding. Then it happened, about thirty feet up, I spotted a little head with its face poking around the side of that tree, and then quickly disappeared. A minute or two passed, and there it was again, only a few feet lower. It was coming down in circles, slowly heading down the tree. It was happening, she was responding. Pound. Pound. Pound. One. Two. Three. I. Love. You. Again and again.

Finally, there it was, just a few feet away. The streetlight was bright enough so that I could see the face clearly—it was the beautiful face of a raccoon, a full-grown raccoon. After all of that emotion, all of the passion and love I could muster up, all I had put into the pounding of the tree, and there she was a few feet away.

Again, with all my being, I extended my hand, thinking but not speaking, offering the thought "Take my hand and let me help you."

In perhaps the most amazing event of my life, the creature moved even closer—and extended its little paw. The bottom of my hand palm up, its paw, palm down. It happened, just standing there for a second of rarified communication. For a split second we touched, our hands touched.

And then I made the mistake of *thinking*, thinking as a human being, of grabbing her and racing to the pet hospital in the middle of the night. That thought, that human thought, broke the trance and suddenly she rushed down the tree and onto the lawn, dragging her limp back legs and scurrying into a hole under the house, perhaps an entrance she was familiar with.

I don't like to think of her dying there, but if it did happen, I pray it was quick. With God all things are possible, and perhaps her wounds rapidly healed. I envision her comfortably sipping a cup of her favorite tea, surrounded by her little raccoon family. In the Koran, God offers this insight: *To know me is to know my creatures.*

The World Symposium on Humanity

Hermosa Beach, 1979. In spite of my split-personality, I was good at what I did: event production. And so in April of '79 I was recruited as a co-producer, one among several, of a mega-event called *The World Symposium on Humanity*, a grand if not grandiose festival and exposition of all things consciousness-expanding.

It was headlined by well-known gurus, best-selling philosophers, and top-rated musicians and artists ... the best of the best as regards the visionary community of the New Age and environment/ecology set.

The event was held simultaneously in three cities—Pasadena, Toronto, and London—and connected via large satellite-beamed screens, quite advanced at the time. My primary function was to market the exhibit spaces for the Pasadena venue, about 200 all in all, and assist as I could in other production matters.

All of this was to be accomplished within a two-month span and without a staff. That's a tall order in that pre-computer, pre-fax era where I had to share a single-line phone with a fellow producer who was recruiting some of the talent, a cool dude about my age named Bob Crosby. Bob lived right off

Topanga Pass in a house that Harry Houdini built, replete with secret tunnels and mysterious niches.

That was great but I would rather have had my own private phone. In spite of these challenges, I got the job done, all 200 of those suckers sold in record time. Sell, baby, sell!

I recall sitting in on one of the earliest brainstorming get-togethers for the show with its organizers up in Vancouver, BC. We met in the headquarters of a group of Sikhs (pronounced seeks) who concocted this multi-media forum and now that I understand more about their philosophy, I can see why they chose to produce such an enlightening event.

That morning we all sat rather smugly in a popular breakfast café with a nice view of a nearby lake. It had old-fashioned, relatively private rounded booths, large enough for the six of us to sit quite comfortably, all with pen and pads in hand.

The leaders of the organization were Canadian Sikhs—go figure—as East Indian as a New York bagel, mostly Jewish cats who had converted to the 3HO philosophy of their founder Yogi Bhajan, his motto being "Happy, Healthy and Holy."

As we were about to complete our meeting and get on with the elementary matter of saving the world, the Main Man, Guru Raj (who we fondly dubbed Garage) sat all-knowingly nodding his Big Turban head and asked with substantial confidence, "What could possibly go wrong?" Immediately a voice, as if booming down from Heaven, pronounced two shattering words: "Human greed."

As it turned out someone eavesdropping from the booth next to us overheard our fanciful ramblings about altering the course of history and so had loudly advised what he felt might just blow the whole thing out of the ether we were floating in.

The guy was on the right track because the show almost did, blow up that is—not because of greed per se, but just too many gurus and not enough devotees. Spoiler alert: folks worked hard, long, and harmoniously—it was really a joy working with all these wonderful people! The show was quite blessed, and had a terrific turnout—it was just one big holistic smile.

Stevie Wonder and the Secret Life of Plants

"I can't conceive the nucleus of all begins inside a tiny seed /And what we think as insignificant provides the purest air we breathe/But who am I to doubt or question the inevitable being/For these are but a few discoveries we find inside the Secret Life of Plants."
—*Journey through the Secret Life of Plants,* by Stevie Wonder

Seattle, 1979, Octoburrrr. About this time, I was riding pretty high. My shows were modestly successful, large-scale events at major venues like the Seattle Center, the Portland Coliseum, and the Pasadena Center, with thousands of folks attending. Keep in mind, they were also very expensive to produce, so I was lucky when all was said and done to have made enough to pay all my expenses and move on to the next event.

My personal life was half decent, in spite of my overindulgence in most everything tasty. I was quite the rake and to the chagrin of Barbara, my mate at the time, I spent way too much time chasing that Most Mysterious Muff, oh Holey Mother of Debauchery and Wasted Loot; that and/or getting plastered at six in the morning at the High Hat Tavern with my rotund bud, FDR.

Anyway, there was a popular book that came out a few years earlier titled *The Secret Life of Plants.* It was written by Peter Tompkins and Christopher Bird, and was described as "A fascinating account of the physical, emotional, and spiritual relations between plants and man." Even then I was a devotee of organic gardening, growing and caring for my own little plot.

I talk to those little guys, veggies and flowers alike, each little seed and seedling, protect them from the insatiable slugs and earwigs, and, year after year in gratefulness they grace my dinner table on the plates and in the vases.

What struck me about the book was that *in a scientific way* it conveyed the notion that indeed plants do have considerable consciousness … and that opens up a whole new can of worms (excellent for soil aeration). In a very earthy sense, layer by layer, the Supreme Godhead might well be a cabbage or lettuce head.

Soooo, after having helped produce the World Symposium on Humanity down in L.A., I returned to Seattle to contemplate my next project. By this time, my head was bigger than the Kingdome football stadium, and was spinning with bravado. My next project had to be bigger and better than anything before. (The word "inflated" comes to mind, though dreaming big is a good thing.)

Event production … something big, with television potential, a soundtrack that would sell … Hmmm. Worldwide. Music. World. Music. Hmmm. *World Music Festival!* … That's it, the best of the best, from countries around the globe. But I would need a headliner for sure. I'd learned that if you snag one big name then suddenly it all starts to fall together. That's what had happened with my poetry festivals and ecology expos.

About this time, I got wind of a new movie coming out, a documentary based on the *Plants* book I just mentioned. In fact, the film bore the same title, with an original soundtrack composed and recorded by Stevie Wonder, called *Journey through the Secret Life of Plants.* Wonder was arguably at his zenith at the time. Headliner. Stevie Wonder. Hmmm.

There was to be a grand opening showing of the film in Los Angeles, with none other than Mister Wonder on the stage. I jumped on a plane and headed south. I didn't have an invitation, but that had never stopped me before and it wasn't going to now. Once I got to the theatre, I managed to weasel my way backstage and, as the presentation ended, I cornered Wonder's assistant.

I described what I had in mind and he said Stevie might very well be interested in participating. He said I might meet *the man* briefly following the show. When the performance was over Stevie, his assistant, and I left through a rear door. As we headed to his limo I introduced myself. He smiled and nodding his head side to side in the Ray Charles tradition, repeated "Toe-moss, Toe-moss." I haiku'd my vision and asked if he would consider participating. Still smiling, he said "Sounds fine, here, here, jot down my agent's number … and have a good night, Toe-moss."

Have a good night? Hell, I had a good week, partying down L.A. way, riding the wave of what I felt sure would be a spectacular accomplishment, my World Music Festival. Build the field and they will come; the dominos will fall in place.

Upon returning to Seattle, I set about lining up a venue, the brand new football stadium named the Kingdome, home of the Seattle Seahawks. I needed a good weekend.

I called their office and because of my success at the Seattle Center I was able to easily secure this new venue. Everyone was more than enthusiastic. After several meetings, I had a pretty good idea of who I would be contacting internationally as performers. Using the bait of the marvelous Kingdome, a television contract and most important, Stevie Wonder as my headliner, I had no doubt all would fall smoothly into place ... what could possibly go wrong?

A few days later, early one Friday morning, I got together with Dennis Riley and, as usual, headed out to our favorite hole-in-the-wall, a Greek smorgasbord and bar called Giorgio's (the High Hat only served beer and wine, and this was a special occasion, time for the hard stuff ... I was preparing to call Stevie's agent). Dennis and I started drinking eight-ish and by ten, I, being of alert and witty mind (or so I thought) and in a sharp business mode, I sloppily slurred, "Denny, let's walk over to my pad an' make *the call*."

By this time I was feeling no pain—a few cups of brandy and coffee and I was bouncing off the wall from all angles. We got to my apartment and I fumbled around in my wallet until I found the card on which I'd scribbled the agent's name and number.

I have long forgotten the fellow's name, and the only thing I was aware of other than the fact he was Stevie Wonder's personal agent was that *I thought* he was a black man, a brother. I'm absolutely embarrassed to confess that the one-sided conversation went something like this:

"Wha's up, my brotha'? Say, this is Toe-Moss, Toe-moss, Stevie prob'ly tol' you 'bout me. Say, I'm gonna be producin' a big-ass happenin' up here in the No'th-wez, See-at-ull, and sheee-it, you know, Stevie done said he be ups to dis jam, so whaz I gots to do?" The phone was silent.

I had tried my old-ass West Fresno street-corner rap on this very sophisticated East Coast attorney, using this blackish accent because I assumed the brother was a brother, was African-American, and that he could identify with my tired-ass street corner jive. Talk about stereotyping!

More silence. Then "click." Huh? Did the phone go dead? Must have. I dialed again. "Click." I had just fucked up the best chance I had ever had to succeed, both financially and personally.

In my drunkenness I just shined it on, made some flaky excuse to Dennis how the phone line had gone dead ... that damned phone company! ... and proceeded to get plastered with Mister Riley. The Not-so-Secret Life of Drunks.

Note: *The Secret Life of Plants* (1973) explores the idea that plants are sentient and despite their lack of a nervous system have some sort of a brain. Recent research has suggested that plants may in fact "remember." This sentience has purportedly been observed through changes in plants' conductivity, shown through a polygraph as pioneered by Cleve Backster. Fascinating stuff. If you haven't, please read the book ... similar in ways to *Messages from Water* and

The Little Book of Bleeps, which are about the consciousness in and of all life, fauna and flora.

And, may I add, the studies of the effect certain mushrooms (psilocybin) on the human brain are promising as to treating addictions and other mental health issues, not to mention the effect of some on other plants and *things*, like oil waste ... they clean it! Of late there have been a spate of insightful documentaries on these little guys, including:

- The critically acclaimed *Fantastic Fungi*
- *The Kingdom: How Fungi made our World*
- *Sacred Mushrooms: A Lost History*
- *The Magic of Mushrooms*
- *A New Understanding: The Science of Psilocybin*
- *Magic Medicine: The Possible Effects of Mushrooms Treating Depression*

You might say the whole field is ... well ... mushrooming.

FDR in a bar? Surely, you jest! ... I know, your name isn't Shirley.

Hey, I hate to shock you, but this is the one and only Ry-lo, *Thee* Fat Dennis Riley, in full drink mode. Yep, that's him all right, all 365 pounds of pure punnery, 366 on Leap Year. Guy's got the biggest heart on the planet and the quickest wit! And this is a real mug shot, as in a mug of beer and a shot of whiskey ... It's called a boilermaker.

By the way, I have no choice but to include this great news: Mr. Riley went on quite a diet as of late and lost over a hundred friggin' pounds! Basically, he made a very difficult choice: keep on with the addictive process of guzzling and stuffing greasy crap down the ol' pie-hole or choose to live. He did the latter and, I am so pleased to report, that man is one happy camper—over 100 pounds happier!

An Achy Breaky Boot

> "Simply irresistible … she's so fine, there's no tellin' where the money went … Simply irresistible … she's all mine, there's no other way to go." —from "Simply Irresistible," as sung by Robert Palmer, bad boy rocker in the music video with the in-sync babes in the background … sex-ayyy!

Seattle, circa '83. It was a cold and rainy night, perfect atmosphere for Snoopy typing his autobiography while atop his doghouse. But certainly not a night to be out on the damp streets of Seattle, broke and broken-hearted.

I had recently had a bit of success with a large event I produced, and when you have success—hate to say it—the babes tend to be more plentiful. When the doors of my show at the Seattle Center closed that Sunday afternoon, I found myself with a pocketful of cash and, exhausted as I was, ready to party.

One thing led to another and as usual I was soon in the thick of raucous debauchery. Not surprising, there was an irresistible gold-digger in the midst, down there at the original "skid row." (The term "skid row," incidentally, was coined in Seattle. "Skid" was in reference to a chute built down the side of a hill for lumberjacks' logs to skid down to the shore of Puget Sound, in what is now Pioneer Square. From the bottom of the chute, the logs would be transferred to ships heading in all directions. When the economy went sour, and out-of-work loggers and others in that industry found themselves destitute, they could still find a little comfort and camaraderie hanging together down around the shanties and bars, down along "skid row" … how 'bout that.)

But back to the gold-digger: She had friggin' playboy bunny looks, and a walk that makes men snap their necks; she had legs that fit nicely over a guy's shoulders. Tall chick, movie star mug, and surely cool to have hanging on your arm. (Yes, I was that lame, that shallow, but hey…) We ended up crashing at her place from the get-go, conveniently close to the watering hole where I met her.

Well, I wasn't lonely, not while there was a playmate and a playpen, not while the money lasted. Set'em up, Joe, for the house! But when the bucks ran out, as they did in short time, things changed dramatically. Arguments ensued about petty matters, like paying the rent, eating canned food, etc. Romance was soon out the window, as were my shoes and shorts ... the wench booted me out, that is, *the lady* requested that I get the hell out or she'd call the fuckin' cops. As the old Charlie Parker lyric has it, "Ro-mance without fi-nance is a nui-sance."

About a week later, I found myself counting my last pennies at the counter of an old-fashioned coffee shop somewhere downtown, contemplating my next wheely-dealy. The guy sitting next to me asks me to pass the sugar. Why sure. Needless to say, a little conversation ensues, and I give him the song and dance of spending all my hard-earned money on this ungrateful creature (my side of the story and I'm sticking to it).

He had heard this tale of woe before ... he had been there. Chuck Streatch was a dapper guy, nattily dressed, in his early fifties ... nice little handlebar mustache. He was out of Alberta, Canada, eh, and had been a jazz trumpet player in his younger years. Gave us something to talk about.

Chuck got over by publishing a little sailing rag titled *Latitude 48°*, a pretty successful monthly tabloid with stories of local sailors and a lot of advertising regarding that industry. (By the way, I say "rag" with great respect for the good ones. They provided a helpful service, be it gossipy and skewed to muckraking, before their rude crushing by the internet.)

Chuck suggested that I consider starting a little mag of my own. I told him that his publishing endeavor seemed great for him, but that I just didn't have enough experience to do something like that. I also said, foolishly but with some understanding, that I could certainly see why some guys just lose it when they hit the bottom of the bottom, sometimes doing something rash like going out and robbing a store or a bank. In retrospect, I think Chuck may have thought I was seriously contemplating such a move, but I certainly wasn't; for me, it was just a matter of time until I'd get on my feet again, get back in my groove.

Turns out Chuck was a small plane pilot and I recall riding with him one day in a convertible he owned, top down. We both noticed a small plane zipping down the freeway above us. For some reason he shook his head and shared this interesting note: "You know, Tomás, they could teach a chimpanzee to fly one of those things. Piece of cake." Still don't know why he mentioned that, but Chuck was anything but a snob. But he may have had a tad of larceny in him.

Just a few minutes after the chimpanzee remark, knowing that I was struggling financially, he tossed out this gem: "You know, Tomás, you're a pretty good-looking guy … Ever think about hooking up with an older woman, one with enough bread to take good care of you?" I didn't waste a second thinking about that one. I said, "You know, Chuck, it's just not in me. I'm afraid I'm one of those idiots who has to be in love." Because of his sailing magazine ol' Chuckie would be aware of such well-seasoned ladies. But no, I was this idiotic romantic. I'm afraid I wasn't very imaginative on this one … hell, is there a law that says you can't love a broad just 'cause she has a few million bucks?

But back to Chuck's concern for me. Before that afternoon was over he carefully articulated the following all-American advice: "Hey, buddy, don't even think that way, about crime as a way out. I've got a much better idea. Why rob a bank when you can do it legally, like I do: go into business." What a concept! … To, as the Mafia have it, "go legit."

In the next few days and weeks Chuck and I would get together for breakfast and coffee, him always grabbing the tab. He was teaching me how to publish a small newspaper, as he was doing—the layout, the editorial side, and more important the advertising (60% should always be ads, said Chuck; sell, sell, sell).

I've always been aggressive when I have an idea, and usually quite fortunate in finding folks to back my wild dreams. Fact is I was up and running within a month or so, with start-up funds invested by a professor buddy of mine, John Wise, who taught at the University of Washington. A tall, cavernous-voiced dude, John even found me free housing at the frat house he was in when he was a student at U-dub thirty years earlier. Wow, that was an interesting experience, living with a bunch of bright White kids who kept their noses in books, not on a mirror.

Based on what I had learned as producer of a couple of major ecology-related expositions there was a whole new industry about to erupt. The adjective "Green" was not in use yet, but there was a real push in that direction. So I called my paper *Energy Times: The News You Can Use.* It was the first and only alternative energy magazine in the Northwest, a free-to-the-public monthly.

In the beginning I did much of the editorial work, hired a couple of salespeople (commission *plus* salary—mistake!), and a distribution manager (my very funny friend Dennis Riley, who was an out-of-work long-haul trucker). The paper ran for about eight months, and grew to about 60 pages and 50,000 circulation. As I recall, the dailies got wind of it (*The Seattle Times* and the *Post-Intelligencer)* and started their own special alternative energy and environment sections. With my limited funds and staff, the big boys in effect put me out of business.

Nonetheless I had learned something very important, and I'd like to share that wisdom with any youngsters who find themselves on "the skids." You might be contemplating robbery or some criminal scheme, but as my bud Chuck said, "Why rob a bank when you can do it legally—go into business." That's what the big boys do.

From Chuck's obit: "Whatever he did in life, Charles Streatch, publisher of *48° North Sailing Magazine*, put everything he had into it. He embraced it all, including his final days that ended June 25, 2006 after a long battle with cancer."

Sittin' on the Dock of the River

1985-ish. I hadn't seen Venus Simms since we were in high school, though as little kids we had spent many a day fishing at the ponds and the lakes of Fresno County. He was a big Black kid with a constant grin to go along with that lazy eye of his. He was the fullback at our high school and later played for Fresno State … I don't recall any guy making fun of his name. Good decision.

Well, I ran into Venus again, hadn't seen him for many a moon, I mean like 20-some years back when we were both in Fresno. Now I was 900 miles north, way up in Seattle living in an historic little cabin built in the mid-1800s on a dock overlooking the Puget Sound.

This modest two-bedroom wooden cottage and dock had a spectacular view of the Olympic Mountain Range, just above the Ballard locks where a nationally-known sea lion named Herschel (a Jewish sea lion … bagels and locks?) ate his way into American history. Turns out he was eating more than his share of salmon and pissed off the wrong folks.

They tried all kinds of tactics to get him out of that part of the river, where the salmon go upstream to spawn. The fish-protection powers-that-be even tried blasting him with ear-bursting hard rock music, but it turned out he liked it … Rock on, Big H. Then they captured him, transported him down to the San Francisco Bay, and guess what? In less than a month he was right back in the Puget Sound chomping away … made the national news! Looking through the window of my little kitchen nook I'd see that joyous critter daily, floating on his back with a flapping salmon in his mouth, rollicking in his infamy.

The little cabin-on-the-dock was magical, hidden beneath a cliff where it couldn't be seen from the street above. At times I'd lay in bed at night and from just a couple of feet beneath me I could hear the splashing of millions of salmon feverishly heading up river.

During the day the local tribe fishermen, who had fought lengthy legal battles to win fishing rights, would pull up to the dock in small motorboats and secure a gillnet that went from one side of the river to the other. In record time that net would be full. I'd of course have a six-pack waiting for the guys next to my barbeque grill ... salmon just don't get no fresher, that is unless you're a bear.

One day I walked up the steep stairs to pick up my mail from the roadside mailbox. Of all things, comin' round the bend is a shiny pickup truck hauling a little fishing boat. That in itself wasn't surprising, but the pickup was driven by ... gasp! ... a black guy. There weren't a helluva lot of "colored" folks in Ballard, Washington, and probably still aren't. I was about the closest thing.

The sight got my attention for sure and—I'll be damned! —to my great surprise it's *Venus Simms*, with that lazy eye of his, the kid I went fishing with when we were nine to ten years old back in Fresno! I jumped up and down and waved like a crazy man (which is easy for me to do).

He stopped and, both of us being quite amazed, just laughed and hugged. Turns out Venus had found a great job building airplanes at the big Boeing plant up in Seattle. We got out the beer and fishing gear (in that order) and walked down to my little dock ... and just sat there like little kids again, feet danglin' off the edge of the dock, waitin' for The Big One.

A Night with Anthony Quinn and George Shearing

Spring, 1986. I lived briefly in West Hollywood during the time I went down there to try to sell a TV script ... wild journey, that was. My small flat above a neighborhood grocery store kept me in vino and vittles ... in that order. While there I got wind of one of my heroes performing in Hollywood ... Anthony Quinn, Anthony Quinn of *Lawrence of Arabia*, *The Guns of Navarone*, *Lust for Life*, and of course *Zorba the Greek*.

He was a hero to me because, for one, out of a humble background he raised himself to greatness (and because his dad, an Irishman from County Cork, had ridden as a revolutionary with Pancho Villa—and Quinn never forgot it). And two, he was a hero to me because throughout his years of award-winning performances and during all those previous racist decades that he played in dozens of films he was never ashamed of being Mexican. Au contraire, he was proud of it.

Most movie goers and classic film buffs remember him from his successful roles, but most don't remember the many so-so flicks dating back to the early '30s where he played a Latin lover, a sheik, a Mexican bandit, a "savage In'jun" (who makes up his own language on the spot), and dozens of "ethnic" villains, roles he was given because of his looks. (Those damned swarthy types! We need to build a wall!)

So, as fate would have it, his lead role as Zorba was reprised, this time in an on-stage musical. He played this character 362 times (the guy was 68 years old at the beginning of this run, and though slower he was still a dancing fool.) The musical had great success on Broadway, at the Kennedy Center, and for two runs in the hometown of his acting career, Hollywood.

And this happened to be a final night of the final run that I was attending, all duded up with a lovely woman at my side whom I'd met at some jazz club—how very fortunate I was in these matters. We had balcony seats near the front row of the center area, perfectly placed for taking in the entire scene.

The show was fittingly produced right there at the corner of Hollywood and Vine, at the palatial Pantages Theatre. Built in 1930 it was an ornate beauty, fully renovated to maintain its art deco, rococoesque flair. What a majestic treat—Quinn at the Pantages! When he first stepped onto that stage everyone stood up and loudly applauded for the longest time. I can still feel the goose bumps.

Mr. Quinn was also quite the artist, with several of his pieces showing in the lobby. So when the play was over we had the opportunity to view some of his art. I confess I hoped that he would grace us with his presence, but that didn't happen. Guess he didn't know I was in the audience … or maybe he did.

No matter. I was thoroughly pleased, delighted, and in a sense honored to even be in the same room. As my de-lovely date and I descended the stairs we walked out into a warm summer night, I thought it would be a good idea to top off this memorable eve with a nightcap at a club I had spotted just around the corner.

I looked up at their sizable sign: Vine Street Bar & Grill, with the word ENTRANCE in all caps. *Thee* renowned Vine Street Bar and Grill, an intimate setting quite beyond forgetting. I had certainly heard of the place but it never entered my mind to somehow get there. But this was it, *thee* place, and it was precisely what it was said to be. To quote *LA Times* jazz journalist Zan Stewart back in 1990, this was "The way jazz was meant to be heard." The cat was hip to it.

I noticed it was pretty dark off to the left of the bar, where most of the tables were set. The place was packed full, but there couldn't have been more than 50 or so folks sitting in that cozy venue. That's the way many of those wonderful jazz joints used to be. When we walked in we were most fortunate to find a couple of stools at end of the bar, the last two remaining as I recall. Kismet, and I was a stranger in paradise.

The drinks certainly weren't inexpensive, but since it was a very special night I was prepared to spend my last cent … fortunately, the lady had a credit card. Everything about that club was by all standards sophisticated. (Why they let me in I still don't know). The maître d', the bartenders, the waiters, probably even the dishwasher, were all wearing tuxes that evening. Real first-class joint.

As we were about to finish our drinks a waiter comes up to us and says ever so politely that the cover charge would be $50. Hell, in those days I could get into the Monterey Jazz Festival for a full day for less than fifty bucks—but I'd usually just jump the fence instead. Barbed wire? I don't see no stinkin' barbed wire!

Anyway, so I kiddingly asked the waiter, "Who's playing? God?" Not quite but as it turned out it was jazz royalty, the incredibly smooth, musically hypnotic George Shearing, *Sir* George Shearing.

The stage was set in that small venue and to my surprise, there were two baby grands arranged back-to-back, just Sir George and his orchestra of one, an accompanying young pianist who never said a word. The oft' heard line, "You could hear a pin drop" was precisely the case. Not a peep, not a clink of a glass. From the first note to the last, every sound, everything was impeccable. The lengthy compositions effortlessly flowed from one to the next, with a little clever commentary between (most folks knew the Great American Songbook melodies and gave a muted applause as each piece began).

Sir George, with his whispery, well-tuned voice, even sang a couple of soft, tasteful tunes. At one point he played a melody that I recognized as a show tune titled *It Never Entered My Mind.* For years I had listened to an album titled *Ella Does Rodgers and Hart*—Ella as in Fitzgerald—and that's where I had first heard this stunningly delicate, hauntingly paced love song—what wonderful lyrics.

As is often the case with jazz, other tunes are briefly blended in. I recognized that Shearing was riffing on Erik Satie's "Gymnopedie No. 1," from which there is little doubt "It Never entered My Mind" originated. The two songs are perfectly interchangeable and mesmerizingly beautiful, as was the entire performance that night.

I apologize for the gushing, but I was so terribly impressed with this pristine concert which gave me an experience that was truly new to me, so much so that I couldn't help but scribble a napkin ditty, tying Shearing and Anthony Quinn into the same magical interlude.

At the end of the first set, the two pianists and a woman from the front row went back into the musician's lounge. I asked the waiter if I might read my little poem to Mister Shearing. The waiter was cool, said he'd ask, and returned shortly with a nod.

There he sat, behind a small desk, dark shades facing up, he and his wife standing behind him, both with pleasant, closed mouth smiles. Seeing as how he was blind he asked that I read my poem (good thing I had a nice little buzz going or I would have been shaking in my boots). My entire piece might've been eight lines or so—and I don't recall a word of it, only that it rhymed, was a little clever, and mentioned my respect for both him and Mister Quinn.

When I finished reading, to my great relief, he and his wife courteously gave a nice little applause. He told her to get me an album (vinyl, of course) and then asked her to guide his hand as he signed it.

Sir George Shearing, how elegant, Anthony Quinn, how wonderfully human, the two in one magical Hollywood night.

So if you're a sensitive sap, please don't go another minute without it—This is not brandy, it's cognac. "It Never Entered My Mind," Shearing, YouTube. Also, if you're so inclined, Clive, drop the jive and check out: George Shearing, Mel Torme, Newport Jazz, YouTube ... That where "A Nightingale Sang in Berkeley Square." Man, that whole set is very, very smooth.

The Money Church of Della Reese

> "The best thing you can do for the poor is not be one of them," sermonized Reverend Ike, who owned 16 mink-lined Roll-Royces and wore huge diamond rings on both hands.

1987. I was alive and reasonably well after having been demoted from Seattle to the lowly burg of Hermosa Beach, California … Please, Br'er Fox, don't you throw me in dat briar patch. Hell, Hermosa Beach was a very desirable destination. Muy hermosa!

Had made a buck or two up in the Great Northwest, but in spite of that, I was damned near broke again. My dreams of selling my TV and movie scripts were shot so I needed to hustle. Going back to my primary trade, I decided to produce a little street fair called The Hermosa Beach Music & Art Festival at a park right there on Highway One.

This could only have been accomplished with the help of the wonderful Moir family, held together under the soft whip of their masterful matriarch Maggie. In a short time, we managed to get this event off the ground and plop a penny or two into my piddly pockets.

The cash was flowing again, and the afternoons were spent sucking suds down at The Poop Deck, sittin' right there on The Strand, a wide walkway along the beach. The Deck was a bird-watchers paradise. They came in droves, on skates, bikes, or just strolling along, usually with a friend. My daily exercise was that of sitting at the window, bending my elbow for the beer, and stretching my neck while checking out the outrageous curves gliding by.

Hey, check out this review of that coastal cantina, with an emphasis on poop: "It's about as divey as dive bars get and there's a bit of a sewage stench near the restroom area, but I HEART it anyway!" My kind of joint!

And in the evenings, just a block away on Pier Avenue, I'd slip back to sip my brandy in the world-famous jazz hang, The Lighthouse … What a delicious venue, with smells of ocean air and smoke. This place was the hub of the mostly-mellow "West Coast Jazz," where blew giants like Chet Baker, Gerry Mulligan, Shelly Manne, Max Roach, Art Pepper, Mose Allison, Ramsey Lewis, the Modern Jazz Quartet, the Jazz Crusaders, and Cannonball Adderley … Mercy, Mercy, Mercy!

About this time, once a week I was attending a little church-of-sorts to cleanse my naughty nights … that and get a free meal. The "services" were run out of the beach house owned by an interesting couple, a fellow named Bill (whose real name I won't disclose for reasons that you'll soon discover) and his gorgeous, red-headed southern belle wife, Deanna. Ol' Bill was an older Jewish guy who was a prominent psychiatrist working near UCLA, and his wife, well, she was pretty much a homebody (and what a body it was!) These two were always at odds over some darned thing. (Come to find ol' Billy was bonking one of his clients, and Deanna's ex-hubby was always just hanging around, pretty chummy … What could possibly go wrong?)

I am reminded of the true but tragic story of a Hong Kong couple, Mr. and Mrs. Al Wong. As it turned out, the husband was a traveling salesman and on one occasion he had to leave the country for nine months or so. When he returned his wife greeted him with quite a surprise … she had given birth to a baby boy.

The man looked down at the squirming kid in the crib, looked down into his bright … blue eyes. Mr. Wong gnashed his teeth and with a look that could kill let his wife have it: "Two Wongs don't make a White!" Tragic, I tell you.

Well, quite apart from the Bill vs. Deanna drama, it turned out that their church was a non-profit front to write off taxable income on a number of items, house payments included. The good news for me is that they had set themselves up as a kind of "New Thought" church, which is a legit spiritual movement that appealed to my free spirit mode because of its openness to all religions. I actually learned a thing or two hanging out with those characters, mostly about what Science of Mind, the Mother Church, had to offer a person with an open and curious mind. (To be clear, this is not Scientology, that dubious creation of sci-fi writer L. Ron Hubbard.)

Folks of this persuasion also speak a lot about "prosperity consciousness," and why this is a good thing. Religious denominations under this umbrella, including Unity, Religious Science, and Divine Science, contend that God supports prosperity. And fifty years later even some of the Protestant mega-churches have jumped on the mucho-banana bandwagon.

However, unlike the prosperity gospel of conservative Christian dogma, which has it that it is only through your commitment to Christ that you deserve wealth, New Thought teaches that God wants people to prosper regardless of religion. Maggie Moir called it "The Money Church."

We'd sit in the living room of our Money Church-at-the-beach—usually four or five of us—and swig wine while munching morsels at their little mandatory weekly meetings. (If you are a church, then by Fed standards you have to show in your books that you meet as a gathering, as a church service, every so often, maybe once a week … I can't help but think that many ministers, even the ones with big buildings and huge followings, might just be headed to hell.)

Anyway, in one of those intimate drink-and-rap sessions, the subject of the great *Touched by an Angel* actress/singer/preacher-lady Della Reese came up … Turns out she was very active as a minister in the New Thought movement, which all centers around the Science of Mind view (again not to be confused with Scientology).

Aaaanyway … we found out that Della was having small meetings in her own home, to which we were somehow invited—*her own little church in the Hollywood Hills.* We arrived one evening and were greeted by Della's handsome hubby, a gentleman named Franklin, and a couple of other folks (some of whom also had a degree of popularity—Gladys Knight and Patty LaBelle, to name-drop two I seem to recall. You never could tell who might just show up.)

What a nice setting, not opulent whatsoever, but very, very comfortable, with a lovely indoor pool and a sizable living room where she held her meetings (this, by the way, was a few years before she landed her starring role as the angel Tess).

She often began by telling her own story, with a heavy emphasis on her near-death out-of-body experience. She had a brain aneurysm in her mid-forties, was taken to a hospital *and pronounced dead.*

While dead she was transported—if that's the word—a few feet above the table on which her body was laying … quite dead! But it was *her spirit* that was levitated. She could see herself lying there, but realized that it wasn't her time, and quickly returned to her body. You might say she was "touched by an angel."

She spoke of the New Testament and what had been lost in translation from the Aramaic—the language of Jesus during His time here—and how in the process mistranslations mightily affected the very real history of Christianity, including how Christians perceive wealth.

In a healthy way, concept-wise, Della echoed the philosophy of televangelist Reverend Ike. Remember him back in the late '60s and early '70s with his decadent cars and jewelry, the original pulpit-pimp who pounded away week after week that money is a good thang? In essence, "God didn't put you on this planet to be po', fool, 'cause that ain't cool!"

At the end of the evening, Della had a message for Tina Turner, who had just come out with a big hit, "What's Love Got To Do With It." Della was damn-near livid. "What's love got to do with it?" What's love got to do with it? Hello. Try *everything*!

Musical Note. Check out Della doing an American pop version of Puccini's *Musetta's Waltz* from *La Bohème.* Back in '59 Della recorded a beautiful song using the Puccini melody titled—not entitled—*Don't you know*? With her operatic range the thing hit the ceiling in record time ... Number One on the R&B chart and Number Two overall. Chick had a set of lungs! "Don't You Know?" Della Reese, YouTube. Go on, treat yourself to a touch of opera.

Can You Dig It?

1987-ish. Down but not out in Van Nuys, CA. Smoggy, flat, endless cities hooked together with fictional boundaries, like the countries of the Middle East ... Pasadena, Glendale, Sherman Oaks, Tarzana (named as a tribute to Tarzan's creator, writer Edgar Rice Burroughs, who settled there in 1919), and beautiful downtown Burbank (as Carson used to quip) ... all the way across the San Fernando Valley to Woodland Hills where coyotes still roam, vestiges of a long-gone time. One back-to-back strip of the same stuff, The Boring Straight, but you can't tell the folks who live there that.

While I was visiting a girlfriend in Pasadena, I went for a short walk early one morning. The smog was so thick you couldn't see the foothills just a mile away ... absolutely true. How thick was it? ... The smog was so thick I thought I was in a barroom back in the '60s! How thick was it ...?

Anyway, here's a guy watering his lawn and I say good morning (Cough! Cough!), and he says Good morning (Wheeze! Wheeze!), nice day says he, and I say, yeah, but damn, I could do without this nasty smog, and he says, yeah, but hell, this ain't nothin', it's *really bad* in Altadena (the city right next to it, less than a mile away!). How we do compensate and adjust.

Well, back to Van Nuys ... I was renting a little mother-in-law unit, you know, the small cottage in the back where couples used to stash their old and/or dying relatives with enough distance where they still had enough privacy to do the hokey pokey without worrying about Judgment Day at the breakfast table.

There wasn't much of a yard, but I have this thing about planting a veggie garden wherever and whenever I can. So there was a little patch of dirt right behind the cottage, I'd say about a three by ten foot area, and it was hard as a rock ... in fact that's pretty much what it was, a whole lotta rocks.

I made up my mind that I'd tackle it anyway and went down to Ace's hardware to buy a shovel and a pick ... That ground really needed to be worked, broken down piece by piece, removing all the rocks, and bringing in a few bags of fertilizer to beef it up a bit ... Beef it up? Cattle manure is too damn hot, go for the horse shit, mo' betta.

I had learned from old Alan Chadwick, the organic gardening guru back in Santa Cruz, that I should dig about three feet down for best results. And then mix it with the good stuff, horseshit, fish emulsion, and the like. Man, getting a few inches down in this ground was a bear, really solidly packed-down rock-hard stuff that hadn't been dug for God knows how long, maybe by a volcano during the Pleistocene.

Clunk. Clunk. Just digging out rocks and throwing them aside into a little pile to be picked up after the toiling. Then, maybe six inches in, I reached down and pulled out this sizable stone that was different from the others ... It had a definite shape that was really quite unusual, and the type of stone was different as well. What the ...? I carried the item over to a small, backyard faucet and washed it off as best I could, and it started to take shape.

The darned thing, about five inches long by three wide, as it turned out, was a dagger, an ancient dagger whose technology was from the very late Paleolithic period. It fit perfectly into the palm of my hand and was very sharp on both edges, like a serrated blade, with a sharp point at the end that had been ever so slightly chipped, probably by my shovel. "Just how old is this thing," I wondered.

Well, to make a short story long, here, today, many years later I decided to finally, with the use of good old Google, see what I could find out about my dagger. Just trying to track this sucker down proved to be quite an adventure.

I typed in "ancient American Indian stone dagger," and the fun began. I've found some photos of similar pieces from that time—arrowheads, meat scrapers, and finally some daggers. The most similar to my "rock" so far is from the Bandera area of Texas. Those things, I am discovering, are from the end of the Paleolithic period, which ended about 12,000 years ago when, our ancestors—mine anyway—came across the Bering Strait and spread down into Canada, the contiguous U.S., and all the way to the tip of Tierra del Fuego ... where they nearly froze their popsicle toes!

They settled here and there along the way, small bands chasing the mastodon, the musk ox and the bison into this glorious undiscovered land. God, what it must have looked like without smoke and roads and the modern human rat overpopulating every niche and cranny.

The knife I had uncovered, though it could scrape the fur from a wolf, could also tear into a nice, juicy mammoth steak or flat out kill a man. It's kind of humbling to hold this chunk of our pre-antiquity, my rock, in my hand, this sturdy, bland gray chunk of chert, wondering just who may have chipped it (a process known as "knapping") into this form. It and the spear and arrow tips of mahogany-colored jasper, and blue-gray hornstone, and shiny black obsidian … were survival tools that evolved in shape and efficiency even as we did.

As I hold my rock, I think of breathing in the fresh air of an ancient time and the absolute thrill of viewing a glistening new horizon, majestic mountains, pure rivers and streams never before seen by men. It is deposited there somewhere, I know, deep in my earlier memory bank. Pristine forests filled with now-vanished creatures. I ponder that though we were hunters of giants, we were simultaneously gatherers of berries and nuts, observing the art of fishing as practiced by the family of bears.

And as I consider the evolving family of man from the very beginning, how we had to be smart and fast and nimble, I come to understand how even the terrible experience—the pain, loss and sheer fear caused by other predators *hunting us*—we developed within ourselves a need for each other which eventually led to compassion and even love.

My rock is a gift to remind me, to remind us, of the immense journey of mankind, and to be grateful to the lot of prehistoric humanity for hanging in there to give us the opportunity to live a relatively civilized life, and not to squander it with frivolous and selfish ways.

Miracle of the Steps

> "I'd rather have a free bottle in front of me than a pre-frontal lobotomy." Heard it—where else? —in a funky bar somewhere between Tijuana and Tacoma.

1988. Meanwhile, back in Hollyrude … I had written a treatment with a couple of episodes for a series that I titled *Help USA.* Even had secured the phone number 1-800-HELP-USA, which back then was a good marketing tool. The idea was to find the great non-profit causes and charities, even the little start-ups, and allow them to have a segment on this one-hour program. Prior to the show we would locate a "surprise guest" who was willing to become a spokesperson and/or sponsor of the organization. That guest would in fact be a famous movie or TV star, a great athlete, singer, or musician.

Also we'd ask for viewers and potential sponsors to call in to our toll-free number and donate or get involved. And to give us ideas for other groups that were doing good work for the public. That was the general idea, still a decent concept I think. (And I still have a couple more strong TV concepts but hang on to them with the hope that one of these days I'll find a taker … there are so many, many more options now. Do I hear a bite of interest?)

Back then you had The Big Four, and that was about it: NBC, CBS, ABC, and a fledgling Fox. The fact that I got through the door to three of the four was amazing, I mean these were the decision makers themselves.

And the reason for this accessibility was that I had found a great partner, a man about my age named Michael Sevareid. He was the son of the great newscaster, Eric Sevareid, an elite commentator for *CBS Evening News*, was one of three anchors America counted on for their info on Vietnam, Watergate, etc. for a couple of decades. So it was Michael who opened those doors for me because he himself was a successful producer and, of course, there was his dad's powerful influence. Michael, thank God, believed in my project.

I distinctly recall us sitting in one of those executive offices pitching the show to the top network executive who had the power to just say yes or no. That's how far it had gone. And what did the fellow have to say after Michael and I had given it our best shot? He almost apologetically explained, "I'm really sorry guys, but the fact is … the fact is that good doesn't sell."

Let me tell you, it bothered the hell out of me that I saw a very similar show on TV about half a year later with an almost identical title: *Heroes: Made in the USA* … stuff like that just wears away at you. Now, the closest thing to it is *CNN Heroes*, and that great program is only once a year.

I remember being in one of those TV executive lobbies a few months later, waiting with a couple of other scriptwriters for our "big chance"—fifteen minutes that could dramatically change our lives (I must again point out, just to get that far takes a lot of doing—the decision makers would have already perused the treatment of your script, so there was a bit of hope).

A middle-aged Jewish woman was seated next to me on this occasion, and I wasted no time kvetching about how I had been ripped off on an earlier script. Her response? She asked me how many scripts I'd submitted. I said two. She all but laughed in my face, shook her head and said, in essence, you just have to keep coming back no matter what happens. You know, that was very good advice.

And so after agonizingly losing my battle to get a TV script on the air, I found myself down and out in L.A., one of the worst places to be financially and psychologically destitute. I luckily located a hole-in-the-wall motel with week-to-week rent, a real dump with rosy-red walls and mirrors in all directions, including on the friggin' ceiling … such a romantic environment.

I'd find fast food on sale (The 2-for-1 Whopper was always a real deal), and that would do it for the day. I had enough for a daily bottle of cheap wine (burgundy, to match the ambiance), and that was about it. Even that horrid joint—The Roach Motel—proved too expensive for me, and I ended up calling a close buddy—Tino Esparza—to wire me a few bucks. All he could come up with was 50 dollars but to me that was God-sent.

It was a long way, however, to cover another week's rent so I called another friend from across town—Bruce Moir was his name, from Hermosa Beach (I had never known an elephant trainer before, and this huge, jovial man was perfect for his occupation). He kindly came over to help me pack my things. In reality I had very little baggage, but I was in such a devastated state—shaky, wobbly and beaten, a real beat-nik—I could hardly make it from my bed to the car.

At forty-five years of age, I found myself lying in a flop 'til-you-drop motel, looking at my haggard body in the ceiling mirror. I was always either drunk or hung-over, with my pancreas always flaring up. This dead-end trap of drinking to soothe the pain, which would cause even more pain and helplessness, brought me to one conclusion: screw it all, I was going to die, and die soon. So I made an executive decision: there's no way in hell that I'm gonna kick the bucket in fuckin' Los Angeleez, if you pleeze.

My final bucket list item was that with the little money I had I'd drive to Santa Barbara, only about a hundred miles up the coast ... and drink myself to death there. No more hospitals for me! I'd rather be in a bar than pee in a jar ... just fuckin' brilliant! I mean this was certainly a classier final chapter, the location that is. Obituary: Tomás Chavez *of Santa Barbara* was found lying dead and naked on the beach.

Bastard that I am though, somewhere deep in me I've always felt that somehow I'd pull through. I thanked Bruce for helping me load my car and then drove to a nearby liquor store where I picked up a jug of on-sale red wine in preparation for my funereal jaunt up the magnificent Highway 1 coastline. How I could have driven that distance is beyond me, and I didn't even have Jesus on my dashboard ... or did I?

It was winter and when I got to Ventura, about an hour south of Santa Barbara, it was already dusk and the rain was coming down heavily. Since it was a beach town there were a couple of parks along the way for summer camping. "Closed," the sign read but I just drove right on through. Not a soul was in that park, not even a Ranger, and so I parked next to a toilet facility where I could take care of my bodily functions. That night I polished off the burgundy and, just tired from everything, fell into a restless stupor.

Early the next morning it was overcast but the rain had stopped, only a light mist. What to do? After gas and wine, I still had about 40 bucks in my pocket ... maybe 41. I remembered that when visiting Ventura a few years earlier I'd seen a seedy group of crazies hanging in a small park near the beautiful and historic Mission Buenaventura, for which the town was named. I remembered because on some level I saw myself in them. There was sure to be a liquor store close by, the supply center for that handful of non-desirable derelicts (I resemble that remark).

Suddenly I had a new plan: screw Santa Barbara, I'll just finish the job here. At that time, you could still find a really cheap, rundown place to rest your head—they were called "cot houses." Cot, not cat. For ten bucks a night you'd get a simple flea-bitten bed or fold-up cot where you'd try to sleep alongside a bunch of flopped sops snoring next to you.

I recalled spotting such a place on that very street. The plan was materializing. Yeah, a cheap room and spend the rest on booze ... that should do it. What a fuckin' genius ... but the truth of it is I've known a few friends, poets and writers, who have done just that.

I arrived downtown pretty early; I'd say seven-ish. I think it was a weekend because there was almost no traffic and no business folks opening up their shops, nothin'. I parked the car and walked toward the area where I thought the hotel might be.

There was a fellow drunk, a kindred spirit, lying on the curb, just lying there on the cement, like an ex-millionaire with a cigar butt in one hand. I figured he might know of the digs I was looking for. "Excuse me, sir, but I believe there's a cheap hotel close by ... yah know where that might be?" He nodded and pointed right up the street, within half a block or so. He sez, "Can't miss it; walk right up those stairs, tell'em Scotty sent yah."

Well, beam me up, Scotty, I'll get this room, get me some hooch an' I'm good to go. I moseyed up the street and lo and behold, there she is, small sign above, a stairway to heaven. I grabbed the banister and pulled my tired ass up those steep steps. I was so exhausted it seemed to take forever to reach the top. I opened the door expecting to find the typical old guy sitting behind an old desk reading a newspaper or drooling over a girlie magazine.

But this was *very* different, eerily so. It appeared that I had walked into a small coffee house of some sort. Maybe this was the hotel's anteroom where they'd make an extra buck or two selling coffee and cigarettes. There was actually a little bar, a couple of tables, and a few chairs here and there. What the ...?

I noticed there was a doorway to a large room in the back, conspicuously open as if to invite folks to walk in. I did just that—and then I stared, semi-shocked. What I saw was a room with a bunch of eight-foot-long fold-up tables, a half dozen or so, with chairs on both sides. The tables formed a "U", and at the front center of the "U" was a podium, and above that podium was a large, lovely painting, a painting of *stairs* leading up to the word, all caps, "HOPE."

Stairs, not unlike those that I had just climbed! At the bottom of the painting, beneath the first step, was the word "DESPAIR." As I recall there were exactly twelve steps in the painting's stairway ... representing what? The twelve months? The twelve apostles? As it turned out, I had walked up *the wrong set of stairs* that drizzly morning ... or did I?

The stairway to this hall was perfectly adjacent, I mean wall-to-wall, to the steps of the flophouse I was looking for. The only difference is that the second set of stairs led up to an Alano Club and A.A. hall: *The Twelve Steps of Alcoholics Anonymous.*

I burst into tears. I mean sobbed, as I am at this very moment. The Muslims say "Allahu Akbar," God is great. Yah think? That morning I told this whole story to the handful of guys there in the front of the A.A. meeting hall, the entry nook. They poured me a cup of coffee and in short time we were all sitting in that back room. "My name is Tomás, and I'm an alcoholic." I was told by an older guy in the fellowship, "Tomás, never stop telling that story … it could save a life." Well, it just had.

I remained in Ventura for about a week, attending meetings a couple times a day and sleeping on some generous A.A. member's couch. I got my health back, but more important than that I developed some self-respect and a real touch of optimism.

I shared with the group that I was originally headed to Santa Barbara—about an hour north—and someone mentioned that a great A.A. club met there daily, and that there was a robust Alano Club as well (a hall where recovering folks can socialize a bit … very low key and always with recovery in mind). I felt healthy enough to make the trek and soon headed up that gorgeous, sunny road.

"Buenaventura" translates to good luck or good fortune … how very, very accurate. In my case, what a blessed oasis it was.

Steppin' on up. Two years later I returned to Ventura specifically to take these photos as a reminder of my miracle at the A.A. hall. Below are two shots, one of the front of the hotel and the other of the front of the AA hall to show how crazy-close those two sets of steps were … just inches apart.

Juan Flew over the Pit Bull Mess

Upon reaching Santa Barbara the following morning, I went straight to the Alcoholics Anonymous watering hole, a combination meeting hall and Alano social club. It was housed in a good-sized older wooden building that may have once been a church or a men's lodge of some sort. I was welcomed by the group and felt immediately at home.

At noon on my very first day there I took in a meeting, which always includes the introduction of newcomers. The newbie is to first cop to being a full-blown alkie, "My name is Tom, and I'm an alcoholic."

Instead, I introduced myself in a non-traditional fashion. Like a humble peasant I lowered my head, sombrero in hand, and said "My name is Tomás and I'm … a Mexican." That got a chuckle or two in this most serious of environments. I then proceeded to briefly tell them about the extraordinary circumstances of my earlier landing in the Ventura A.A. hall. The members nodded their heads, knowing that what I had shared was true and that it fell into what might qualify as The Miraculous.

Following the meeting a Chicano fellow walked up to me and said, "So you're looking for a place to live for a while … I might just have something that'll work for you, at least for now." His name was Juan, a stout middle-aged guy who shaved his head to a gloss … with his well-worn tats, he looked like he was probably a bad-ass in his day. He understood perfectly well what I'd been through and that I was trying my best to get my act together.

He lived just two houses away from the A.A. hall—how cool is that?—and he offered me a tiny room in the very back of the old house that he lived in. That ten-by-ten space is where I lived for several months as I put the pieces back together. The house was old enough that it could have easily fit into the run-down neighborhood I grew up in back in West Fresno. But Juan kept it very clean and organized and simple. Not even a TV set. I think "Spartan" would fit here.

Within a week I had found work selling books over the phone for a small publishing company. I had to get up pretty early because many of the phone calls were to the East Coast, three hours ahead of Pacific Time. I didn't have a wind-up or electric alarm clock, but I did have an organic one: an unusually loud but punctual rooster. Juan said that the old guy had lived in his yard for years. That sucker would awaken me every morning at the first light of the morning sun, his salutation to the dawn. It felt good because it was familiar from my childhood, and too, it gave me a sense of being in the country, in nature.

My small window facing the back yard looked over Juan's very Mexican domain: a couple of tree-sized cactus plants, with prickly pears galore that he would periodically harvest; a small but productive tomato and chili patch; and a doghouse for his beloved pet, a shit-brown pit bull.

Oh, yeah, and that other critter, the cocky rooster, who had an uncanny ability to sense the dog moving in on him. That damned dog would go racing towards the rooster as he pecked the ground, and time and again, the rooster would, in essence, say fuck you and just fly up into the trees. (Yes, chickens can fly … when they have to, and so can you … when you have to.)

Into my third month at Juan's pad, I woke up one morning to one hell of a ruckus. The squawking of the rooster and the growling of the dog. It was primal and it was terrible. I looked out the window and the dog had been laying low that morning, planning his revenge and desire for blood after years of torment. He had the rooster by the throat, but he wasn't immediately intent on killing him, just torturing for the joy of it, much like cats will paw and gnaw at birds they've caught without killing them for a while.

I yelled to Juan to come with me into the back yard to try to save the rooster that he so loved. We ran out there and Juan reached down to pull the pit bull away. He had raised that dog from puppyhood, and deeply loved her also. That damned pit without an iota of hesitation turned on Juan and went for his hand! As Juan kicked the bitch (female dog, no PC here) and finally got her to let go of him, in a fraction of time she tore the chicken's neck in two.

I have friends who've owned pit bulls and they swear that it's not their fault, that they've been taught to be mean. Bullshit. Many are killers at birth, bred for generations and trained to be aggressive; under certain circumstances they have done great harm to people, including the elderly, children, and other dogs—even killing them. There are no shortages of such incidents. Who the hell in their right mind, especially if kids are around, would raise these canine sociopaths? They remind me of the little gangsters who beat my father to a pulp, to death, just for the hell of it. Yes, there are pit bulls among us.

Death of a Rooster

On the morning of feathers
as the sun was still rising
the drama unfolded
he crowed his last crow.

The hound had him cornered
on the morning of feathers
with nowhere to fly
and nowhere to go.

He was tough, an old fighter,
taunting and gritty,
fearless in the ring
but not in the city.

He was the stuff
of pride and cocksureness,
Manolete, Dominguín,
and the sway of El Cordobés.

He was goose bumps from La Negra
on the Day of Liberation,
he was Marines in The War,
the pride of a nation.

Bruised beak and talons,
his death a pure pity,
a warrior lost
in the streets of the city.

The Man with a Million Minds

> "A man needs a little madness, or else … he never dares cut the rope and be free."—Nikos Kazantzakis, author of *Zorba the Greek* and *The Last Temptation of Christ*

Part One, 1990. Harry Kislevitz was arguably the craziest son of a bitch on the planet. Yeah, but crazy like a fox at times.

I was en route in my little '66 off-white Volvo sedan heading north out of Santa Barbara to the Bay Area. What a joy, taking the winding and stunningly gorgeous Highway One along that long, slow coastline.

When I got up to Big Sur, about 200 miles north, I noticed a small wooden cabin on the right with a sign, Henry Miller Memorial Library, where the brilliant and sexually notorious (for his time) Miller had lived and loved a few years earlier.

Tropic of Capricorn, *Tropic of Cancer*. There, along with the periodic company of a handful of marvelous mad men and/or women, he had also experienced intellectual intercourse, if you will, with a fellow writer, the exotic, erotic Anaïs Nin—who was hardly a nice nun.

Talk about bohemian ambience, Oh, this historic habitat! A sure trip to beatnik hell in Squaresville if I passed it up. Besides, it was time to pull over, take a hit and swig down some lukewarm brewskis (which, sad to say, I had returned to drinking by this time).

Then I walked through that fateful door. I'll be damned, there stood a good ol' buddy, a fellow named Jerry Kamstra whom I'd met in North Beach a few years earlier. He had somehow become the manager of this wonderful little piece of history. (The library's still there, by the way.)

Jerry was quite a character, big handlebar mustache and a stylish Mexican straw hat, a tall guy and the boots he wore made him look even taller. He was an original for sure, and had written a couple of tasty novels including *The Frisco Kid*.

What a mind … A few years earlier, he had taken the money advanced to him by some large magazine (*Look*, I believe it was), a few thousand dollars to do a story on pot smuggling from Mexico. He decided that the best way to get this story written was to, well, do a bit of a field study. And so he took all that bread and went to Mexico to do his research, actually buying a tremendous amount of marijuana which he then smuggled into the U.S. … Damn! And more than once. He then turned his adventures into *Weed: Adventures of a Dope Smuggler*—a novel twist indeed.

When I first met Kamstra, he was living with his wife and two kids on the upper half of Lawrence Ferlinghetti's two-story Victorian, there on Potrero Hill. Ferlinghetti by this time was nationally known, not only as a tremendous poet and owner of City Lights Book Store, but because he had made national news and literary history by being tried for publishing Allen Ginsberg's influential and infamous *Howl and Other Poems.* The charge was literary obscenity ... ah-fuckin'-mazing! 1956, a magical time to be alive in San Francisco, for sure. I was still picking my nose and cutting cheese back in Columbia Elementary in Fresno.

But back to the Miller Library. Turns out Kamstra was boning this chubby goddess I'd met somewhere in my earlier travels ... What the heck was her name? Anyway, the three of us hugged, Jerry pulled out some uninhibitualizing imbibements (as if we needed them) and we settled into what one might expect in Henry Miller's library. He locked the doors—We don't need no stinkin' tourists! —and the three of us howled into the night like horny werewolves.

Sometime during that deliciously delirious evening I mentioned to What's-her-face that I was headed to San Francisco to try to find a gig of some sort, she asked like what, and I said hell I don't know, I'm a pretty good little writer at times, maybe something to do with writing. She said she had an idea that just might work, but that I was heading in the wrong direction, map-wise that is. She sez, "So, you've been in Santa Barbara for a few years, ever heard of Crazy Harry?"

Crazy who? Well, that was the start of it. Turns out Crazy Harry was in fact Harry Kislevitz, a multimillionaire toy manufacturer from New York, the creator and owner of Colorforms play sets, who had settled in Montecito. Right at the ocean, this was an enclave of the rich and famous, the ritzy part of Santa Barbara (which was hardly a slum itself).

Harry lived there long before Oprah Winfrey and other notable beach bums, before Carol Burnett, Brad Pitt, Kevin Costner, and one of The Beach Boys, Mike Love (whom I once visited with sax man Charles Lloyd). On any given day down at the overpriced deli you might be sitting next to Jane Russell (she of celebrated knockers), a tanned Richard Widmark, and a handful of other ancient movie stars whom I'd seen on the silver screen as a kid. They'd mosey in now and then, and I'd just sit there at a nearby table thinking, like a little kid back at the White Theatre, "Wow-wee!"

But back to Harry. Mr. Kislevitz owned three sizable houses in Montecito, each with a brand new Mercedes parked in front of it, perfectly normal, right? But if you look in any dictionary for the definition of eccentric, you'll find Harry Kislevitz as the prime example. In reality, though, *eccentric* is an extreme understatement—Kislevitz was Krazy with a Kapital K! You name a mental malady, he had it: paranoia, depression, tri-polar, attention deficit disorder (ADD), grandiose delusional disorder (GDD), grandiose omnipotent disorder (GOD), and then some. In other words, S.O.S. (• • • – – – – • • •) ... Save Our Souls! This guy was a real work.

Anyway, my friend What's-her-face (the name will come—the "Butterfly Lady"... she sold butterfly art and outfits at New Age fairs ... SteveAnne somebody). Anyway, she was sharp as hell and a full-bosomed beauté to boot and she tells me that Harry, a wealthy *and* generous nut she had met back in S.B., is looking for a writer to help him with his memoir and fulfill other duties as his "private scribe"—that's what his title for the gig was. Well, I had just about enough gas to get me either to The City *or* make a significant U-turn back to Santa Barbara. How very, very tempting.

She gave me his number and I called him the next morning after the three of us had enjoyed breakfast at a café walking distance from the Miller cabin. Harry answers the phone, I tell him a little about my background and ramble on, I'd like to do a little work for you, whatever you need, etc., and he sez "Can you come for dinner?" Heck yes, I sez. He sez well come on down, we're having dinner early, 4-ish, here's the address.

Now that was a real no-brainer. I thanked Jerry and The Butterfly Lady and headed back to where I had just left the day before ... beautiful scenery, especially when you got a good buzz and great prospects. I arrived a little earlier than dinnertime and things went quickly from that point on. Harry, already in his early sixties, was a gaunt Jewish cat with a Jimmy Durante schnoz, wispy long, gray hair and wild eyes. He greeted me, sat me at the table, and launched right in, trying to convey his muddled, manic notions about saving the planet (turns out he and I had a lot in common). I'll say this: the guy didn't fiddle-fuddle around ... if he liked you, you were soon on board and that was that.

All that said, thank God for Ron Scalia, Harry's all-around manager. Ron was a terribly bright middle-aged man, a UK-born Italian, a sweet and quiet soul who had his finger on the pulse of everything in that mind-messing milieu. He taught me the Kislevitz Maneuver, a real survival technique in LooneyLand. Basically, it went something like this: When you see Harry coming, hide. I soon found out why.

Part Two. That very night I was driven by Ron to one of Harry's three houses, all of them priced in the millions. Mine was a one-story, sprawling Spanish style five-bedroom place, relatively new, with nice furniture but not a lot of it. Everything was top-drawer, as it were ... including the only other inhabitant, a petite dancer whose bedroom was on the extreme opposite side of the house from mine.

The dancer was a Russian prima ballerina of some renown, the real deal. Turned out to be a truly nice young thing who was hungry to learn American ways. Nasdrovia!, sez I, I vill teach you, my dahlink. Crazy Harry had somehow snatched her from the then Soviet Union, where he had been visiting earlier that year. It soon became evident as to why, but that's another story. Snatched?

Early the next morning there was Ron knocking on the door, bright and frisky. He'd arrived in a new Mercedes station wagon, whose motor was running in the driveway. "Ready to go?" ...Wha? Turns out Harry had a hair up his ass about something going on at his newly acquired property—an entire town called New Cuyama. I threw water on my face, dressed and rushed out to the car.

Ron and I scooted up the street and picked up Mister K and his wife-to-be, an attractive singer named Sidney Gay, half his age, who relished her role as a millionaire's moll. (Harry wasn't a very attractive man and some have had the nerve to insinuate that money may have had a little to do with her presence ... the noive!) We headed out, with Harry yakking a mile-a-minute.

New Cuyama is a desolate place about a hundred miles northeast of Santa Barbara with no easy way to get there, other than by small plane. (In fact there was a tiny pothole-pocked airstrip, essentially non-functional, which Harry now owned along with almost every other piece of commercial property in that town.) Up the freeway we went, to Santa Maria, then across Highway 166 to this tiny burg of a hundred or so. It was located right on the highway, and one of the few sources of income was the flow of semi-trucks whose drivers would stop there for a cold beer and a greasy burger en route to Bakersfield, Fresno, and beyond.

When I say Harry bought the town, I mean just that. He bought the only restaurant, bar, merchandise store, a couple of power companies, and the airstrip which was on the sizable chunk of land that came with it. There was a big one-story World War II-era building on that parcel that had obviously been related to the airfield at some point. That structure was still habitable, though it had no furniture at the time. This was to be headquarters of Global Cities, Harry's latest brainstorm. (One thing I can surely say is that the man thought big and put his money where that crazy-ass brain was.)

His idea was this: he was going to convert this very rural hick town into a self-sufficient, 100% organic, solar-powered, counter-culture community, a utopia in the desert. This was back in 1984, which just happened to be the name of the George Orwell book about a dystopian society headquartered on Airstrip One … coincidence, you ask?

In Harry's paradise everyone would build their own houses with the help of the rest of the community, à la Habitat for Humanity—in essence it would be a commune. (So *that's* what he was doing back in the U.S.S.R.)

New Cuyama was to be a model for similar cities where Harry was beginning to buy property, large chunks of remote and empty land. Needless to say, it was easy to recruit long-hair types, still-hopeful hippies that were ready to move out there into the middle of nowhere with nothing but grasshoppers, rattlesnakes, and lumbering big-rigs pulling in now and then for a fill-up.

The first thing Harry did that day was to walk into the small restaurant—the only restaurant in town in which was the only bar in town, and unceremoniously fire the cook, the bartender, and the waitress … You can bet that went over really well in that little community. He replaced the cook with a couple of flakey back-to-nature Euell Gibbons freaks who had convinced him that they had culinary experience. Their specialty? Brown rice, soy cakes, and bean sprouts, a bastardized macrobiotic hodgepodge … yummers.

He went on to replace the bartender with a little Japanese guy who served up bizarre organic drink concoctions that would make your head spin. (You'd need a drink after some of that shit!) The new guy poured the hard liquor into the sink (alcohol abuse!) and replaced even the beer with some pretty outrageous bottled beverages, mostly foreign with arcane names.

I'll never forget the looks of those truckers' faces when, after a hell of a long, hot drive, they sat down for their regular cold brew and a thick, juicy bacon burger. The most appetizing thing on that damned menu was an Ostrich Burger, terribly dry and tasteless … and I'm surprised the hippy-dippy chefs even let that on the menu.

I can go on with how, in record time, Harry arrogantly proceeded to fuck up that whole town. And it's not that his ideals about a self-sufficient community weren't honorable … certainly the concept had been tried hundreds of times, here and around the world, sometimes with considerable success. It's just that Harry, besides being inconsiderate of the townsfolk, was so thoroughly into his own aggrandizement that it was impossible for him to get a damned thing done.

To illustrate the point, this tall, thin man had commissioned a 12-foot-tall painting of himself as Uncle Sam with the body of Dwayne "The Rock" Johnson, holding a shovel in one hand and a hammer in the other … I gotta say, that outrageous portrait was mucho impressive, which was of course the point.

Above is an old photo of Harry dressed as Uncle Sam in front of a humongous painting of himself … as Uncle Sam. Pretty creative, I must say.

Anyway, back to ol' Harry's Utopia in the Desert. The guy managed to disappoint a lot of good people who thought, "At last we'll have something." Shades of a certain President, huh? The psychological term is Narcissistic Personality Disorder, and that was one of his more stable features. Yet Harry had a heart of gold and that makes all the difference in the world.

From day-to-day, almost minute-to-minute, Harry would change his mind about everything … *everything*. And then come back a few days later and do it all over again. Maddening for the folks who were addicted to their paychecks, and in time I was the first to say "Yessir. Yessir." There was no debate, early or late we all learned to go along with the whim of him.

The fact is at some deep level, Harry had no intention of completing a damned thing … a reality he shared with me in one of his clearer moments, a kind of fear of accomplishment. The man had very severe problems that complex psychological terms would have a hard time defining. He had been through dozens of shrinks and when he was through with them, they needed a shrink. Medication seemed to only make him worse.

A hairy note: He sold his New Cuyama properties after a period of time, within a couple of years … That the town ever returned to normal is dubious. I hear they eventually got a community swimming pool and a Coke machine.

Part Three. ***Harry does Hawaii.*** On an otherwise perfect day, The Mad Hatter got a hare (sic) up his ass, and with very little warning, as was his wont, he declared that we were hopping off to the island of Oahu. Seems he had an idea about how his concept of Global Cities could work on a remote Hawaiian island.

The man could be very convincing, what with his successful Colorforms toy company as part of the door opener. So, as it turned out, he had contacted a major Japanese-owned bank and real estate conglomerate that was headquartered in Honolulu and told them he wanted to buy up a massive amount of land in the Hawaiian jungle. They must have thought this expansive son-of-a-Bernstein might just be serious about laying out a shekel or two for some remote real estate.

Next thing you know he and I are on a plane bound for Hawaii, me with a bright new white suit and colorful silk shirt to boot. Harry brought along his, as always, unpressed everything and one of his splashier straw hats. He had reserved a couple of swank rooms on the beach and so we kicked back the first night, me with my pad and pen, ready to jot down whatever nutty shit he might come up with (and to be fair, periodically some of his ramblings were ingenious, even coherent).

Next morning, we were driven by a limo sent for us by our hosts. We took the elevator to the top floor of a sparkling new Honolulu skyscraper, which had huge windows and a majestic view. At that time it seemed that the Japanese had bought up half the island, including the prime hotels on Waikiki … How ironic, considering the relatively recent history of World War II. Harry was unusually quiet all this time.

We were greeted by a sweet, soft-voiced receptionist, who had the demure demeanor of a geisha girl. She escorted us to a large meeting table where a group of Japanese businessmen (six or seven) were standing, mostly bankers, with a couple of real estate brokers and developers. Per their custom, each bowed as they introduced themselves. I made my little bow, but Harry just stood there staring at them. The stage was certainly set.

The leader of the group gestured with his hand that we should all sit and proceed with the meeting. Everyone took a seat except Harry, who was situated at the head of one end of the massive conference table. His not sitting just stopped everything dead in its tracks. As it turned out, he had no intention of sitting, period.

Harry was a fairly tall man, six feet at least, but that day he seemed much taller—and not because all the Japanese were short guys. While the businessmen stood in bewilderment, Harry took off his hat, walked up to the table's edge, and to everyone's amazement pounded his fist onto it making a thunderous noise causing everyone there to squirm in their chairs.

With the stern and menacing scowl of a samurai warrior going into battle, he scanned each man with a cold stare; he then screamed at the top of his lungs, "Remember Pearl Harbor!!!"

Holy fucking shit! We're talkin' stunned, all of us. I had foolishly thought that he couldn't possibly be crazier than what I had previously experienced. But just maybe this wasn't as mad as it seemed, just one hell of an expensive therapy session. He stormed out of the room as I sheepishly gestured to the group like, geez, hey, I didn't say that, and then followed him back to the waiting limo.

That night I had a few Mai Tais at a bar on Waikiki while I grappled with what it might have been like to be there on December 7, 1941. The absolute shock of that surprise attack was truly unimaginable. I knew perfectly well what the place looked like and felt like in peacetime—Honolulu, Schofield, Hickham, Pearl Harbor—because I had been to all of these places when I was in the Army back in '62. But the scope of the assault that December day, the panic and horror, was far beyond any experience I could possibly imagine.

I surmised that Harry as an older New York Jew might well have had relatives and friends who were tortured and murdered by the Nazis who, after all, were cohorts with the Japanese in that war. Or it may have been closer, maybe relatives of his in the Navy were harmed in Pearl Harbor. Or maybe he himself had been in the service back then.

For all of his madness, Harry was an exceptionally sensitive being and at his age in some fashion he certainly experienced that lengthy war on a personal level. In any case, I'll wager those poor bankers never knew what hit'em ... Talk about a sneak attack!

Part Four. ***Harry loved to play house.*** By that I mean, again at the drop of a hat (and he loved his hats...the mad hatter, the had matter), he would decide to move the furniture, *all of it*, from one house to another. He had a Mexican crew of worker bees who loved him … Hell, he paid them well to load up his things in that big old truck of theirs and, like musical chairs, play musical houses. "A" would go to "B," "B" would go to "C," and "C" would come back to "A." Sometimes to "D", that being all the way to New Cuyama, a hundred miles away. Same thing every month or so. The Mexicans would just shake their heads and laugh, of course never to his face; they would just get on with the work. I think maybe Harry, in his own way, was creating much-needed employment for these dedicated "illegals."

I was no exception. Every Friday, I'd turn in whatever I had written—which he almost never read—and then pick up a nice little check. At any given time there were, not including the Mexican workers, at least a dozen folks on his payroll, which really wasn't a payroll but more of an on-going Christmas bag.

They'd come from out of the woodwork with all kinds of Looney Tune notions and, more often than not, he'd fund them if he liked the person. He even dished out the bucks for one of my projects, a large environmental expo—twenty grand, just like that.

In that way Harry was a real mensch (a Yiddish term for "a decent responsible person with admirable characteristics"). In some kind fashion, this was his way of sharing his substantial wealth. He did go out of his way to help people, and God bless him for it.

Part Five. ***Talk about sharing the wealth!*** After the New Cuyama fiasco, Harry bought a huge chunk of property in Costa Rica, right on the coast, where again he intended to build one of his "Global Cities." He and a close, mutual friend, a filmmaker named Bob French, flew there to make the arrangements. Bob, like all of us, knew this was yet one more of Harry's grandiose dances but, hey, it was his band and his dance hall.

So here yah go: While down there on business (if it could be called that), Bob and Harry decide to have a little good Christian fellowship with the natives, that is to find the local cathouse and proceed to test the wares. (Tangent: Harry, by the way, had ten children that he was aware of … end tangent.) Anyway, Harry decides that it is the madam herself, the Queen of the Scene, that tickles his fancy and so ends up tickling her fancy throughout the night.

After a bit of hanky-panky she tells him what a tough life she's had, why she turned to prostitution, about being hustled by pimps, etc. The next morning Harry and Bob go back to the little hotel where they are staying. Immediately Harry calls his New Jersey headquarters to have them wire him $50,000. That's 50,000 American friggin' dollars back in the early '90s.

That morning he goes to a bank somewhere nearby and is able to pull out the money *in cash.* Bob had no clue what was going on but went along for the ride … not that he had a choice. Harry puts the entire sum—$50,000 cash!—in a large brown paper bag and goes to the doorstep of the madam. No one answers the knock. He tries a handful of times, and with no success, he looks at Bob, smiles a little, and with a little note attached he just leaves the bag on her doorstep! 50,000 cash dollars!

That's how Bob, who is an honorable man, told it and if you knew Harry, that's exactly how it was.

As I gathered, it wasn't too much later when his ex-wife and grown kids, realizing he was squandering *their* inheritance, took some legal action, took over the business, set aside money for his retirement, and sent him a sizable monthly stipend. That's pretty much how it came down as I best recall. He never let them forget, though, that the fortune came from his original hard work and out-of-the-box, out-of-his-mind brilliant/crazy mad marketing creations.

From the Guadalajara Times, September 2009:

> Ajijic resident Harry Kislevitz died at a local nursing home on September 1 at the age of 82. Kislevitz was a philosopher and inventor and today three generations learn and play with his invention of Colorform Toys to coordinate memory and building skills. He and his wife, Sydney Gay, moved to Ajijic, Mexico from Santa Barbara in 2005. Kislevitz is survived by his wife and ten children."

Finally, in 2020, Harry was inducted into the Toy Manufacturers Hall of Fame … He had deserved it all along but, alas, Harry was Harry. Yah know, I miss the guy … God bless that wonderful one-of-a-kind character.

Signs of the Holy Ghost

Following are three rather amazing experiences I have had with what might be termed "kundalini energy." The stories are true and seem to fit the notion that there exists a force, a very real but subtle force, that has much to do with our spine, and energy that moves from the base of the spine all the way up to the top of our head and out. I would like to begin with three definitions that are central to this story; they are taken practically verbatim from Wikipedia, with a bit of my commentary that will shed light on my experiences with this blessed energy:

Chakras: Rotating vortices of subtle matter, which, according to traditional East Indian medicine, are considered the focal points for the reception and transmission of energies. Seven major chakras or energy centers (also understood as "wheels of light") are generally believed to exist, located within the subtle body. These form the basis of yoga.

Kundalini: literally means *coiled*. In Indian yoga, a "corporeal energy," an unconscious, instinctive or libidinal force or Shakti, lies coiled at the base of the spine. It is envisioned either as a goddess or as a sleeping serpent, hence a number of English renderings of the term such as "serpent power."

The Holy Ghost: The meaning of Holy Spirit and Holy Ghost are identical. Holy Ghost was the common name for the Holy Spirit in English prior to the 20th century. "Pneuma" is the Greek word for *spirit* and is found 385 times in the New Testament. It is used in the general sense of *spirit* as well as the Holy Spirit, and can also mean *wind* or *breath*.

Story # 1: *An Odyssey with Telemachus*

San Francisco, 1972 or so. One morning I was returning to Santa Cruz after one hell of a week-long bender in San Francisco, which included a heavy duty acid trip and gallons of booze to bring me down off of my first serious LSD bummer (the term bummer is hardly adequate for the horrifying experience of taking bad acid.) My understanding is that after the popularization of LSD in the mid to late sixties, several elements of society got into the act, the Mafia amongst others.

There wasn't a great deal of morality about all of this; it was hardly for God-consciousness or even psychedelic bliss … it was business, dirty business, and some of that acid had been cut with meth-like "speed" and God-knows-what to manufacture it on the cheap. But the shit was just that, and it would have your head spinning out of control and your heart pounding like it was ready to burst outside of your chest … Strawberry Fields in hell!

The previous night I'd gone trolling, so to speak, and caught nothing but a good cold. As John Lennon understood, "Nobody loves you when you're down and out." I was so damn broke I ended up attempting to get a little shut-eye in the Greyhound bus terminal down off of Market Street. I sat on a bench and tried to snooze, but every few minutes the Greyhound security cop would walk by and kick me on the foot … "No sleepin' here." I told him I was just waiting for someone, but, nonetheless, every time I started to zonk out here comes the kick.

Finally I said screw this, there's gotta be a better set-up, so I went to the men's head, went into one of the stalls, locked the door, sat my ass down and fell asleep on the stool amidst the delicate fragrances (eau de toilette) and refined pastoral art. When I woke up, maybe an hour later, I was a little more sober and, digging through my pockets, found to my amazement that I had enough fare to get me back to Santa Cruz.

The bus arrived in an hour or so and I boarded, still sleepy, still half drunk and way hung-over … and now very weak as well. The acid I had dropped the day before had drained me dry. As we headed south, I began freaking out amid out-of-control emotions. I was becoming incoherent, from a number of factors: too much of everything—maxed out debauchery, little food and little sleep for several days. I was relatively young, but the body can only take so much.

By the time we made a stop in the tasteful little town of Los Gatos, where I'd previously lived, I really lost it, was almost as nuts as I had been back in Fresno and, man, that's scary, like your mind and body are separated, floating out there in space somewhere. I jumped off the bus because I was panicking and needed some human comfort. I had an acquaintance there in town, a wise man whom I knew to have a deep knowledge of the body and mind. The guy actually knew the meaning of pneuma and how it could be applied in a case like this.

His name was Telemachus Graneus (Telemachus was, in Greek mythology, the son of the hero Odysseus). He was a well-groomed gentleman with a handsome mustache, welcoming smile, and piercing dark eyes. When I showed up at his porch and shared my plight, he welcomed me in and poured a cup of tea. My hands were shaking to the point where I could hardly hold the cup.

By this time, it was late morning and being a chilly day in early spring the sun brought a welcome warmth. Telemachus asked me to walk out to the back yard with him. There were steps down his back porch, four or five of them and, as I stepped down, he asked me to take a moment, to just sit there on the stairs. He also asked me to listen closely to him and do as I was asked. At this point he could've asked for anything and I would have done it.

His direction went something like this: "Tomás, do you feel the sun, the warm rays of the sun? Just feel the warm rays of the sun."

"Tomás, now follow me closely, feel the warm rays on your feet, do you feel the rays on your feet? Imagine the light of the sun on your feet."

"Now, feel upward, do you feel the light on your knees, do you feel the light on your knees?"

This process continued, upward to butt and waist, to the stomach area, the chest and finally to the head … "Do you feel the light moving up to your head?"

Immediately he asked if I felt better, and I surely did. He then suggested we repeat the process. He repeated the instructions, and I did my best to follow them. From feet, to legs, to torso, to head, I could *actually feel* that loving energy healing my body. The energy was smooth, flawlessly flowing and effortless. And after only the third time I felt amazingly well. This all happened within ten minutes!

I then gave him a very thankful abrazo, a full-armed embrace that we Latinos are wont to do, and headed back to the bus depot. I felt so good I had totally forgotten the fact that only minutes earlier I was in unholy hell.

Story # 2: *Don't Sweat It.*

1972, Pleasant Hill, Oregon. Up at Kesey's ranch, Jimmy D. and I had been given the exciting task of raising money for The Honorable High Priest of Acid, His High-ness Timothy Leary. Kesey had told us that Leary was "The Captain of the Team," and that we needed to raise consciousness about him being locked up in Folsom Prison on trumped-up drug charges, and that a few bucks and some good PR could help do just that.

I had already produced a sizable poetry/music event at Glide Memorial Church in SF called Alleys of The Valley and suggested we try something like that, but on a much grander scale, what with Kesey's fabulous connections and all. After some discussion about venue, we all agreed that the sizable auditorium in Santa Cruz was the ideal spot for the event.

Jim and I returned to Santa Cruz, our home at the time, eager to do our promotional work on the gig. I called top poets from Ken's list and recruited a handful of locals. What an amazing line-up of readers who came that stormy Saturday night for this literary hullabaloo: Kesey, Ginsberg, a woman named Blue; Ferlinghetti, Snyder, and Paul Krassner, too … and those were but a few.

Jim and I passed our press material out to every damned media outlet from Frisco to San José. We created flyers and posters, and tacked them up everywhere … especially in the girls' dorms up at UC Santa Cruz.

Suddenly Jim became very ill … one of those dangerous pneumonia-like sicknesses. I mean the guy could hardly walk, in fact was flattened out for a few days (come to think of it, might've had to do with his trips to those UC dorms).

Within a day, after drinking from the same bottles and smoking the same joints with Jim, I started experiencing similar symptoms: headache, weakness, high temperature, the works. I recall going to sleep the first night of contracting that whatever-it-was—I knew it was serious and with both Jim and I out, the show wouldn't go on.

My lady and I lay in bed, she on her side facing away from me, and I, head propped up, watching television. I turned the TV and lights off, and lying there on my back thought about The Light that Telemachus had taught me about. I proceeded to pray, "God, help me and Jim get well, this is really an important event and I think we all need something good like this to happen."

Immediately upon finishing my prayer I felt an immense energy forming at the bottom of my feet; then in an intense but not painful rush it flew up my legs, my spine, throughout my entire body, and up through the very top of my head.

It had such force that there was a considerable crackling sound as it left my body from the top of my head, so loud it awakened my lady friend from a deep sleep. "What in the world was that?" she asked. I quickly responded, "Oh, nothing, just the TV going off."

How could I explain what had just happened? In seconds I was lying there in an absolute puddle of sweat, I mean a puddle so wet it drenched my pillow and the sheets all the way down to the mattress. So drenched we had to get up and change the bedding.

I then went back to sleep and woke up feeling perfectly healthy and energized! The Santa Cruz Poetry Festival turned out to be, at that time, the largest poetry event in American history.

Story # 3: *Holy, Moley!*

Fresno, 1990. That blistering summer I'd regularly mosey down to the Tower District and partake of a brew or two … or three or four or more.

Well, anyway, this particular evening I found myself in a local fern bar called Livingstone's, then a yuppie-esque environment with a comforting dark ambiance. As I was sitting there, I noticed a young Latino man, I'd say somewhere in his mid-twenties, seated in a corner.

I hazily recalled partying with him and his friends the previous night, the neo-beat hipsters of Fresno … yep, even ol' Frez has some of us. The kid was already a boozer, a shame I say as one who has seen his life go to hell because of alcoholism. Nonetheless he was really bright, charming and was a seeker of spiritual truth. I joined him at his table.

He had already found a path to his liking, a mystical Christianity, if you will. By that I mean not necessarily a path of Church dogma, but of the more esoteric or occult leanings. (If you're interested, read Aldous Huxley's *The Perennial Philosophy*, an amazing anthology of obscure writings dealing heavily with Western mysticism.)

During the young man's practices along these lines, he'd had an experience which had convinced him that there was more to Christianity than meets the eye. There is a beautiful line in Antoine de Saint Exupéry's sweet and profound gem of a book *Le Petit Prince*, when the wise fox tells the Little Prince, "One sees clearly *only* with the heart. The essential is invisible to the eyes."

I asked him what he meant by "an experience" and he said that he had literally felt the Holy Ghost, the very same spirit spoken of in the Old and New Testaments.

From the time I began my own spiritual quest in my late teens, I've always been open to what some would call arcane knowledge, preferably firsthand … which is pretty much the only way we can really know matters such as these.

As we sat there in the corner of the bar, right in the middle of his attempt to describe the phenomena that had opened his eyes, I felt a soft, serene "breeze" blowing up my spine like the light tickle of a feather, not from the outside but from *within my body*, from the tip of the backbone and up to the tip of my head. It was most subtle but very, very tangible in its presence. There was no doubt that this wonderful little wisp of pure, sweet energy, which took but a second, had entered and left my body in response to the very conversation we were having. He looked over at me, his eyes quite open now, and said, "Did you feel that, did you feel that?"

"Well, yes, are you telling me you did too?"

What is amazing here is that two separate people had the identical spiritual experience simultaneously ... How could that be? In the very same moment, we both felt that wisp of pure goodness flow up our spine. I find it striking that in John 3:8 The Spirit is likened to the "wind that blows where it will."

The three stories above have one thing in common ... What Eastern mystics refer to as "kundalini," which as I have mentioned literally means "coiled," like a serpent ready to strike. When it "strikes" it heads straight up your spine, from the bottom of your backbone to the top of your head.

After my aforementioned experiences with kundalini and the Holy Spirit, it has again and again occurred to me that there must be a means by which individuals might tap into this marvelous energy to heal ourselves and to expand our consciousness; that there must be a way to convey this awareness to large numbers of people.

This train of thought which says "God is in you" has a considerable history, dating back to early Hinduism in the Vedanta teachings, which today can also be found in the teachings of non-duality, transcendental meditation and various mystic schools of thought.

Strikingly we hear this refrain in "Mind-cure Churches" (so coined by William James in *The Varieties of Religious Experience*). New Thought founders Phineas Quimby and a patient of his, Mary Baker Eddy, launched Christian Science and spawned a plethora of New Thought churches, such as Science of Mind, Unity, and Church of Divine Science. How fine it is that our blessed mind has the potential, under the certain circumstances, to do our bidding for self-healing.

How fine it is that indeed the Holy Spirit is alive and well within each of us, willing, under the proper circumstances, to do our bidding for self-healing. So there is a means of self-healing. In Christianity we are taught in Matthew 7:7 NIV, "Ask and it will be given to you; seek and you will find; knock and the door will be opened to you."

Heart-Mind

There is a word, a term, a concept in the Tibetan language that has been in existence before the times of Christ and Buddha. That word is *Yab-Yum*. It literally means father-mother, the yin-yang dance of the male and female elements of all life, dancing in unison in creative bliss. It is also a Tantric sexual position in which the female sits on the male's lap.

Yab-Yum laid the groundwork for a logical holistic vision because the early Tibetans felt that at the very basis of human physiology and psychology the heart and the mind indeed are one joined organ. Are they not in fact thoroughly connected, parts of one beautiful and miraculous form? I have read that the heart itself has over 40,000 specialized cells that are "brain-like," and I don't find that surprising. It seems that there is more of a connection than we have previously considered.

Though it is only in our minds that we are separate, we do much damage to ourselves, to others, and to the overall environment when we behave with a fragmented outlook. So often this stems from teachings that place emphasis on differences rather than our common source, and from our own inherent arrogance and ignorance—Adam and Eve in the garden, a metaphor for man's rebellion and ignorance in the light of The One.

In 1948 the great American poet Robinson Jeffers wrote *The Answer* that speaks of this unity, this union:

> Integrity is wholeness,
> the greatest beauty is organic wholeness,
> the wholeness of life and things.
> The divine beauty of the universe.
> Love that, not man apart from that,
> or else you will share man's pitiful confusions,
> or drown in despair when his days darken.

There is now a vast amount of information, not just of spiritual nature, but from the most advanced sciences that illuminate and illustrate our oneness with all. When all is said and done, each one of us is quite unique, quite wonderful, and simultaneously *of the same magical, mystical stuff.*

Ultimately, we are not apart from anything, the environment, from the rest of humanity and certainly not from the various parts of ourselves. The seemingly different components of our body/mind are simply the strings of one sublime, divine organ, an instrument in the most grand of symphonies.

I wrote the following poem when I returned home from the César Chavez funeral march, April 30, 1993, in Delano, CA.

El Camino Real

In the sacred field of roses,
In the scorching fields of summer,
In the frozen soil of winter and toil in the fall,
May the Spirit of the Harvest bless the hands that feed you,
May the prosperity of Heaven be shared with us all.

From the dust of flat Delano and the orchards of the valley,
From the corridors of Berkeley and the barrios of L.A.,
Past the wild dogs of Gallo and the sour grapes of Safeway,
Past the sneers and jeers of farmers
And gendarmes in San José,
Rose a flower of compassion, a fountain of wellbeing,
A signpost on the highway pointing out the way.

With him the families huddled
And spoke of things not dreamed of,
Spoke of simple matters, clean water and no shame,
Spoke of better housing on the dirt floors of Delano,
Spoke of education for the children with no name.
On the dirt floors of Delano a match was lit one evening
That scorched the field of summer and set the fence aflame.

From him the world is better, the heads of workers risen
Above the prison of the endless rows
Of peaches, grapes and cotton,
From him we've seen the highway
That leads us to the mountain,
He has shown us the pathway, the pattern and the plan.
Onward to The Vision, we have seen the Royal Highway
And the leader lives within us,
And the leader says we can!
¡Sí, se puede! … ¡Sí, se puede! … ¡Sí, se puede!

A Romp with a Well-Rounded Rump

After the César Chavez march, I reacquainted myself with a well-rounded lady, educationally and otherwise, Loretta O … Ohhh! About twenty years earlier as student at San José State—replete with rumpled tweed jacket, crumpled Kangol hat, and a copy of *On the Road*—I taught a poetry class and lovely Loretta was one of my eager students. You may use your imagination as to the results of that.

I didn't have a degree, but was published in a minor way, poems and the like in a couple of anthologies. In those days, the professors were very liberal … Little did they know of the anarchistic ambiance I had set up for my "mini-happenings." I got creds for my poetry and then more for teaching this class in my own home … Cool.

I would conduct the sessions up in my cramped little garret to give the students a sense of "bohemian lifestyle." I'd get out a joint (some of these kids had never experienced "reefer madness"), pass the wine bottle around (nice fat jug of burgundy), and, you know, just be spontaneous as I am told was the manner in which those crazy beatniks were wont to behave (frankly, it was just the way I lived). I encouraged them to bring flutes, drums, and anything they could beat on … hell, I would like to have taken that class myself, still would.

As fate would have it, Loretta and I hit it off again after meeting at the Chavez ceremony …¡Que viva César! Soon after our relationship was somewhat resumed, I found that Mizz L was very conscious of the weight she had gained … silly girl. She was a very beautiful Latina and in my opinion not overweight whatsoever … pleasantly plump maybe. Sadly she had been bludgeoned by the Anglo skinny-is-beautiful hammer.

Loretta, for all her beauty, intelligence, and musical abilities (a wonderful guitar player with a rich, sensuous voice), was as well a fundamental Christian. In time she straight up told me she loved me but that it would never work because she and her entire family were immersed in Christ … Jesus! I'm telling you, brother, this is as close as I ever got to converting on the spot. Halleluiah!

Anyway, here's the lyrics to a jazzy little poem/song I wrote with her as the inspiration. It has been recorded, and most folks enjoy the sappy snappiness of it. By the way, you can hear the tune at www.ZenMatador.com.

Chubbette: A Pen Chant for the Rubenesque

You seem to think that men all want
That sleek and slinky look,
You seem to think The Princess came
From a fairy tale book,

Her wedding maids all slim as sticks,
The Prince, a stringy star …
Put away that silly book, my friend,
I love you as you are.

When we met, my pet, in that small dinette
And talked and talked until dawn,
After the breakfast steak and the chocolate cake,
After your car was long, long gone,

I thought of you, my dear,
If only you, my dear, clearly understood …
I thought of you, my dear,
If only you, my dear, loved *you* as I could.

Don't you know, Chubbette, it's your soul, Chubbette,
It's your smile, and your laugh, and your pout,
It's your nose, Chubbette, and your toes, Chubbette,
Not your clothes that knock me out,

Nor the pounds, my pet, but the sounds, my pet,
Of your breath on my neck in the morn …
Please don't fret, Chubbette, it's your heart I met,
It's the very spot you were born.

From the day we met in that small dinette
You've been my only wish,
Don't say nyet, Chubbette, when I ask, my pet,
If you'll be my gourmet dish.

A Cold One with Philip Levine, Poet Laureate of the United States

1995. Fresno, oddly enough, has over the years become quite the mecca for for-real teachers and a slew of serious poetry students. How seriously strange is that?

> Who would have thought that a dusty railroad town in the middle of a desert would become a world-renowned center of poetry? But that is just what happened in Fresno. More than 75 poets with ties to Fresno have achieved national or international reputations, including the poets laureate of two states and a Pulitzer Prizewinner.—from Community Alliance/Fresno Website, July 1, 2010. Author not cited.

The writer didn't know at the time that two more Fresno poets were destined to be selected as Poet Laureate of the whole danged U-S-of-A! Juan Felipe Herrera (2015-2017), … a Chicano homeboy from the tiny town of Fowler, a few grape fields down the road from Fresno. Served two terms. Yep, he and Philip Levine, a mentor of Herrera's, who held the honor from 2011 to 2012. And mustn't forget Garry Soto, who won more poetry awards than you can shake an iambic pentameter at.

I had first met Phil back in '72 when I was producing a poetry reading in San Francisco's Glide Memorial Church. As a fellow Fresnan I had made my invitational call to Mr. Levine while he taught at California State University, Fresno, and had the great fortune of his picking up the phone and taking the time to chat with me about my event. Over the years he also agreed to read at the big Santa Cruz events, fully knowing that he would be surrounded by those—gasp!—damned beatnik poets.

Philip, born back in '28, was a poor Jew growing up in Archie Bunker Detroit, which was both anti-Black and anti-Semitic. He really worked hard at his chosen and beloved craft to earn his various degrees, and eventually earned a scholarship in poetry to Stanford University.

Over time he taught at various prestigious schools but found his home teaching for thirty years at Fresno State, all the while helping build the phenomenal poetry culture that exists to this day. But the ultimate salute to his poetic prominence here in America was the title of Poet Laureate.

While I was in Fresno attending my meditation classes and getting slammed at Fred's Tavern on weekends, a friend of mine all the way back to the early Café Midi days and a well-respected poet in the Fresno area for many years, Chuck Moulton, passed away. He was in fact the founder of the still-happenin' Fresno Poets Association.

I threw a little going away party for him at Fred's, with a mix of music, munchies and, of course, poets, both the scurrilous scoundrels and the poetically pristine. I invited Phil and he graciously agreed to read at this not-so-solemn farewell to Chuck.

As he and I sat at a little table having a cold one before the stage show got under way, we had a chance to reminisce a bit. We spoke about his reading at the big Santa Cruz events I had produced when, years before his national stature, he had the chance to rub shoulders with the likes of fellow readers Lawrence Ferlinghetti, Allen Ginsburg, Michael McClure, William Burroughs, Diane di Prima, Ken Kesey, and many other famous/infamous wordsmiths of the Beat Generation.

Maybe it was the beer combined with the raw atmosphere of an Irish wake but Mr. Levine, knowing my bohemian heart, had a confession to make as to the poetically pure. I cannot quote him verbatim, as I was certainly in no pain. But it went something like this: You know, Tomás, I want to share something with you about The Beats as poets. I didn't think much of their poetry for some time … but looking back I was wrong. They're as good as any, just have their own style. I hope I got that close, Phil.

So my impression from this confession, what I've come to believe, is, hell, it's all poetry, all swell, all's well from Hip-Hop to Hamlet. No one, not even the King of Harlem, can decree to what degree it be or not it be. Philip Levine passed away on Valentine's day of 2015. Sweet day for a sweet man.

P.S. I encourage my young readers to pick up a funky paperback of *On The Road, Howl, Coney Island of The Mind,* and/or *The Beats,* by Seymore Krim … yeah, put it in your hands, feel it, smell it, go to a coffee house and, like, digest it. Find an old copy, if you can, that reeks of weed, wine, and wisdom.

Japanese Scroll description found on eBay

> Honorable note from the Japanese seller of a lovely old scroll being offered on eBay: "They're old goods, but I don't know how long it's an old one. Please see and judge a picture. This product is used goods. There are a bruise and dirty. This becomes only a little wavy. Please accept it and bid."

I bid $48.50 for this treasure and still don't know how that happened. It was meant for me, apparently, and I honor its presence in my humble abode. Please see and judge a picture, the above colorful painting/scroll by Nakajima Kaho (1866-1939).

It is presented in the sizable kakejiku wall-hanging fashion (this one is 72.12" H × 20.74" W). It has an ornate glossy golden silk frame about three inches wide, designed with intricate, jade-colored flowers on delicate branches. I must say, in spite of the seller's considerate warnings, it looks very new and unblemished … and the only waves are on the lake.

It now hangs on the wall of my office directly in front of my desk. It constantly inspires me. It reminds me of the Cold Mountain poems of the hermit Han Shan (approx. 720 to 780 CE), as translated by Gary Snyder, Bill Porter (Red Pine), and a handful of others who pine for that quiet time and place. Here is my cave-scribbling haiku-esque snapshot inspired by the scroll:

Han-Shan Dawn

In the misty hills
fog floats amidst the tall trees
like good-natured ghosts.

With a sharp-edged stone
a hermit writes a poem
on the mountain wall.

His laughter echoes
like crows first taking to flight
in the morning dew.

In Search of the Diamond Sutra

"Only in the transcendent state, beyond the domain of opposites, is truth realizable."—from the W.Y. Evans-Wentz foreword to *The Diamond Sutra,* Shambhala Press

Basic Buddhism. I wish to clarify a little on the general topic of Buddhism for those to whom the subject is new:

First, a sutra is a scriptural narrative, especially a text traditionally regarded as a discourse of, or about, the Buddha.

Second, the practice of Buddhism is a therapy for the alleviation of suffering—that which is caused primarily by our own faulty thinking. It centers around the development of a holistic consciousness and a healthy lifestyle.

This knowledge and direction is contained within the central tenets of *The Four Noble Truths*, of which the *Eightfold Path* is the Fourth Truth.

Third, Zen is a school of Buddhism that focuses on attaining absolute clarity as to the nature of reality. Its study and practice leads to the lucid realization of non-duality and with that, the liberated state of Nirvana.

Fourth, Nirvana, as summarized at Britannica.com, is "The goal of the Buddhist path. It is used to refer to the extinction of desire, hatred, ignorance and, ultimately, of suffering and rebirth. Literally, it means 'blowing out' or 'becoming extinguished,' as when a flame is blown out or a fire burns out."

And Fifth, Buddhism is not a religion per se—though some schools have inferred the presence of a spiritual backdrop, like that of the Tibetans whose ceremonies are imbued with a sense of sacredness. Though it is independent of a deity-based belief system, it is true that for some the experience of Nirvana, the attainment of enlightenment, is so all-encompassing, so liberating, that it is difficult not to perceive it through a spiritual lens.

Buddhism provides a process to see reality as it really is for the purpose of ending unnecessary pain, our own and that of others. The realization of Nirvana may be attained directly through dedicated Buddhist study, meditation, focus, and living on the righteous Eightfold Path.

As stated by Buddhist scholars Robert E. Buswell Jr. and Donald S. Lopez Jr. (*10 Misconceptions about Buddhism*), "Ch'an [Zen in Japan] practice does not involve any progress. The absolute essence is free from all extremes and representations. In one realization, all is realized. In one flash of cognition, all is cognized."

In labeling this experience as religious we attempt to quantify it; we give it a name. We try to link it to something. But this is-ness is beyond measure of any sort; it is simply incomparable. This is why in our attempt to understand enlightenment it is essential to let go of our feelings of selfhood and individuality. Attaining this state without a high degree of selflessness and humility, to use a New Testament example, is more difficult than it is for a camel to go through the eye of a needle. It is impossible.

Seek and ye may stumble onto It. It all started in a bar—surprise! —in Santa Barrr-barrra, 1994-ish. I was in my late forties. As usual I was blathering up a storm with the bartender and somehow got on the subject of Zen teaching, though I had no depth awareness of what this meant other than intellectual knowledge from various readings and a touch of intuition. You might say I couldn't see the universe for the stars.

However, I did manage to communicate what I *thought* Zen was all about—enough apparently for a fellow about my age sitting down the bar a bit to walk up to me and mention that he had an inkling of what I was getting at.

Then it came. He asked me if I had ever read *The Diamond Sutra*. He said that what I was expounding was essentially in the right direction, and that this sutra might be of real interest to me. In retrospect, he knew I wasn't "there" but was sincere enough that I might be ready for some real insight on the subject. When he said "Diamond Sutra," I literally lit up, akin to the old miner who finally hits a vein of the glittery stuff. There are times that even beyond instinct there's a certain undeniable sense of what is true. I knew that I must find this book.

A few days later, without conscious planning, I walked into a corner bookstore down on State Street, one of those warm, friendly establishments of yesteryear. I was poking around in the Eastern Religion section, at this particular moment not really expecting to find the book the fellow had spoken of. I looked up to the top shelf on the bookcase and—voilà!—I found myself in front of not one but a row of Diamond Sutra books, six or so copies of the same book. Ah ha!

There was a moment of real excitement. Could this possibly be …? All were with the same spine and from the same publisher, Shambhala. I pulled the first copy out and opened the first page. I was stunned to find that I couldn't read it because … well, because it was upside down. Or that I had somehow picked it up upside down … but that didn't make much sense either.

I went back to the cover and went through the whole process again. That whole blasted book was upside down! I proceeded to pull out every other copy and not one of them was printed in this manner. How to explain this? The covers and inside content were all "normal" except for this particular book.

That blast of synchronicity was letting me know that this was indeed it, The Book, for my journey at this point of my life; and this was the information I had been searching for, seeking, for a lifetime. Little did I know that this teaching would *turn me upside down* before all was said and done. I went straight to the clerk, bought it, and settled into one of those big, old chairs that you could once find in cozy little bookstores.

Every now and then I'd look up to the strange stares of passers-by. Seeing only the cover (upside down), I'm sure that they thought I was quite mad … and the reality is they were quite right but not for that particular reason.

It is said that for a person seeking spiritual wisdom, it shall be found. There will be no doubt about it, you will surely know. Both the extraordinary Swami Yogananda and his spiritual master-to-be, Sri Yukteswar, knew their relationship with a single glance. That sudden synchronistic appearance generally comes in the form of a living teacher, a guru.

Oddly enough my guru was not alive, not in this time or place. He came from a culmination of what I had learned and experienced in a lifetime of seeking (some would argue *lifetimes*); he came from the repetition of the koan-esque *Diamond Sutra*; and he came from the teaching of the sixth century founder of Zen, Hui-neng.

Two books, one message. The book was in fact two books in one, the first being *The Diamond Sutra* written during the fourth century CE, 800 years before the time of Prince Siddhartha Gautama who, through his great sacrifice and relentless dedication to eliminate the suffering of all people, was to become The Buddha. No one knows to what extent *The Diamond Sutra* reflected his exact words but the practice in India was for the bodhisattvas (the priestly devotees) to daily recite the words of their master. There is comfort in the knowledge that the message was well preserved.

What stands out in this sutra are the repetitive concepts, the teachings, always building for the student's self-realization on nearly any given stanza.

The particular edition that I had mysteriously found, as mentioned, contained a second book, *The Sutra of Hui-neng,* also known as *The Platform Sutra.* Hui-neng lived from 638 to 713 CE in China, about 1,200 years after the life of The Buddha.

The Diamond Sutra, according to the back cover of this edition is "… one of the most treasured works of Buddhist literature and the oldest extant printed book in the world. It is known as *The Diamond Sutra* because its teaching is said to be like a diamond that cuts away all dualistic thoughts, releasing one from attachment to objects and bringing one to the further shore of enlightenment."

The same copy describes *The Sutra of Hui-neng* as "… the autobiography of this pivotal figure in Zen history and some of the most profound passages in Zen literature." Hui-neng is regarded as the father of Zen, whose transcribed lectures ultimately laid the groundwork for its teaching and practice throughout the world.

That evening I dipped my toe into a stream that was headed to the further shore. I was on the verge of becoming a "stream entrant," which is similar to the concept of "beginner's mind." Both refer to the point of initial enlightenment, where once initiated you do not become *more* enlightened. There is no such differentiated state. In fact we come to realize "there is nowhere to go, no one to be." This is a notion taught by ninth century Zen Master Lin Chi, and it is in that tradition that famed author Thich Nhat Hanh has carried on.

Either you are in the stream or not in the stream—once in the stream you are cognizant of *this*, this boundless, inconceivable reality that surrounds us and is us, every single one of us. It is the peace found when attachments and false beliefs are left behind.

In W.Y. Evans-Wentz's introduction to *The Diamond Sutra* I read what to me still stands as pure beauty in concept and in direction. He quotes the great Tibetan yogi Milarepa:

> Time is fleeting, learning is vast;
> No one knoweth the duration of one's life.
> Therefore use the swan's art of extracting milk from water
> and devote thyself to the Most Precious Path.

In my fumbling way I did my best throughout my adult life to heed this advice, that is to keep on searching. "Seek and you will find," we are taught and that is gospel. Considering the unruly nature of my vagabond ways and my lifelong addictions (that's plural), it seems that my spiritual consciousness grew in spite of me.

About a year after this wondrous discovery—finding *The Diamond Sutra*—I moved back to Fresno because I just didn't have the finances to cover the rent of my studio apartment near the beach in Venice. I was kindly put up in a little 12-foot trailer by an old buddy from my youth, Ed Perez.

After being there for a brief span I returned to my profession as an event producer. I developed a new show that I could produce out at the Fresno County Fairgrounds, a "new age" fair of some sort, and shortly after putting those wheels in motion the funds (and the beer) began to flow. I soon moved into a one-room apartment in the Tower District, the very one I'd lived in thirty-some years earlier when I was a barista at Café Midi and a student at City College.

How strange and wonderful this was, filling me with memories of dear friends and great times. The place was within a few blocks of that magical coffee house where I had worked as a young man, where I had first spread my bohemian wings. Unfortunately the café had closed but, as I was to find, younger hipsters still hung in the streets of the vibrant Tower District.

I soon began taking a 16-week meditation course (one evening per week, plus daily practice) which was broken into two sessions, the first eight weeks being *Basic Meditation* and the second being *Advanced Meditation* (which in retrospect was more of the same, but with some cursory notes about the benefits and history of meditation).

The teacher was of the Vipassana school, here in the U.S. often referred to simply as "insight meditation." And of late it has morphed into the more palatable term "mindfulness." Meditation is at the core of Buddhism; it is a means by which one may tame the raging bull. And the reality is that all Buddhist branches are very similar in their basic beliefs, taking refuge in the "Three Jewels": the Buddha (teacher), the Dharma (teachings) and the Sangha (community).

All branches use the breath, not the mantra as do the Hindus, to quiet and focus the mind in meditation. (I do both, but mostly have used the two-syllable mantra. Because my mind wanders so incessantly I find the mantra is a stronger medium, a heavier anchor if you will, to help me focus.)

And now I practice an additional method that I've recently developed. I call it *Silence Meditation*. It is one that I was inspired to develop as a result of decades of meditation with so very little attainment of pure silence. Many of my teachers have pretty much just given up on maintaining any consistent period of quietness of mind, being satisfied with the sporadic moments they experience.

But I have discovered that the mind, if given the opportunity, would just as well hush the monkey chatter altogether. Simply explained, while in my traditional meditation posture *I tell my mind to be quiet*. I am a stern but not harsh teacher. I simply command, "Silence." The mind, it appears, is more than willing to follow my instruction … at least for a few moments, and then without fail I hear my self-centered rambling again.

I have just begun this process, but in this short span I have considerably less "blah-blah-blah, I-me-mine" blather, as neurologist Gary Weber calls it, and more pure silence; in fact, more quiet space than I have had in the many years I have practiced. (You may wish to give it a shot.)

But even here we should be cautious of developing the belief that the voidness we may experience in any type of meditation—the thorough emptiness we experience in our silence—is not necessarily Samadhi (total self-connectedness) or being in the transcendent state of Nirvana. Sitting with a simply blank mind of voidness is hardly enlightenment—it may be closer to a boring escapism. It is just sitting like a frog on a log with little consciousness other than the desire to snag a fly. It is hardly being aware of essence of mind, hardly consciously living in the now.

The Zen Zap

1995, when I was a mere lad of fifty. At the completion of the two consecutive eight-week Vipassana courses mentioned above, I found myself sitting at home alone one summer morning. I had just finished my daily 20-minute meditation session and, as part of my personal ritual, I read from the Diamond Sutra/Hui-neng book.

By this time I had been through *The Diamond Sutra* portion several times, reading and repeating many of the stanzas. And yet the writing still seemed so abstruse, remained so mysterious and, forgive me, struck me as so inscrutable. Strangely, I dearly loved what I was reading but just didn't "get it."

This particular day I decided to move on to the second half of that book, the Hui-neng portion. Bay Area philosopher Joe Miller in his foreword to the Shambhala 1969 edition wrote of the *Sutra of Hui-neng*, "If you let this sutra happen to you, you will enjoy unendurable pleasure indefinitely prolonged. Fall awake, my friend!" "Unendurable pleasure indefinitely prolonged"—simply irresistible. Perhaps not what one might immediately conjecture, but possibly a treasure more pleasurable than pleasure.

I do not wish to tempt you with these comments, for they may create expectations; I can only relay the experience I have had in this realm. The pleasure that Mr. Miller speaks of is to a great extent the enormous release of the mental and physiological suffering caused by our many attachments and false beliefs. They are what hold us back from true liberation.

The first lesson of the Buddha in *The Diamond Sutra* teaches that "No bodhisattva who is a real bodhisattva cherishes the idea of an ego entity, a personality, a being, or a separated individuality." ("Bodhisattva literally means an 'enlightened being.' Bodhisattva is an aspirant of Buddhahood who works for the enlightenment of all sentient beings."—C.D. Sebastian at springer.com)

What was said was that a Bodhisattva *should not cherish* these notions of ego and selfhood. These ideas have no ultimate basis and are in fact unhealthy when out of control. We wrap ourselves in a ball of nerves because of false, immature, and foolish views and we harm many others in the process.

Some, it must be said, may just find this foreign thought too difficult. And many are frightened, even angered, by the threat of this clear thinking because it challenges their deeply imbedded ignorant beliefs. It does take courage and perseverance to let go of long-held beliefs, but when we allow ourselves to focus on the right practice of meditation and the right teaching of liberation there is nothing remotely as clear and rewarding.

Blown out. As I read that morning, Hui-neng was an impoverished and illiterate young man born in 538 CE in a small province in China, not far from what is now Hong Kong. He became a woodcutter to earn money for himself and his widowed mother. One day while finishing his work at the local market he overheard the recitation of a certain sutra. Upon hearing the words, he states, "As soon as I heard the text of this sutra my mind became at once enlightened. Thereupon I asked the man the name of the book he was reciting and was told it was *The Diamond Sutra.*"

I found this quite striking, that an illiterate youth immediately experienced and understood *enlightenment* upon merely hearing this sutra. After my years of digging around in the Zen sand garden of my mind—reading Alan Watts, D.T. Suzuki, going to meditation retreats, etc.—I never grasped it. Yet this uneducated kid got it just like that.

I consoled myself with the caveat, "How many lifetimes, though, had he been preparing?" As it turns out, there may have been a lot more to my question than I knew. Further, there's no shortage of pure genius among children … but mind you, "getting it" is not simply a matter of intelligence; it is also having the willingness to let go of all of our preconceived notions and telling the ego to hush up.

I dug into his sutra, first the brilliant and beautiful forewords by Christmas Humphries and Joe Miller. Then, to my surprise, the Hui-neng book was not primarily *about* the patriarch but was for the most part educational addresses given *by* him—of course, the *Sutra of* Hui-neng. He, like the Buddha before him, was lecturing to a sizable crowd, about a thousand in the temple hall. It begins thusly:

> Learned Audience, our essence of mind (literally self-nature), which is the seed or kernel of enlightenment (bodhi), is pure by nature and by making use of this mind alone we can reach Buddhahood directly. Now let me tell you something about my own life and how I came into possession of the esoteric teaching of the Dhyana (early Zen) school.

Hui-neng proceeds to share his life as a young man and how he attained his initial enlightenment experience. He then tells the story of how he came to meet the Fifth Patriarch of the Dhyana discipline and how and why he was chosen to succeed him.

These first pages are fascinating and poignant, and alone have the primary elements for one's initial enlightenment experience. But it goes on, page after page, line after line, similar in so many ways to *The Diamond Sutra* because on any given page one may discover the information needed to fully awaken.

I truly believe that each person who pursues this path diligently, with heart-mind dedication, will sooner or later reach the desired goal. I would like to share with you the story and the precise line that struck me so powerfully and forever changed my life when I'd just turned 50.

After Hui-neng had been handed the robe and begging bowl that acknowledged him to be the newly designated Sixth Patriarch of the Ch'an school, he is ordered by his predecessor to travel to another city and to be careful, "lest someone should do you harm." And that nearly happens as he is pursued by a jealous monk who is aware that he possesses valuable items, namely the revered robe and begging bowl of previous heads—the Patriarchs—of this order of Buddhist monks in China.

This most tenacious monk, Hui-ming, who in his lay life had been a military general, is described by Hui-neng like so: "His manner was tough and his temper was hot."

From here I will take the great liberty of extensively quoting this particular passage because I choose not to tamper with it in any way in order to best convey my own experience to you. It is from the Dih Ping-Tsze translation from Chinese to English (1930). It takes place when Hui-neng is finally caught by the general, Hui-ming:

> When he was about to overtake me, I threw the robe and the begging bowl on a rock, saying, "This robe is nothing but a symbol. What is the use of taking it away by force?" I then hid myself.
>
> When he got to the rock, he tried to pick them up but found that he could not. Then he shouted out, "Lay brother, Lay brother … I come for the dharma, not for the robe." Thereupon I came out of my hiding place, and squatting on

> the rock, he made obeisance and said, "Lay brother, preach to me, please."
>
> "Since the object of your coming is the dharma," said I, "refrain from thinking and keep your mind blank. I will then teach you." When he had done this for a considerable time, I said "When you are thinking of neither good nor evil, what is at this particular moment, venerable Sir, your real nature [literally *original face*]?" As soon as he heard this, he at once became enlightened.

It is on this line—"When you are thinking of neither good nor evil, what is at this particular moment, venerable Sir, your ... *original face*?"—that I, like the general, finally experienced being fully blown out. In a timeless flash I realized what came before the stars and what is the nature of all things. In this Big Bang fraction of a second it was all very clear, every line of *The Diamond Sutra*, and all of my previous readings along these lines, the Oh! and the Ah! of haiku, the reason for the clever evasiveness of koans ... all clear and lucid ... Oh! I had taken the question "What is your original face" quite literally and set out to find it. Funny thing happened on my way to now.

For me the experience, this insight, was far more impactful than I could have possibly imagined and yet, once realized, was so very simple and thoroughly uncluttered. Transcendent consciousness labeled as Nirvana, Moksha, or Enlightenment, call it what you may, is essentially beyond description, incomparable, and with no boundaries whatsoever. Our human senses cannot define it because they are limited in this matter. They can only hint around "That which has no name."

For my linear mind it was, for lack of adequate words, an instantly cleansing experience that allowed my consciousness to flow out like a spiral nebula expanded to the point of total obliteration, leaving me with only the unencumbered totality, conscious yet without thought. "Flow down and down in always widening rings of being," wrote the Persian poet Rumi.

I cannot compare my experience to Dorothy landing in Oz, transforming from a 1930s black-and-white theatre film suddenly to full-color, three-dimensional virtual reality. And I cannot compare it to a magical spaceship carrying me and Neil deGrasse Tyson to every corner of this universe. I cannot compare it because there is nothing to compare, nothing whatsoever comparable.

The unruly senses, including a false sense of self, are part of what leads us to a belief in self as apart from what non-duality philosopher Rupert Spira calls "The single indivisible reality." He tells us we all experience this highest consciousness in the forms of love and beauty, *qualities that have no opposites and are inherently transcendent.*

I have explored ways of conveying this rather amazing experience, and perhaps it needn't be so complicated. I have thought that one way of describing my path that led to this phenomenon of awakening is, as I did, to imagine *traveling back through time*, back through all ancestry, all genetic connections, and beyond any possible past incarnations; through and beyond all past lives, and the lives of the creatures from which I have evolved; past all evolution of the creature I call myself. Back, back through all time and space, beyond any and all "Big Bangs" and whatever was before that, so thoroughly emptied I found myself in this vast void of here and now. There came a point where I just "jumped into" this new view of looking at reality. In that thoroughly liberated second "all is realized" as we see our "original face." Frankly, I don't believe flashing back in time was the way Hui-neng intended the process, but nonetheless it accomplished the same result.

By exercising this meditative peeling of time and space, or by silently transcending such dualistic concepts as good and evil, one *suddenly* concludes that there is nothing tangled whatsoever, no confusion, pure unbounded consciousness … love beyond opposites. The Beatles were right, you know, "Love is all there is."

A Baptism into Mysticism. For me, the instantaneous Zen burst had an element of an amazing event that happened in the school swimming pool when I was eleven. While I was being held under water by a bully in the school swimming pool, in a fraction of a fraction of a second, my entire life spun before me in vivid detail. It was like a holographic movie in my mind—every single second of my life from birth up to the moment of being nearly drowned. Just what was it in me that observed that experience?

I use this example to show how our normal senses of time and space—our perceptions—are not always as they appear to be. There are theories, incidentally, that attempt to rationalize such phenomena as a mental reaction, suggesting that people just "think" they had such an experience, that it is a matter of brain function and lack of oxygen, and that it does not actually occur. That is incorrect.

When it happens to a person in real time you absolutely know that this exponentially accelerated visual biography is precisely what is occurring. What happened to me took place in a blink of an eye, yet every single solitary "frame" of my life was visually observed in my mind's eye, the internal camera that exists in all people. I have read about others who have had the same experience, and recently met such a person. When it happens you know it to be true—it is not a movie, not a mental fantasy, it is you, your life, taking a rapid-fire journey back through time. This is all acceptable when you are no longer attached to the illusory schedule of time, and it is made more understandable when you accept the consciousness that is all about you and within you that is not attached to your material body.

Matter is matter-less. What Buddhists term as "The Great Void" is the recognition of "nothingness," and it is just that: no-thing-ness. That being the case, then what is all of this stuff around me and within me—my fingers on this computer, this computer, my cat in her box, her box, etc. … just what is all this *stuff*?

From ScienceAlert.com we are told, "But it might humble you to know that all of those things—your friends, your office, your shiny car, you yourself, and even everything in this incredible, vast Universe—are almost entirely, 99.9999999 percent empty space." I disagree. In a final analysis *it is all empty space*, including the mass we think our world is composed of.

An equation like E=MC2 is just that, an equation; this equals that—but it does not really tell us what "this" or "that" is composed of or what is the nature of inertia, let alone why these forces exist at all. Science can tell you what the properties of particles are, but what is the force at the core of those forces? What is gravity? In truth, existence is but the indefinable process of spirit; it is The Tao, with its elegant symbol of yin-yang. Here it is clear that black and white are not really separate but rather swirling variations of energy at play, interdependent aspects of the one merged reality in motion, the cosmic player being Consciousness itself.

For me that experience of enlightenment was incomparably beyond night and day, beyond any idea or thing, beyond any hallucinogenic, psychedelic-induced experience I had ever had. Again, there is literally no comparison. No wonder I never got it … there is nothing to get. Yet "it" is all there is. As Alan Watts put it in the title of one of his books, *This is it.*

In this place there is nothing to hide, nothing hidden, all clearly here and now, the source of power, the essence of beauty, the transcendence of good and evil. What utter wonder that all of this is at once no-thing and not no-thing. As *The Diamond Sutra* announces, *It neither is nor is not.*

Yet *this* is totally alive, hardly a void nothingness, bursting with eternal brilliance in the midst of seemingly black and empty space. The whole bloomin' universe is ... well ... bloomin'. Birth, decay, re-birth—the whole process holy.

This was the key that I had long sought and at least for that second the door of perception was wide open. I had found my guru for this "pathless path" and his name is Hui-neng.

All of the above said, not a thing had really changed other than my perception of reality. In a way, it was the same perception I had as a child playing in the piddly puddle by the dripping faucet that had grown mint, moss, and dinosaurs. To quote The Sixth Patriarch:

> Who would have thought that the essence of mind is intrinsically pure! Who would have thought that the essence of mind is intrinsically free from becoming or annihilation! Who would have thought that the essence of mind is intrinsically self-sufficient! Who would have thought that the essence of mind is intrinsically free from change! Who would have thought that all things are the manifestation of the essence of mind!

Being captured by this sutra, I was thoroughly humbled by the absolute magnificent illumination of it all and the fact that indeed this *un-ness is-ness* is a magnificent interactive *one-ness.* Wonderful beyond words. That experience is always here for those who seek it. As the *Precepts of the Gurus* share, "It is great joy to realize that the path to freedom that all the Buddhas have trodden is ever existent, ever unchanged, and ever open to those who are prepared to enter it."

I cannot adequately honor the two-in-one book *The Diamond Sutra & The Sutra of Hui-neng.* When the time is right the teacher will arrive. Perhaps your teacher awaits you at this publisher's website: www.shambhala.com.

Note. Known as "The Perfection of Transcendental Wisdom," Prajnaparamita sutras suggest that all things, including one's self, appear as thought-forms, i.e., conceptual constructs. In Buddhist terminology paramita literally translates to perfection, or crossing over "to the other shore," the place of enlightenment. The paramis are practices that can lead one to the sublimity of certain virtuous or ennobling qualities.

They are practiced as a way of purifying karma on the path to enlightenment. In the Mahayana tradition of Buddhism there are six paramitas: generosity, morality, patience, effort, concentration, and wisdom. The objective of these practices is to live in a state of tranquility and to achieve the attainment of Nirvana here and now. Not near-vana but here-vana.

The Other Shore

There is no other fruit to taste,
No scent, no touch, no flavor,
No words are near nor birds to hear,
Nor nectared wine to savor;

There is no time for sun-kissed glow
On that distant beach;
Nor space between the ebb and flow,
No other shore to reach;

There is no lost horizon,
No primordial lagoon
Shimmering in the laziness
Of a summer moon;

On this shore all words are mute,
Moot in silence, grand …
The beauty is the nothingness
Hidden in its sand.

A Visit by the Hummingbird King

March 16, 1999. I was living in the little town of Rodeo, just northwest of Richmond. It's a strange environment, close to major metropolitan areas (Oakland, Berkeley, and San Francisco) but still seemingly stuck back in the Fifties.

This small community (its tiny-ness is what I liked about it) is, in spite of its quaintness and direct bay access, surrounded by oil manufacturing companies (which is what I didn't like about it). On any given day I would hear the loud and eerie emergency sirens go off as if we were about to be nuked … But what this warning was really all about was that one of those humongous oil tanks had gone haywire and we all needed to stay inside until it was safe to breathe. Real comforting.

I chose to move there because you could find a nice older home on the cheap in this Hideaway by the Bay. I lived in a house that had probably been built in the late '20s/early '30s, with large windows and tall ceilings, a beatnik pad perfect for my modus operandi.

My dear boy Tino, a chocolate Labrador retriever still in his early puppyhood, and I lived quite happily there for a while. We had a large backyard with a gloriously generous fig tree and plenty of room for a large vegetable-and-flower garden. Tino, with his soft mouth, would pick the tomatoes and deliver them to my doorstep, skin unbroken, and line them up as perfectly as if he had used a yardstick.

One spring day a couple of Black kids—nine, ten years old—rang the doorbell selling odds and ends for some charity. Even though I was damned near broke I found it hard to turn them down. What I chose was a set of lovely wind chimes made of tin and fishing line, the plastic line we used to call "catgut."

The individual chimes hanging on the fishing line—four of them—were designed as tiny, tin like hummingbirds, turquoise and silver, thin glittery pieces of metal that were about the same size as actual hummingbirds.

I hung them in a window overlooking the backyard, a window that was in the back of the sizable walk-in kitchen pantry. There was no screen there, just that large window situated between two lines of shelves on each side of the room. I purposely left the window open so I could hear the crisp tinkle of the chimes when a soft wind blew.

One morning soon after I had hung them up, I heard a commotion coming from the pantry ... There was no wind to speak of so why were the chimes making such a ruckus? I headed back there and beheld an amazing sight: a hummingbird was caught in the hummingbird chimes! I can only think that he—I know the guy was male—had been attracted to the three little silver cuties hanging in the window.

It immediately occurred to me that the thin plastic line could easily cut him to shreds, just about the right thickness to do just that if he moved rapidly as hummingbirds are wont to do. What an experience that was to hold him in one hand as I very, very slowly took down the chimes and that delicate little creature.

I placed him on the kitchen table and, like a skilled surgeon, ever so slowly and methodically removed the terribly tangled fishing line. Fortunately for him only three of the four lines were wrapped around him.

Once that was done, he just stood there, shocked I'm sure, because he didn't move. Then suddenly he began flying, zipping around just under those high ceilings, from room to room he flew. I ran around the house opening all the windows and doors I could, but he insisted on hanging out at the very top, near the ceiling. Finally, after many attempts, I managed to catch him in a paper grocery bag.

I then took him out to the backyard where there was an old-fashioned redwood picnic table and bench. I sat on the bench, put the bag on the table, and opened it. Slowly he walked out and just stood there for a moment, looking at me. How very unusual.

I was just pleased that he was unharmed and, hopefully, could still fly. As I sat for a moment filled with curiosity and concern, he looked up and then abruptly took to the air. He flew in circles over my head a couple of times, wider and wider, and then headed towards the giant fig tree where he disappeared from sight. I've seen him a few times since, in different towns and parks—pleasant little chap.

Hummingbird Note:

I went online to find out more about hummingbirds, and one of the first images that popped up was a photo of one of the little critters enjoying a large pink flower with this caption: "*A coincidence is when God performs a miracle and decides to remain anonymous.*" It's God saying, "Helloooo. Anybody awake out there?" And really, it wasn't all that anonymous.

The Hummingbird King

Trapped in my window with a wind chime of four,
A wind chime of hummingbirds I bought at my door,
He, this tiny fellow, on a bright day of spring
Came to my kitchen, bejeweled little king.

What nectar did he seek in a pantry so dry?
What mission of merit in cobwebs so high?
His little heart pounding as fast as his wings,
Trapped in my window in this world of things.

To the ceiling he rose, trapped in the lines
Of linear walls, of serpentine minds,
From the black sun of riddles
and the flow of lost rhymes
flew the tiny bird-king of lemons and limes.

Of birth and re-birth, he spoke as he flew,
Of a world of oneness, a nectar-filled view,
He shared only of flowers, of wind, and of sky
And the wonders awaiting when we learn to fly.

There in the window, with a large paper sack
I nudged his tiny body to the paper sack back,
And closed his little world, eclipsed the black sun,
In resignation he lay, no movement, not one.

"A king should never be captured or chained,"
I heard him cry, his little heart drained.
To the back yard I raced and on an old wooden chair
I placed the tiny bird-king as he sat with a stare,

His virescent lime vest and necklace of gold
Sparkled in the sunlight, a fortune to behold!
And before he soared to his home in the trees,
His kingdom of nectar and honey and bees,

"Thank you, my friend," he hummed as to share,
"Your world forever is here and not there,
Your world is beauty, your world is bright!"
And with that he flew to his kingdom of light.

Meeting Joel Rothschild

"As to me, I know of nothing else but miracles."
—Walt Whitman

It has occurred to me time and again that there are no accidents. My brief acquaintance with Joel Rothschild certainly would qualify under that theory. Not so much the actual meeting, but the man's story and how hearing it came at a perfect time in my life.

On arriving in Sacramento following my episode with that delightful little fellow, The Hummingbird King, I produced a major health fair in which there were local and national exhibits, and a fine group of speakers. Among them was Mr. Rothschild. He had been recommended to me by his publisher, Marc Allen, as a man who had two important stories to tell. First, he was the world's longest survivor of the AIDS epidemic, and equally astounding, he experienced beautiful encounters with his mate *after* the man had passed away! He calls them "signals," hence his book's title, *Signals: An Inspiring Story of Life after Life.*

As publishers often do, Marc sent me a copy of Joel's book, a tidy 160 pages but for those of us in awe of such merciful messages, an amazingly significant work. I didn't know quite what to expect but as I read the dust jacket, I was more than intrigued. To begin with, the kudos were from a Who's Who list of New Age luminaries, including Deepak Chopra, Joan Borysenko, Neale Donald Walsh, and Bernie Siegel, M.D. I have no doubt there were many that didn't make it onto the cover. Here's what Marianne Williamson had to say: "*Signals* stands as a bright beacon. Through his encounter with a world parallel to the one we perceive as real, Joel's story stands as a testimony to love's infinite power."

And here is the description from the cover copy: "*Signals* is the extraordinary true story of two friends, both living with AIDS, who made a pact: whoever died first would try to contact the other. Joel Rothschild, the more skeptical of the two, was the one left behind. His book chronicles a series of miraculous experiences and encounters that tell an amazing story and offer wonderful proof of an afterlife."

A series! Were this a singular incident of synchronicity one might shrug and say, hey, just another little coincidence. But throughout his writing, powerful "mini-miracles" are chronicled that lead, I would think, even a skeptic to take a second thought. As you know, my life has been riddled with substantial incidents of a synchronistic nature, not the least of which was my most recent lengthy meeting with a certain endangered hummingbird.

Reading Rothschild's book reinforces my theory that these are certainly not accidents at all, but a means by which the Highest Power interacts with us. Just the fact that these remarkable phenomena can occur on any occasion, anywhere, gives us all a reason to be joyous.

I do not intend to reveal the details of *Signals*, in hopes that you take the time to read this brief, well-written book for yourself. It's a narrative you will never forget, but more importantly it contains information that will strengthen you in times of tragedy and loss.

What got my immediate attention was one small aspect that was personal to me that I'd like to share. Here's how it goes: To begin with, each chapter starts with an icon, a small drawing of a … hummingbird. Hummmm. Of course, this captivated me, but why I wondered, did Mr. Rothschild choose it? Again, I don't wish to reveal details about this amazing tale but let me say just this: Against all odds, Mr. Rothschild experienced some most uncanny encounters with hummingbirds. As he explains it, they were direct messages from his recently lost lover who had vowed to be in contact even after death … and the hummingbird incidents were only some of the continuous streams of astounding messages he received.

As fate would have it I chose Joel as the keynote speaker for the health expo I was producing. He was flying into Sacramento and needed a ride from the airport. And though I had surrogates, I chose to personally pick him up in hopes of having a conversation relevant to his incredible experiences regarding life after death … and share my own hummingbird story.

I walked into the airport and greeted him. He was, I thought, an unusually handsome man with a champion's smile in spite of the horrendous losses he had experienced. I didn't know at the time that he had been a very successful bodybuilder, who had attracted celebrities like Arnold Schwarzenegger and Bruce Springsteen to his health spa (his own strength and stamina had to be of great help in his survival with AIDS).

As we drove to the event, we chatted briefly about hummingbirds, reinforcing our shared belief that these little guys have some phenomenally good vibes, and seem to come around just when you need a friend.

The Mouse that Soared

> "My confidence comes from knowing there is a source, a power, greater than myself that I am a part of and is also a part of me." —Oprah Winfrey quote from her awe-inspiring documentary series *Belief.*

Since first being shocked and awed by Hal, the menacing mega-computer in the film *2001*, I developed a fear of computers and as far as I was concerned a mouse was just a pesky rodent. But as we all know, it ain't always the way we want it … like in those monotonous lyrics, "I never promised you a rose garden." And when my little business in Rodeo went belly up, I couldn't even afford my rent, let alone my part-time secretary.

The computer was there for her to work on my business, because I sure as hell didn't want to deal with the business of business … hell, that sounds like work.

Here it was in the late '90s and I had such disdain for The Thing from Some Nerd's Brain that I had refused to learn how to use it. My old hippy paranoia was afraid that someday computers would hack into our personal lives … yah think? Survival has a way of making folks do stuff that they would rather not, in this case my forcing myself to learn how to use a computer because without my secretary, I now needed the damned thing.

So on her last day of work, I asked Wilma to come over to my house/office and show me the basics. Within the first few minutes an icon popped up. At the time we were on AOL and there was a program called "NetFind."

"What's this?" I inquired, already thoroughly amazed at the overwhelming world I was on the verge of discovering. "That's a way," she responded, "of finding people practically anywhere. People out of your past, old friends …" Before she could finish her sentence, my mind was racing. All of my adult life, since the horrible breakup and divorce with my wife and loss of my daughter I had wanted to find them.

Among other things, my daughter was the only blood relative I was aware of, and even without real knowledge of family, I still knew there was something important about our connection. I felt she needed to know about me, no matter how complicated, difficult or embarrassing she might consider my life.

I have to admit there is something to the visible, tangible bond of blood, an inherent though unconscious commitment like bees have with their queen. I had, at one point, before the advent of sophisticated and affordable computers, hired a private investigator to find my daughter, to no avail. Nonetheless I did try again on a couple of occasions, but found nothing but dead ends, and just let the matter dissolve into my endless cocktails.

Astounded by the new possibility that the computer seemed to offer, I asked Wilma to show me how to use this amazing people-finding tool. "Nothing to it", says she: "You go here, type in a name and answer as many questions as you can." All these years I had carried the full name of my father-in-law. I always figured that M would remarry and that it would be tough locating her, but good old Bill, her father, was another matter. The guy was pretty solid, a reliable family man, and all-in-all a good egg.

Right then and there I typed in his full name—William rather than Bill—and his last name, which wasn't common at all. When it came to the question of which city he was in I had no idea, but I figured that they'd likely still be in California.

So there it went, and poof, in a nano-second—I couldn't believe it!—up popped his full name, which belonged to three, count'em, three people in the State of California. I intuitively figured he and his wife might have headed north. Only one of the three was upstate from Fresno, the other two were in the L.A. area.

It was late in the evening by this time, so I decided to wait until morning to call. It was one of the most restless nights of my life. Is it really possible I might find my daughter after all these years—35 years? I paced throughout the night and finally fell out. I awakened early and tried my best to be patient about the call. Finally, I dialed the number.

A woman's voice meekly answered. I've always remembered my former mother-in-law's name because she was a real sweetheart, "Is this Joannie?"

"Yes," she slowly replied, wondering who the heck this might be at eight in the morning. I said, being aware of her age.

"Joannie, is there a chair close by, you might want to sit down." In retrospect I shouldn't have said that. I just wanted her to be comfortable, but my suggestion probably made her far more on edge.

"Joannie," says I, "This is your ex-son-in-law, Tom, you know, your daughter's ex." Thoroughly beside herself, she literally screamed. Excitedly, the first darned thing she said was, "You know, Tom, if you ever did a good thing in your entire life, you have a beautiful daughter, Gina, who is beautiful in every way." Thanks, Joannie, for the vote of confidence. But the astounding realization that I had found my daughter after all these years just blew me away.

Joannie went on to tell me that just the week before, on Easter Sunday, my daughter had been at their home, insisting on finding anything and everything that they still had regarding me. Tucked away out in the garage they had found a few old guess-who's coming-to-dinner photos from the wedding, and M's wedding dress. Joannie said that she'd convey the news of my calling to Gina, though I really wanted to have the honor.

What an amazing experience it was the next day to finally talk with my long-lost daughter, and then to actually drive up and meet her … difficult to convey. Joannie was right in every way; Gina is smart, funny, and lovely … and to top it off has two terrific kids. (I'm a grandfather!) For the first time in my life, I almost felt … normal (though "normal" is a state I remain unimpressed by). So, OK, I'll cop to it, and give credit where credit is due—it was a damned computer that opened that long-closed door … that and some astounding coincidence.

Bill, my ex-father-in-law, passed away within a month and his name disappeared from AOL's NetFind shortly thereafter. I would never have found him, and thus my family, just a few weeks later. We speak of miracles and to me this was one for sure.

Believe me, living a lifetime without a single relative, no matter how well I've rationalized and covered it up, left me with a sizable hole in my being. When, for example, folks would head out to be with their families on holidays, I'd usually head to my favorite bar where I'd go nuts with my adopted family of zany maniacs.

It strikes me that most folks take having a biological family for granted. In gratitude I stopped drinking for a couple of years … The primary reason was not wishing to be a total slob in the presence of my very young grandkids. In fact, my daughter in no uncertain terms let me know to cool it on the hooch in their presence … Good goin', Gina-Beana!

It was about that time when I asked her if she knew of what racial background she was from, me being a Mex and her mom being heavily German. She didn't and so like a good parent I shared the makings of her ancestry, "Gina," said I, "You're a beaner- schnitzel."

You know, as eternally grateful as I am for this amazing gift, when I think about all the good friends I've had throughout my life, well, the fact is I was pretty well cared for. Scattered along the West Coast, my friends have been my family, folks whose friendships have, I would hope, been mutually joyous and reassuring.

At times they were like a rope tossed out to a guy stuck in quicksand—not a replacement for what I didn't have, but a for-real family nonetheless. For me it remains true that though blood may be thick, love is boundless. How blessed are those who have both.

Throwing Sand on Rocks

July 21, 2003. On a perfect afternoon with overcast clouds that mellowed what otherwise would have been a blazing sun, I found myself sitting atop a large rock at the edge of a marvelous sparkling lagoon on the North Shore of Lake Tahoe.

As I sat there with foolish thoughts of equanimity, from the cool water of the shoreline came two very young girls—five years old or so. They approached my perch of a rock, hands filled with sand. Giggling, they proceeded to throw that gritty substance at the rock on which I was sitting.

Like a couple of skinny-legged sandpipers they scurried to the edge of the water and then back a few feet onto the beach, and then up to the rock with their fingers dripping gobs of sand. This process was repeated time and again. Over and over they'd return with hands full of sand; each time they'd vigorously fling the fine grain at *my* rock, screaming with the high-pitched screech of little girls in absolute mirth.

What is this magical ceremony, I wondered? Is it a secret ritual that they had mutually agreed upon while laying on their cartoon-strip beach towels, deciding that this was a dance of sorts to salute the god of mud pies? Were they building something in their mind's eyes, not like the boys who would construct mighty sand castles but for them the palace of a fairy princess?

My curiosity soon got the better of me. I took a moment to carefully craft a delicate question. Ah, that's it! That's the question! And so I waved my hand as they approached my rock once again, their little hands loaded for yet another salvo.

And then I asked *the* question: "Excuse me, young ladies, I was just wondering … *what are you girls doing?*" The response from the one closest to me, the wise older one, was immediate: "Throwing sand on rocks."

Parking at the Big Fair

(A Synchronistic Meeting with Life-After-Death)

> "What luck," I said, "to find myself lunching with you today." "Nothing ever happens by chance," Hesse answered, "Here, only the right guests meet. This is the Hermetic Circle …" —from *A Record of Two Friendships*, by Miguel Serrano about his remarkable meetings with Hermann Hesse and Carl Jung

Summer of 2005. The delightful town of Santa Rosa has, like most towns across America, an annual fair. Cotton candy, hot dogs on a stick, circus barkers, horse racing, pig shit, and a hell of a time finding free parking.

My lady and I must have driven around the blocks adjacent to the grounds for half an hour. We thought we had finally found a good space in front of a tidy old house in a nearby residential neighborhood. Relieved, we pulled up, parked, and got out of the car.

About this time a tall, slim fellow in his, I'd say, mid-eighties came out of the house where we'd parked and walked directly over to us. Uh-oh. In a soft-spoken voice he told us that we shouldn't park there because we'd be given a ticket, even that far away from the fair on a Sunday afternoon. He also advised us where there was a safe place to park just around the corner.

We thanked him, and I said something to the effect of "What great luck meeting you." He replied that he didn't think it was luck at all. Without prompting, and with no apparent reason, he began telling us a story of his death, *not near death*, but *certified* death from a heart attack he had recently suffered. It was eerily similar to the story I'd heard a decade earlier from the famed actress and singer Della Reese.

"The coroner", he said, "had pronounced me dead." He described the experience immediately following his death in detail. It was, well, heavenly. It was a "Clear Light" moment … bright, glorious light that he walked through.

He said that he was perfectly healthy in that state, that in a brief span he met old friends who had died before him, and he had, for lack of a better term, been in some sort of communion with God. (It is important to recognize that the brain is not the mind and that consciousness is also non-local; it is not simply a matter of physical being but rather a pervasive force.)

The old gent said he was so thoroughly and ecstatically content that he didn't want to leave, but was told that it really wasn't his time. Suddenly he found himself quite alive on a gurney in the emergency room … astounding! And what I found equally assuring was that this "accidental meeting" was a "coincidence" arranged to communicate to Dru and me what a wondrous time we'll have at the *Big Fair* down the road.

Heavenly Herd by Tosa Hirokata, Circa 1450

Postcard from Heaven

Valentine's Day, February 14, 2010. My dear friend Barbara Temple died of an asthma attack on February 5th. She was as good as they come, and I hope to see her at "The Big Fair." Her mate of several years, Pete, died shortly afterwards—within a week, a healthy man, of a heart attack. And that it was, for she was his heart. His death was beyond normal physicality—I think, very simply, he loved the woman so deeply he could not go on without her.

Not long after Barb's passing, I was sorting through boxes of some very old correspondence, and lo and behold I found a very interesting postcard dated back to 1991. I had never noticed it, but for years I would stack cards, letters, and the likes, and when they were cluttering my room I'd throw them into a storage box with the idea that I'd eventually get around to them.

This particular card had a humorous note from Barbara on one side, as usual, but also an amazing and strikingly interesting piece of art on the other. *I had never seen this card before*, though I had it tucked away for almost 20 years.

The picture on the card was taken from a painting by Tosa Hirokata from mid-14th century Japan. What did it depict? Well, of course—a Zen Matador! Never mind the fact that there had never been Spanish-style bullfights in Japan, and certainly not in the 14th Century. And why is the bullfighter depicted as a lovely, graceful, and commanding woman wearing a robe of the Upper Warrior class?

There is no way that twenty years earlier Barbara *Temple* would have had the foggiest notion—nor did I—that I would eventually be writing a book titled *Zen Matador*, and that the grand finale would be titled *The Temple Within … temple … within.* What are the chances that the very morning of my discovering this card I was discussing a potential cover for my book that would somehow reflect the idea of … not to be repetitious … a Zen matador?

However, there it was on the postcard: The image of a fine painting of what appears to be a Japanese bullfighter, female at that, in the ring with *nine* bulls. These are not confrontational beasts at all but subdued animals just walking away from her, being *herded.* The appearance is that the bullfighter has tamed them, has them under her control. At first, I found this baffling and thoroughly incongruous. A Japanese woman bullfighter?

Later it dawned on me that the painting was a creative if subtle homage to the *Ten Bulls* or *the Ten Ox-herding Pictures.* I had learned about this popular allegory from a tidy little book, *Zen Flesh, Zen Bones* (1957) on Zen and pre-Zen writings compiled by Paul Reps and translated by Nyogen Senzaki. I'd read it in my mid-twenties, part of my curriculum for Beatnikism 101.

Wikipedia describes *Ten Bulls* as "a series of short poems and accompanying drawings used in the Zen tradition to describe the stages of a practitioner's progress toward enlightenment, and his or her return to society to enact wisdom and compassion."

These revered depictions were best illustrated and formed as poetry by Kuoan Shiyuan in the 11th Century, and from that time grew in popularity as a teaching device to convey the Buddhist message. So of course the artist Hirokata would have been well aware of them, as they were essential lessons of early Zen in Japan. *The Ten Bulls* inspiration is evident in the painting's title, *Heavenly Herd.* (It has occurred to me that we only see nine bulls in the painting because at the advanced stage of this process the bull becomes invisible ... the student realizes that all is void.)

This "text of non-dual practice" according to a Thrift Books overview, "... became an instant sensation with an entire generation of readers who were just beginning to experiment with Zen." It may well have been influential in the thoughts/writings of the Beat icons, like Alan Ginsberg, Jack Kerouac, and Gary Snyder, who art like in Nirvana. Here's a sampling:

The Bull Transcended. The above drawing represents the seventh stage of enlightenment according to the Ten Bull allegory. "Astride the bull, I reach home. I am serene. The bull too can rest. The dawn has come. In blissful repose, within my thatched dwelling I have abandoned the whip and ropes."

The Reps/Senzaki transcription is written with a simple elegance, as no doubt was the original, bringing forth the humility and clarity of the teaching. It is still in print and well worth a bone or two. *Zen Flesh, Zen Bones,* Charles Tuttle & Company

The Old Hippy Get-together

April 2012. I recently returned from a delightful three-day event in San Francisco. It was called the New Living Expo, but a better name might've been the Old Hippies Never Die Fest. I mean the place was crawling with lively, colorful codgers … like me! Wall-to-wall happy-faces, I mean way groovy! I recognized some of those folks from similar shows I had produced in Seattle, Portland and L.A. 35 years earlier … a bit slower but they hadn't changed a heck of a lot, with those same mellowed-out I-love-everybody-and-everything eyes. Back at yah!

Saucer-believers with tie-dyed T's; lovely young ladies with long, ochre gowns who looked like they'd stepped out of a hobbit movie; tofu-munching old guys that still had all their yoga moves intact; and a handful of Grand Poobahs of the Guru Kind, mostly Americans who had managed to pick up highfalutin' Hindu handles along the way, Swami So-n-So and Maharishi Muckymuck. Hell, I bought some of their books and incense … seems most of these ol' guys had learned something of interest and value along the way … yep, they were onto something.

As you by now know, I'm very open to this kind of ambiance with all its airy-fairy nuances and higher power innuendoes. Except for a brief atheist jag when I was about 20, I've always believed that something, some supreme energy/entity, exists and is a part of us all—not only transcendent but here all the time in plain sight.

I came to this philosophy not through religious study or devotion, not with a singular "leap of faith," but because of my own constant inquisitiveness and astounding personal experiences, those, and because of a love affair with Nature herself. Added to the similar experiences of countless others I have heard or read about I'd be a full-blown idiot not to "believe."

For me it is perfectly reasonable to accept God *without blind faith*, rather a matter of pure logic and transcendent experience. However, I do find great merit in those who have faith even without personally witnessing the miraculous, yes, that's pretty impressive. As Jesus told Thomas—doubting Thomas, no less—who had insisted on seeing his wounds after He had returned from the dead, "Because you have seen me, you have believed; blessed are those who have not seen and yet have believed."—John 20-29 NIV

Backed by an absolute mountain of testimony from those who have experienced the miraculous nature of it all, so many of us are compelled to accept the Divine Face both beyond and within this human existence. I have no doubt there is an interaction of consciousness between this energy field we call our bodies and that force that moves worlds, galaxies and all the marvelous interactions of our personal lives, all the time leaving wiggle room for us to decide if we wish to create our own moves in the whirl of Lila, the playful dance of The Absolute with the contingent world.

If we follow this logic to its ultimate conclusion, then there must be a method behind that with which we are blessed to have interaction with us *in this realm*. And that method is for the spiritual evolution of life, the growing—purifying—of our consciousness to the point where we are readied for the total reunion with our Source, a glorious respite from mortality's suffering and loss. It is communion.

How fortunate I am/we are to have, as in no other time in history, access to the transpersonal visions, mystic writings, and deeply wise seminars. What an array of incredible teachers, whether at an expo, a conference, or an enlightened church sermon; whether online from the likes of Ted Talks, Oprah's Super Soul Sunday, or the Institute of Noetic Sciences, the parapsychological research group founded by astronaut Edgar Mitchell. (see www.ions.com)

So what, you may ask, does all of this have to do with old hippies? Well, to begin with, that whole '60s movement owed a lot to psychedelics—acid, mescaline, mushrooms, peyote, etc. Many folks reported experiences of elevated consciousness and there is no shortage of studies, articles, and books on the spiritual effect of these drugs ... and maybe I just tend to ramble from the lingering effects of those quite astounding trips.

Little Miracles

The Blessed Language of Synchronistic Incidents

> "Unless all existence is a medium for revelation, no particular revelation is possible." —William Temple, Archbishop of Canterbury from 1942 to 1944.

Part One: *Synchronici-tree.* If you have read this book from the beginning, you've probably noticed that time and again I have personally experienced—at times in the most strikingly blatant of ways—what the renowned psychologist

Carl Jung termed "synchronicity." There are countless stories like mine, for they have occurred every day of the year in all parts of the world since human beings have had the capacity to recognize them. We can safely say millions upon millions of people have been touched by some form of this uncanny phenomena.

Admittedly even contemplating the nature of synchronicity is daunting because it forces us to dig beyond what we view as real, beyond what we perceive as logical. And further, if one has not directly, *personally*, had a powerful synchronistic experience, it's all the more easy to shoo away the very idea like an unwanted fly. My feeling is that most everyone has these experiences but sets them aside as mere coincidence, fearful of the profound message that they bring.

Carl Jung died in 1961 in his home in Zurich, Switzerland. I find it noteworthy that immediately following his death a great tree on his property was struck and split by lightning … a tree that he for many years had sat under, he, the champion of synchronicity. (This incident is noted in the aforementioned book *Jung & Hesse: A Tale of Two Friendships.*)

Part Two: *Synchronicity as a message from God.* Jung referred to the phenomenon as "meaningful coincidence." If it is meaningful—that is it has value, focus and reason—if that's the case, then what is at the basis of this meaning and who or what is the original force?

What is common is the mystifying nature of the event. When analyzed these occurrences could only happen with the involvement of an "outside force" that would be capable of shifting time and space (space-time) and physical matter (matter, as the "new physics" implies isn't really matter as we perceive it; it has no substance, no ultimate solidity, but rather is a form of invisible energy).

This baffling activity of synchronicity must be to affect a desired outcome, that being our realization that *we are being communicated with* by a force that is necessarily omnipotent, omniscient and omnipresent … in effect, the powers that we attribute to God. Nothing else might possibly have the capacity or force to perform these otherworldly occurrences, these "little miracles."

Why, then, would this force, the highest consciousness in this and all universes, choose to affect our lives by involving us with an experience that could only have been nurtured and administered by a power on Its level, which is both beyond and within all levels of existence? Why would God interact with individual human beings in so obvious—and, at times, mischievously subtle—ways?

To go further it's necessary to ask the question, "Who or what is God?" It is the only way we can make sense of this. I find it frightening to even ask this question, but we must be brave and ask. It simply follows that to understand the nature of synchronicity, it is necessary to have an inkling of understanding as to the nature of God, synchronicity's source. This would in turn lead us to the reason for God's decision to interact with humanity in any form, in this case via synchronicity.

D.T. Suzuki, the Japanese philosopher who heavily influenced the influx of Zen thought into the Western World, in one of his writings opined that God created man so that He could see Himself. He reflected along these lines: God, the Unmanifest, created us, humanity and the consciousness we possess, as a mirror, if you will, to observe His own existence.

The logic goes something like this: God was lonely … when one is "all one" then one is "alone" … all one, for there is no "other." (I am paraphrasing here, and don't recall from which book I read this material many years ago. I believe the ideas, in any case, stand.)

Being all there is there is nothing to compare one's self with, no other thing, no "other" on which to reflect upon. Being all there is there is no "self." Being the whole, God could hardly see/experience Him-Her-Its-self, as there were no parts of that Self. It's a little like the human brain, my brain, your brain. If we were only in our own body, with our brain busily buzzing, but never saw a photo, a picture or some sort of image of another person's or of another animal's brain, then an image of our own brain would be impossible for us to imagine.

God created man so that God could become conscious, conjectured Carl Jung; conscious, like the mythical Adam and Eve in The Garden, that fateful bite being *the act that God actually wanted us to do.* Paradise is meaningless without the concept of an opposite, at least for a fragment of time, a foil, a righteous ruse, that fateful moment when we become aware of our nakedness. It seems that we need to be apart in order to come together, a full cycle dance.

Human consciousness would allow unmanifested God—being the Great Unconscious—to envision parts of Itself, at least on this planet and plane. Without this "break" there would be no dance, no beauty, no play. In the Hindu religion this is referred to as Lila. (Sanskrit: "play," "sport," "spontaneity," or "drama.") This term has several meanings, most focusing in one way or another on the effortless or playful relation between the Absolute, or

Brahman, and the contingent world, within which we live in ignorance until the point of self-realization, which is the consciousness that resides within each individual, not the small self but the Great Self.

In Jungian terms this process might be considered the first step of individuation, if you will, of God Itself. Individuation means the observation and understanding of the separation of the conscious and unconscious mind with the intended result being integration, a return to wholeness.

For God, The Unmanifest, The Invisible, to see itself, to experience itself, it must also become God, The Manifest, the visible, the tangible in the form of beings and things. All the ugliness and beauty in the world would hardly be aware of itself but for the eyes of sentient beings. We have a purpose. The realization of this seeming break followed by its synthesis, that is for us to again become whole. That is the psychological and metaphysical goal.

Returning to The Whole, The Transconscious Void, all opposites are reconciled … wholly, holy. (This is of course a matter of our mind's spiritual evolution because we are never merely a part, we are never apart. But when we return, we are not the same … this is the flowering, we are a new flower in a fresh bouquet.)

We now find from the great telescopes and expansive formulas of astronomers and quantum physicists that when all is said and done over 90% of all matter in space is invisible "dark matter." And to the remaining 10%, and somewhere within this whole wild dance are you, me, Fido, and Kitty. The ancient Greek word "atomos" refers to "that which can't be split," what was believed to be the tiniest of all things, and the conclusion was that an atom was so tiny it was invisible

In a final analysis that is the case for this whole ball of nothingness. But keep in mind, there is absolute wonder here even if all is ultimately empty. Think about it.

It is no Secret

February 20, 2015. Lying in bed early this morning I found myself reminiscing about the lyrics of an old song that I'd heard on radio when I was really young, about five or so. As thoughts often do, they just pop into our brains from God knows where. I thought, wow, how true this message is if people would just take it to heart.

In those days if a song was good the handful of local stations in any given city would play it again and again, to the point where these great old tunes were really imbedded in our young minds (good thing most of the sounds were snappy and upbeat). A little later that morning as I returned to this manuscript, I decided that I needed a certain quote from Carl Jung.

I was looking for a line from his famous letter to A.A. co-founder Bill Wilson to use in a vignette I was developing. So I went online and found a wonderful site that, unlike most of the others on this topic, had a copy of the actual typewritten letter sent by Dr. Jung to Mr. Wilson. It gave me chills because here you could almost feel and see that marvelous old gent sitting at his manual typewriter laying out the profound spiritual cornerstone (typos and all) of what was to become Alcoholics Anonymous.

When I heard the music playing in the background on this website even more goose pimples popped up. Of all tunes it was an instrumental version of the very song I had been contemplating that morning with the thought of somehow fitting it into this book (That moment darn near brought me to tears.) Here are partial lyrics of the above-mentioned song, and if you're interested you can find a wonderful rendition by The King himself on YouTube "It is No Secret," by Elvis Presley.

> It is no secret what God can do
> What He's done for others He will do for you
> With arms wide open He'll pardon you
> It is no secret what God can do.

This was the first cross-over gospel, country, and pop ballad ever recorded, reaching the number one spot on all three charts! And there's a heck of a story about the country-western songwriter who composed the piece back in 1950. The fellow's name was Carl Stuart Hamblen, a hard drinkin', hell raisin' womanizer until he saw the light.

He even previously wrote a drinkin' man's song that became a top hit with the lyrics starting out with "I won't go huntin' with you, Jake, but I'll go chasin' women … The moon is bright and I'm half tight and life is just beginnin'." Pretty funny tune, story of my life. You can find it on YouTube sung by that sausage feller, yep, ol' Jimmy Dean himself. A real hoot!

Also turns out a friend of Hamblen's who went by the stage name of John Wayne (yep, that pilgrim) and a young preacher by the name of Billy Graham (yep, that travelin' tent feller) were instrumental in this musician's conversion to the clean melody of a wholesome Christian life. The guy went on to write many a tune into his old age. Real uplifting stuff.

Notes: Some folks are out-and-out non-believers, atheists; and some say they just don't know, the agnostics. For "higher power" healing to work it does take that leap of faith or at least an attempt to believe. Just call out His name and He'll be there ... yep, "You've got a friend."

The basic point I'm trying to convey is that this spiritual energy exists simultaneously beyond us and within us, even if we are "out of synch." But the body responds to our thoughts, and so it is a matter of upgrading our thoughts. When at various stretches in my life I wasn't poisoning my mind with alcohol it just made sense that I was not only thinking clearer but feeling great. Attending AA was for me literally Godsent.

I wish to be very clear that there are a number of effective self-induced "positive thinking" therapies that do wonders, whatever your belief system might be. There are also well-established programs like Self-Management and Recovery Training (SMART) and other Cognitive Behavioral Therapy (CBT) processes that are quite successful without being faith-based. Still ...

An Angel from the Outfield. But I see it like this: If you're in the seventh game of the World Series, the bottom of the ninth with two outs and the score is tied, and you have a batter like Reggie Jackson—Mr. October—in his prime, why put a rookie in? I am that rookie and frankly, I can't handle the heat. So I say, God, would you please go to bat for me?

PROF. DR. C. G. JUNG

KÜSNACHT-ZÜRICH
SEESTRASSE 228

January 30, 1961

Mr. William G. Wilson
Alcoholics Anonymous
Box 459 Grand Central Station
New York 17, N.Y.

Dear Mr. Wilson,
your letter has been very welcome indeed.
I had no news from Roland H. anymore and often wondered what has been his fate. Our conversation which he has adequately reported to you had an aspect of which he did not know. The reason was, that I could not tell him everything, was that those days I had to be exceedingly careful of what I said. I had found out that I was misunderstood in every possible way. Thus I was very careful when I talked to Roland H. But what I really thought about, was the result of many experiences with men of his kind.
His craving for alcohol was the equivalent on a low level of the spiritual thirst of our being for wholeness, expressed in mediaeval language: the union with God.[1]
How could one formulate such an insight in a language that is not misunderstood in our days?
The only right and legitimate way to such an experience is, that it happens to you in reality and it can only happen to you when you walk on a path, which leads you to higher understanding. You might be led to that goal by an act of grace or through a personal and honest contact with friends, or through a higher education of the mind beyond the confines of mere rationalism. I see from your letter that Roland H. has chosen the second way, which was, under the circumstances, obviously the best one.
I am strongly convinced that the evil principle prevailing in this world, leads the unrecognized spiritual need into perdition, if it is not counteracted either by real religious insight or by the protective wall of human community. An ordinary man, not protected by an action from above and isolated in society cannot resist the power of evil, which is called very aptly the Devil. But the use of such words arouse so many mistakes that one can only keep aloof from them as much as possible.
These are the reasons why I could not give a full and sufficiant explanation to Roland H. but I am risking it with you, because I conclude from your very decent and honest letter, that you have acquired a point of view above the misleading platitudes, one usually hears about alcoholism.
You see, Alcohol in Latin is "spiritus" and you use the same word for the highest religious experience as well as for the most depraving poison. The helpful formula therefore is: spiritus contra spiritum.

Thanking you again for your kind letter
I remain
yours sincerely

C. G. Jung.

[1] "As the hart panteth after the water brooks, so panteth my soul after thee, O God." (Psalm 42,1)

Above is Jung's letter to Bill Wilson, which I found here: www.barefootsworld.net/jungletter.html. I went to this site and heard that sweet tune that sounded so familiar. Well, all I can say is *it is no secret.* Yes, that was the music playing in the background! I feel so blessed to have these on-going synchronistic experiences … Thank you, thank you, thank you.

The website where I found Jung's letter to Bill Wilson is the creation of someone who goes by the name Barefoot Windwalker—How cool is that? His profound, unedited words on the site include these: "I must state, once again, there are no political, economic, 'religious' or military solutions to what is primarily a *spiritual problem* in the world today, the We-Them syndrome. We, all of mankind, must realize We are all ONE." Windwalker, who passed onward and upward in 2009, also wrote this: "To solve our problems we must rise to a level of consciousness above our norm. For us that level is one of humble sober-minded Spiritual Awakening." Check the ol' guy out at: http://barefootsworld.org/somethingtoponder.html

Addicts Unanimous: Recovery for All of Us!

Throughout this memoir I refer to many incidents where I was in a learning process and battling my addiction to alcohol. I have put considerable energy and money on how to conquer it.

Like the Second World War hero and classic western movie star Audie Murphy, I have been *To Hell and Back.* Not once or twice, but throughout my adult life. You see, I am an alcoholic, and life for me has been a hellacious roller coaster of illusive elation and lucid exhilaration, the difference between night and day. I call it Dr. Jekyll and Mr. Hernandez.

In writing my memoir I've been given the opportunity to get a pretty good look at myself and, though painful, I must say there's a lot to be said for honestly looking back. That is why I have kept fighting the damned thing, addiction that is, and again I have a few years—seven as of Valentine's Day, 2025—of absolute sobriety under my belt. It is stunning what a magnificent world this is!

Over the years I have tried some of the most popular therapies, like AA and SMART, and they are both excellent programs … as they say in Alcoholics Anonymous, "It works if you work it."

But I have found in my efforts and my studies that "One size does not fit all." For many, there is a universal reality for lasting sobriety and peace—when we ally ourselves with "Higher Power" in whatever form it may take. That may be Jesus for some, or Allah, or Buddha … or some mind space that is beyond our smothering ego, which is always at the source.

To do my best to educate others as to their many options, I have set up a small non-profit, and I am building a website for any sincere person who has made the decision to change. Here they'll find the many options available, and then go on to apply a simple 10-page "Personal Recovery Plan." This "Plan" template is written by a top-notch psychotherapist and author, Rita Milios. With the education learned in this directory of all-things-recovery, a person may begin to build an uplifted and fulfilled life.

This dramatic change is possible, I know, and the rewards are great. This directory is a work in progress, but there is certainly enough info gathered even now to hopefully put a person on the right path. If you (or a loved one) is struggling with addiction you might wish to visit: www.recoverydirectory.org.

How it all Came to Be

Enlightenment, it appears, means different things to different people. A great guru like Ramana Maharshi spent most of his life in a cave to discover the Truth of it all; another may wish to use his great vision to feed the world. Another may be quite happy washing dishes.

To maintain a state of Nirvana we need to practice, practice, practice, because our minds, like all things, are impermanent … everything is changing.

Live what you've learned. Healthy body. Healthy mind. The door to Higher Consciousness may be open for us to experience but you still have to walk through it. You have to live the life that you now know to be true.

In my case, I had hit a high point of my consciousness back in 1995, yes, thoroughly blown out without peppy uppers or psychedelic boosters, just meditation, study, and a resolute commitment to overcoming my most terrible attachments, namely alcohol and out-of-control sex.

Shortly after that transcendent leap back in 1995 I was again drowned in my addiction-of-choice, good ol' booze. Everything you could imagine about the effects of addiction clobbered me, even the dread shingles—a veritable Tommy-Tsunami. In other words, I was a total wreck.

Just mind-boggling how strong my urges had become! Considering the dark, downer existence of an addicted life there is little place for the clear light to continue to shine through. I attempted to abstain, and I enjoyed periodic bouts of sobriety, but when The Call of The Wild whispers in my ear I'm like a tiny needle that is suddenly within inches of a giant magnet—it's called a "trigger." Wham, you're knocked clear off that clean-n-sober wagon and sucked back into another bender!

Had it not been for the kindness of dear friends, Dru, Laura and others, I could well have been living—and dying—under the freeway bridge with the others whose lives are destitute for any number of reasons. Alcohol and drugs seem to be a common denominator for those folks and, given their circumstances, it's hard to blame them … a certain cyclical hell.

Laura was considerate to the point of offering a crash pad in her new home. It was a large suburban, three-bedroom crib that felt like a valley where you could hear your echo. She hadn't moved in yet but there was a room that was set up for her son to eventually live in—in fact, within a month. She offered me that room with the stipulation that one month was precisely the time I had to live there. She also supplied me with my medicine: a little bottle of brandy every day.

Sitting there in that essentially empty house, for the first time in my life I felt in-depth loneliness combined with a sense of despair. God, what terrible emotions. For me, just nervous, pacing energy with a where-the-hell-do-I-go-from-here knot in the gut. Laura did have a telephone there—Hallelujah!—but no internet, that wonderful hub of instant connections. I had my computer but the only use of it was as a word processor … in essence, your basic typewriter. Did I say … typewriter?

I hadn't written a thing in years, not even a simple poem, but I was suddenly inspired. I went to my storage space and dug through all the stacked boxes looking for the one marked "poetry." There I found the "magic box," sheets of lined paper, typed paper, napkins from dozens of bars I had frequented in years past with scribbled, hardly legible notes, old letters from chums and pissed-off girlfriends, and a handful of photos and sketches. My, my, what a busy boy I had been and a wild one at that.

I had kept all of these tattered bits and pieces of my past so long that the cardboard storage box they were in was falling apart and mildew had given the paper the feel of long-lost scrolls. I had dragged that treasure chest of baloney, babble and tales of travel with me from place to place over the decades.

When the notion hit, it was only a matter of minutes for me to jump on it. Like a cold rat with an old newspaper, I tore through those frayed parchments thinking to build a home for my true-to-life expressions, something to leave behind. There it is, there's my book: an autobiography!

It was a jig-saw puzzle … What memory came first? And how does it all fit together? Mind you, these pieces were but a fraction of what was to come, but it was a start. It quickly began making sense: get a title, even a temporary one, and get busy. Within a month—my brief stint at Laura's—I was up to

60-some pages and a pretty substantial table of contents. (I had told my lady friend, Dru, that I'd be quite happy with a tidy little book of about 120 pages, so hey, I was already halfway there.)

Then I made the blessed move to a buddy's soon-to-be-foreclosed-on pad. He and his family had moved out a month prior and I was allowed to stay there for $500 cash a month, that is until the bank chose to put a lock on the doors. This, mind you, could have happened on any given day. Nasty sense of insecurity, but it was a familiar setting: a large empty pad with few amenities other than electricity, water, and my beloved old-but-functional typewriter in the form of an antiquated Mac.

Shortly thereafter I got phone and internet service and was back in business peddling my events with little time for writing. Still, within a couple of months the manuscript was way over my initial goal. The darned thing was rapidly expanding to over 200 pages. In spite of my circumstances, the writing itself kept me not only alive but marvelously excited. There was a great catharsis in process, though my sobriety was sporadic. Yes, I was starting to feel it … one day at a time.

Over time I slowly began to decrease my drinking. A day, a week, eventually a month. I could not have imagined that the time would come when I would reach over six years of clean & sober. It may not sound like much but for an old guy who had been living the nutso night life for over 40 years, believe me, it was and is a quantum leap to a glorious new world.

All of this somehow propelled me into being very conscious of the great fortune of just being alive and having a roof over my head, temporary as it may be. In a word, I feel *blessed.*

I now gaze out my window looking into the backyard where I planted a sizable garden this spring with a variety of vegetables, herbs and flowers; where an old wooden fence leans against a crepe myrtle tree. I sketch a branch and write a haiku.

Crepe myrtle blossoms
splashed across the summer sky …
Who can paint so well?

Around the River's Bend

Around the bend
at summer's end
the glimmer of a town;
Daffodils and daisies dozing
and hollyhocks, like ladies, posing
with their faces down.

I dock the boat
where white geese float
along the lapping shore;
And wander in
where I've never been—
but I've been here before.

A coin I find
locked in my mind,
but now's the time for spending;
A smile of wine,
with my hat tipping,
Auld lang syne,
my glass slow sipping—
a toast to never ending!

I trek the trail
'cross fern and dale,
then saunter to the river;
The end I hear,
my friend, is near,
the full moon is a sliver.

The Great Mystery

What is God? Decades ago up in Seattle I met the wise and kind Father Jack Fulton (formally Father Joseph John Fulton, OP), the pastor of Blessed Sacrament Church and the author of *Love Grows in Brooklyn*. This lovingly nostalgic autobiography chronicles his great odyssey from Brooklyn, across the U.S. as a parish priest, to West Coast cities, parts of Europe, and ultimately to return to his beloved home for the final stretch ... a touching and inherently sweet sharing.

In a small room near the front of the church he and I held a handful of "sessions" of therapy, philosophy and, I must confess, charity on his part (I was flat broke at the time and he would generously lay rent money on me after our short meetings ... I will not swear that all of the money went for rent, for that would most surely send me to a blistering fate.)

One afternoon, I believe the last time I saw him, I asked the most candid question, "What is God?" His unquestioning instant response was "God is love." This was not a robotic, indoctrinated answer—it was from his soul. It was striking in its simplicity and astounding in its implications. In all these years no other characterization of God has resonated so vividly. God-ness is Goodness. Period. That is why Jesus adamantly exhorts us to love God with all of our being—in other words, the commandment is to *love Love*. How beautiful. And in that very same message He tells us to love others as we would like to be loved.

From Matthew 22:37-40 we read, "You shall <u>love</u> the Lord your God with all your heart and with all your soul and with all your mind. This is the great and first commandment. And a second is like it: You shall love your neighbor as yourself. On these two commandments depend all the Law and the Prophets." His words are undeniable and He has made them easy to understand. He has pinpointed a strong and clear position for his followers. He has said, "Just do these two things," but do Christians pay heed? That is what has led author C.K. Chesterton, author of the "Father Brown Stories," to observe, "Christianity hasn't failed ... it hasn't been tried."

Do this without the desire for reciprocity, without asking for anything in return. Just express your love and your gratefulness, that's all. How fortunate we are to be able to communicate with this Great Spirit and to be able to receive love in return. How amazing that we have a mind that if opened allows us to truly care about all sentient beings and just be part of the wonder of life. (You know, strange and wonderful things begin to happen when we do just that.)

My Daily Prayer

I would like to share with you my daily prayer along with related commentary.

I have learned after decades of morning meditation to seat myself in a proper meditation pose, back straight, but not rigid. I place my hands in my lap, one over the other. From this seated position I now begin my prayer.

> Dear God, I pray
> that we all find peace today,
> that we are all
> growing in consciousness,
> in kindness to others,
> in a healthy love of ourselves,
> and in a great love of you.
> I pray that I too
> am growing in these ways.
> Amen.

As I say these words I remind myself that I am not in an empty room, but rather I am in the presence of The Divine, The Great Spirit. In these quiet moments I sit in gratefulness for God's compassion throughout my life. I remind myself that I am not just a body-mind of this world, but the underlying spirit of all existence. I am of the pure spirit found in all sentient beings—it is what poet Walt Whitman observed in a blade of grass. The nature of God is the God of nature.

When asked about his religious belief, Albert Einstein replied it was that of Dutch philosopher Spinoza, who believed in pantheism—here meaning God in everything. In this sense, we can say that we too are composed of God. As popular author and philosopher Alan Watts put it, "We are not a drop in the ocean—we are the entire ocean in a drop."

With this poignant Self-realization, insignificant enemies and self-induced fears gradually fade away as we come to live our daily lives as the blessed beings that we are. When we come to find our own essence, our true self, and as we continue to grow into this radiance, we are liberated from divisive dualistic thought. Freed from the illusion of separation, we realize that we are and always have been one with God.

Artwork courtesy of Stephen Morath

This Is

This is the Goddess,
her selective generosity and subtle silhouette,
the moon, the muse, and her daughters.

This is the civilization of quiet knowledge,
mud drying and footprints on the stars,
the flight of turtles and the torch of Neptune,
the mermaid that got away.

This is the palm reader and her exotic teas
foretelling the destiny of dynasties,
an old man on a bicycle
purposely lost where time does not exist.

This is a merciful encounter
on the dark side of the self
and veneration in the tradition of fish.

This is an oasis of polite conversation
in the mirage of a bustling city,
the blood of the bull in the shifting sand
and the matador's duty to bring up the sun.

This is a million migrating monarchs
landing on the fingertip of our imagination,
It is a free ticket for big trains with big whistles,
It is walking through walls of museums
and living in statues of exquisite marble.

This is the season for waterfalls
and hummingbird nectar,
the graceful dance of soft rain
amidst the vernal wind,
It is the color turquoise created to be seen.

This is the Eternal Flower,
the Golden Flower,
its endless blossoming,
the blossoming of openness,
The Lotus of The Lake.

This is the permeating chord
of an angelic choir
and the sweetness of supposed accidents,
It is the deliverance of emptiness,
The deliverance.

This is the bird's cry
of good morning and good night,
This is the promise
of love that never dies.

Handsome Dog. Tomás and Tino, the Happy Hound. Tino's the good-looking one on the left—with the mesmerizing eyes. No! Stop! Don't look into his eyes!

Though a champion of the finest pedigree, he is a mongrel at heart (loves those kitty-dropping Tootsie Rolls). Along with his acclaimed cookbook on canine cuisine, *Bone Appétit,* Tino is writing his own memoir, *Zen Muttador.*

Read more about Tommy, Tino, and Louie the Cat in the exciting sequel, ***Signals from the Sombrero Galaxy.*** Coming soon to a planet near you!

CONTACTING THE AUTHOR

Mr. Chavez is the Founder, President and Treasurer of the *Beatnik Retirement Organization* (BRO), a non-profit front for his own failed retirement plans. When not in the depth of Nirvana (Nirvana Garcia, his sleazy girlfriend), he offers his services as a lay theologian—lay?

He periodically finds himself available (fortunate for his immense fan base ... by rare appointment, mind you) for poetry recitation, amateur psychiatric sessions (him as counselor or client), seminars on pan fried Buddhism (What is the sound of one chop sticking?) ... and whaaatever. He may be booked by his agent, Joseph Mahma, at 1-800-JOE-MAHMA.

Mr. Chavez, with a true bohemian disdain for all electronic communications (a non-text Mex), prefers correspondence via snail mail. He longs for the return of the Pony Express. However, you may find the email address of his secretary, Ms. Tomassina Chavini, on the website **www.ZenMatador.com**

Having attained perfective enlightenment, Swami Havabanana (formerly Tomás Chavez) is now Director of Marketing for the ***Zen Matador*** fine line of way-out clothing, caps, and other cool stuff.

www.ingramcontent.com/pod-product-compliance
Lightning Source LLC
LaVergne TN
LVHW090547110826
845146LV00001B/44

* 9 7 9 8 9 9 2 9 6 4 6 0 8 *